Time and Trauma

NEW HEIDEGGER RESEARCH

Series Editors:

Gregory Fried, Professor of Philosophy, Boston College, USA
Richard Polt, Professor of Philosophy, Xavier University, USA

The New Heidegger Research series promotes informed and critical dialogue that breaks new philosophical ground by taking into account the full range of Heidegger's thought, as well as the enduring questions raised by his work.

Titles in the Series:

Time and Trauma

Thinking Through Heidegger in the Thirties

Richard Polt

ROWMAN & LITTLEFIELD INTERNATIONAL

London • New York

Published by Rowman & Littlefield International Ltd
Unit A, Whitacre Mews, 26-34 Stannary Street, London SE11 4AB
www.rowmaninternational.com

Rowman & Littlefield International Ltd. is an affiliate of Rowman & Littlefield
4501 Forbes Boulevard, Suite 200, Lanham, Maryland 20706, USA
With additional offices in Boulder, New York, Toronto (Canada), and Plymouth (UK)
www.rowman.com

British Library Cataloguing in Publication Data

A catalogue record for this book is available from the British Library

ISBN: HB 978-1-78661-049-2
       PB 978-1-78661-050-8

Library of Congress Cataloging-in-Publication Data

Names: Polt, Richard F. H., 1964– author.
Title: Time and trauma : thinking through Heidegger in the thirties / Richard Polt.
Description: Lanham : Rowman & Littlefield International, 2019. | Includes
    bibliographical references and index.
Identifiers: LCCN 2018049764 (print) | LCCN 2019002514 (ebook) | ISBN
    9781786610515 (Electronic) | ISBN 9781786610492 (cloth : alk. paper) | ISBN
    9781786610508 (pbk. : alk. paper)
Subjects: LCSH: Heidegger, Martin, 1889–1976. | Ontology.
Classification: LCC B3279.H49 (ebook) | LCC B3279.H49 P654 2019 (print) |
    DDC 193—dc23
LC record available at https://lccn.loc.gov/2018049764

∞™ The paper used in this publication meets the minimum requirements of American
National Standard for Information Sciences—Permanence of Paper for Printed Library
Materials, ANSI/NISO Z39.48-1992.

Printed in the United States of America

Contents

Acknowledgments

Work on this project was supported by a faculty development leave from Xavier University in fall 2017.

Initial versions of portions of this book appeared in the following publications; I thank the publishers for permission to reissue the texts in revised form.

"Arendt and the Space of Action." *The Point* 1:1 (Spring 2009): 65–68.

"Being and Time." In *Martin Heidegger: Key Concepts*, ed. Bret W. Davis. Chesham: Acumen, 2010. © Individual contributions, the contributors. Reproduced with permission of The Licensor through PLSclear.

"Being at Issue." In *After Heidegger?* ed. Gregory Fried and Richard Polt. London: Rowman & Littlefield International, 2017.

"Beyond Struggle and Power: Heidegger's Secret Resistance." *Interpretation* 35:1 (Fall 2007): 11–40.

"The Black Notebooks as Thought Journals." In *Zur Hermeneutik der "Schwarzen Hefte,"* Heidegger-Jahrbuch 11, ed. Alfred Denker and Holger Zaborowski. Freiburg: Karl Alber, 2017.

"The Burning Cup: Or, *Im Anfang war die Tat*." *International Journal of Žižek Studies* 1:4 (December 2007).

"Drawing the Line: Political Thought in Heidegger's Lecture Courses and Seminars of 1933–35." In *Heidegger's Question of Being: Dasein, Truth, and History*, ed. Holger Zaborowski. Washington, DC: Catholic University of America Press, 2017.

"From the Understanding of Being to the Happening of Being." In *Division III of Heidegger's "Being and Time": The Unanswered Question of Being*, ed. Lee Braver. Cambridge: MIT Press, 2015.

"Heidegger in the 1930s: Who Are We?" In *The Bloomsbury Companion to Heidegger*, ed. François Raffoul and Eric Sean Nelson. London: Bloomsbury Academic (UK), an imprint of Bloomsbury Publishing Plc, 2013.

"Heidegger, Reason, and the Burden of Being." *Argumenta Philosophica* 2 (2017): 35–48.

"Heidegger, the Scourge of the Enlightenment." *Acta Philosophica* 25:2 (2016): 342–45.

"Hitler the Anti-Nihilist? Statehood, Leadership, and Political Space in Heidegger's Seminar of 1933–34." *European Review* 22:2 (May 2014): 231–43. Reproduced with permission.

"Inception, Downfall, and the Broken World: Heidegger Above the Sea of Fog." In *Heidegger's "Black Notebooks": Responses to Anti-Semitism*, ed. Andrew J. Mitchell and Peter Trawny. New York: Columbia University Press, 2017. Copyright © 2017 Columbia University Press. Adapted from and reprinted with permission of Columbia University Press.

"Meaning, Excess, and Event." *Gatherings: The Heidegger Circle Annual* 1 (2011): 26–53.

"Propositions on Emergency." *Philosophy Today* 59:4 (Fall 2015): 587–97.

Review of *Ponderings II–VI: Black Notebooks 1931–1938*, by Martin Heidegger, trans. Richard Rojcewicz. *Notre Dame Philosophical Reviews*, June 2016.

Review of *Hölderlin's Hymns "Germania" and "The Rhine,"* by Martin Heidegger, trans. William McNeill and Julia Ireland. *Notre Dame Philosophical Reviews*, June 2015.

"The Secret Homeland of Speech: Heidegger on Language, 1933–34." In *Heidegger and Language*, ed. Jeffrey Powell. Bloomington: Indiana University Press, 2013.

"Self-Assertion as Founding." In Martin Heidegger, *On Hegel's "Philosophy of Right": The 1934–35 Seminar and Interpretive Essays*, ed. Peter Trawny, Marcia Sá Cavalcante-Schuback, and Michael Marder. London: Bloomsbury Academic (UK), an imprint of Bloomsbury Publishing Plc, 2014.

"Traumatic Ontology." In *Being Shaken: Ontology and the Event*, ed. Michael Marder and Santiago Zabala. Palgrave Studies in Postmetaphysical Thought. Basingstoke and New York: Palgrave Macmillan, 2014. Reproduced with permission of Palgrave Macmillan.

For inviting me to present or publish work that contributed to this book, I thank Jesús Adrián Escudero, Lee Braver, Ron Bruzina, Bret W. Davis, Alfred Denker, Pedro Erber, Giorgio Faro, Robert Gingerich, Gary Gutting, Michael Marder, Andrew J. Mitchell, Eric Sean Nelson, Diane Perpich, Jeffrey Powell, François Raffoul, Marcia Sá Cavalcante-Schuback, Marc Sable, Ted Schatzki, Paul Taylor, Jonny Thakkar, Peter Trawny, Facundo Vega, Jon Wittrock, Santiago Zabala, and Holger Zaborowski.

For his generous encouragement and provocative thoughts on this project and others, I am always grateful to Gregory Fried.

Abbreviations

The following texts are cited parenthetically in this book. Other texts are cited in notes and listed in the bibliography.

HC: Hannah Arendt, *The Human Condition*, 2nd ed. (Chicago: University of Chicago Press, 1998).

NHS: Martin Heidegger, *Nature, History, State: 1933–1934*, tr. Gregory Fried and Richard Polt, with essays by Robert Bernasconi, Peter E. Gordon, Marion Heinz, Theodore Kisiel, and Slavoj Žižek (London: Bloomsbury, 2013). This translation includes the pagination of the German text: "Über Wesen und Begriff von Natur, Geschichte und Staat," in *Heidegger und der Nationalsozialismus I: Dokumente*, Heidegger-Jahrbuch 4, ed. Alfred Denker and Holger Zaborowski (Freiburg: Karl Alber, 2009).

SZ: Martin Heidegger, *Sein und Zeit* (Tübingen: Niemeyer, 1953). The pagination of this edition is included in GA 2; in *Being and Time*, tr. John Macquarrie and Edward Robinson (New York: Harper & Row, 1962); and in *Being and Time*, tr. Joan Stambaugh, rev. Dennis J. Schmidt (Albany: State University of New York Press, 2010). All translations from SZ are mine, but I generally stay close to Macquarrie and Robinson.

GA: Martin Heidegger, *Gesamtausgabe* (Frankfurt am Main: Vittorio Klostermann, 1975–). Cited in the following format: (GA volume number: German page / translation page). Not all translations listed below include the entire contents of the corresponding GA volumes. In cases where texts from a GA volume appear in more than one English volume, an abbreviation for the English volume is used. Pages from translations are cited only when a translation is quoted or when the GA pagination is not included in the translation; "tm" indicates that the translation has been modified. Translations are mine if not otherwise credited. All emphasis in quotations is original.

GA 1. *Frühe Schriften* (1912–1916). Ed. Friedrich-Wilhelm von Herrmann, 1978.

GA 2. *Sein und Zeit* (1927). Ed. Friedrich Wilhelm von Herrmann, 1977.

GA 3. *Kant und das Problem der Metaphysik* (1929). Ed. Friedrich-Wilhelm von Herrmann, 1991. / *Kant and the Problem of Metaphysics.* Tr. Richard Taft. 5th, enlarged ed. Bloomington: Indiana University Press, 1997.

GA 4. *Erläuterungen zu Hölderlins Dichtung* (1936–1968). Ed. Friedrich-Wilhelm von Herrmann, 1981, 2012 (rev. ed.). / "Hölderlin and the Essence of Poetry." In *The Heidegger Reader*. Ed. Günter Figal, tr. Jerome Veith. Bloomington: Indiana University Press, 2009.

GA 5. *Holzwege* (1935–1946). Ed. Friedrich-Wilhelm von Hermann, 1977. / *Off the Beaten Track.* Tr. Julian Young and Kenneth Haynes. Cambridge: Cambridge University Press, 2002.

GA 6.2. *Nietzsche II* (1939–1946). Ed. Brigitte Schillbach, 1997. / EP = *The End of Philosophy.* Tr. Joan Stambaugh. New York: Harper & Row, 1973. N4 = *Nietzsche*, vol. IV: *Nihilism.* Tr. Frank A. Capuzzi, ed. David Farrell Krell. San Francisco: Harper & Row, 1982.

GA 7. *Vorträge und Aufsätze* (1936–1953). Ed. Friedrich-Wilhelm von Herrmann, 2000. / EP = *The End of Philosophy.* Tr. Joan Stambaugh. New York: Harper & Row, 1973. QCT = *The Question Concerning Technology and Other Essays.* Tr. William Lovitt. New York: Harper & Row, 1977.

GA 8. *Was heißt Denken?* (1951–1952). Ed. Paola-Ludovika Coriando, 2002. / *What Is Called Thinking?* Tr. J. Glenn Gray. New York: Harper & Row, 1968.

GA 9. *Wegmarken* (1919–1961). Ed. Friedrich-Wilhelm von Herrmann, 1976, 1996 (rev. ed.). / *Pathmarks.* Ed. William McNeill. Cambridge: Cambridge University Press, 1998.

GA 11. *Identität und Differenz* (1955–1963). Ed. Friedrich-Wilhelm von Herrmann, 2006. / "The Principle of Identity." In *The Heidegger Reader*. Ed. Günter Figal. Bloomington: Indiana University Press, 2009.

GA 12. *Unterwegs zur Sprache* (1950–1959). Ed. Friedrich-Wilhelm von Herrmann, 1985. / *On the Way to Language.* Trans. Peter D. Hertz and Joan Stambaugh. New York: Harper & Row, 1971.

GA 13. *Aus der Erfahrung des Denkens* (1910–1976). Ed. Hermann Heidegger, 1983, 2002 (rev. ed.). / TP = "The Thinker as Poet," in *Poetry, Language, Thought*, tr. Albert Hofstadter (New York: Harper & Row, 1971). WS = "Why Do I Stay in the Provinces?" Tr. Thomas Sheehan. In *Martin Heidegger: Philosophical and Political Writings.* Ed. Manfred Stassen. London: Continuum, 2003.

GA 14. *Zur Sache des Denkens* (1927–1968). Ed. Friedrich-Wilhelm von Herrmann, 2007. / *On Time and Being.* Tr. Joan Stambaugh. New York: Harper & Row, 1972.

GA 16. *Reden und andere Zeugnisse eines Lebensweges* (1910–1976). Ed. Hermann Heidegger, 2000. / FT = "The Rectorate 1933/34: Facts and Thoughts." Tr. Lisa Harries. In *Martin Heidegger and National Socialism: Questions and Answers*, ed. Günther Neske and Emil Kettering. New York: Paragon, 1990. HC = *The Heidegger Controversy: A Critical Reader*, ed. Richard Wolin. Cambridge: The MIT Press, 1993. HR = *The Heidegger Reader*, ed. Günter Figal. Bloomington: Indiana University Press, 2009. HS = "Heidegger and Schmitt: The Bottom Line," *Telos* 72 (Summer 1987): 132.

GA 18. *Grundbegriffe der aristotelischen Philosophie* (1924). Ed. Mark Michalski, 2002. / *Basic Concepts of Aristotelian Philosophy.* Tr. Robert D. Metcalf and Mark Basil Tanzer. Bloomington: Indiana University Press, 2009.

GA 19. *Platon: Sophistes* (1924–1925). Ed. Ingeborg Schüßler, 1992. / *Plato's "Sophist."* Tr. Richard Rojcewicz and André Schuwer. Bloomington: Indiana University Press, 1997.

GA 20. *Prolegomena zur Geschichte des Zeitbegriffs* (1925). Ed. Petra Jaeger, 1979, 1988 (2nd, rev. ed.), 1994 (3rd, rev. ed.). / *History of the Concept of Time: Prolegomena.* Tr. Theodore Kisiel. Bloomington: Indiana University Press, 1992.

GA 21. *Logik. Die Frage nach der Wahrheit* (1925–1926). Ed. Walter Biemel, 1976, 1995 (rev. ed.). / *Logic: The Question of Truth.* Tr. Thomas Sheehan. Bloomington: Indiana University Press, 2010.

GA 24. *Die Grundprobleme der Phänomenologie* (1927). Ed. Friedrich-Wilhelm von Herrmann, 1975. / *The Basic Problems of Phenomenology.* Tr. Albert Hofstadter. Bloomington: Indiana University Press, 1982.

GA 25. *Phänomenologische Interpretation von Kants Kritik der reinen Vernunft* (1927–1928). Ed. Ingtraud Görland, 1977. / *Phenomenological Interpretation of Kant's "Critique of Pure Reason."* Tr. Parvis Emad and Kenneth Maly. Bloomington: Indiana University Press, 1997.

GA 26. *Metaphysische Anfangsgründe der Logik im Ausgang von Leibniz* (1928). Ed. Klaus Held, 1978, 1990 (2nd rev. ed.), 2007 (3rd rev. ed.). / *The Metaphysical Foundations of Logic.* Tr. Michael Heim. Bloomington: Indiana University Press, 1984.

GA 27. *Einleitung in die Philosophie* (1928–1929). Ed. Otto Saame and Ina Saame-Speidel, 1996, 2001 (rev. ed.).

GA 28. *Der deutsche Idealismus (Fichte, Schelling, Hegel) und die philosophische Problemlage der Gegenwart* (1929). Ed. Claudius Strube, 1997.

GA 29/30. *Die Grundbegriffe der Metaphysik. Welt—Endlichkeit—Einsamkeit* (1929–1930). Ed. Friedrich-Wilhelm von Herrmann, 1983. / *The Fundamental Concepts of Metaphysics: World, Finitude, Solitude.* Tr. William McNeill and Nicholas Walker. Bloomington: Indiana University Press, 1995.

GA 31. *Vom Wesen der menschlichen Freiheit. Einleitung in die Philosophie* (1930). Ed. Hartmut Tietjen, 1982, 1994 (rev. ed.). / *The Essence of Human Freedom: An Introduction to Philosophy.* Tr. Ted Sadler. London: Continuum, 2002.

GA 32. *Hegels Phänomenologie des Geistes* (1930–1931). Ed. Ingtraud Görland, 1980. / *Hegel's "Phenomenology of Spirit."* Tr. Parvis Emad and Kenneth Maly. Bloomington: Indiana University Press, 1998.

GA 33. *Aristoteles, Metaphysik Θ 1–3. Von Wesen und Wirklichkeit der Kraft* (1931). Ed. Heinrich Hüni, 1981, 1990 (2nd rev. ed.), 2006 (3rd rev. ed.) / *Aristotle's "Metaphysics" Θ 1–3: On the Essence and Actuality of Force.* Tr. Walter Brogan and Peter Warnek. Bloomington: Indiana University Press, 1995.

GA 34. *Vom Wesen der Wahrheit. Zu Platons Höhlengleichnis und Theätet* (1931–1932). Ed. Hermann Mörchen, 1988, 1997 (rev. ed.). / *The Essence of Truth: On Plato's Cave Allegory and "Theaetetus."* Tr. Ted Sadler. London: Continuum, 2002.

GA 35. *Der Anfang der abendländischen Philosophie: Auslegung des Anaximander und Parmenides* (1932). Ed. Peter Trawny, 2011. / *The Beginning of Western Philosophy: Interpretation of Anaximander and Parmenides.* Tr. Richard Rojcewicz. Bloomington: Indiana University Press, 2015.

GA 36/37. *Sein und Wahrheit* (1933–1934). Ed. Hartmut Tietjen, 2001. / *Being and Truth.* Tr. Gregory Fried and Richard Polt. Bloomington: Indiana University Press, 2010.

GA 38. *Logik als die Frage nach dem Wesen der Sprache* (1934). Ed. Günter Seubold, 1998. / *Logic as the Question Concerning the Essence of Language.* Tr. Wanda Torres Gregory and Yvonne Unna. Albany: State University of New York Press, 2009.

GA 39. *Hölderlins Hymnen "Germanien" und "Der Rhein"* (1934–1935). Ed. Susanne Ziegler, 1980, 1989 (rev. ed.). / *Hölderlin's Hymns "Germania" and "The Rhine."* Tr. William McNeill and Julia Ireland. Bloomington: Indiana University Press, 2014.

GA 40. *Einführung in die Metaphysik* (1935). Ed. Petra Jaeger, 1983. / *Introduction to Metaphysics.* Tr. Gregory Fried and Richard Polt. 2nd ed. New Haven: Yale University Press, 2014.

GA 41. *Die Frage nach dem Ding. Zu Kants Lehre von den transzendentalen Grundsätzen* (1935–1936). Ed. Petra Jaeger, 1984. / *The Question Concerning the Thing: On Kant's Doctrine of the Transcendental Principles.* Tr. James Reid and Benjamin Crowe. London: Rowman & Littlefield International, 2018.

GA 42. *Schelling: Vom Wesen der menschlichen Freiheit (1809)* (1936). Ed. Ingrid Schüßler, 1988. / *Schelling's Treatise on the Essence of Human Freedom.* Tr. Joan Stambaugh. Athens: Ohio University Press, 1985.

GA 43. *Nietzsche: Der Wille zur Macht als Kunst* (1936–1937). Ed. Bernd Heimbüchel, 1985.

GA 44. *Nietzsches metaphysische Grundstellung im abendländischen Denken: Die ewige Wiederkehr des Gleichen* (1937). Ed. Marion Heinz, 1986. / *Nietzsche*, vol. II: *The Eternal Recurrence of the Same.* Tr. David Farrell Krell. San Francisco: Harper & Row, 1984.

GA 45. *Grundfragen der Philosophie. Ausgewählte "Probleme" der "Logik"* (1937–1938). Ed. Friedrich-Wilhelm von Herrmann, 1984. / *Basic Questions of Philosophy: Selected "Problems" of "Logic."* Tr. Richard Rojcewicz and André Schuwer. Bloomington: Indiana University Press, 1994.

GA 46. *Zur Auslegung von Nietzsches II. Unzeitgemäßer Betrachtung "Vom Nutzen und Nachteil der Historie für das Leben"* (1938–1939). Ed. Hans-Joachim Friedrich, 2003. / *Interpretation of Nietzsche's Second Untimely Meditation.* Tr. Ullrich Haase and Mark Sinclair. Bloomington: Indiana University Press, 2016.

GA 47. *Nietzsches Lehre vom Willen zur Macht als Erkenntnis* (1939). Ed. Eberhard Hanser, 1989.

GA 48. *Nietzsche: Der europäische Nihilismus* (1940). Ed. Petra Jaeger, 1986.

GA 49. *Die Metaphysik des deutschen Idealismus. Zur erneuten Auslegung von Schelling: "Philosophische Untersuchungen über das Wesen der menschlichen*

Freiheit und die damit zusammenhängenden Gegenstände" (1809) (1941). Ed. Günter Seubold, 1991, 2006 (2nd rev. ed.).

GA 50. *Nietzsches Metaphysik; Einleitung in die Philosophie—Denken und Dichten* (1941–1942, 1944–1945). Ed. Petra Jaeger, 1990, 2007 (2nd rev. ed.).

GA 51. *Grundbegriffe* (1941). Ed. Petra Jaeger, 1981, 1991 (rev. ed.). / *Basic Concepts.* Tr. Gary E. Aylesworth. Bloomington: Indiana University Press, 1993.

GA 52. *Hölderlins Hymne "Andenken"* (1941–1942). Ed. Curd Ochwadt, 1982.

GA 53. *Hölderlins Hymne "Der Ister"* (1942). Ed. Walter Biemel, 1984. / *Hölderlin's Hymn "The Ister."* Tr. William McNeill and Julia Davis. Bloomington: Indiana University Press, 1996.

GA 54. *Parmenides* (1942–1943). Ed. Manfred S. Frings, 1982. / *Parmenides.* Tr. André Schuwer and Richard Rojcewicz. Bloomington: Indiana University Press, 1992.

GA 55. *Heraklit* (1943, 1944). Ed. Manfred S. Frings, 1979, 1987 (rev. ed.). / *Heraclitus: The Inception of Occidental Thinking; Logic: Heraclitus's Doctrine of the Logos.* Tr. Julia Goesser Assaiante and S. Montgomery Ewegen. London: Bloomsbury Academic, 2018.

GA 56/57. *Zur Bestimmung der Philosophie* (1919). Ed. Bernd Heimbüchel, 1987, 1999 (rev., expanded ed.). / *Towards the Definition of Philosophy.* Tr. Ted Sadler. London: Continuum, 2000.

GA 60. *Phänomenologie des religiösen Lebens* (1918–1921). Ed. Matthias Jung, Thomas Regehly, and Claudius Strube, 1995, 2011 (rev. ed.). / *The Phenomenology of Religious Life.* Tr. Matthias Fritsch and Jennifer Anna Gosetti-Ferencei. Bloomington: Indiana University Press, 2004.

GA 61. *Phänomenologische Interpretationen zu Aristoteles. Einführung in die phänomenologische Forschung* (1921–1922). Ed. Walter Bröcker und Käte Bröcker-Oltmanns, 1985, 1994 (rev. ed.). / *Phenomenological Interpretations of Aristotle: Initiation into Phenomenological Research.* Tr. Richard Rojcewicz. Bloomington: Indiana University Press, 2008.

GA 62. *Phänomenologische Interpretationen ausgewählter Abhandlungen des Aristoteles zu Ontologie und Logik.* (1922). Ed. Günther Neumann, 2005.

GA 63. *Ontologie. Hermeneutik der Faktizität* (1923). Ed. Käte Bröcker-Oltmanns, 1988. / *Ontology—The Hermeneutics of Facticity.* Tr. John Van Buren. Bloomington: Indiana University Press, 1999.

GA 64. *Der Begriff der Zeit* (1924). Ed. Friedrich-Wilhelm von Herrmann, 2004. / CT1 (tr. of pp. 3–103) = *The Concept of Time: The First Draft of "Being and Time."* Tr. Ingo Farin. London: Continuum, 2011. CT2 (tr. of pp. 107–25) = "The Concept of Time." In *Becoming Heidegger: On the Trail of His Early Occasional Writings, 1910–1927.* Ed. Theodore Kisiel and Thomas Sheehan. 2nd ed. Seattle: Noesis Press, 2010.

GA 65. *Beiträge zur Philosophie (Vom Ereignis)* (1936–1938). Ed. Friedrich-Wilhelm von Herrmann, 1989, 1994 (rev. ed.). / *Contributions to Philosophy (Of the Event).* Tr. Richard Rojcewicz and Daniela Vallega-Neu. Bloomington: Indiana University Press, 2012.

GA 66. *Besinnung* (1938–1939). Ed. Friedrich-Wilhelm von Herrmann, 1997. / *Mindfulness.* Tr. Parvis Emad and Thomas Kalary. London: Continuum, 2006.

GA 67. *Metaphysik und Nihilismus* (1938–1939, 1946–1948). Ed. Hans-Joachim Friedrich, 1999.

GA 68. *Hegel* (1938–1939, 1942). Ed. Ingrid Schüßler, 1993. / *Hegel*. Tr. Joseph Arel and Niels Feuerhahn. Bloomington: Indiana University Press, 2015.

GA 69. *Die Geschichte des Seyns* (1938–1940). Ed. Peter Trawny, 1998, 2012 (rev. ed.). / *The History of Beyng*. Tr. William McNeill and Jeffrey Powell. Bloomington: Indiana University Press, 2015.

GA 70. *Über den Anfang* (1941). Ed. Paola-Ludovika Coriando, 2005.

GA 71. *Das Ereignis* (1941–1942). Ed. Friedrich-Wilhelm von Herrmann, 2009. / *The Event*. Tr. Richard Rojcewicz. Bloomington: Indiana University Press, 2013.

GA 73.1 and 73.2. *Zum Ereignis-Denken* (1932–1970s). Ed. Peter Trawny, 2013.

GA 74. *Zum Wesen der Sprache und Zur Frage nach der Kunst* (1935–1960). Ed. Thomas Regehly, 2010.

GA 75. *Zu Hölderlin—Griechenlandreisen* (1939–1970). Ed. Curd Ochwadt, 2000.

GA 76. *Leitgedanken zur Entstehung der Metaphysik, der neuzeitlichen Wissenschaft und der modernen Technik* (1935–1955). Ed. Claudius Strube, 2009.

GA 77. *Feldweg-Gespräche* (1944–1945). Ed. Ingrid Schüßler, 1995, 2007 (2nd rev. ed.). / *Country Path Conversations*. Tr. Bret Davis. Bloomington: Indiana University Press, 2010.

GA 78. *Der Spruch des Anaximander* (1942). Ed. Ingeborg Schüßler, 2010.

GA 79. *Bremer und Freiburger Vorträge* (1949, 1957). Ed. Petra Jaeger, 1994. / *Bremen and Freiburg Lectures: Insight into That Which Is and Basic Principles of Thinking*. Tr. Andrew Mitchell. Bloomington: Indiana University Press, 2012.

GA 80.1. *Vorträge 1915 bis 1932*. Ed. Günther Neumann, 2016.

GA 81. *Gedachtes*. Ed. Paola-Ludovika Coriando, 2007.

GA 82. *Zu eigenen Veröffentlichungen* (1936–ca. 1950). Ed. Friedrich-Wilhelm von Herrmann, 2018.

GA 83. *Seminare: Platon—Aristoteles—Augustinus* (1928–1952). Ed. Mark Michalski, 2012.

GA 84.1. *Seminare: Kant—Leibniz—Schiller* (1931–1936). Ed. Günther Neumann, 2013.

GA 86. *Seminare: Hegel—Schelling* (1927–1957). Ed. Peter Trawny, 2011. / Tr. of pp. 59–184 in *On Hegel's "Philosophy of Right": The 1934-5 Seminar and Interpretative Essays*, ed. Peter Trawny, Marcia Sá Cavalcante Schuback, and Michael Marder, tr. Andrew Mitchell. London: Bloomsbury, 2014.

GA 87. *Nietzsche: Seminare 1937 und 1944*. Ed. Peter von Ruckteschell, 2004.

GA 88. *Seminare (Übungen) 1937/38 und 1941/42: 1. Die metaphysischen Grundstellungen des abendländischen Denkens; 2. Einübung in das philosophische Denken*. Ed. Alfred Denker, 2008.

GA 89. *Zollikoner Seminare* (1959–1969). Ed. Peter Trawny, 2017. / *Zollikon Seminars: Protocols—Conversations—Letters*. Tr. Franz Mayr and Richard Askay. Evanston: Northwestern University Press, 2001.

GA 90. *Zu Ernst Jünger* (1934–1954). Ed. Peter Trawny, 2004.

GA 94. *Überlegungen II–VI (Schwarze Hefte 1931–1938).* Ed. Peter Trawny, 2014. / *Ponderings II–VI: Black Notebooks 1931–1938.* Tr. Richard Rojcewicz. Bloomington: Indiana University Press, 2016.

GA 95. *Überlegungen VII–XI (Schwarze Hefte 1938–1939).* Ed. Peter Trawny, 2014. / *Ponderings VII–XI: Black Notebooks 1938–1939.* Tr. Richard Rojcewicz. Bloomington: Indiana University Press, 2017.

GA 96. *Überlegungen XII–XV (Schwarze Hefte 1939–1941).* Ed. Peter Trawny, 2014. / *Ponderings XII–XV: Black Notebooks 1939–1941.* Tr. Richard Rojcewicz. Bloomington: Indiana University Press, 2017.

GA 97. *Anmerkungen I–V (Schwarze Hefte 1942–1948).* Ed. Peter Trawny, 2015.

GA 98. *Anmerkungen VI–IX (Schwarze Hefte 1948/49–1951).* Ed. Peter Trawny, 2018.

Introduction

How do we become the ones we are?

—Martin Heidegger, Martin Buber[1]

For Martin Heidegger, becoming who he was going to be meant undergoing a tumultuous transition after the publication of what he had envisioned as the first half of *Being and Time* in 1927. That project was never completed. Instead, a series of questions drew the restless Heidegger into a dark new philosophical and political landscape. He experienced a crisis, an emergency, and emerged from it with a new approach to these very themes: emergency, self-transformation, and the question of who one is. This book tries to understand the problems that brought Heidegger into a new phase of his thought, and to think through the concerns that drove him during that period.

To "think through" a thought can mean to analyze it; to get over it and come out on the other side; or to think with its help. I aim to achieve all three: to work out some interpretive issues, to work through certain problems and deficiencies in Heidegger's thought, and to work on my own philosophical ideas while drawing on the more promising aspects of his thought.

My focus is the period that begins with the so-called turn after *Being and Time* and includes his much-discussed and lamented entanglement with National Socialism. For convenience, we can refer to this phase as "the thirties." But how should we delimit it philosophically?

This distinctive and troubled period in Heidegger's philosophical career is marked by a shift "from the understanding of being to the *happening of being*" (GA 40: 218/233 tm). Instead of describing the temporal structures that allow us to understand being, as he intended to do in *Being and Time*, he now

1

looks to the happening in which we come into our own as those who stand in the truth of being. The emphasis is no longer on our constitution—human nature, in traditional terms—but on a transformative event that seizes us and thrusts us into the condition of "being-there" (*Dasein*).[2]

Such an event could involve the founding of a new political order—and the thirties are notoriously the decade of Heidegger's overt political engagement, including his 1933–1934 tenure as Nazi rector of the University of Freiburg. For several years, he is intensely concerned with action, decision, and the awakening of the German *Volk*. By the end of the decade, however, his view of politics is considerably jaundiced; in the forties he will develop a philosophy of *Gelassenheit* or "releasement" that lays aside power and will in order to await the gift of being. The thirties, then, are marked by his attempt to leap into a singular, transformative event that would bring Germany into its own.

By late 1929, Heidegger is ready for a metamorphosis: "Now I am finally at the decisive inception, and am ready to turn the deconstruction against myself."[3] We can say, not completely facetiously, that his "thirties" began on a weekday evening in that December.[4] We can pinpoint the moment when he allows himself a fateful step into the political: halfway through his lecture course *The Fundamental Concepts of Metaphysics*, he asks about "*our* Dasein," "*the Dasein in contemporary man.*" He claims that we are sunk in profound boredom, insulated from distress (GA 29/30: 242–44). This moment is the beginning of a theme that often recurs in the thirties—the idea that his times suffer from "the emergency of the lack of emergency." He has leapt into the divination of a shared situation and into a cultural critique.

This juncture in Heidegger's lectures is the start of what soon becomes a political-philosophical worldview that gets woven into a metanarrative about Western history. This story becomes increasingly difficult to disentangle from the question of being itself, which Heidegger now approaches "ontohistorically," in terms of the history of beyng (*seynsgeschichtlich*).[5] "Dasein" is also historicized: it is no longer the human condition in general, but a possible transformation of the human—a new way of relating to all that there is (GA 29/30: 509; GA 65: 3, 9, 248, 294, 300; GA 82: 22, 56–57, 74).

It was in 1930, by Heidegger's own account, that he began to believe that National Socialism could generate a new inception for the West (GA 95: 408). Before this, he may very well have had political predilections, but they stayed out of his philosophy, which focused on describing what seemed to be universal human conditions.

What provoked this change in Heidegger's thought and attitudes? One could speculate about his new professional circumstances after the publication of *Being and Time*: he gained a chair in philosophy and no longer needed to obey academic conventions. One could also point out the panic that so many in Germany and elsewhere were feeling as they beheld what looked like a failed experiment in liberalism and capitalism. (The American stock market began to crash on October 24, 1929.)

But to judge from his journals, known as the *Black Notebooks*, Heidegger himself might prefer to think of the change in his thought in terms of the requirements of philosophy itself as a risky adventure. He writes, at the outset of the thirties, "Only if we actually err—*go* into errancy—can we run up against 'truth'" (GA 94: 13/11 tm). Thinkers must learn "long useless straying"; "the history of philosophy is in itself an erring" (GA 95: 227/176).

In trying to understand Heidegger's transition into the thirties, we should not wipe out this element of experimentation and risk. The transition should not be smoothed over in retrospect and turned into a logical extension of his earlier thought. However, we can identify some crucial spurs that urged him to think differently. One is the question of the origin of our temporality. Others include the themes of emergency and shared selfhood, which were present in *Being and Time* but become more urgent.

As for the end of the "thirties," it is more gradual. Heidegger draws back from his political or quasi-political discourse of leaping, deciding, and founding. His enthusiasm for struggle and power cools. During the Second World War, he moves toward a nonwillful letting-be.

Although the transition to Heidegger's "late" thought was incremental, it eventually led to a stark personal and philosophical collapse. After the defeat of Germany and his removal from teaching, he experienced a depressive crisis from which he had to recover in a sanitarium. He had to build a new, humbled way of thinking on the ruins of his former thought, trying to describe "things" in a deliberately simple, unpresumptuous way, as if he were seeing the world anew.[6] Philosophically, the collapse of the "thirties" could be highlighted in two dramatic reversals. In a lecture from 1945, "Poverty," he defines *Not* (urgent need or emergency) as being forced to focus on what we require for survival, and claims that freedom lies in *Not-wendigkeit*, turning away from such compulsion (GA 73.1: 878–79). Emergency is no longer a requirement for appropriate existence. The other reversal is a postwar passage in the *Black Notebooks* that says the "talk of the history of beyng is an embarrassment and a euphemism" (GA 97: 382). With such statements, one can say that the "thirties" have been left behind.

To be sure, Heidegger still understands the West as suffering from a certain crisis that must be understood in terms of its entire history. And short of certain extreme breaks, one does not simply become a new person—or a new philosopher. Several themes and concerns run throughout sixty years of Heidegger's thinking, and a case can be made for a unified interpretation of his trajectory.[7]

Why, then, focus on the thirties?

Although the path from *Being and Time* to the thirties is tangled and far from obvious, the thirties radicalize certain tendencies in that book. To remain within Heidegger's thought-world of the twenties would be to neglect these more radical implications. In particular, *Being and Time*'s concepts of the moment, ecstasis, existence, and history imply an embrace of the thinker's own historicity that is not fully explicit there. *Being and Time* claims we must find possibilities to retrieve from our heritage, but it remains at the general level of "existential" ontology, avoiding the particular, "existentiell" question of *which* possibilities to retrieve. At the same time, any response to this question seems arbitrary in the face of anxiety, which confronts us with the ultimate insignificance of all things and roles, reminding us of our exposure to death. Thus, as Heidegger's students quipped, "I am resolved, only towards what I don't know."[8] In the thirties, however, he makes choices, leaving behind the detached viewpoint of *Being and Time* and acting as a member of a community at a particular historical juncture. This choice of who to be is, in his view, intrinsically linked to the philosophical act of asking the question of being. Heidegger acts—and in the ensuing turmoil, develops a wealth of intriguing ideas.

Heidegger's choices were, in my view, first deeply wrong (joining the Nazi movement) and then unsatisfactory (withdrawing from all politics). But his failed attempt to act politically at least gives us an occasion for thinking about the political realm as such and reflecting on concrete decisions, which was not possible within the ambit of *Being and Time*. The thirties represent his attempt to participate in history, radicalizing the thought of historicity and engaging in his times. Maybe, then, this period could be a fertile source for our own practical thought. It is during the few years when he has faith in action that his concepts are potentially most illuminating for our attempts to think and act today. Potentially—but with the constant danger that we will be seduced by the phantoms that tempted him into evil. This is one reason why the thirties must be thought through.

Of course, we should be cautious if we appropriate any ideas from a philosopher who sympathized with Hitler. Just how much of a Nazi and an antisemite was Martin Heidegger? Interpreters differ widely, and often acrimoniously, on whether his Nazism was a passing aberration or a long-term commitment, and whether it was due to a character defect or a philosophical error. As a biographical and psychological question, the issue of his Nazism has legitimate but limited interest. It is easy to find numerous vices in him that he shared with millions who have lent their support to tyrannies, scapegoated minorities, and lied both to others and themselves. But as a question of philosophical interpretation, the issue is more important, as it helps us see the implications and limitations of his ideas.

It was never wholly accurate to describe Heidegger as a convinced Nazi, since from the start he hoped for a questioning more radical than any party slogan. As early as 1934, he begins to view mainstream Nazi ideology as an instance of the domineering and reductive metaphysics of modernity. However, this metaphysical critique is not accompanied by a moral or political one, and he even explicitly dismisses such points of view (GA 95: 13). In texts such as the *Black Notebooks* he portrays all modern movements and forces, including the phantasmagoric power of "world Jewry," as instances of one and the same machinational metaphysics. Modernity's forgetting of its roots is associated in his discourse with the traditional prejudice against Jews as supposedly nomadic cosmopolitans. Despite his critique of Nazism on the theoretical level, he does not resist it, but submits to it (GA 95: 408). As we will see, he seems to view Nazism as the ultimate modern destiny, an extremity of willfulness that must be played out to its catastrophic conclusion before a new inception can become possible (GA 95: 50, 417).

Clearly, then, there is good reason for concern. Heidegger's ambiguous but close relationship to Nazism is not just a personal failing, but a disturbing knot in his thoughts of the thirties. As we think through those thoughts, can we be certain that our own thought is not being "infected" with Nazism?[9] We cannot. Philosophers never understand themselves completely. However, if Heidegger's thought in the thirties offers significant questions and insights, we need to think through them—maybe even especially because they are entangled in error and evil. Instead of avoiding a problematic philosopher— and how many great philosophers are unproblematic?—we should take the problems as occasions for better thinking.

What of Heidegger's late work? As valuable as it often is, I find it politically inadequate. After he is disappointed by his intervention in politics, he retreats from the sphere of the political altogether. He turns ever farther away from concrete struggles, power relations, and emergencies, in order to focus on the remote and epochal happening of being itself, which lies beyond both power and powerlessness (GA 66: 83, 187–88). He deemphasizes founding, and patiently awaits a new dispensation that can come only from being. His postwar writings seem to abandon *praxis* altogether in favor of a pastoral "dwelling" that claims to be the true "ethics" but is essentially contemplative (GA 9: 356–58/271–72).[10]

In the *Contributions to Philosophy* (1936–1938) he could endorse a "will to ground and build" (GA 65: 98/78) and a "will to the event of appropriation" (GA 65: 58/46 tm), but in the forties he identifies the "will to will" as the essence of a modern subjectivism that must be set aside (e.g., GA 5: 235/176). The *Country Path Conversations*, composed in the final phase of the war, suggest that will itself may be evil (GA 77: 208). Willfulness springs from a malignancy in being—a blockage and concealment within the very process of presentation. Heidegger can only recommend "pure waiting," a releasement to the event that releases us into the open (GA 77: 217/140). We have already almost reached the famous statement from the *Der Spiegel* interview of 1966: "Only a god can still save us" (GA 16: 671/HR 326). Calculation and action cannot rescue humanity, because the illusion of self-sufficiency is just an effect of the very devastation from which we need to be rescued.

There are various difficulties in this project of setting aside the will. First, Heidegger has to assume that a certain free will is crucial to the human condition: even if oblivion has come upon us, we have some freedom either to resist it or to let ourselves fall all too far into it. (As Plato puts it, we all have to drink from the river of Carelessness on the plain of Lethe, but some of us drink a little deeper than we have to: *Republic* 621a.) Secondly, Heidegger's attempt to understand evil is unsatisfactory. He holds that evil will is essentially the manipulative approach to beings that is typical of modern technology; this approach embodies a "devastation" that has been "sent" to us as our destiny and that stems from the self-occlusion of being.[11] But as Bret Davis points out, the deepest evil is not the technological "faceless defacing" that perceives everything as an object and ignores the face of the other; profound evil is "face-to-face defacement."[12] The sadist knows that the other is there, and willingly treats her as if she were an object in order to enjoy her horror at her own objectification. Sadism is not a misunderstanding, but deliberate and knowing abuse. This fact is the downfall of all theorists who identify evil with ignorance or oblivion. This line of thought also suggests that will, including the possibility of evil will, is not just a phase in Western history; it is an essential dimension of the human condition.

If we want to think about ethics and politics, then, Heidegger's late period is likely to leave us dissatisfied—not to mention that his evasive way of dealing with his own past and the Nazis' crimes leaves a great deal to be desired. He may escape from Plato's cave, but he never comes back down to develop appropriate judgments about particular human relations. Retrieving ethics and politics after Heidegger means resisting the detachment that characterizes his later thought and drawing selectively on his thoughts of the thirties to develop better concepts of decision, will, and initiative. Action must be recovered as a central topic of post-Heideggerian philosophy.

Despite Heidegger's misguided choices and his failure to appreciate particular situations, his writings offer many opportunities to reflect on the deeper ground of ethics and action.[13] After Heidegger, it is harder to place our confidence in conceptions of action as pure self-determination, or will as autonomous choice. One lesson to be learned from his late thought is that we always remain indebted to a disclosure that we did not make, that we cannot harness, and that calls for our response but cannot be exhausted by this response. The most responsible action will always involve a certain responsiveness to what Heidegger in the thirties calls *das Ereignis*, "the appropriating event."

As I have argued in my study of the *Contributions*, the greatest promise of the thought of *Ereignis* lies in its possible application to concrete phenomena: we must each discover the appropriating events of emergency in our own lives and communities.[14] Here I pursue this idea. Although Heidegger focuses on the rare emergency that would found a world and an era, we can apply some of his thoughts to the smaller shocks and reversals that are frequent elements of our individual and collective lives—developing a "traumatic ontology" of human beings and their understanding of being. I also attempt to retrieve politics with the help of Hannah Arendt's concept of action as an event that both discloses and develops the actor, initiating unpredictable relationships. The political realm can be a seedbed for such events—for the emergence of selves in emergencies large and small.

The challenge is not just to interpret Heidegger, but to think and act today. The twenty-first century is witnessing a disturbing resurgence of neofascist movements, complete with an intelligentsia that draws on right-wing theorists of the past, including Heidegger.[15] To denounce these developments in the name of morality and liberal democracy is correct and necessary, in my view, but this is no answer to the ideas of those who reject these standpoints. A more adequate and philosophical response goes through Heidegger to grasp the theoretical inadequacies of his stances toward politics, and to show that his best insights of the thirties can be appropriated in support of a pluralistic and free society.

Chapters 1 and 2 of this book are primarily interpretive, chapter 3 is critical, and chapter 4 is constructive.

Chapter 1 sheds light on some motivations for Heidegger's shift after *Being and Time*. No longer content with describing human temporality as the horizon for our understanding of being, he pursues the possibility that our temporality itself originates in a crucial moment. This time when time arises is bound up with the experience of emergency and the question of who we are.

Chapter 2 examines seminars, lecture courses, journals, and other manuscripts in which Heidegger attempts to work out fundamental political questions in light of his new philosophical orientation. These texts reflect both his initial support for Nazism and his later critiques of it, as the decade of the thirties sees him leap into the event of revolution and then pass through the political into the mysterious "event" of being itself. I consider his conceptions of political founding, the role of silence in his political thought, and his analysis of the metaphysics of struggle and power that is reflected in Nazi ideology.

The chapter ends with a close look at the *Black Notebooks*, which illustrate his ambiguous relationship to Nazism and other contemporary phenomena.

Chapter 3 unfolds a philosophical critique of Heidegger's political thought, drawing on Arendt's views on action and plurality. At stake here are not only his temporary enthusiasm for National Socialism and his antisemitic tendencies, but his permanent antiliberalism and his failure to appreciate political realities. Again, his attitudes richly deserve moral condemnation, but I focus on theoretically retrieving politics as a sphere of action.

Chapter 4 draws on Heidegger's thought of the thirties to sketch a temporal ontology along the lines of what might have been included in *Being and Time*, Part One, Division III, and then to supplement it with a traumatic ontology—an attempt to understand human beings and our relation to being itself that hinges on transformative encounters with what exceeds established sense.

The appendix, "Propositions on Emergency," lays out the fundamentals of traumatic ontology in the style of Spinoza's *Ethics*. This text is an experiment in thinking deductively about the issues at stake and testing the consistency of a possible system of traumatic ontology. Such an "axiomatics of being-there" (GA 73.1: 255) is very un-Heideggerian (GA 42: 56–57/32–33), and deliberately so: it is meant to draw us out of Heidegger's ambit and explore whether ideas with Heideggerian roots can survive in a different philosophical atmosphere. But since the very spirit of traumatic ontology resists systematization and conceptual fixation, the text is written with tongue partly in cheek; it ends (with a nod to Wittgenstein's *Tractatus*) by demonstrating the inadequacy of all systems of propositions.

Chapter One

Into the Happening of Being

Heidegger's move away from *Being and Time* is overdetermined, and any reconstruction of what is happening in his work of 1927–1930 must beware of retrospective oversimplification.[1] His own accounts of his transition (e.g., GA 66: 411–17) and his later interpretations of *Being and Time* (e.g., in GA 82) must also be read with some reservations, since they are typically couched in his later language and emphasize only certain features of the development.

I, too, will be selective in this chapter and will trace just three threads in the tangle, including some little-known strands—but these threads lead us to some of the most distinctive and crucial themes of the thirties. First, Heidegger comes to focus on certain intense moments when human temporality itself can be said to arise; this will lead him to a conception of history centered on such "inceptions." Secondly, he comes to view such times as moments of crisis or emergency, and identifies the lack of explicit emergency as the implicit emergency of his historical moment. Finally, he associates both of these themes with the question "Who are we?"—the experience of becoming a problem for ourselves.

These are not the themes most commonly discussed in accounts of the shift from "Heidegger I" to "Heidegger II," or of the faltering of the project of *Being and Time*. More frequently, commentators emphasize Heidegger's attempt to overcome subjectivity and his turn toward "being itself." This issue is important, but if one understands the "turn" too simplistically, as a pivot from being-there to being, this may obfuscate the fact that Dasein continues to play a central role in Heidegger's thought in the thirties. In fact, individual and collective selfhood becomes a burning issue for him, because it is through becoming ourselves that we become open to being. "*Because* the inquiry into being is grounded most intimately in the inquiry into Da-sein and vice versa . . .

the inquiry into Da-sein must be made anew" (GA 66: 414/367). The "that-it-is [*Daß*] of being-there" is also "the *birth of being*" (GA 73.1: 11). This double happening is Heidegger's most distinctive concern in the thirties—a happening in which politics is not incidental to philosophy.

BEING AND TIME ON TIME AND BEING

Some essential points from *Being and Time* and related texts will set the stage for these developments.

The title of *Being and Time* expresses what Heidegger later described as his "sole lightning bolt" of insight (GA 82: 355; cf. GA 98: 279): presence stems from the present. Being is available thanks to time; temporality is the context in terms of which we can encounter anything as something that is, instead of nothing at all. This thesis is not fully developed in the work as it stands, but the book does show that there are several distinct ways of being: what it means for a "present-at-hand" entity to *be* is to be given as an object to a theoretical gaze; a "ready-to-hand" entity, such as a tool, *is* when it fits into a meaningful network of purposes and functions, or a "world"; and we ourselves *are* by existing as "being-there"—we are entities for whom our own being is at issue as we go about inhabiting the world, and who are thoroughly temporal. That is, we have always already been "thrown" into some situation, we "project" possibilities, and we dwell among other beings in a present world. Our temporality is also historical, as each of us is a member of a community. Heidegger suggests that through "communication and struggle," a group may find a way to forge a destiny from its heritage (SZ 364).

These points are all linked to the insight that our temporality gives us access to being. Our projective reach into possibilities, our thrown dependence on what we have been given, and our engagement in a current world make it possible for anything to make sense to us as what is, rather than what is not. Presence-at-hand, which the Western metaphysical tradition has generally identified with all being, should be unmasked as only one type of being—a narrow, objectified mode that is made available within the present. An insight into the broader dimensions of temporality should make it possible for us to acknowledge and comprehend more types of being, including our own, in some unified way.

Let us look more closely at this idea and its elements: (a) beings, (b) being, (c) Dasein and its temporality, (d) time as the horizon for being.

(a) *Das Seiende*, often translated as "beings" or "entities," or more literally as "that which is," embraces everything that is something at all, and not nothing. It is not limited to "things" in the narrow sense (individual objects or substances). Nearly everything with which we concern ourselves, theoretically or practically, is a being. This would include a particular cat, the species cat, the cat's act of running, the number pi, absolute monarchy, the religion of the Hittites, Baroque music, cryptocurrency, quasars, a love affair, and so on.

(b) It is considerably harder to explain what Heidegger means by "being" (*das Sein*), sometimes translated as "Being" to distinguish it more clearly from an entity. Serious interpreters disagree.[2] In order to have a truly clear concept of being, we would need to have completed the project of *Being and Time* itself, which remains unfinished. However, as Heidegger emphasizes from the outset, we already have an implicit, vague understanding of being that we can work with. The following remarks, then, are inexact elucidations of his usage of the word *Sein*, not strict definitions.

First, he often uses "being" as one might use "essence" or "nature": to examine "the kind of being that belongs to living things as such" is to establish what characterizes something as alive (SZ 10). Heidegger calls this "what-being" (*Was-sein*, SZ 42).

He also refers to *Sosein*, being-such or being-thus (SZ 5, 7, 14). This seems to be a broader category, including not only essences but also nonessential qualities or predicates, as when we say that the cat *is* asleep.

"Being" also has the sense of "that-being" (*Daß-sein*, SZ 5, 7, 14). An entity, something that is, is something instead of nothing. In traditional (medieval and modern) terms, this sense of being is existence, as contrasted with essence (GA 24: 108–71).

These usages of "being" cohere as long as we are willing to challenge the doctrine (found in Kant and frequently repeated in analytic philosophy) that the term "being" conflates several logically distinct operations. In particular, universal quantification ("every platypus *is* a mammal") is distinguished from existential quantification ("here *is* a platypus"). The problem with this doctrine is that what it is for something to exist (that-being) may depend on the sort of entity it is (what-being), and vice versa.[3] "What-being is that-being" (GA 74: 6); or more precisely, for different kinds of entities, there is a special sort of "actuality which is prescribed for [their] respectively determined what-being" (GA 33: 223/192). A platypus does not exist in the same way as a number, freedom, or *Paradise Lost* exists. The differences among their ways of existing are precisely the essential differences among these kinds of entities. Admittedly, describing what it *means* for something to exist is distinct from asserting that it *actually* exists; but the point is that there is no single, simple sense of existence or actuality. If we keep what-being and that-being utterly separate, we easily end up assuming that that-being (existence, actuality) applies in just the same way to all kinds of entities (GA 6.2: 374–75/EP 11). That is precisely the unquestioned, reductive understanding of being that

Heidegger finds pernicious. Partly in order to avoid such reductionism, *Being and Time* reserves the term "existence" for Dasein's distinctive way of being, in which we are concerned with our own being and inhabit a world.

Heidegger also emphasizes that being is not an entity. It "is" not, but it is given to Dasein as the entity who understands being (SZ 183). Being is essentially related to Dasein's understanding; it is that in terms of which Dasein understands entities as entities (SZ 6). For instance, we understand the cat in its catness, or being-a-cat; this being-a-cat is not itself an entity that forms part of the cat, but the context in which the cat makes sense to us as a cat.

Thus, without Dasein, being would not be given (SZ 212). No entities can be understood without an entity who can understand them. Without that entity, there is no understanding and thus no context for understanding. This may sound viciously relativistic, but Heidegger insists that interpretations of being can be better or worse: they can either impose a restrictive, misleading framework on beings or provide a context that allows beings to display themselves richly (SZ 150).

In order to suggest the multiple yet related senses of "being" and being's essential relation to Dasein, we can gloss being as the difference it makes that there is something instead of nothing. There is no such difference without someone (Dasein) to whom the difference can be made. The difference has an "existential" sense but also an "essential" one, for entities display their various essences in the particular sorts of difference it makes for them to be something instead of nothing. As we tease apart their ways of being, we discover the differences it makes that there are, for instance, artworks rather than nothing, or atoms rather than nothing.

Even though "we are always already operating within an understanding of being" (SZ 5), being usually goes unrecognized. At first and for the most part, it does not show itself directly, but lies in the background of the overtly self-showing phenomena. But being can be brought out: it can be revealed as having already been showing itself indirectly as the "sense and ground" of the overt phenomena, and as "belonging" to these phenomena (SZ 35). The sense of a phenomenon is the context that allows it to be understood (SZ 151).[4]

One of Heidegger's favorite techniques for revealing being is the interpretation of certain overt phenomena as "deficient modes" of a more fundamental phenomenon. The absence of historical research is a deficient mode of historicity (SZ 20). The essential usability of shoes becomes clear when my shoes do not fit (SZ 73–74). Indifference to others is a deficient mode of caring for them (SZ 121). These are exceptions that prove the rule: their function is to extrapolate an ordinary "ontic" concept, which pertains to entities, into an "ontological" one that grasps their being. Heidegger hopes that his redescription of the ontic negatives (lack of usability, history, or caring) as deficient ontological positives will draw our attention to underlying phenomena that have always already been making it possible for the overt positive and negative phenomena to show themselves. Then "care," for instance, no longer refers to a particular state that we may or may not be in, but to the human condition as such, and we may recognize that it is only thanks to this condition that we can become careless, carefree, or uncaring. (A shoe is neither caring nor uncaring, but altogether lacks ontological care.)

However, uncovering being is not just a matter of performing a few dialectical tricks, for we inevitably draw on a tradition that makes it difficult to acknowledge and articulate some distinctive aspects of entities (SZ 20–22). In particular, traditional philosophy, science, and common sense often assume that to be is to be present-at-hand—to subsist as an actual object with given properties that can be theoretically specified. But this assumption cannot do justice to the many dimensions of what there is: the utility of tools, the familiarity of a dwelling, or the oppressive endurance of a tradition, to name a few.

One more point about being: according to *Being and Time*, there cannot be anything that lies hidden "behind" being (SZ 35–36, 152), because being is not the partial disclosure of some nonmanifest entity, but what enables the manifestation of entities in the first place. If there were no manifestation, then being would not go into hiding, like an undiscovered entity, but simply would not occur at all. However, there is something "behind" being in another sense: we can ask what *gives* being, or makes it possible. Again, the thesis of *Being and Time* is that being is given by temporality. In the thirties Heidegger will try to push past this answer, but the question endures. He is interested not only in describing how we understand entities, but in finding what enables us to understand them at all. This question is not just about the being of beings, but about the source of "being as such."[5]

(c) *Dasein and its temporality* can be properly understood only if we free being from its restriction to presence-at-hand. Again and again, well-meaning attempts to distinguish soul from body, or subject from object, have ended up merely positing a different kind of present-at-hand thing, because such theories fail to rethink what it is to be in the first place. Dasein is not a present-at-hand thing with present-at-hand properties.

Dasein is not a thing: it is the "there," an opening or disclosure (SZ 133, 135, 220–21). In this sense, Dasein *is* its own world (SZ 364): it provides the meaningful forum, the illuminated space within which all entities can be discovered. To be the "there" is to engage with what is, to exist as the field in which beings can make a difference. Such an opening cannot be understood as if it were simply one item available *within* the opening.

Dasein has no properties: it has possibilities that engage with its situation. Our being is an issue for us: we have always adopted a position on who we are, and are perpetually challenged to renew our position. Our existence remains a problem, and our selfhood never crystallizes into a rigid identity. To own up to this condition is to exist in a self-owned or authentic way (*eigentlich*)—not with properties, but properly. To evade or forget this condition is to fall, to exist inauthentically.

Dasein is not present-at-hand: it is temporal. The point is not just the truism that we change—philosophies of becoming are among the most hackneyed metaphysical standpoints. Dasein's time is better understood in terms of three "ecstases" (SZ 329).[6]

(1) Deliberately or not, we are engaged in possible ways to be. Heidegger calls this our understanding, our projection of possibilities. Futurity essentially involves our concern with who we are: Dasein is "*being out toward what it is not yet, but can be*" (GA 64: 46/CT1 38 tm). Thus we always understand ourselves and our surroundings in terms of the possible (SZ 43, 86). The future is marked, however, by the constantly looming possibility of the extinction of possibilities—mortality, or "being-toward-death" (SZ 262).

(2) In turn, we are claimed by our circumstances, which are thrust upon us as given. This is our thrownness, our past as a having-been that we are challenged to take over or reclaim.

(3) Through projecting possibilities while being claimed by the past, we arrive at the present: we dwell at home in the midst of things in our current world.

These three "ecstases" allow us to "stand out" from any determinate spatiotemporal point. Temporality is the original "outside-itself" or *ekstatikon* (SZ 329). "The human being is a creature [*Wesen*] of distance" (GA 26: 285/221, cf. GA 9: 175/135) who reaches past current confines into a broader and richer space and time. "Man is not a thing that stops at its skin."[7] It is impossible to understand anything human simply by inspecting a particular cross-section, as it were—its properties at an instant—or even a massive set of such facts ("big data," as we say). Dasein is always more than it factually is: it cannot be reduced to its present-at-hand characteristics, but demands to be understood in terms of the world it inhabits and the possibilities it pursues (SZ 145, 236).

We are not just *in* time, then; "*each Dasein is itself 'time'*" (GA 64: 57/CT1 47). Dasein is its own present, in which it encounters and deals with present entities, and it is also its having-been and its to-be. It is "*thrown possibility through and through*" (SZ 144). Since we inhabit time with others, participating in a heritage and destiny, it can also be said that "Dasein is history" (GA 64: 86/CT1 73). Time and history are neither obstacles to our fulfillment nor simply arenas in which we happen to act; they are the heart of our own being. To avoid a misunderstanding: Heidegger's terms "fate" (*Schicksal*) and "destiny" (*Geschick*) have a non-"fatalistic" meaning. They are not inevitable outcomes, but senses of individual or shared selfhood that provide some clarity and purpose by finding an appropriate connection between what we irrevocably have been and what we can still be.

The threefold ecstatic structure of time can be summed up as the future that presences as having-been (SZ 326, 350). Although the ecstases are interconnected, the future is primary (SZ 329, 339). By virtue of the future, Dasein is confronted with its own being as an issue. It is faced with the question of *who* it is because it must adopt some possible way of being. In terms of this ultimate possibility, or "for-the-sake-of-which," our more immediate options gain their sense, as do the possible ways of being of the other entities we encounter (SZ 43, 86, 145).

The present as well as the past thus gain their significance from possibilities. The future brings the other ecstases into relief. "Only insofar as Dasein itself *is* as 'I-*am*-as-having been,' can it come toward itself futurally in such a way that it comes *back*. . . . Having-been arises, in a certain way, from the future" (SZ 326). Adopting a possible way to be requires making something of what one already finds oneself to be: one has to take up one's own past as a burden and an inheritance. Dasein "*is* its past, whether explicitly or not" (SZ 20). Dasein "has in each case already gotten itself into definite possibilities" (SZ 144) or "abandoned itself" to them (SZ 270). A "resolute" stance discloses these possibilities as such (SZ 298) by "retrieving" them (SZ 339, 385)—appropriating them as guiding interpretations of existence. This does not mean mere "iteration" (GA 69: 22/22), but creative adaptation.

Our present is an opportunity for action and discovery. The authentic, futural retrieval of the past is "the right way of becoming contemporary" (GA 64: 94/CT1 80): it "discloses the current situation of the 'there'" (SZ 326). Presence, then, is at its fullest not when time is suspended or when we live only in the "now" (as if such things were possible), but when we draw most authentically on the future and past. Heidegger thus denies presence its traditional ontological priority, since it becomes available to us only through the interplay of future and past (SZ 350–51). The traditional focus on presence is not simply an intellectual error, but is due to "falling," or Dasein's tendency to shirk its responsibility for itself and get absorbed inauthentically in the present (SZ 328).

Time is datable and significant: it is oriented by events that play meaningful roles in our lives. The phenomenon of the *right* time—the appropriate moment—is primary. There can also, of course, be wrong times and so-called senseless events, but these are more exceptions that prove the rule: we understand them in terms of appropriateness. We can also measure change chronologically and lay out a timeline, but sequence is founded on significance, not the other way around. The common representation of time as a linear continuum comprising pointlike "nows" is a theoretical abstraction from the ecstatic and meaningful character of temporality (SZ 408).

Because it is mired in oblivious modes of temporality, everydayness is insensitive to the genuinely unique; nothing seems to happen for the first or last time (GA 64: 75–76; SZ 370–71). In contrast, primordial time plunges us into "the unique thisness and one-time-ness [*Diesmaligkeit*] of [our] being-*there*" (GA 64: 82/CT1 70 tm). The urgency of our own existence is diluted in everydayness, and we tend to notice only the changes occurring in the entities we encounter, changes that lend themselves to measurement by the clock. In order to reconnect to primordial temporality, I must become authentic; I cannot simply ask, "What is time?" but must ask myself, "*Am* I time?" (GA 64: 83/CT1 71). Am I being properly temporal?

The self is ineluctably temporal, whether one properly acknowledges time or not, because time allows us to discover or create who we are and where we stand. Augustine comes close to this insight through his concern with the temporality of sin and redemption (GA 60: 175–246), but his Christian Platonism orients him toward the eternal and leads him to see time itself as fallen. Augustine does anticipate Heidegger's ecstatic concept of temporality when he writes that it is through recollection and anticipation that the soul extends beyond the infinitesimal now and has a past and future (*Confessions* 11.27–28). However, Heidegger attempts to dig deeper into Augustine's idea (GA 83: 73) and find a more fundamental structure that underlies these particular, explicit forms of awareness. Thus, both remembering and forgetting depend on the ecstasis of having-been (SZ 339): only what can matter to us as part of our pastness can be forgotten or recalled. Similarly, anticipation, along with every other relation to the possible, depends on the ecstasis of the future; thus, projection is not planning or envisioning, but a movement that is in effect whenever particular anticipations arise (SZ 145). Heidegger finds the ontological basis of the acts of consciousness described by Augustine (GA 82: 301).

Much the same point can be made about Heidegger's conception of ecstasis and Husserl's phenomenology of "internal time consciousness"; such consciousness, along with all intentionality, is grounded on the "outside-itself," a temporal transcendence proper to Dasein's way of being (SZ 366). Husserl's paradigmatic example of temporal experience is listening to a series of tones—a case of disengaged observation that sheds no light on temporal phenomena that grip us personally, such as guilt or fate. Heidegger, who edited a volume of Husserl's lectures on time,[8] never explicitly criticizes his mentor's approach, but he must have seen it as derivative and limited.

For Heidegger, the entry into authentic temporality takes place in an *Augenblick* or "moment" (SZ 328, 338). In the moment, an insight into one's situation breaks through the fallen time of everydayness and confronts one's own, authentic and historical time. This concept echoes the classical *kairos* as critical moment or opportunity (GA 18: 188–91; GA 19: 163–64; GA 62: 383–84); the Christian *kairos* as a transformative time when the world is revealed anew in relation to God (GA 60: 150); Kierkegaard's conception of the decisive moment;[9] and Nietzsche's notion of the moment as the transfiguring "hour of midday" (GA 44: 149).

Augenblick is literally a glance of the eye, and vision has often been understood as beholding the present-at-hand. But Heidegger broadens the "moment" into an encounter with one's own temporality in its full scope. Dasein is brought face to face with the situation and what it requires (SZ 338, 410). Dasein meets its fate by resolutely bringing itself back to the "there" (SZ 386).

The moment breaks through the fallen, restricted, and often dull temporality of everydayness (GA 29/30: 224). In the everyday experience of time, every "now" is familiar and routine. In objectified, scientific concepts of time, all "nows" are identically present-at-hand and measurable. The moment of vision is also a form of the present, but it is superior and unique; from this vantage point, one can survey one's current world, acting in light of what has been and may be (SZ 338, 410; GA 29/30: 226). The instantaneous "now" derives from the ecstatic moment (GA 24: 407–9).[10]

(d) *Time as the horizon for being:* As Heidegger saw in his "lightning bolt" (GA 82: 355), the problematic concept of presence-at-hand can point the way to its own overcoming. What if presence in general, as a sense of being, depends on the temporal present and thus on time? Time, then, would not be just another entity, but would be the "horizon" for being, and thus the matrix for all interpretations of entities (SZ 1, 17, 235). (A "horizon" is a higher-order analogue to "sense": it is the context in which being can be understood.)

We might then overthrow the ideal of intuition (*Anschauung*, literally looking-at) that has guided traditional Western metaphysics. The act of intuiting is directed toward a particular mode of being, presence-at-hand (SZ 147), but it has inappropriately served as the standard by which all modes of encountering beings and being have been judged. Intuitive "seeing" has crowded out other ways of behaving and perceiving. The concept of time as the horizon for being could liberate us from such restrictions.

This concept might also untangle certain conundrums about time and being, such as whether time itself exists: it seems to consist of what is no longer, what is not yet, and what is only for an infinitesimal instant.[11] Heidegger's approach allows us to "show from the perspective of 'time'" that "we can no longer pose the question in this way" (GA 64: 61/CT1 51). When we ask whether time "is," we presuppose some understanding of being—and almost inevitably, we understand presence as the primary or central sense of being (GA 64: 101; SZ 25–26). But if our access to presence is itself made possible by time, time cannot be subordinated to presence.

Metaphysics tends to privilege the timeless over the temporal, which is understood as a decline from eternity. Plotinus writes:

> At first—before this "first" was generated or the "after" was wanted—time was not, but was at rest with itself in what *is*, and itself kept quiet in what *is*. But there was a busy, active nature, wanting to rule itself and be its own, choosing to seek more than the present, that moved itself, and time moved too; and always moving on to the "next" and the "later" and to what is not the same but one after another, we turned our journey into a long stretch and fabricated time as an image of eternity. For there was an unquiet power of soul that always wanted to transfer what it saw there into something else, that was unwilling for the whole to be present to it all at once.[12]

For both Plotinus and Heidegger, time is tightly linked to our concern with our own being. Because we must decide who we are, there has to be a gap between our given being and our possible being, between facticity and futurity. But Plotinus, harking back to Parmenides, sees the primal event that distances the present from the future as a fall. Full presence, full being, would be self-contained plenitude without distance. Against this tradition, Heidegger asks why we understand being as presence in the first place, and proposes that this understanding is made possible by our extension into future, past, and present. When we take presence as the definitive sense of being, we lose sight of its roots in time, and misunderstand ourselves; this absorption in the present, not the loss of eternity, is the true fall. Heidegger thus seeks his founding insights not in a putative state of full presence, but in the moment that realizes our deep temporality.

"Is there time-free 'being'? No. Are there timeless beings? Yes. Not just the mathematical is timeless, though, but also whatever is not *Dasein*."[13] Only Dasein is ecstatically temporal, and this enables Dasein to understand being—including the being of other entities, which lack such temporality.

How far did Heidegger get with the project of establishing time as the horizon for being? Part One, Division III of *Being and Time* was to have shown that Dasein's temporality provides "horizonal schemata" that delimit and unify the possible senses of being (SZ 365; GA 24: 429–44). The ecstasis of the present directs us to a horizonal schema that he designates as *Praesenz* (GA 24: 305). This schema enables us to understand not only what is present, but also what is absent, such as an unavailable ready-to-hand thing (GA 24: 306, 311). The past and future temporal schemata can be called "*having-been*" and "*the for-the-sake-of-itself*" (SZ 365). The for-the-sake-of-itself provides "futurity as such, i.e., possibility pure and simple. Of itself the ecstasis does not produce a definite possible, but it does produce the horizon of possibility in general, within which a definite possible can be expected" (GA 26: 269/208).

This is all, literally, schematic: it sketches a new "language game,"[14] but gives us little indication of how the particular questions Heidegger reserved for Division III would have been worked out.[15] How is being given, if it is not an entity (SZ 230)? How can we properly conceive of it (SZ 39)? What are all the "variations" of being (SZ 11, 241, 333)? How are they all connected (SZ 45)? (One may assume that as a good reader of Aristotle, Heidegger would never expect a univocal sense of being, but rather an organically linked family of senses: cf. GA 33: 27–28.)[16] Why, among these variations, does presence-at-hand tend to emerge as the primary sense of being (SZ 437)? How does being relate to truth (SZ 230, 357)? How does it relate to beings (SZ 230)? How does it relate to nonbeing (SZ 286)? Does time have its own way of being (SZ 406)? How does time relate to space (SZ 368)? How does Dasein's temporality make intentionality possible (SZ 363n23)?

What is clear, at least, is that Division III would stand in the tradition of transcendental philosophy, even though the term "transcendental" appears only rarely and ambiguously in *Being and Time* (e.g., SZ 38–39).[17] Just as Kant describes the forms of our sensibility and understanding as conditions of the possibility of experience, Heidegger wants to describe Dasein's temporality as the condition of the possibility of any encounter with entities as such.[18] When he calls time a "transcendental horizon" (SZ 39), he implies that it is the sole and necessary context in terms of which we must understand being. In retrospect, he will even describe the problem of *Being and Time* as a "transcendental question squared" (GA 82: 350–52): the book inquires not just into being as the condition of possibility of the experience of beings, but into time as the condition of possibility of the understanding of being.

But why did this project of temporal ontology falter? Why did Heidegger decide to cast his manuscript of Division III into the flames (GA 2: 582, GA 66: 413–14, GA 94: 272) just as the first two Divisions were being typeset (GA 49: 39)?

One difficulty is that *Being and Time* provides no clear account of the derivation of ordinary, sequential time from the supposedly more primordial ecstatic temporality. How would the teleological order of Dasein's possibilities determine a chronological sequence of events?[19]

It might also be objected that Heidegger is not always clear on whether ecstatic temporality requires authentic existence—so that an authentic moment, in some sense, *generates* the threefold ecstases—or whether ecstatic temporality is a structure that is presupposed by any existence, authentic or inauthentic. As von Falkenhayn puts it, the moment is "the way the resolution temporalizes, and the temporalization [*Zeitigung*] of the unity of the ecstases of temporality."[20] *Zeitigung* normally means coming to fruition; in Heidegger, it means how time essentially occurs, or what time does, so to speak (SZ 304)—much as, in other texts, "worlding" is what the world does and "nihilating" is what the nothing does. Could "temporalize" be taken in a transitive sense, so that the moment, as it were, *creates* the ecstases, or is the "temporalization" of the moment just a greater illumination of an ecstatic structure that is already fully in place? The latter possibility is more consistent with the approach of *Being and Time*, which focuses on existential necessities more than on particular, existentiell moments. But the text does credit the moment as "the *authentic present*" with the power of "allowing one to *encounter for the first time* what can be ready-to-hand or present-at-hand 'in a time'"—even though Heidegger's footnote to this sentence claims that the existentiell moment presupposes a more primordial temporality (SZ 338). In the thirties we will see him going farther in conceiving of the moment as the genesis of ecstatic time.

The underlying difficulties must have something to do with the transcendental character of Heidegger's investigation, for this is an aspect of *Being and Time* that he comes to criticize in particular. By 1930 he is telling his students that "transcendental philosophy . . . must fall" (GA 29/30: 522/359). In the *Contributions to Philosophy* he says that the transcendental approach was merely "provisional" (GA 65: 305/241). It is overly indebted to a conception of being as a universal that serves as the condition of possibility for beings (GA 65: 250, 468). This line of thought is merely a preparation for "the turnaround and the leap" (GA 65: 305/241) into the "grounding of the essence of truth" (GA 65: 455/359).

But what exactly is he criticizing? Is it a misreading of his earlier thought? *Being and Time* gets "misinterpreted as transcendental philosophy" (GA 67: 25). — Or is it the misleading language in which his thought was couched? Division III "was held back because thinking failed in the adequate saying of this turning and did not succeed with the help of the language of metaphysics" (GA 9: 328/250). — Or is it an erroneous aspect of that thought itself? *Being and Time*'s transcendentalism-squared blocks an appropriate approach to "the truth of being" (GA 82: 352).

One might take Heidegger's shift away from a transcendental approach as rejecting an overly subjectivist conception of Dasein. This can be defined as a view that takes the understanding of being as an achievement of the subject, whose way of being is wrongly assumed to be self-determining and self-sufficient. Such a conception is a form of "subjectity," an understanding of being as such that privileges underlying, independent things (GA 5: 133/100, 146/109). It misunderstands the very being of a self, which is indebted, relational, and permanently problematic.

Certain forms of transcendental philosophy are in fact subjectivist, and Heidegger repeatedly rejects this way of thinking. For example, a standard interpretation of Kant's transcendental idealism is that *a priori* synthetic principles are not objective facts, but accomplishments of subjectivity; they are not, of course, voluntary choices, but they are ways in which the subject's consciousness necessarily constitutes itself. Versions of this subjectivist transcendentalism have been developed by thinkers such as Fichte, the neo-Kantians, and Husserl. In the *Contributions* Heidegger claims to have left such subjectivism behind for good (GA 65: 259), so that there is no possibility of understanding being as a product of Dasein. Instead, Dasein is thrown into belonging to being; it is indebted to the event of appropriation that first brings Dasein into its own (GA 65: 250–51). Heidegger's later texts further emphasize our dependency and our receptivity to being, our need to wait and listen rather than imposing ourselves.

Did he come to view *Being and Time*, then, as hopelessly infected with a subjectivist point of view? Did he destroy Division III because he decided at the eleventh hour that he had fallen prey to such a view?

This cannot be the whole story, since *Being and Time* already repeatedly forswears subjectivism (SZ 14, 106, 110, 227, 420). For all his later criticisms of the approaches and vocabulary of *Being and Time*, Heidegger is never willing to say that the project was essentially subjectivist.[21] In the thirties he claims that in *Being and Time*, "'Dasein' is the word for the entity that we in each case are—the human 'subject'—but with the intention of eliminating this very 'subject' in its subjectivity" (GA 82: 22); in this project "not just the subjectivity of man but the role of man is shaken, as one will recognize someday" (GA 67: 90). In 1953 he writes: "the 'transcendental' [in "time as the transcendental horizon for the question of being," SZ 39] does not pertain to subjective consciousness; instead, it is determined by the existential-ecstatic temporality of being-there" (GA 40: 20/20 tm).

In order to assess such statements, it makes sense to return to Heidegger's pre–*Being and Time* interpretations of Kant. His contrarian reading of what Kant's texts can teach us does not exalt the activity of the subject at all. In fact, in his 1925–1926 lectures (GA 21), Heidegger already takes the approach that he will develop in his post–*Being and Time* interpretations of the first *Critique* (GA 25, GA 3): against the neo-Kantians, he argues that time, which is shown in the Schematism to be essential to any comprehension of experience, is available to us through our receptivity and is in no way the product of subjectivity (GA 21: 225, 230–31). Experience depends on our receptive openness to time.

Given this evidence, it is implausible to charge *Being and Time* with a subjectivist point of view. In fact, the text avoids ascribing the fundamental features of Dasein to some primal activity, even when it comes to the projection of possibilities. Projection is not a plan that we construct (SZ 145), or a necessary act of synthesis; it is a forwardness that underlies any human activity, a happening in which we are always already involved. Heidegger makes the point clearly in a discussion of *Being and Time* in 1941: "My being is not transported into the future because I have a representation of the future; I can represent something futural only because my being as Da-sein essentially happens in the fundamental way of letting what is coming come toward it, of being transported into the coming" (GA 49: 50). Similarly, "the significance-relationships which determine the structure of the world are not a network of forms which a worldless subject has laid over some kind of material" (SZ 366). The subject does not generate significance, either voluntarily or necessarily, but finds itself drawn into a world.

Thus, Dasein's temporality is not an active achievement of Dasein, but the way in which Dasein is essentially drawn out and drawn in. We are drawn out to the reaches of time: to the possible, the preestablished, and the present. We are thereby drawn into a world, a field in which beings can be for us. It would be inappropriate to construe the horizonal schemata as products of Dasein, as the effects of the subject's spontaneous self-positing. Willful and constructive forms of consciousness are certainly possible, but what makes them possible is a prevoluntary, preactive transcendence—a happening that primordially engages and opens us. This transcendence is the deeper basis of the Kantian "transcendental" problematic (GA 9: 139/109; GA 41: 246). Unlike subjectivism, the view of the self in *Being and Time* acknowledges that the self is dependent, relational, and problematic: selfhood is proper to an entity that finds itself thrown into a world and into the need to pursue some possible way to be.

To sum up: subjectivist transcendental philosophy holds that the (necessary) activity of the subject generates the conditions of possibility of experience. Heidegger never subscribed to such subjectivism, but instead developed a nonsubjectivist type of transcendental thought in *Being and Time*. The horizonal schemata of time serve as conditions of possibility of experience, but they are not products of Dasein's activity; instead, time happens to Dasein, so to speak. We find ourselves constituted by temporal ecstases that operate on a level more basic than any subjective activity. To discover the temporality that enables all experience is not to set ourselves up as the creators of being, but to understand how we are temporally drawn into transcendence.

Why, then, did Heidegger become uneasy with his project in Division III?

THE TIME WHEN TIME ARISES

I propose that Heidegger began to feel the need for a new line of thought. He came to believe that he had to address the origin of ecstatic temporality itself, and he sought such an origin in a mysterious, founding event. This would be the time when time arises—"the moment when time opens itself up in its dimensions" and is "torn open into present, past, and future" (GA 4: 39–40/122). History bursts open at rare "moments of temporalization" (GA 69: 116/98 tm). This theme could not be encompassed in a transcendental inquiry, even a nonsubjectivist one. The temporal ecstases described in *Being and Time* might be called an ongoing "happening," but the event that plunges us into this ecstatic condition is a more radical happening—an eruption of time itself. Such a moment is not just a greater awareness of ecstatic time, but its source—and if being is temporal, then being too arises in this event. By the early thirties, Heidegger is referring to a "happening of being" (e.g., GA 94: 6/6, 32/25, 59/45) and to "the inceptive disclosure of beings as a whole," which takes place "in a 'time' which, itself unmeasurable, first opens up the open region for every measure" (GA 9: 190/145 tm). The movement "from the understanding of being to the *happening of being*" (GA 40: 218/233) can be revealed in some key passages of texts from the late twenties and thirties that we can follow like breadcrumbs that lead us to the thought of *das Ereignis*, the appropriating event.

Heidegger's initial puzzlement about the ground of time is couched in transcendental language. In 1927 he wonders: if we understand entities within the horizon of being, and being within the horizon of time, then does not time also need to be understood in terms of some further horizon? Are we not faced with an infinite regress (GA 24: 396–97/280)? His first answer is that time needs no further horizon because primordial time is finite:

> The series . . . of projections . . . has its end at the horizon of the ecstatic unity of temporality. We cannot establish this here in a more primordial way; to do that we would have to go into the problem of the finiteness of time. At this horizon each ecstasis of time, hence temporality itself, has its end. But this end is nothing but the inception and starting point for the possibility of all projecting. . . . Temporality as origin is necessarily richer and more pregnant than anything that may arise from it. . . . Within the ontological sphere the possible is higher than everything actual. [GA 24: 437–38/308 tm]

He returns to the question near the end of these lectures:

> Because the original determinant of possibility, the origin of possibility itself, is time, time temporalizes itself as the absolutely earliest. *Time is earlier than any possible earlier* of whatever sort, because it is the basic condition for an earlier as such. And because time as the source of all enablings (possibilities) is the earliest, all possibilities as such in their possibility-making function have the character of the earlier. That is to say, they are a priori. But, from the fact that time is the earliest in the sense of being the possibility of every earlier and of every a priori foundational ordering, it does not follow that time is ontically the first being; nor does it follow that time is forever and eternal, quite apart from the impropriety of calling time a being at all. [GA 24: 463/325]

What might Heidegger mean? First, it is clear that time is "the origin of possibility" because of futurity: I understand possibility and potential because I am drawn into possible ways to be. But futurity is finite, because it is shadowed by mortality—our possibilities are always faced with the threat of complete negation.

What would it mean, then, to understand time? Time allows us to grasp things, but it itself cannot be grasped. It allows us to seize possibilities, but cannot itself be taken up into some higher possibility. We can do nothing with time, we can do nothing about it; we find ourselves caught up in it far beyond the power of our action and thought. Just as we did not bring ourselves into the temporal condition of having possibilities, and cannot overcome the mortality of that condition, we cannot project some further possibility that embraces temporality itself. In one sense, time is implicitly understood as a basis for whatever else we may understand (GA 24: 307–8). Yet in another sense, time cannot be understood. To stand over time, as it were, is impossible. To "understand" our own temporality is to run up against it as a primordial given that we cannot transcend, to collide with its facticity and opacity.[22] "Earlier than everything earlier, and earlier than the earliest, is [temporality, which] makes possible earlier-ness as such."[23]

End of story, one might conclude. But the more Heidegger runs up against the sheer givenness of time, the more he is inclined to wonder about it. "What does it mean to say that time is a horizon? . . . we do not have the slightest intimation of the abysses of the essence of time" (GA 29/30: 219–20/146). "Being . . . is *understood in the light of time.* How does time come to perform this illumination? Why precisely time? . . . *What is time itself,* such that it *can expend this light and illuminate being?* . . . with the catchcry 'being and time' we have ventured the leap into this abyss, such that we now stand in utter darkness, lacking all support and bearings" (GA 31: 114–15/80).

In 1927 he denies, as we saw, that "time is forever and eternal" (GA 24: 463/325). This suggests a time when time arises. But from a transcendental viewpoint, that would confuse a condition of possibility of experience (temporality) with something that appears within experience (an event). As Heidegger wrestles with the question of the source of time, the transcendental structure appears to be cracking. One might try to widen that crack by resisting his subordination of natural, linear time to the ecstatic temporality of Dasein: after all, was there not a time before Dasein?[24]

The event of birth is not discussed in *Being and Time*, despite a few remarks on Dasein's stretching between birth and death (SZ 233, 373–74, 390–91). Heidegger's concern is the fact that Dasein "exists natally" (SZ 374), or has *been* born, rather than the actual occurrence of being born (and even the phenomenon of existing natally requires much more attention than *Being and Time* gives it, as he observes at GA 27: 124). Similarly, *Being and Time* avoids the question of whether Dasein's ecstatic temporality might itself have ontical roots in the linear time of events within the world. The only issue is the transcendental one: ecstatic time is the condition of possibility for making sense of linear time (SZ 330–31).

One can thus speak of *Being and Time*'s "temporal idealism."[25] Realism and idealism may be superficial categories—yet idealism has the advantage of recognizing that being cannot be reduced to beings, "but is already what is 'transcendental' for every entity" (SZ 207). Similarly, Dasein's temporality is transcendental for every event within time. Tracing our temporality back to a set of facts in serial, objective time would be a reductive myth (cf. SZ 6). There can be no empirical account of the origin of Dasein's time, because Dasein's time makes all accounts possible.

Heidegger's later remarks on the topic seem, at first glance, to fit the temporal idealism of *Being and Time*. In 1935 he asserts that "we cannot say there was a time when there *were* no human beings. At every *time*, there were and are and will be human beings, because time temporalizes itself only as long as there are human beings" (GA 40: 90/92). He makes a similar claim three decades later: "Strictly speaking, we cannot say what happened before the human being existed. Neither can we say that the Alps existed, nor can we say that they did not" (GA 89: 737/55–56). His point is not the triviality that there would be no one to say or know anything if no one existed. Neither is he arguing that it is false or meaningless to claim that there are entities in themselves, independent of us. Instead, this claim is both meaningful and correct (SZ 227), but its meaningfulness always presupposes the fundamental significance and disclosure that belong to Dasein's temporal existence. Factually correct statements about pre-human nature cannot be asserted or understood without the human temporality that allows them to be intelligible. This implies that such statements cannot explain human temporality itself; our time cannot be reduced to empirical facts.

So does the question of the origin of our temporality make sense? Again, from a transcendental point of view, the question seems unanswerable, and maybe even meaningless. Time must simply be accepted as a fundamental structure of our experience. In Kantian terms, time is a form of sensibility, and to ask for the cause of time is to ask for an impossibility: causality has sense only when applied to objects as perceived *within* our temporal sensibility. The *a priori* conditions of experience and thought cannot themselves be traced back to some further ground, because grounding—like all thinking—is itself governed by these conditions. This would seem to be a category mistake. Time cannot emerge from within itself. Time is not itself an empirical happening.[26]

But the transcendental point of view is undercut by another theme in *Being and Time*, if we take it radically enough: facticity. "The concept of 'facticity' comprises the being-in-the-world of an entity 'within-the-world' such that this entity can understand itself as bound up in its 'destiny' with the being of the entities that it encounters within its own world" (SZ 56). I cannot separate who I am from what I find around me: I have to come to terms with my surroundings as I decide how to be. Any attempt to understand oneself apart from other entities is doomed.

This is not only a point about human life, but affects philosophy itself, for §63 of *Being and Time* emphasizes that existential analysis has an existentiell basis: philosophy always springs from one's own attempt to come to grips with who one is in a situation. We can think only because we are thrown and indebted; "philosophizing is essentially an affair of finitude" (GA 26: 198/156).

Does *Being and Time* do justice to finitude? Heidegger writes that the temporal sense of thrownness and facticity is having-been (SZ 326). But if we understand having-been just as a dimension of Dasein's temporality, which is the horizon in terms of which all being is intelligible, then we have not fully embraced facticity: we have not acknowledged that Dasein and all its horizons are radically indebted to something other than themselves. Even if we give lip service to facticity, and even if we understand the ecstases of temporality as drawing us out rather than as being produced by subjectivity, the transcendental way of thinking can still suggest that we are essentially untouched by our concrete situation. But we do not hover over other beings; we are part of what there is. Dasein is an entity amidst entities, even though it is extraordinary because it has some understanding of being. It is both the "there" *and* an entity within the "there."

This predicament is described under the rubric of "metontology" in *The Metaphysical Foundations of Logic*:

> the entity "man" understands being . . . the possibility that being is there in the understanding presupposes the factical existence of Dasein, and this in turn presupposes the factual presence-at-hand of nature. . . . As a result, we need a special problematic which has for its proper theme beings as a whole. This new investigation resides in the essence of ontology itself and is the result of its overturning, its *metabole*. I designate this set of questions *metontology*. [GA 26: 199/156–57 tm]

We need a way to think about the dependence of our understanding of being on an ontic ground from which it emerges. The realm of sense cannot be explained by the things we encounter, but it is indebted to those things.

One reason, then, why Heidegger became uneasy with his transcendental approach in *Being and Time* may be that he suspected it could not address the question of how Dasein comes to be from the finite context into which it has been thrown—in other words, how ecstatic temporality arises. This question comes alive as he enters the thirties. Ecstatic time is no longer simply primordial, and natural time is not simply derivative; we are indebted to nature, but are raised above it at founding moments that generate ecstatic, meaningful time. In the language of the mid-thirties, the world emerges from the earth.

A related line of thought will radicalize *Being and Time*'s concept of historicity. The book asserts that we are profoundly historical, but its fundamental thesis that time is the horizon for being seems rather ahistorical, as if a fixed essence of Dasein determined, once and for all, the range of senses that being can have. This way of thinking does not reflect our indebtedness to the movement of history, which can thrust new senses of being upon us as our ecstatic temporality is born and reborn in clashes between earth and world. Dasein is claimed by the happening of being and participates in its unfolding destiny.

These developments do not imply that we have to discard all the insights of *Being and Time*, but they do imply that the transcendental framework of those insights must fall away. What would be left? Consider the distinctive phrases *immer schon* (always already) and *je schon* (in each case already) that appear throughout *Being and Time*. The word *schon* emphasizes that we are not in a position to lay the foundation for our own being. Our activity presupposes a thrownness that we cannot master. As for *immer* and *je*, they suggest universality and necessity: in no case can we ever lay our own foundation. This is the aspect of *Being and Time* that smacks most strongly of traditional transcendental philosophy, with its quest for *a priori* knowledge of necessary limits. But, ironically, that very quest sets us up, in effect, as knowers who *can* establish a firm and certain ground: a clear conception of our essence and its inevitable finitude. At the same time, as we have seen, the transcendental approach blocks any attempt to inquire into the origin of ecstatic temporality in an event that may be profoundly contingent. Ultimately, then, transcendentalism must be considered a residual attachment to presence and a vestige of modern metaphysics. The *immer* and *je* should be dropped. And in fact, by the time of the *Contributions* phrases such as "always already" have almost completely vanished from Heidegger's thought.[27] We are left with the *schon*—a description of how we, in fact, find ourselves existing. We can notice the thrown, temporal character of experience without taking any stand on whether experience is possible *only* by virtue of that temporality. So even when we let the overtones of necessity fade away, *Being and Time* retains much of its thought-provoking power simply as a description of our current ways of encountering beings in their being—an attempt to tell it like it is, whether or not it has to be.

How do we get into ecstatic temporality, then? As Heidegger says in 1928, "the primal fact . . . is that there is anything like temporality at all. The entrance into world by beings is primal history pure and simple," which happens in "primal time, i.e., the time that begins with primal history itself" (GA 26: 270/209 tm, cf. GA 83: 21–22). We can speak and think of this primal time only by actually engaging in "the extremity of the moment" (GA 29/30: 227/151, cf. 252/170), as he puts it in his 1929–1930 lectures. We must *"prepare our entering into the happening of the sway [Walten] of world"* (GA 29/30: 510/351 tm), which is also the "fundamental happening" of the distinction between being and beings (GA 29/30: 524/361 tm).

The "unused preliminary studies" for these lectures show Heidegger ruminating on the origin of world and temporality.

> In transcendence a surpassing—but what *transcends* must be preserved from *overreaching* (Hegel). . . . But *pulling it back from this overreaching* [. . .] leads to the authentic task of letting the *engagement in* beings happen. *Irruption and liberation—actual philosophizing.*[28]

> The happening of transcendence: *self-pervading sway* [*Sichdurchwalten*] *of time and space in the word—fundamental movedness*. . . . In the surpassing—the there, and being in the there with and amidst *beings*. The *amidst* and its wholeness in each case—the *world*. The *sway* of beings as a whole.[29]

Temporality

It is not just a fact, but itself is also the essence of the fact: facticity. The fact of facticity (here the root of the "overturning" of "ontology").

Can one ask, "How does time arise?" To answer in the scheme of traditional ontology: through the deformation and restriction of eternity? With *time* in each case the first possibility of origination. . . . What then is the sense of the impossibility of the problem of the origination of time![30]

What *belonging-together* of Dasein with beings manifests itself here? Is it achieved with the "irruption" and manifestation? How is Dasein outside itself? Is there a standpoint that interrogates and sees Dasein and non-Dasein beings in their belonging-together, or all this only in *transcendence*, in such a way that it lays claim to its own eccentricity [*Exzentrik*] for itself and its transcendental relation?
. . . With Dasein, world first happens. Dasein breaks in, and beings are revealed.[31]

The transcendental tries to "lay claim to its own eccentricity," that is (Heidegger may mean) to assimilate the other to itself. Instead, we must understand how Dasein and disclosure take place as an "irruption," an "engagement" in the "*sway* of beings as a whole." Significantly, he refers here to the word; poetic naming might have everything to do with the outburst of Dasein's ecstatic time.

What does he mean by calling temporality "the fact of facticity"? Recall that facticity is how our own destiny is wrapped up with the entities around us. The question, then, is how this destiny emerges among entities. How does the very phenomenon of destiny arise within destiny-less, non-Dasein entities? What is the origin of Dasein's time?

Let us read a little farther in the statement from *Introduction to Metaphysics* that initially seemed to defend a transcendental standpoint: "time temporalizes itself only as long as there are human beings. There is no time in which there were no human beings, not because there are human beings from all eternity and for all eternity, but because time is not eternity, and time in each case temporalizes itself only at one time, as human, historical Dasein" (GA 40: 90/92). In order to conceive of the particular times when time "temporalizes," one has to abandon the strictly transcendental point of view. However, this point of view retains some limited legitimacy: as long as we have already originated, temporality does enable our experiences.

Since humans are not eternal, it seems legitimate, in fact irresistible, to ask: when, precisely, did human time originate? Heidegger only occasionally raises this question, much less answers it. One might assume that ecstatic temporality and historicity began in "prehistoric" times, long before chronicles were recorded. But I have found only one page where he speculates briefly and inconclusively about the awakening of "imagination" during the "Ice Age" (GA 73.1: 405). Perhaps such speculations are necessarily mythical, in a nonpejorative sense: "'myth' is the word that is supposed to name the pre-inceptive realm in which being has not yet come into the open" (GA 74: 34). There is no "gradual crossing-over . . . from prehistory to history.

There is always the leap of the inception, which one grasps precisely when one refrains from making this leap understandable. . . . The leap of the origin, according to its essence, remains a mystery."[32]

In the essay "On the Essence of Truth" he proposes a much later date, and many of his subsequent texts hint at a similar view: being becomes an issue when Greek philosophy gets under way. "The ek-sistence of historical human beings begins at that moment when the first thinker takes a questioning stand with regard to the unconcealment of beings by asking: what are beings?" (GA 9: 189/145)—the question that guides Western thought.[33]

At that moment, he elaborates in a 1932 course, some human beings take the fateful step into understanding being and relating to beings *as such*.

> Beings as a whole, previously concealed from self-manifestation, find *for the first time* and henceforth . . . the site and the room in which they can step forth out of their concealedness in order to be at all as the beings they are. . . . Thus, what *is* comes to its being. It does so only if and insofar as the understanding of being happens. . . . Through this original questioning and only through it, being becomes what is at issue above all, and for all that is. Inasmuch as being comes into understanding in this way, beings as such are empowered to themselves. Henceforth they can come to light as the beings that they are. Yet now they can first also thrust themselves forward as what they are not and can thereby be disguised and covered over. . . . The questioning concerning being is the *basic act of existence*; with this questioning, there begins the history of humans as existing. [GA 35: 93–95/71–72 tm]

Once the "transition to existence" (GA 35: 93/70) or "liberation to existence" (GA 35: 95/73 tm) has taken place in philosophy, Dasein stands close to this origin (GA 35: 97) even if we have forgotten the question of being that the inception granted us (GA 35: 96). "Who then are we . . . ? We exist, in our being we are constructed on the understanding of being—even more, on the already-asked question of being. . . . Insofar as we exist, that inception *keeps happening*" (GA 35: 98/74 tm).

The suggestion that human beings did not truly "exist" before Greek philosophy—that they were not being-there, did not have an understanding of being that transcends beings—is a bizarre surprise for any reader of *Being and Time*. That text ignores the question of when Dasein began, and there is no suggestion there that philosophy is required in order to get Dasein going. To the contrary: the explicit question of being grows from the understanding of being that is always already implicit in every human experience and act. As Heidegger still puts it in 1930, "philosophy cannot find what it asks about by *inventing* it. It must somehow *find itself before* it" (GA 29/30: 516/355). *Primum vivere, deinde philosophari.*

But the 1932 lecture course claims that "being is found through invention [*erfunden*]—poetized—formed" (GA 35: 95/72 tm), and that only those human beings who inhabit the world opened up by philosophy actually "exist." The Eurocentrism of the idea is startling, and seems philosophically indefensible: how can it be that people who live beyond the realm inaugurated by early Greek thought are not exposed to beings as such? But Heidegger is quite clear: "Not all humans who are actual, were actual, or will be actual do 'exist,' have existed, or will exist—*in the sense* we understand existence" (GA 35: 84/64, cf. GA 45: 212–13).

> Humans and human lineages are and have been and will be, without their being having been determined as existence, without humans occupying themselves with their stance, i.e., without humans taking themselves as beings in the midst of beings who comport themselves to beings as such. There is a being of humans, since they move in the highest simplicity and in the harmony of their needs and abilities with the powers that shelter humans and re-attune them. By way of such harmony and such shelter, nothing breaks open as regards beings as such. Humans *are*, and yet they do not *exist* in the stipulated sense of existence. [GA 35: 92/70 tm]

The transition into "existence" would also, presumably, thrust us into ecstatic temporality. Heidegger seems to be making this point in a semilegible note where he speaks of "an interception of the *inception*. Pressed forward [?] into temporality—*taken possession* of it—*grounded*" (GA 35: 257/195 tm, editor's question mark).

But the idea that Dasein and its temporality did not exist until the inception of philosophy is not the most radical position that Heidegger will adopt in the thirties. In the 1936 *Running Notes on "Being and Time,"* he proposes that *no* human beings have yet achieved the status of being-there. A crucial step was taken with the Greeks, but Dasein now requires the "second inception." "Ecstatic-horizonal temporality is not to be made accessible through exhibiting it [phenomenologically], but through a leap into Dasein" (GA 82: 26–27). "Through the leap into Da-*sein*, *being*-human is first essentially transformed *beyond* what has been so far" (GA 82: 56). "Being-in-the-world is no 'structure' in itself, which was already 'there' up to now, but *historizes* [*geschichtet*] and is only a coming transformation" (GA 82: 57).

> Where does the "there" come from, and does it essentially occur "for itself"? Or is it something *given as a task* and given with and for being-human as historical . . . first grasped and grounded in (appropriation) [*(Ereignis)*] . . . a turning point in history itself—*there-ness*—essentially occurring only as *being*-there. . . . Properly taking over being the there, and in this first creating it, is an

extraordinary moment of history, in the preparation for which we are standing.
[GA 82: 74]

Being and Time's talk of the "foundations" of Dasein (SZ 197) makes it seem
as if these foundations "were present-at-hand and had merely been hidden up
to now! instead of projective grounding of Da-sein—not as substratum and *ontological background, but as the space where a second inception can play out
[Spielraum], a space that is thrown ahead*" (GA 82: 100). In short, as Heidegger
puts it in a 1941 text, "a future humanity is delivered over to being-there" (GA
82: 320–21). Man may be a "transition" (*Übergang*), as he already says in 1931
(GA 32: 215–16/149), echoing Nietzsche's prophecy of the *Übermensch.*
     Most of Heidegger's texts of the thirties are less blunt; they speak of an
origin of Dasein's ecstatic time without deciding whether it happened or will
happen at some particular juncture. The *Contributions*, I have argued, adopt a
"future-subjunctive tonality" without usually being as stark and direct as the
texts we have just considered.[34]
     Whether or not we can date the origin of Dasein, Heidegger wants to
conceive of it as an "inception" (*Anfang*) rather than a mere "beginning"
(*Beginn*). This distinction runs throughout the texts of the thirties.[35] As he
says in his Rectoral Address: "The inception still *is*. It does not lie *behind us*
as something long past, but rather stands *before* us. The inception, as what is
greatest, has in advance already passed over all that is to come and thus over
us as well. The inception has invaded our future; it stands there as the distant
injunction that orders us to recapture its greatness." (GA 16: 110/HR 111 tm).
In 1934, he writes:

> The beginning is immediately left behind; it vanishes as a happening proceeds.
> The inception—the origin—by contrast, first appears and comes to the fore in
> the course of a happening and is fully there only at its end. One who begins
> many things often never attains the inception. Of course, we human beings can
> never start inceptively at the inception—only a god can do that. Rather, we must
> begin with—that is, set out from—something that will first lead into or point to
> the origin. [GA 39: 3–4/3 tm]

According to the 1941 text devoted to this theme, *Über den Anfang,*

> inception . . . at first means as much as "beginning," and this means a distinctive
> position and phase in the course of a process. But . . . here the word "inception"
> is supposed to name the essence of beyng. . . . The inception that seizes is the
> appropriating event. [*Der An-fang ist Er-eignis.*] To start inceptively [*Anfangen*]
> is to seize oneself and raise oneself up in the appropriating event itself, the event
> as which the clearing essentially happens. [GA 70: 9–10]

Only in an inception does a clearing open against concealment; in inception, the difference between being and nothing takes place. An inception is a history-founding ground of intelligibility. It generates interpretability, but cannot itself be interpreted in any established terms. It emerges from the earth, but founds a new, ecstatic temporality that spreads open a world. In the sudden moment of the inception, history irrupts into the ontic sequence of nature, and *Homo sapiens* is "de-ranged" (*ver-rückt*) into being-there (cf. GA 65: 372; GA 73.1: 74). Our mission is to participate creatively in this event that is the source of truth, worldhood, history, and our existence itself.

We will not be able to describe the inception of our temporality as if it were just another incident within time (this much is true in the transcendental point of view). The event from which meaningful time and being erupt is mysterious.[36] All understanding is itself temporal, so the arising of time can be understood only in its very opacity. It is not to be reduced to scientific findings about nature, since science itself depends on temporality. Primal time must emerge from nature as earth.

The concept of earth is developed in "The Origin of the Work of Art" (1935). A great artwork embodies the strife between a world—the articulated constellation of senses that orients and illuminates a people—and the earth, or the concealed, uninterpreted basis of these senses (GA 5: 35/26, 50–51/37–38). Earth intrinsically eludes and exceeds sense; it is the prime example of what I will call "excess" in chapter 4. The world struggles to display the earth, to interpret and control our roots, but the earth resists the world: we cannot exhaustively grasp our own facticity. The work of art would remind us of the earth—if there were any artworks today. Art "first brings out the open through strife: the clearing in whose light we encounter beings as such, as if on the first day";[37] but there are "no current works that would be works of art."[38]

The emergence of a world that depends on the earth yet wrestles with it is the origin of Dasein's time. In the moment when time arises, a clearing opens against concealment; meaningful time comes to be in a way that cannot be reduced to the natural sequence that precedes it.

> The luminosity of the great moment that gathers everything in the simple clarity of the essential happening of being. This moment is the lightning bolt into the nothing.
>
> Insofar as, and if, the there illuminates and conceals itself by this luminosity, and thus lets the *earth* shine out in a world—insofar as, and if, the there *thus* comes to stand, the appropriating event essentially happens as being.
>
> That we know transfiguration and its possibility has its basis here—in this moment (*time*). [GA 73.1: 172]

> Why is this sudden moment of "world history" essentially and abysally other than all the "millions of years" of worldless processes? Because this suddenness lights up the uniqueness of beyng, and that which, outside [the distinction of] entity and nonentity, neither was nor was not, receives the abyssal ground of a grounding as what is. . . . The "moment" is the origin of "time" itself—time as the unity of [ecstatic] transport [*Entrückungseinheit*] . . . The moment has no need of "eternity" . . . [GA 66: 113–14/90 tm]

Time, then, is "not the *nun* [now] and not the *eternal instant*—but the *suddenness* of history*" (GA 73.1: 266).

Despite his claim that the moment does not need the eternal, Heidegger does occasionally use the word "eternity" (*Ewigkeit*) to describe the moment. This does not mean a *nunc stans* (GA 66: 114), or an atemporal or unchanging state, but a time at the origin of time—time at its most intense. Eternity is "the deepest oscillation [*Durchschwingung*] of time" (GA 95: 120/93). It is not ahistorical, but the birth of history. "Originary temporality [is] the 'temporalizing' of the eternal!" (GA 73.1: 15).

The inceptive moment emerges from the earth and founds a new, ecstatic temporality that spreads open a world. "Only since 'torrential time' has been torn open into present, past, and future, has it become possible to agree upon something that lasts. We have been *one* conversation since the time when there 'is time.' Ever since time arose and was brought to stand, we *are* historical" (GA 4: 39–40/122). What was only obscurely suggested in *Being and Time*—that the moment of vision is the origin of the temporal ecstases—is affirmed here and placed within a vaster, darker, telluric time.

Heidegger often thinks of inception as a poetic event. His prototypical poet is Hölderlin—author of the line, "But what endures is founded by the poets." Heidegger glosses this saying as follows:

> Poetizing is founding, a grounding that brings about that which remains. The poet is the one who grounds beyng. . . . Through the poet, the beckoning of the gods is, as it were, built into the foundational walls of the language of a people, although the people may not even suspect this at first; insofar as this happens, beyng is founded in the historical Dasein of the people, a pointer and directedness are placed into this beyng. [GA 39: 33/32 tm]

"Poetry is the fundamental happening of beyng as such. It founds beyng, and has to found it . . . Poetry, as founding—as that creating that has no object and that never merely sings about something what lies at hand—is always an intimating, a waiting, a seeing come" (GA 39: 257/233 tm). "Poetry makes beings more beingful [*seiender*]" (GA 34: 47/64) by naming them; it "nominates the beings to that which they are" (GA 4: 41/123–24). If being is the difference it makes that beings are something instead of nothing, the poet finds ways to highlight that difference, to allow it to touch us more deeply.

Poetry happens when time itself happens most intensely. These poetic "peaks of time" are the origin of ecstatic time (GA 39: 52/50, 56/53).

> Within this prevailing forward of that which has been into the future—which, directed backward, opens up that which earlier already readied itself as such— there prevails the approach of a coming and a still essentially happening (future and having-been) in one: originary time. The temporalizing of this time is the fundamental happening of that attunement in which the poetizing is grounded. This originary time transports our Dasein into future and having-been, or better: brings it about that our being as such is a transported being—provided that our being is authentic. Inauthentically, it is always—in contrast to such transport— merely sitting tight on an ever-changing present-day. . . . In such time . . . 'there comes to be' time; there comes about that right time, which is no inopportune time [*Unzeit*]. [GA 39: 109/100–101 tm]

Calculated time is the *Unwesen* of time, its counter-essence or "corrupted essence"—which is "not nothing, but is a power in its own right, and one that belongs to the essence of time" (GA 39: 112/102).

A great poet, then, is an inceptive founder of time and being. This founding event has a past, of course, but it retrieves that past and draws on it in a way that opens a new world. This is why "the poet is never contemporary" (GA 38: 170/142). The poet is not a maker in the technical sense, nor a god-like creator of new beings, but one who can institute an original relation to being. "Original" here does not simply mean innovative, but close to the origin. This is *"the event [Ereignis] of a decision about the essence of truth"* (GA 51: 21/17 tm).

Earth and world can also clash outside art and poetry; beings can become more beingful through many ways of engaging in freedom (GA 34: 60) and history (GA 45: 201). So poets are not the only founders; in the mid-thirties Heidegger typically speaks of the poet, thinker, and statesman. "Founding" is, among other things, a political concept, and it is no coincidence that he is thinking about the founding of time during a period of revolution and political "inception." What is at stake, as he says in 1934, is "a transformation of our entire being in its relation to the power of time . . . this transformation depends on . . . how we temporalize time itself. . . . [we] *ourselves are time*. We are the temporalizing of time itself" (GA 38: 120/100). "Time in its formation of time (temporalization) [*Zeitbildung (Zeitigung)*] is that power in which alone the happening of our Dasein happens in history" (GA 38: 125/104).

As early as the spring of 1932, according to Heidegger, he began to focus these lines of thought on *das Ereignis* (GA 66: 424). *Ereignis* normally means "event," but it also echoes *eigen* (own, proper). According to the *Contributions to Philosophy (Of the Event)* (1936–1938), which we will consider more closely in chapter 2, the appropriating event is the event of the grounding of the there (GA 65: 183, 247) and "the truth of the essential happening of beyng" (GA 65: 74/59 tm). (For more on *Ereignis* as "the happening of being" or "fundamental happening," see GA 73.1: 107, 224, 264; GA 82: 196.) In this event, we would come into our own as we were seized by an inception. We could then properly "be there," and things could gain their proper places and significance.

The appropriating event would take place at a "site of the moment" where "time-space" would emerge.[39] Heidegger's tentative description of time-space (GA 65: §242) is not a transcendental account of the "formal concepts" of time and space in general (GA 65: 261/205), but an attempt to speak of what "takes place in the uniqueness of the appropriation," in a moment that would inaugurate, or perhaps reinaugurate, meaningful time and space (GA 65: 74/59; cf. GA 71: 271). Time-space is an "abyssal ground" that opens a domain of unconcealment, yet denies this domain any absolute foundation. Time-space ties us back to "the first inception" of the revelation of being among the Greeks, readies us for "the other inception" that may bring a new destiny of being, and ties us to the present as the site where the current "abandonment" of being must be endured.

As these thoughts suggest, being is not constantly given; "beyng is at times" (GA 70: 15). It emerges only sporadically and unpredictably—and only as an inception, not as a beginning. "Being does not begin and end, nor does it subsist 'perpetually' in the duration of beings. Being has an inception, and essentially so: it *is* the appropriating inception" (GA 71: 147/127 tm). How often do these inceptions come? Has one ever fully taken place? The answers are elusive. "When and how long being 'is' cannot be asked" (GA 69: 145/124; cf. GA 98: 160). If we could know how often appropriation has taken place (or will do so), we would not need to think the uniqueness of beyng (GA 65: 488).

In sum, while the transcendental aspect of *Being and Time* suggests that temporality is a fixed structure that we occasionally recognize, Heidegger now presents it as gushing forth at great historical moments that establish a way of existing for a people or an age. He has made the transition from the understanding of being to the happening of being. This happening is not just an ongoing movement in which we are engaged, but the founding of such a movement, an abyssal ground that must remain a mystery, yet can still be acknowledged in its very mysteriousness. The peaks of time are inceptions, breakthroughs, or events of appropriation when a world is founded. Such founding events are not chronologically first, but they are so transformative that they inaugurate new domains where entities can be discovered. Among those entities are we ourselves—and we find that we are indebted to the "earth," to a basis that we cannot fully interpret. We are an outburst of ecstatic time, but we are also tied to the natural time from which we emerged.

We might picture the relationship between natural and ecstatic time as follows. A line can represent the "'millions of years' of worldless processes" (GA 66: 113/90 tm), the ontic surroundings in which we are embedded. From this linear time, a peak of time may rise up (GA 39: 52, 56). From that peak, ecstatic time may erupt, spreading a horizon within which beings become meaningful and understandable. But the horizon is finite: it will never embrace all that is. It is also incapable of fully explaining its own origin—the extraordinary peak from which it sprang.

This line of thought is characteristic of the thirties. Eventually, however, the author of *Being and Time* appears to have shied away from time. In 1930 he saw "no further possibility" of finding a problem more primordial than being and time (GA 31: 128/89), but by the mid-thirties he sees time as only a preliminary answer (GA 82: 12, 21, 33–34, 36, 81, 101, 125, 134–35; GA 74: 9). By the late thirties he speaks of following "time" (in quotation marks) as a "hint" (GA 73.1: 87, 176). This hint leads to *Ereignis*: "the essence of temporality is determined from out of beyng as the *clearing* of eventuation [*Ereignung*]" (GA 46: 94/77). *Ereignis* is "not just the full and more original 'time'" (GA 73.1: 159), but some source beyond time itself.

In contrast to the *Contributions*, which frequently describe *Ereignis* as an inceptive or inaugural happening (e.g., GA 65: 57, 183, 247), several postwar texts insist that it is not a happening at all (GA 11: 45/292; GA 12: 247/127; GA 14: 25–26/20; GA 98: 161, 341). "Time and Being" (1962) proposes that appropriation is the source of time, and warns us not to misconstrue appropriation—"something which is not temporal"—as an event within time (GA 14: 57/47). It would seem that *Ereignis* is no longer a historical inception from which truth and being erupt.[40]

With such thoughts, Heidegger has apparently returned to something like a transcendental standpoint. We cannot pursue this development here, but will stay with the distinctive thought of the thirties.

THE EMERGENCE OF EMERGENCY

In addition to the question of the inception of time, the thirties are ushered in by *Not*. The word has no perfect English equivalent, but in many cases it could be translated as "emergency." For example, a *Notausgang* is an emergency exit, to be used in cases of urgent need. *Not* is a pressing distress that arises at a particular juncture. It could also be translated as "urgency," "plight," or "needfulness"—but the kind of need that interests Heidegger should not be confused with "needs" (*Bedürfnisse*) that stem from bodily requirements, urges, wishes, and cravings (GA 51: 4–5/3–4).

For Heidegger in the thirties, salvation depends on recognizing a profound emergency that determines what is "necessary" (*notwendig*) for human beings, what they need to do in order to find their destiny. Who we are is not a given, but needs to emerge in an emergency in which it is urged forth (*er-nötigt*, GA 82: 101).

Already in the twenties, Heidegger holds that at times of crisis the greatest insights may become possible. The moment of vision, as we have seen, is a turning point when the whole world can be transfigured. Such a moment can emerge in an emergency: the significance of our being-in-the-world as a whole comes into view most clearly when it is threatened in anxiety (SZ 184–91). An anxious confrontation with the ultimate darkness of "nihilation" can bring the sense of being to light (GA 9: 88–96/111–22). This experience sharpens sense by exposing it to what I will call "excess": what eludes or resists our current interpretive abilities.

In December 1929, Heidegger extends this point of view from the extraordinary experiences of an individual to a collective condition. After elaborating an almost comically prolonged phenomenology of dullness (based on experiences such as waiting for a train), he identifies the fundamental mood of his times as "*profound boredom*" (GA 29/30: 115/77, 239–49/160–67). He had noted in *Being and Time* that moods can be shared (SZ 138), but this is a new venture into broad cultural diagnosis. In profound boredom, nothing seems urgent; the question of who we are has not come alive. This underlying disengagement is not evident at first glance, but it is the key in which we hear the tune of our whole existence.

Heidegger's goal is to alert his audience to profound boredom so that it may become anything but boring. Instead, it may be experienced as a crisis, an alarming absence of "oppressiveness" (*Bedrängnis*) (GA 29/30: 244–46/163–64). Then the mood may be transformed in a moment of vision. This course thus offers us the first instance of a theme that recurs frequently in the thirties: *die Not der Notlosigkeit*, the emergency of the lack of emergency (e.g., GA 45: 183; GA 94: 148–49).

To the objection that there are emergencies everywhere—social, political, religious—Heidegger replies that these particular crises and the fights against them repress the emergency of "*being left empty as a whole*" (GA 29/30: 243/163). What is lacking is "the rooted unity of essential acting" and the "mystery" of the "inner terror . . . that gives Dasein its greatness" (GA 29/30: 244/163–64, cf. 531).

The emergency of the absence of oppressiveness challenges the human being to face the task of *"being there"* (GA 29/30: 246/165). This means freeing "the *essence* of man," letting *"the Dasein in him become essential . . .* loading Dasein upon man as his ownmost burden"; this attainment of Dasein is the *"tip of the sharpest moment"* (GA 29/30: 248/166 tm). What is striking here is the implication that we are not always already Dasein; Dasein is a possibility that we fully enter only in a moment of vision. What was described in *Being and Time* as a moment of authentic insight now seems to be the very inception of being-there.

Perhaps not coincidentally, 1930 is the year when, by his own account, Heidegger put his faith in Nazism (GA 95: 408). This decision was his response to a deep emergency. As he puts it in 1932, "Today there is only *one* clear line that sharply divides left and right. Half-measures are a betrayal."[41] "What the Greeks called *acme* is penetrating our being-there. The knifeblade on which everything has been cut and decided, where the particularity of the individual wants to become something essential within the whole."[42]

Emergency demands the grounding of our highest possibilities (GA 65: 46; GA 66: 235; GA 76: 100). But not everyone recognizes the urgency of the moment and the need to choose. "We still sense nothing of the spiritual emergency of being-there. . . . *How do we bring about the great necessitation into the greatest emergency?* . . . When will we create the true encounter between the German 'worker' and the German tradition that belongs to him and his people?" (GA 94: 148–49/109 tm). If the Germans do not face the crisis, "the spiritual strength of the West" may fail and our "illusory culture [may] suffocate in madness," he warns in his Rectoral Address (GA 16: 117/HR 116). In lectures from 1934–1935, he speaks of the "threat to our spiritual and historical Dasein" as the "innermost and most far-reaching emergency" (GA 39: 113/103 tm) that faces the people at a time when "the West [is] hovering at the edge of the abyss" (GA 39: 222/202). The "supreme emergency" faces us in the form of a decision as to whether the people will find its gods (GA 39: 146/128 tm)—whether the dimension of the holy will open for the community, if only as a question, or whether that dimension will be completely occluded.

By the later thirties, Heidegger's political impulse has become more muted and skeptical, but the theme of emergency is taken to new heights. In some notes for a 1937–1938 seminar, he describes the lack of emergency as a state in which "everything is familiar and accessible and answered—and everything can be managed and handled." The experience of this condition "must stem from emergency and remain in its lineage, so much so that it first necessitates the emergency" (GA 88: 40).

Emergency is not only at the heart of our being-there, but is crucial to the emergence of the "truth of beyng" itself (GA 65: 46/38).

> The emergency we mean here is *not knowing the way out or the way in . . .* out of and into what, through such knowing, first opens up as this untrodden and ungrounded "space." This . . . is that "between" where it has not yet been determined what is in being [*seiend*] and what is not in being. . . . This emergency explodes beings, still veiled as such, in order to enable the space of the in-the-midst of beings to be occupied and founded as a possible standpoint of man. This emergency . . . is the *casting asunder* of what will be determined forthwith as beings in their beingness over against non-beings—assuming that the emergency necessitates a necessity in man that is adequate to it. [GA 45: 152–53/132–33 tm]

> Not just any "emergency"—a lack—a misery—a grievance and an inconvenience—but "emergency" as *being-there.*
>
> *The emergency*—in the fullest power of *necessitating* into the extremity of being human—*of grounding and withstanding the essential happening of being.*
>
> What is the essence of this *emergency?* . . . The most un-canny—the most unique . . .
>
> Emergency as beyng's *lack of home and hearth. . . .*
>
> Emergency—is not our wretched worries—but the emergency of being itself—*being in emergency!* [GA 73.1: 278]

Heidegger comes to see the lack of emergency as an effect of the abandonment of being—not simply our neglect of being, but being's self-concealment or turning away from us (GA 65: 119; GA 66: 358). There is a risk that "the emergency as which being essences in its necessitation may never historically, for man, become the emergency that it is." The problem is how "this emergency as such can properly reach man, in his essential distance from himself" (GA 6.2: 355/N4 245 tm). The only way out is to experience the lack of emergency as itself an emergency that pertains to being (GA 67: 251). In order to allow ourselves this experience, we must overcome "anxiety in the face of anxiety" (GA 67: 252) and face the terror of nihilation. Sense can be retrieved only if we first feel it recede.

A further recurring thought in the thirties is that every necessity is rooted in an emergency (GA 65: 45, 97). One would traditionally assume that necessity is established by universal physical, metaphysical, or logical principles, and is thus prior to any particular crisis to which an individual or a group might be exposed. Heidegger's reversal of this priority, which is part of his rethinking of the "modalities" (GA 65: 279–83), reflects his view that all logic, physics, and metaphysics are manifestations of a "history of being" in which disclosures of the world are given to human beings. If this is so, then emergency is the more fundamental issue: we can grasp necessary aspects of beings, or necessary relations among the assertions we make about beings, only because historical emergencies challenge us to receive and wrestle with senses of being.

An adequate response to the emergency must include philosophy (GA 65: 45) and a confrontation with the philosophical tradition (GA 66: 80). We need to experience the emergency of our times in terms of the looming collapse of "the first inception" (the inquiry into the being of beings inaugurated by the Greeks) and the dawning of "the other inception," a new kind of thinking that would ask how being itself essentially happens (e.g., GA 65: 5–6/7, 171/135 tm). The transition from the first to the other inception is a *krisis* in the root sense, an urgent decision. Transitional thinking may require rereading the thinkers of the first inception in a way that anticipates the other inception, as when Heidegger translates Anaximander's *to chreon*—usually taken as physical or metaphysical necessity—as *nötigende Not*, "emergency that necessitates" (GA 51: 106/91 tm). But above all, the very act of philosophy must be rooted in emergency: "I have always been in a crisis, since I began to philosophize! For philosophizing consists in being in a crisis and bringing one about" (GA 82: 180).

With the concept of "releasement" in the 1940s, which sets aside willful choice, and after the defeat of Germany, Heidegger's writings convey less of a sense of acute crisis, and instead aspire to be set free from urgent require-ments (GA 73.1: 878–79). As the thirties fade away, emergency settles down.

THE BEING WHOSE BEING IS AT ISSUE

The third theme that inaugurates the thirties, along with the inception of time and emergency, is collective selfhood. Heidegger moves from *Being and Time*'s general analysis of the fact that Dasein's being is at issue for it to ask-ing, with mounting agitation, who "we" are. The issue is crucial to the very existence of a community: "We are, insofar as we seek ourselves. . . . We seek ourselves insofar as we ask who we are" (GA 36/37: 4/4). "The ques-tion 'Who are we?' includes the question of *whether* we are" (GA 65: 51/41).

Heidegger lays the basis for this question in the twenties. As he writes in 1924, if the being of Dasein has a reflexive, self-problematizing character, "then being-there would be being questionable" (GA 64: 125/CT2 210 tm). Dasein is the being whose own being is an issue for it (SZ 41–42). We are always, deliberately or by default, taking a stand on our being and adopting a way of existing. We thus have a relation to our own being that other entities seem to lack. We have been handed a burden that may feel heavy or light, that we may recognize or disregard, but that, as long as we exist, we cannot simply put down—for this burden is our existence itself.

But our relation to ourselves also affects our relation to all other beings: since we exist by being-in-the-world, and we encounter other entities within the world, the question of how to exist marks our interpretation of entities other than ourselves (SZ 12–13). What beings signify to us is tied to who we take ourselves to be. Because our own existence is a problem, and because we exist in the context of a world, what it means for *everything* to be is also a problem—and we have an intrinsic mission to discover, question, and enrich our own understanding of being.

Let us look more closely at the elements of this idea. First, to say that Dasein's own being is at issue for it (*es geht um seinen Sein*) means that each of us is ineluctably concerned with *who* he or she is. Each of us is thrown into a concrete heritage, inhabits a meaningful world, and projects possible actions in terms of some ultimate "for-the-sake-of-which"—a way to be that structures one's world (SZ 84). Without my projection of selfhood, nothing would make sense to me. To put it in Kantian language, the "who am I?" must be able to accompany all my representations.

Our ultimate possibility is not necessarily an explicit choice. In fact, we ordinarily forget and even avoid it. Most of the time we do not agonize over our selfhood; we simply accept who we are, and get on with the business at hand. We act as typical members of our group, adopting the default behavior of the "they" (*das Man*). Some of us never experience an existential crisis at all. But this is all consistent with Heidegger's idea; his view is that this normal way of existing is a "fallen" condition in which the question of selfhood appears to have been settled once and for all, or remains mute. From a more insightful point of view, fallenness testifies to a higher calling. What seem to be cases of indifference to one's own being—recklessness, ennui, automatism, the unexamined life in all its variations—are really just deficient modes of care. Only an entity whose being is at stake for it can fail to take up the challenge, seek to unburden itself from itself, or forget its own responsibility.

In moments of lucidity, we realize how far we have fallen. But waking up to oneself does not mean retreating to a disembodied, noncommittal mind, for Dasein is always already being-in-the-world. "In" means engaged in, as when we say that someone is "into" politics or music (SZ 54). "World" means a network of meaningful and purposive relations (SZ 86). Each of us is into the network. I may care about my home, my family, my neighborhood, and my city; I operate in these environments, interpret myself in terms of them, and encounter things and people as relevant because they play a part in these significant webs. Even the experience of anxiety, where all the nodes of my network seem to recede into insignificance, does not destroy the network or my caring involvement in it. It is like standing atop Mount Everest, with an unparalleled view of the landscape, knowing that you will freeze or asphyxiate unless you descend. Anxiety shows us that our involvements cannot ground an identity that defines us as if we were a present-at-hand thing; our being remains at issue. But any viable response to the question of our being, any answer to the question of "who," no matter how provisional, must take the form of reengaging with the world.

Because I am-in-the-world, then, what is at issue for me is not my own being in isolation, but the being of everything that matters to me within my significant network. The question of who I am cannot be answered by navel-gazing. If I am into music, then I am engaged with what it means to be an instrument, to be a musician, and to be a good or bad piece of music or performance. How I interpret music is part of how I interpret myself—how I manage to be somebody. If we extrapolate from this example and include lesser degrees of engagement, we see that every Dasein is concerned with beings as a whole and as such. No matter how circumscribed one's world may be, it forms some totality in which one plays a part and where things have their places. No matter how distant we may be from theoretical questions of ontology, it makes a difference to us that beings *are* at all. And just as one's own selfhood is never settled, the sense of all other beings remains in question: our interpretation of every region of entities is susceptible to a paradigm shift, and the sense of the whole keeps calling for new responses. In this way, the question of being springs from the human condition itself. It is not the invention of philosophers, but is implied in the fact that our own selfhood is in question and that we can be someone only by engaging in a world where we care about entities as a whole.

Since being is at issue, we are constantly exposed to questions that cannot be definitively answered: What is the sense of being? Who am I? Who are we? Although we often use the word "identity" to refer to who we are, the word misleadingly suggests that we are identical to some definite content. "Selfhood" is preferable, as long as we keep in mind that it is a relation to oneself and one's world as problems, not a simple selfsameness. Heidegger thus insists that Dasein is a "who" (a self) rather than a "what" (an identity), and that the "who" is essential to all the features of our way of existing (SZ 45).

This thought insists on a tension and incompleteness within our own being: rather than having a fixed character that we can simply discover, our selves are permanently at stake. Particular goals (the "toward-which" of an activity) can be completed: I can finish building a house. But the "for-the-sake-of-which" cannot be fulfilled: one never *finishes* being an artist, a Christian, or a parent, even if one gives up on these ways of life and turns to others.

Heidegger's position combats "subjectivity," in his sense, which is a form of "subjectity" (GA 5: 133/100, 146/109)—a view that displaces the self in favor of a self-certain *subjectum*, an underlying, present thing with ascertainable, identifiable attributes. Subjectivism, which would impose the parameters of a subjective identity on the sense of all beings, has to be rejected if we deny that selfhood is identity. As I argued earlier in this chapter, Heidegger's transcendental thinking in *Being and Time* was never subjectivist. As we will see in chapter 2, his antisubjectivism plays an important part in his evolving view of Nazi ideology.

Because being-there is always being-with (SZ 118–25), the question "Who am I?" implies the further question, "Who are we?"—a decision about the destiny of a group. My world is shared: the network constantly implies others, even if they are not currently on the scene. My habits are cultural, my language is dialogical, the traditions to which I am indebted were developed by others. To grapple with my own existence is, at the same time, to address what it means to be a member of my community.

In §74 of *Being and Time*, Heidegger refers to the joint happening of Dasein as a *Volk* whose destiny is discovered, in his resonant but unexplained phrase, through "communication and struggle" (SZ 384). Some kind of communal authenticity is possible, he suggests: being-with is not simply the anesthetized irresponsibility of *das Man* or the cultural background against which an individual develops authenticity. Some genuine shared response to the question of "who" can emerge.

In the thirties, he continues to affirm that Dasein is a "who":

> Now, if we ask about man, we see that this question was up to now always posed in the form: *What* is man? . . . here it has already been decided that man is *something* constituted in such and such a way, which has these and those components that belong to it. One takes man as an entity that is put together out of body, soul, spirit. . . . The real revolution in the question must be that the question as a *question* must already be posed in a different way. We do not ask, "*What* is man?" but "*Who* is man?" [GA 36/37: 215/163 tm]

But he also wants to ask who "we" are within a concrete place, time, and community, rather than simply referring to an abstract "man" or "Dasein." The question recurs obsessively in these years: "Who are we?"

The question first comes to prominence in the same course that introduces the theme of emergency, the lectures of 1929–1930. The project of awakening a fundamental mood that thoroughly attunes us presupposes some decision about this "us": are "we" the people in Heidegger's classroom? Students? Germans? Europeans? Should we define ourselves still more broadly, as today's humanity? Paradoxically, as the circle of the "we" expands, our task becomes both more indefinite and more urgent (GA 29/30: 103–4).

The triumph of National Socialism in 1933 seems to have given Heidegger, for a while, a reply in practice to the question, "Who are we?" Nazism offered what he took to be an authentic bond to his primary community: Germany. According to Rector Heidegger's inaugural address of May 1933, by taking its place in the new political order, the university is performing an act of "self-assertion." This kind of self-assertion is not arbitrary license, but positive commitment (GA 16: 113–14). Dedicated work is supposed to unite the Germans in a shared mission.

Nevertheless, he wants to maintain "Who are we?" as a question, and not simply answer it with a political and practical identity. In fact, his Rectoral Address is notoriously vague about the content of the new German mission. With his increasing distance from the Nazi party, which we will trace in detail in the next chapter, he comes to see the "who" as a deeper and more difficult predicament, requiring a philosophical and poetic struggle that may never eventuate in a solution. Already in late 1934, he insists: "We exclude ourselves from the poetic . . . if we do not . . . first let the question of who we are become a *question* in our Dasein: one that we actually pose—that is, sustain—throughout our entire short lifetime" (GA 39: 59/55).

The "who" question must remain open, and it is tied to a series of other open questions:

> What should we do?
> Who *are* we?
> Why should we *be*?
> What are beings?
> Why does being happen? [GA 94: 5/5]

> *Are we?*
> *Who* are we?
> Where are we?
> In what moment are we?
> Who are *we*? . . .
> Who decides about "being"?
> Or does being decide about every "who" and all questioning? And how does it do so? What is being? How should being be unveiled and be brought into its truth? What is truth? [GA 69: 8/8]

These passages, so typical of the thirties, illustrate how the project of thinking of the happening of being is entangled with the question, "Who are we?"

* * *

We have seen how three themes—the inception of time, emergency, and self-hood—play key roles as Heidegger moves into the thirties. How are they connected? *Being and Time* argued that the fact that our being is an issue for us is essential to temporality and to our understanding of being. There, Heidegger describes moments when we recognize our being as an issue, and stop evading the burden of having to be someone. But how does our being first come to be an issue? A disruptive event must originally force us into the question of who we are. This moment when our being becomes an issue is an emergency, a crisis, a problematic juncture. It is the inception in which Dasein's selfhood emerges, along with ecstatic time and the understanding of being.

One might object that the prominence of these themes in the thirties is not really a shift in Heidegger's thought. *Being and Time* already characterized Dasein as a "who" and described the possibility of anxiety. These are *existential* features of Dasein's way of being. In contrast, questions such as "Who are we?" or "What is our current crisis?" are *existentiell* questions, issues to be worked out in the existence of a particular individual or community. By raising these questions, Heidegger may be attempting to live more authentically or inspire others to do the same, but he is not breaking any new ontological ground, one could argue. If we adopt this point of view, we may still take interest in the thirties as a phase in Heidegger's life and thought, but we will not see it as a change in his fundamental standpoint.

However, even in *Being and Time*, some difficulties stand in the way of a neat division between the existential and the existentiell. Heidegger claims that "those characteristics which can be exhibited in [Dasein] are in each case possible ways for it to be, and no more than that" (SZ 42). This would seem to undercut the very distinction between necessary structures and contingent possibilities.

He also claims that the roots of existential insights are ultimately existentiell (SZ §63). This might be taken as a platitude: Plato, Aristotle, or Descartes would agree that one must dedicate oneself to a certain way of life before one can make philosophical progress. But Heidegger means the statement more radically: philosophical insights always remain bound to who one is; they necessarily form part of one's way of existing at a certain historical juncture. This implies that the vision of human existence laid out in *Being and Time* is itself part of Heidegger's choice to take a stand in a certain way. This is not a narrow historicism that would limit the validity of his insights to Germany in 1927, but it does imply that if we choose to adopt these insights, we are making a certain decision about who we are and how we are. Our articulation of the existential structures is part of an existentiell moment in which we glimpse and project them.

In the years following *Being and Time*, Heidegger emphasizes that asking about being means asking who we are. This question and the emergency that provokes it are indissociable from the content of thinking. A couple of passages from the thirties will drive home the point that Heidegger wants the question "Who are we?" to be more than simply existentiell; it is crucial to philosophical insight, and even to the arising of Dasein's time itself.

> The poet says: "Since we are a dialogue." "Since"—'since the time that. . . .' If we do wish to look for a so-called 'definition' of man here, then it is a historical one, relating to time, and . . . to the time of the peoples . . . that time which . . . comes to be only if we ourselves become 'partakers,' partaking in the dialogue, and only if we ourselves decide in favor of that which historically we can be. We understand the word of the poet only if, and only so long as, we ourselves enter into this decision and stand within it. [GA 39: 69/63]

"The real question, 'Where do we stand?' which is to be asked concomitantly with the question, 'Who are we?' . . . concerns the standing-up [*Erständnis*] of space-time itself from the inceptive experience of the truth of beyng" (GA 96: 226/178 tm).

There are dangers, to be sure, in overturning the distinction between the existential and the existentiell. For one, we might be concerned about the ethical implications of placing a certain standpoint or way of being above a general conception of the human essence: Does this not discount certain people as less than Dasein, since (we can tell ourselves) they have not adopted the proper stance? Heidegger himself, in his postwar years, was more given to speaking about the human condition in general than to insisting on decisions. But our criticisms should be postponed until we have followed the course of his thinking in the thirties.

That thinking is necessarily political, given the themes that we have been tracing. According to Heidegger, if a genuine emergency impels us to ask "Who are we?" our own being, and the being of all beings, will become an urgent issue. He thus desires a transformative event that will cast his community into the problem of being. What if a group that shares an inherited world could recognize its fragility and creatively cultivate its meaning? What if the community could free itself from intellectualist abstractions—principles with no living roots in the emergence of sense? This would imply a politics that would have to be nationalist in some sense—grounded in the living, shared world of a particular group and inciting that group to ask who it is. The community would have to come alive to itself as a problem, so that it could participate in the happening of being.

Chapter Two

Passing Through the Political

In chapter 1 we encountered three key themes of Heidegger's thought in the thirties: inception, emergency, and selfhood. They are undeniably pertinent to politics: the question of shared selfhood—"Who are we?"—is motivated by an emergency that calls for a new inception. Such an inception is the founding of a community. How could such a founding take place? If inceptions are concealed, would a founding be accessible to language and discussion at all? Could a movement that emerged from the founding maintain collective selfhood as a question, or would it degenerate into an identity, a mass subjectivity? If it did degenerate, should it be rejected, or would there be a role for it even in its degeneracy, in its distorted version of the truth?

Heidegger answers "yes" to this last question. According to his own testimony in an entry from the late thirties in the *Black Notebooks*, from 1930 to 1934 he believed that National Socialism could bring about a new inception of Western history. He admits that this view was a misunderstanding of the movement's "authentic forces and inner necessities"; nevertheless, he tells himself that Nazism must be "affirmed" (GA 95: 408/318 tm).

Those bare facts already make it impossible for any responsible reader to accept Heidegger's thought without trepidation. He is an ambiguous and problematic philosopher, and will remain so. The controversy over his relation to Nazism is not simply a question of historical and textual accuracy; it will always require philosophical reflection, and by the same token, it cannot be put to rest. The uncomfortable task of reflecting on his politics is a permanent part of interpreting his philosophy. The questions cannot be settled by any single fact, such as the fact that he joined the Nazi party and never resigned—we would have to ask what party membership meant to him. They cannot be settled, either, by a concatenation of complex

49

facts—the mass of documents that lies before us. The question demands that we think.[1]

Even the interpreters who admit this point sometimes assume that the challenge is to identify Heidegger's beliefs. We then decide whether they should be labeled "Nazi." But things cannot be so simple, since Heidegger rightly rejected the notion of philosophy as a set of beliefs—something that one "has." Philosophy is something we do and something that happens to us—a journey along paths that may well turn out to be "woodpaths" (*Holzwege*) or dead ends. The challenge in interpreting Heidegger is to travel with him, noticing various positions he takes along the way but being wary of identifying any of them as the essence of his philosophy. If there is any proposition to which he remains true, it is that truth is not a property of propositions. Truth is not the correctness of an assertion, but the happening of unconcealment—a happening that assertions can intimate, but that ultimately eludes all propositions and beliefs. So what we should ask is not simply whether he held Nazi beliefs, but which of his thoughts end in blind alleys, concealing more than they unconceal, and which are journeys worth continuing.

From the ethical point of view, it is clear that as he wandered, Heidegger fell short in empathy, moral imagination, honesty, and respect for his fellow human beings; from the political point of view, he is culpable for supporting a genocidal dictatorship. But in these regards, he is just one of countless contemptible people, including many intellectuals, who have been implicated in tyranny over the ages. We do not learn much that is new and distinctive when we recognize the immorality in Heidegger's life and thought. In this regard, a phenomenological critique may be more interesting and philosophically fruitful than the ethical one. In this chapter, then, I will follow his attempts in the thirties to characterize political action and the political sphere. In chapter 3, I develop some criticisms of these paths on the grounds that they fail to disclose political phenomena.

Heidegger's political thought in the thirties defies easy summary or strictly chronological exposition. There are various kinds of questions to be asked, and they are best answered through different kinds of textual sources. Those sources are now abundant, and I make no claim to completeness. I have chosen the texts that I find most telling and that are tied most closely to the themes I traced in chapter 1: the inception of time, emergency, and the "who."

We will examine some lecture courses and seminars from Heidegger's most political phase in order to watch him reflecting on how to found a community, as well as on how language and silence play a part in the roots of politics. None of his reflections coalesce into a doctrine, but by following his teaching, we can see how he tries to make inroads into the political realm.

In order to follow his growing distance from that realm, we will turn to some posthumously published meditations in which he critiques the metaphysical basis of National Socialist ideology. From Heidegger's point of view, this ideology hardened into a collective subjectivism. The Nazi themes of struggle and power had attracted him in the mid-thirties as elements of emergency and inception. But by the late thirties, he views the will to power as an expression of late modern subjectivity that would need to be set aside in a new inception.

However, this does not mean that he simply rejects Nazism. For insight into his ambivalent stance toward the events of the thirties, we will consider his thought journals, the *Black Notebooks*, which are most explicit about his own attitudes. He comes to see National Socialism and its traits, such as "machination" and "brutality," as an *Un-wesen* or "counter-essence" that he "affirms" despite its negativity. These texts also provide insight into the dynamic of inception and downfall in terms of which he views history.

In these lectures, manuscripts, and journals, we can watch Heidegger plunge into the political and pass beyond it. He does not emerge unscathed. His perspective, by the end of the thirties, is embittered and remote. In chapter 3, we will look for better ways of understanding and appreciating politics, without either overestimating or denigrating the political sphere.

Before we study these texts, let us reflect on why Heidegger's enduring concern with the question of being has a political dimension at all.

We might take a fresh look at his general project by considering the process of so-called representational drawing. The skillful artist must decide which points are the indispensable references in a scene, which lines mark the crucial boundaries. As shapes and contours emerge, the scene comes to life on paper; the drawing evokes the being of what is pictured. Dürer's drawing of a hare brings out its hareness and its animality. Not only that, but the particular hare seems to be there for us in the drawing, to live on the paper. Dürer has evoked both the essence and the existence of the hare—to invoke an all-too-easy distinction that is overcome in this work of art that reveals a singular entity.[2] What-being and that-being bleed into each other when we draw out the being of a thing. If we try to draw only *what* a thing is, we get a so-called left-brained picture, a schematic diagram. This is what most children's drawings are: not natural, uncultured expressions, but representations of the cultural symbols they have learned. Children rarely draw what they see; they draw the prisms through which they see it. The mature artist also draws the what-being, but in constant dialogue with that-being. The lines of a good drawing allow the thing they delineate to present itself anew.

Presence, then, is essential to drawing; but drawing does not just re-present what is present in the present. In one respect, the draftsman never draws what he sees, but only what he has seen: he glances from the subject to the paper, drawing what is fresh in his memory. Even the most recent memory is selective, a look back at what has presented itself, identifying the crucial contours of its "being what it was," in the Aristotelian phrase. In another respect, the draftsman is looking forward, into possibilities: from the infinity of possible lines, he can select the limits that make it possible for the thing he is drawing to be. The presentation of the drawing happens through the interplay of looking back and looking forward. Drawing stands out into future, past, and present.

Although all the work of drawing is in the hands of the artist, the artist cannot arbitrarily create art from nothing. Representational art, at least, can fail—not because it is not photographically accurate, but because it falters in its selection of features; it does not draw out the being of the thing. We cannot give rules for successful drawings, but we have all seen bad ones. Drawing is neither purely active, then, nor purely passive. It is an attentive, discerning response that is drawn out by the being of the thing drawn, at the same time as it draws out the thing's being.

We can extend these points to the understanding of being as such. Being is given to us thanks to our extension into future, past, and present. Everything we do draws, or redraws, a line between being and nonbeing. But most of our behavior takes this relation to being for granted: we glance at a scene or use the things in it, taking them in or taking them up without taking the time to draw out their being with care. We act as if things were simply, self-evidently handed to us. For a purely technological attitude, the presence of beings becomes flat, calculable data that can be transformed and reproduced ad infinitum in accordance with our will. Things become resources. Form becomes information.[3] We take the that-being and what-being of entities for granted. We forget that being, including our own, is at issue for us.

However, it is possible to draw the line between being and nonbeing more thoughtfully and deliberately. At its best, this is an attentive and creative responsiveness, not an imposition of subjective will: "Where the limits are— where the concealed begins—*in every case, this is decided by the way in which beyng essentially happens*—and not by the particular kind of human capacity and knowledge, although this is not incidental, either" (GA 73.1: 34).

How, then, do we draw the line between being and nonbeing? What difference does it make to us that there is something instead of nothing?

As we saw in chapter 1, what being means to us goes hand in hand with who we are, since we are ourselves by encountering the being of all the beings in the world we inhabit. So we must also ask: How do we draw the line between who we are and who we are not? What are the contours of our selves?

Whoever we are, we are part of a "we"—a community whose members have to draw on shared, inherited senses within a shared realm of possibilities as they draw the lines of who they are. Thus, although the thirties are Heidegger's most overtly political phase, some broadly political dimension has to form part of his question of being.

Heidegger told Karl Löwith in 1936 that the root of his political engagement was his concept of historicity.[4] What can this mean? Section 74 of *Being and Time*, on authentic historicity, speaks in brief, abstract, but emphatic terms of the need for a generation to discover the destiny of the *Volk*—to draw the line that separates who we are from who we are not—through communication and struggle (SZ 384). Presumably, this could not take the form of everyday idle talk (SZ §35), but would require shattering the complacency of the "they" (SZ 129). If primal truth surges from a moment of disclosive resoluteness, an intersection of possibility and heritage that reveals the present as a "situation" (SZ 299), one must act decisively in order to rally one's community to a new vision. We can speculate that such acts would not be encouraged by liberalism: elections and guarantees of personal liberties would do nothing but reproduce the chatter of the day and reinforce the illusion that a people is nothing but a sum of individuals. When we combine *Being and Time*'s concept of historicity with its talk of resoluteness, choosing a hero (SZ 385), and "leaping ahead" (SZ 122), it is not difficult to read the text as National Socialism *in potentia*.[5]

However, the danger in reading these passages in retrospect is that such an interpretation reduces the possibilities of Heidegger's text to the actuality in which they were realized in 1933. A possibility is recognized as such only when it is maintained as possibility; it cannot be reduced to the particular acts or happenings in which it becomes manifest (SZ 145, 262). *Being and Time* opens possibilities; it does not call for a particular choice or act, but encourages its readers to ask how their community can be defined.

We cannot say, then, that Heidegger's concept of historicity is essentially Nazistic, but we can certainly say that it played a key role in his transition to the happening of being. We have seen that he comes to perceive his account of time as the transcendental horizon of being as too ahistorical, too insulated from inceptive moments. Dasein must be explored and chosen as a historical possibility. Philosophy cannot stand above historical happening and describe it in a neutral language, but must grasp itself as acting within the very history that it is trying to understand. Philosophy requires "engagement": "seizing a necessary possibility, exposing oneself to the *necessity* of fate, complying with the freedom of a resolution" (GA 36/37: 78/62).

We can feel Heidegger's own desire to engage, his restlessness and apprehension, when he says in his lectures on Plato's allegory of the cave in 1931–1932: "The philosopher must remain solitary, because this is what he *is* according to his essence. . . . Isolation is nothing to be wished for as such. Just for this reason the philosopher must always be there in decisive moments, and not give way. He will not misunderstand solitude in external fashion, as withdrawal and letting things go their own way" (GA 34: 86/63 tm).

The National Socialist revolution appeared to provide an opportunity for decisive, disclosive action. As Heidegger saw it, the movement that had come to power had the potential to become appropriately historical: it was based not on abstract principles, but on the particularity of a people. It did not call for chatter and calculation, but for resolute struggle. It would force the Germans to wrestle with their own selfhood, to draw the line between being and nonbeing.

In 1933, then, he seizes his opportunity to intervene. "The present happenings . . . increase the will and the certainty . . . of assisting in the construction of a world grounded in the *Volk*. For a long time the pallor and shadowiness of mere 'culture' and the unreality of so-called 'values' have sunk down to nothingness for me; I have sought the new basis in being-there."[6]

The moment, as Heidegger sees it, does not call for debate and calculation, but for resolute struggle. Only by participating in this moment of emergency, when the German destiny is being decided, can he fulfill his dedication to truth. Of course, there is risk in this venture: "Speaking out from solitude, [the philosopher] speaks at the decisive moment. He speaks with the danger that what he says may suddenly turn into its opposite" (GA 36/37: 183/141).

Let us look a little more closely at how he could imagine that Nazism was the right way to draw the line, taking our clue from a 1936 lecture course in which he describes Hitler and Mussolini to his students as antinihilists. These two men "have introduced countermovements [to nihilism] on the basis of the political formation of the nation or the people." He comments that they are both "essentially influenced by Nietzsche," although in their politics "the authentic metaphysical domain of Nietzschean thinking has not directly come to fruition" (GA 42: 40–41).[7]

What could Heidegger mean by calling Hitler an antinihilist? In the 1935 *Introduction to Metaphysics*, he defines nihilism as a condition in which being has seemingly lost all sense, and appears to be empty in contrast to the richness of beings.

> Everywhere we are underway amid beings, and yet we no longer know how it stands with being. We do not even know that we no longer know it. We are staggering even when we mutually assure ourselves that we are not staggering, even when, as in recent times, people go so far as to try to show that this asking about being brings only confusion, that it has a destructive effect, that it is nihilism. . . .
>
> But where is the real nihilism at work? Where one clings to current beings and believes it is enough to take beings, as before, just as the beings that they are. But with this, one rejects the question of being and treats being as a nothing (*nihil*), which in a certain way it even "is," insofar as it essentially unfolds

[*west*]. Merely to chase after beings in the midst of the oblivion of being—that is nihilism. Nihilism thus understood is the *ground* for the nihilism that Nietzsche exposed in the first book of *The Will to Power*.

In contrast, to go expressly up to the limit of Nothing in the *question* about being, and to take Nothing into the question of being—this is the first and only fruitful step toward the true overcoming of nihilism. [GA 40: 211–12/226 tm]

Heidegger's one-upmanship with regard to Nietzsche illuminates a certain reservation in his reference to Hitler and Mussolini the next year: although these men are influenced by Nietzsche, they have not yet understood the "authentic metaphysical domain" of Nietzsche's thought—which is to be found not through Nietzsche's own concepts but through Heidegger's meditation on being and nothing. Furthermore, a "countermovement" may be merely reactive and may reproduce the essential features of what it struggles against (GA 7: 74/EP 89); this was eventually to become Heidegger's predominant view of Nazism.

Heidegger's studies of Nietzsche in the thirties and forties (GA 43, GA 44, GA 46, GA 47, GA 48, GA 50) end by characterizing Nietzsche as the last metaphysician, who thinks the essence of beings as the will to power but fails to think of being itself. He is "the final victim of a long-standing errancy and neglect," because he conceives of being as a mere "vapor" (GA 40: 39–40/40). Nietzsche is a nihilist, by the definition presented in *Introduction to Metaphysics*.

But this is a rather abstruse and ontological definition of nihilism. What does nihilism mean more concretely, as a phenomenon in human life? Another passage from *Introduction to Metaphysics* brings us closer to understanding:

Dasein began to slide into a world that lacked that depth from which the essential always comes and returns to human beings, thereby forcing them to superiority and allowing them to act on the basis of rank. All things sank to the same level, to a surface resembling a blind mirror that no longer mirrors, that casts nothing back. The prevailing dimension became that of extension and number. *To be able*—this no longer means to spend and to lavish, thanks to lofty overabundance and the mastery of energies; instead, it means only practicing a routine in which anyone can be trained, always combined with a certain amount of sweat and display. In America and Russia, then, this all intensified until it turned into the measureless so-on-and-so-forth of the ever-identical and the indifferent, until finally this quantitative temper became a quality of its own. By now in those countries the predominance of a cross-section of the indifferent is no longer something inconsequential and merely barren, but is the onslaught of that which aggressively destroys all rank and all that is world-spiritual, and portrays these as a lie. This is the onslaught of what we call the demonic. [GA 40: 49–50/50–51]

This passage evidently shares Nietzsche's antiegalitarianism and his admiration for overflowing strength—but in Heidegger, these attitudes are linked to the question of being. The image of a "blind mirror" suggests that in the late modern world, qualitative differences of depth and excellence are no longer recognizable; all beings are represented as quantifiable objects that are essentially the same, and this representational paradigm is no longer even recognized as such. Blind mirroring is the opposite of drawing—a creative, responsive tracing of being. An impoverished understanding of what-being and that-being is taken for granted by individuals and states, all of which focus their energies on organizing and controlling beings. This process obliterates the qualitative differences that it ignores; it is a devastating worldview, laying waste to people and things. Germany, caught between the "pincers" of American and Soviet nihilism, must find a way to resist (GA 40: 40/41).

Heidegger was persuaded, then, for some time, that in order to fight nihilism, "we" had to redraw a clear line between being and nothing, a line that had become blurred and senseless. Drawing that line would require distinguishing who "we" are from who "we" are not. A nationalistic and dictatorial movement, whether or not it understood its own metaphysical basis, seemed to him for a while to supply the appropriate means of drawing such a line. But just how could a new way of being for the Germans be founded?

FOUNDING THE *VOLK*

Our best sources for this question are Heidegger's lecture courses and seminars from the most politicized years of the thirties. Here we can see him struggling with the question of how an authentic community of the people is to be inaugurated and with the ontological foundations of politics. How can a new inception of history take place? How can it respond appropriately to emergency and awaken the question of collective selfhood?

As we have seen, Heidegger himself dates the beginning of his faith in National Socialism at 1930 (GA 95: 408). There are indications of this orientation in the first version of his lecture "On the Essence of Truth," from July of the same year: truthfulness requires rootedness (*Bodenständigkeit*), which includes "natural connection to the soil, provenance from an ethnicity [*Stammesart*], and being woven into the landscape" (GA 80.1: 338), as well as "saving the people [*Volkstum*] and protecting the homeland" (GA 80.1: 339).

However, "rootedness" disappears in subsequent versions of "On the Essence of Truth" (composed October 1930 and later), and Heidegger's lecture courses of 1930–1932 offer no clear indications of nationalistic or atavistic sympathies. He appears to be goading his audience to ask, "Who are we?" in regard to philosophy rather than politics. Some key passages in these lectures vividly show that this question has become a matter of more than "existenti-ell" importance: it is central to the very project of thinking of being.

In *The Essence of Human Freedom* (1930), Heidegger argues that the con-cepts of negative and positive freedom both invite reflection on the general question of what it means to be (GA 31: 6–7, 30–31). But he does not sub-ordinate the problem of freedom to the problem of being: to the contrary, the question of being is itself a "problem of freedom," not only theoretically but in a concrete sense, since it requires one to "become essential in the actual willing of [one's] own essence" (GA 31: 303/205).[8]

Our own essence must be chosen from finite possibilities, as Heidegger insists in one of his many confrontations with Hegel, his 1930–1931 reading of the *Phenomenology of Spirit*.[9] Are "we," with Hegel, those who presume to possess absolute knowledge (GA 32: 71), or are knowledge and being not absolute at all for us, but finite (GA 32: 55, 145)? Hegel affirms an abso-lute point of view that exposes all partial standpoints in their limited truth and subsumes them in a systematic whole. He denies that he imposes the absolute on the finite; the finite standpoints themselves imply a dialectical process that points to their supersession in the absolute. Heidegger, however, asserts that Hegel presupposes his conclusions—as all philosophers do (GA 32: 43). Even in the examination of sense-certainty that begins the *Phenom-enology*, Hegel has already assumed that "we" are absolute knowers (GA 32: 66). This means that "we have already let go of what is ours in the sense of what is humanly relative" (GA 32: 71/50 tm). If being is finite, Heidegger implies that "we" must retrieve our finitude by acting and thinking from a unique historical situation. The title of *Being and Time*, he says, already implies that philosophy is not a "science" that aims at a system of absolute knowledge (GA 32: 18/12–13); it is an effort of historically situated, finite human beings. Time empowers concepts, not vice versa (GA 32: 144). This means that every philosophy is *einmalig*: it is a singular effort that happens only once, which is precisely what allows it to be retrieved creatively in a singular confrontation (GA 32: 105). Since humans are radically finite, and being is revealed only for and in human temporality, being itself is finite (GA 32: 56, 145). Being is "single, simple, singular"—a finite donation to finite humanity (GA 32: 60/42 tm).

We will soon analyze a seminar in which Heidegger confronts Hegel on a directly political level, but some political implications of his anti-Hegelian-ism are already evident. If we are essentially finite, and the very meaning of "we" is a matter that must be decided by a particular group on the basis of its unique historical situation, then politics cannot be founded on transhistorical principles such as human rights or on rationally constructed theories of the

social contract; politics has to be based on "what is ours" (GA 32: 71/50)—
the particular heritage and vocation of a group, which must struggle against
anything and anyone that threatens its communal destiny.

In other lecture courses of the early thirties, Heidegger tries to reveal "*what
remained un-happened*" in the tradition (GA 34: 322/228) through readings
of key texts such as the *Critique of Pure Reason* (GA 31, GA 41) and Book
Theta of Aristotle's *Metaphysics*, which argues for the priority of actuality
over potentiality (GA 31: 107; GA 33). Heidegger, in contrast, continues to
affirm the possible over the actual: it is only in terms of possible ways to
be—which are always finite and shadowed by death—that we can encounter
any actualities (SZ 262).

Heidegger's account of the history of Western philosophy is deepened
through the beginning of his intense interest in early Greek thought (GA 35),
which can remind us of the inception of the West and suggest paths not taken.
In the premetaphysical thinking of Heraclitus, Anaximander, or Parmenides
we can witness an encounter with the gifts of truth and being. Yet because
the Presocratics were unable to ask about the source of these gifts, they could
not prevent philosophy from degenerating into a series of metaphysical positions—attempts to ascertain general truths about beings, without meditating
on truth and being. Here, too, the question of shared selfhood arises: Who are
we when we look back at the inception of Greek philosophy (GA 35: 43)? As
we saw in chapter 1, Heidegger also asserts that only those human beings who
live in the legacy of that inception "exist," in his sense: only they are exposed
to the question of being (GA 35: 92, 95).

The common thread in his reflections during these years shortly before the
Nazi regime is the need to draw the line: to make a free but situated decision
that would reorient our own being and, in this way, establish a fresh relation
to being and history. He senses the need for a new founding. With Hitler's
rise to power and Heidegger's ascension to the rectorate of the University of
Freiburg, these reflections on freedom and possibility become exhortations to
embrace the German destiny.

The Fundamental Question of Philosophy:
A Call for Founding

The Fundamental Question of Philosophy (Summer Semester 1933) is Heidegger's first lecture course as rector. It begins with a dramatic description
of the historical moment: the German people is finding itself by finding its
vocation (GA 36/37: 3). This discovery is not factual knowledge of the future, which would suffocate all action by removing risk (GA 36/37: 4), but
a readiness to ask who we are and to take up the mission we have inherited.

Heidegger asserts that we *are* by asking *who* we are: a community does not truly exist until it recognizes its own being as an issue. We must demand what will be, quarrel with what *is* in the accepted present, and honor what has been (GA 36/37: 4). This triad clearly reflects the dimensions of ecstatic temporality, which Heidegger hopes will be reborn at this revolutionary moment.

We have inherited the legacy of the "inception," which is never exhausted by what comes after it and enjoins us to "create the spiritual world that is still latent in the happening that is coming to be" (GA 36/37: 7/6). At the time, German academics were often critical of liberal democracy, but mistrusted the violent, anti-intellectual tendencies of the National Socialists; the call was to *vergeistigen* the revolution, that is, provide it with some intellectual content and cultural direction. Heidegger's colleagues may have thought he might provide a scholarly bulwark against Nazi crudity, but he turns out to have no interest in defending what he sees as a bankrupt academic establishment, for according to him, intellectuals have no true concept of what spirit is. He glosses *Geist* as "breath, gust, astonishment, impulse, engagement" (GA 36/37: 7/6).

As they create the new world that is half-awake in the spirit of the revolution, the Germans should look to Greek thought as *"the ceaseless questioning struggle over the essence and being of beings"* (GA 36/37: 8/7 tm). Such a struggle is never complete, for philosophy "arises from the *ownmost urgency and strength of humanity*, and *not* of God. It is not absolute knowledge either in its content or in its form. Proper to it is the *highest essentiality*, and thus *necessity*, but not therefore infinity" (GA 36/37: 10/8).

Obviously Heidegger is again opposing his thought to Hegel's, and soon the aim of this lecture course becomes clear: a confrontation with Hegel, who represents the culmination of the tradition that was built on Greek thought but fell away from the original emergency of the Greek inception. If we fail to come to grips with this decline and seize our destiny, then—Heidegger repeats a passage near the conclusion of his Rectoral Address nearly word for word—the West will crack at its joints and collapse (GA 36/37: 14; GA 16: 117).

After a critique of Descartes and pre-Kantian German metaphysics, Heidegger has to conclude his course without adequately confronting Hegel, but he ends with a strong contrast between Hegel and the origin of philosophy. In the Greek inception, we find the *"deepest emergency of questionworthiness* in the struggle with the unmastered powers of truth and errancy"; at the end, with Hegel, we find the "empty eternity of the decisionless" (GA 36/37: 77/61 tm). There is no emergency anymore; nothing is really at stake.

Heidegger ends with a call to engage "in the essentially uncertain" (GA 36/37: 79/63). We must leap into the obscure new reality and create a new world, including a new metaphysics. The German people, he concludes, has not lost its metaphysics and cannot lose it—because it has never had it! (Apparently the metaphysics of Wolff, Baumgarten, Kant, and Hegel are not genuinely German.)

There is little in this lecture course that can be called specifically National Socialist, except perhaps the emphasis on the *Volk* and the rejection of modernity, and thus implicitly of modern liberal politics. Much of what Heidegger says here could have been said at the moment of any revolution. We can taste the fervor, the sense of momentous decisions and great opportunities—but this revolutionary mood is not linked to particular policies or ideological schemes. One could almost take him to be celebrating an abstract revolutionary spirit rather than this particular revolution and its programs.

Nature, History, State: Founder as Führer

In contrast, the 1933–1934 seminar *On the Essence and Concept of Nature, History, and State* puts Heidegger's thought directly into the service of a nationalist dictatorship. This seminar stands as his most concerted attempt to develop a political theory and to tie his political commitments explicitly to his fundamental philosophical ideas. The text consists of student protocols that he reviewed and kept. We cannot count on it as a verbatim transcript of what he said; however, it seems reliable as a record of the general train of thought that he developed in this seminar. Here is the closest thing we have to a Heideggerian political philosophy—a philosophy that resists nihilism, as he understands it, by emphasizing human finitude and qualitative difference.

Although it seems to have begun in a relatively Socratic fashion, the protocols suggest that the seminar soon became another lecture series by Heidegger, where he attempts to lay the foundations of a political philosophy that is in tune with the new regime. This is done by means of a series of characteristically Heideggerian reflections on nature, history, and state. His technique is to propose that standard concepts in these three domains consist of traditional prejudices that have covered up a more original experience of the essence of the phenomena. He distinguishes human, historical existence from the natural world and argues that a people can attain its full, distinctively human being only through its state, which is to be ruled absolutely by the will of a born leader. He also offers an account of political space that distinguishes between the local homeland and the "interaction" that connects it to a broader territory.

The first four of the seminar's ten sessions seem to have been intended to fend off a naturalistic interpretation of human being by questioning the essence of nature, providing historical perspective on the concepts of *physis* and *natura*, and emphasizing the qualitative differences between historical and nonhistorical beings. This is the only aspect of the seminar that Heidegger mentions in a circa-1945 retrospective on his teaching: it was a "critique of the biologistic view of history" (GA 86: 898). Historical, human time requires decision; in this sense, animals have no time (NHS 33). Of course, animals change, so they, along with all nature, are in time in the sense that they undergo various processes (NHS 28–29). For the ancients, this natural process of becoming might mean the emergence of the characteristic presence of an entity with an inner principle that guides its activity. For the moderns it might mean only the change of location of a material object, a change that can be measured and calculated. Neither approach, however, captures the distinctively human and historical experience of time.

Heidegger turns abruptly to the state in the middle of the fifth session. He avoids traditional approaches to political philosophy—questions such as, "What is the state's purpose?" "What is its origin?" or "Who will rule?"— because they do not yield fundamental insights into the essence of the state (NHS 38). An ontology of the state demands that we reflect on the people, since the people is "the supporting ground" of the state. He mentions the racial concept of the *Volk* as "the tie of the unity of blood and stock," but this is only one concept among others (NHS 43).

What it means for a particular people to be must be established through its state. While he leaves open the question of what a people in general is, he claims that the state is not just "grounded in the being of the people" (NHS 46 tm), but *is* the being of the people (NHS 46, 53, 57). "The people that turns down a state, that is stateless, has just not found the gathering of its essence yet; it still lacks the composure and force to be committed to its fate as a people" (NHS 46). A stateless people *is* not yet; it has not yet found fulfillment as a community.

This conception of the state transcends any description on the level of mere beings. We might compare this passage from *Introduction to Metaphysics* (1935): "A state—it *is*. What does its being consist in? In the fact that the state police arrest a suspect, or that in a ministry of the Reich so and so many typewriters clatter away and record the dictation of state secretaries and ministers? Or 'is' the state in the discussion between the Führer and the English foreign minister?" (GA 40: 38/39). If we follow the reasoning of the 1933–1934 seminar, it is a mistake from the start to assume that a state is an entity, something that *is*. Instead, the people is the fundamental entity, and the state is the being of the people. The concrete acts that are the business of government are incidental, and may even distract us from the state's essence.

The seminar elaborates on the people-state relation through an analogy to individuals. Because individuals' own being is an issue for them, they have consciousness and conscience. They care about their own being, want to live, and love their own existence. In just the same way, the people loves its state: "The people is ruled by the urge for the state, by *erōs* for the state" (NHS 48). This is why we care about the form of the state, or the constitution—which is not a contract or a legal arrangement, but "the actualization of our decision for the state"; constitutions are "factical attestations of what we take to be our historical task as a people, the task that we are trying to live out" (NHS 48–49). The erotic urge and decision for the state is to be distinguished from "drive" as felt by lower animals; bees and termites are instinctively driven into cooperative formations, but this nonhuman phenomenon is not genuinely political (NHS 48; cf. Aristotle, *Politics* 1.2, 1253a8–9).

Heidegger briefly contrasts his concept of the political to two others. Carl Schmitt's view that the essence of the political is the friend-enemy relation comes in for some criticism when Heidegger emphasizes that for Schmitt, "the political unit does not have to be identical with state and people" (NHS 46). A group based on solidarity against an enemy is less fundamental than a *Volk*. He also criticizes Bismarck's concept of politics as "the art of the possible," which depends too much on "the personal genius of the states-man" (NHS 46).

But this remark should not lead us to expect an antidictatorial point of view; in fact, Heidegger's views as presented here easily lend themselves to a personality cult. He claims there can be a born leader, an individual who "must be a leader in accordance with the marked form of his being" (NHS 45 tm).[10] A born leader needs no political education, but he ought to be supported by an educated elite, a "band of guardians" who help to take responsibility for the state. Heidegger seems to envision something like Plato's "complete guardians," the philosopher-rulers, but here they are in service to a leader who knows what to do not as a philosopher, but as a creator. This leader not only understands, but actually "brings about" what the people and the state are. Notably, this expression was penciled in by Heidegger himself on the student protocol (NHS 45, cf. 46). The born leader drafts the state and people: he draws the line between who "we" are and who "we" are not. The focused will of the leader provides the clear identity that a vague urge cannot.

There is no room for debate and disagreement within Heidegger's com-plex of people, state, and leader. "Only where the leader and the led bind themselves together to *one* fate and fight to actualize *one* idea does true order arise." He envisions "a deep dedication of all forces to the people, the state, as the most rigorous breeding, as engagement, endurance, solitude and love. Then the existence and superiority of the leader sinks into the being, the soul of the people, and binds it in this way with originality and passion to the task." In this unified whole, which recalls "the medieval order of life," citizens are ready to sacrifice themselves in order to defeat "death and the devil—that is, ruination and decline from their own essence" (NHS 49 tm). This passage puts the notions of decision and emergency that are so pervasive in Heidegger's thought in the thirties in the service of a totalitarian and purist point of view.

In the eighth and perhaps most original session of the seminar, he focuses on the political meaning of space. In all of his thought, space is meaningful: it is not a geometrical abstraction, but a complex of places where things and human beings belong—or fail to belong. In *Being and Time*, he describes the spatiality of Dasein and of the things in our environment as a field that comprises qualitative differences in importance, a gathering of appropriate and inappropriate relations. "The homogeneous space of nature shows itself only when the beings we encounter are discovered in a way that has the character of a specific *deworlding* of the worldliness of the ready-to-hand" (SZ 112). Space appears to be an undifferentiated repository for mere present-at-hand objects only if we disregard the significance and purposes of the things we meet.

In the seminar, Heidegger develops two aspects of the space of a people: homeland (*Heimat*) and territory. He indicates the latter with a variety of words: *Land, Herrschaftsgebiet, Territorium*, and *Vaterland*. (The term "fatherland" is mentioned only one other time in the seminar [NHS 52], where Heidegger implies that it reflects an inadequate relationship to the people.) The immediately familiar homeland, the locality into which one is born, is small, not just in its measurements but in the coziness of its familiarity. The proper relation to it is *Bodenständigkeit*: groundedness, standing steadfast and rooted in the soil. But there is another impulse, working out into "the wider expanse," that opens the space of the state, the territory. Only when rootedness in the soil is supplemented by "interaction" (*Verkehr*) does a people come into its own (NHS 55).

The passage could be seen as an example of a dialectic between the familiar and the strange that is at work in many of Heidegger's texts.[11] In *Being and Time*, one must experience the uncanniness of anxiety before one can return authentically (*eigentlich*, "own"-ly) to one's familiar environment. If we were completely ensconced in our surroundings, they would be our habitat and we would be nothing but animals. The key to authentic dwelling is the recognition that this dwelling is finite and contingent. Accordingly, "When one is put out of the home . . . the home first discloses itself as such" (GA 40: 176/186). The concept of "interaction" also involves a readiness to step out beyond one's comfort zone—but in this case, we do not step out into the nothingness of anxiety, but into a *Herrschaftsgebiet* or "sovereign dominion" (NHS 55), a territory that can be controlled by the state and that borders on other states.

What are the concrete implications of Heidegger's thoughts on political space? He makes two telling remarks. First, Germans who live outside the boundary of the Reich cannot participate in the extended space of state-governed interaction. If the state is the very being of the people, these groups are being "deprived of their authentic way of being"—prevented from fulfilling themselves as Germans (NHS 56 tm). Their politico-ontological eros is being thwarted. He does express some reservations about the slogan "people without space" (popularized by Hans Grimm's nationalistic novel *Volk ohne Raum*): a people necessarily has some space of its own (NHS 53). Still, his comments fit all too easily with the Nazi call for *Lebensraum* and Hitler's ambitions to unify all Germans under a single state.

Secondly, different peoples have different relations to their spaces and affect the landscape in accordance with these relations. Heidegger contrasts a rooted (*bodenständig*) people to a nomadic people that not only comes from deserts, but also tends to lay waste to every place it goes. He adds that perhaps "Semitic nomads" will never understand the character of "our German space" (NHS 56).

Heidegger's remark does an injustice to nomadic people, who can be very much at home in the landscape through which they travel, and whose practices may well be ecologically superior to those of settled agriculture. But his primary target is surely not traditional nomads, but the Jews, who are represented here as rootless aliens. His comment demonizes German Jews: he implies that they destroy the richness of local life, and thus are "demonic" as defined in *Introduction to Metaphysics* (GA 40: 50/51); they are the "devil" that causes "decline from [the German] essence" (NHS 49).

Heidegger's cutting comment thus fits all too easily with the characterization of modern rootlessness that one finds in many of his texts and with the antisemitic stereotype of the wandering Jew. But did we not just say that homelessness is a prerequisite for genuine homecoming? Is Heidegger's own thought not nomadic, in this sense? No, because the nomadic rootlessness that he denounces is an intellectualized mentality that no longer feels homesickness at all; it takes all things as merely present-at-hand, as senseless objects to be manipulated in a shallow world where nothing and no one belongs—where the very question of belonging no longer resonates. This is what Heidegger understands by devastation and how he understands the Nietzschean line "the wasteland grows" (cf. GA 8: 31/29–30).

Heidegger's statement on Semites and space is a relatively mild formulation of a cliché that Schmitt was to express with full venom during the war:

> The peculiar misrelation of the Jewish people to everything that concerns soil, land, and territory is grounded on its style of political existence. The relation of

a people to a soil formed by its own work of settlement and culture, and to the concrete forms of power that result from this, is unintelligible to the mind of the Jew. And he does not even want to understand all this, but only to dominate it conceptually in order to put his own concepts in their place. *Comprendre c'est détruire* [to understand is to destroy], as a French Jew has admitted. These Jewish authors, of course, were as little responsible for creating the theory of space up to now as they were for creating anything else. But here, as elsewhere, they were important in fermenting the dissolution of concrete, spatially determined orders.[12]

Heidegger's remark on "Semitic nomads" certainly scapegoats the Jews as agents of destruction, but one can argue that, when expressed at a certain level of generality, his views are not necessarily anti-Jewish. The idea that a people needs a state and a space of its own would, of course, be endorsed by Zionists.[13] Heidegger also warns his students not to assume that he is referring to measurable territory (NHS 53), so we should not be too quick to identify specific implications of his remarks on space. Still, it is fair to say, at least, that he is experimenting with a philosophical justification of Nazi expansionism and of antisemitic notions of what it means to be German.

Returning to the relation among state, people, and leader, Heidegger raises the question of the nature of the will of the people, but does not resolve it, resorting instead to a disappointingly vague remark: it is "a complicated structure that is hard to grasp." He prefers to emphasize the inseparable, "single actuality" of people and leader (NHS 60). To be led is not to be oppressed: the true leader will show the path and the goals to those who are led, rather than forcing them (NHS 62). "The true implementation of the will [of the leader] is not based on coercion, but on awakening the same will in another, that is . . . a decision of the individual" (NHS 62).

But what about individuals who cannot recognize the path, or who disagree with the goals? Heidegger seems not to care what will become of these dissidents. Instead he looks to the glorious deeds that manifest "the soaring will of the leader" (NHS 62). He briefly discusses resistance, or will that opposes the leader's, but seems to see it purely as a negative phenomenon that requires reeducation. Education at all levels "is nothing but the implementation of the will of the leader and the will of the state, that is, of the people" (NHS 63). Complete unanimity is the ideal: even if community depends on individual decisions, any such decision that contradicts the will of the state, which is identical with the will of the leader, is out of order and amounts to a betrayal of the people. It is ultimately the Führer who decides who "we" are. The only alternative, as Heidegger sees it, is confusion and collapse. A "higher bond," such as a bond to the *Volk*, "creates the highest freedom, whereas lack of commitment is negative freedom. One has sometimes understood political freedom in this latter sense, and thus misunderstood it" (NHS 63).

Heidegger ends the seminar by praising the *Führerstaat* as the culmination of a historical development that has reconstructed community after the Middle Ages were dissolved by modernity. National Socialism promises reintegration and the revival of a sense of being:

> . . . three great disintegrations . . . have occurred many times since the dissolution of the universal commitments and obligations of the Middle Ages:
> 1. The collapse of dogmatic-ecclesiastical faith, of the concept of creation, occurred in the wake of the first dissolution of a great bond: man became a self-legislating being that wills to, and must, found his own being himself. This is the source of Descartes' search for a *fundamentum absolutum*, which he found in the conviction *ego cogito, ergo sum.* The being of man is based on reason, that is, mathematical *ratio*, which is elevated to the decisive power of the world.
> 2. The second disintegration consists in the disintegration of the community—the fact that the individual in himself is the final court of appeal.
> 3. Descartes carries out the sharp separation between mind and body. . . .
> Of the three domains that we touched upon in the course of our explanations and questions—nature, history, and state—the state is the narrowest, but it is the most actual actuality that must give all being new sense, in a new and original sense. The highest actualization of human being happens in the state.
> The Führer-state, as we have it, means the completion of the historical development: the actualization of the people in the leader. [NHS 64 tm]

This passage (and a similar one at GA 16: 290) reminds us of Heidegger's debt to Catholic antimodernism. This is not to say that in 1933–1934 he is still a Christian, or that he wants to return, literally, to medieval conditions—but he feels the loss of the integrated, structured existence of the Middle Ages. Medieval man inhabited a world where things had not sunk into a "blind mirror" (GA 40: 49/50) but were rich in significance; qualitative differences were reinforced by bonds that transcended arbitrary, individual choice. What Heidegger hoped for in National Socialism, then—its "inner truth and greatness"—was the revival of a rooted, hierarchic way of life, against the nihilistic condition in which all beings are reduced to an unquestioned ontological indifference and are evaluated in terms of rootless abstractions. Similarly, Heidegger writes in the *Black Notebooks* that "socialism" means the "commitment of all to their task in each case, according to their responsibility and type within the entirety of the people, dividing all according to their places and levels" (GA 94: 124/91 tm, cf. GA 16: 304). The idea recalls the medieval social order as well as political justice as defined in the *Republic*.

What stands out most in the seminar is the notion that rootedness can be implemented from above: the Leader animates the state, which is the very being of the people. The people truly begins to be—it responds to the question,

"Who are we?"—only when a supreme leader rises up from the people and takes power. The *Volk* is founded from the top down.

On the Essence of Truth: Founding and Enmity

The lecture course *On the Essence of Truth* (in GA 36/37), from the same Winter Semester 1933–1934, is largely based on Heidegger's 1931–1932 course on Plato's allegory of the cave and *Theaetetus*. He would usually prepare a whole new course every semester, but evidently the duties of the office of rector made this impossible. He does improvise some new material, which has been recorded in student notes, and he begins with an extensive and important introduction. Why repeat this particular course? It is not accidental that the *Republic* explores the relation between politics and philosophy, that there is a significant political dimension to the allegory of the cave, and that Heidegger saw himself in a somewhat Platonic light (consider the echo of the three classes of Plato's just city in his rectoral address).

In his introduction to the course, Heidegger raises the question of the essence of truth, and immediately addresses the objection that this is an impractical, abstract inquiry, remote from the urgent needs of the people (GA 36/37: 83). The objection assumes that essence is an abstraction, a universal representation, whereas essence is disclosed only when human beings "*put* essence to *work*" (GA 36/37: 87/70).

But what *is* the essence of beings? We can answer the question only by appropriating the Greek inception in a German way. Here Heidegger indulges in his own version of Nazi rhetoric: we must "draw on the fundamental possibilities of the proto-Germanic ethnic essence [*des urgermanischen Stammeswesens*] and [. . .] bring these to mastery" (GA 36/37: 89/71).

In his previous course, Heidegger had characterized the Greek inception as the ceaseless struggle over being. He now focuses on struggle itself by selecting Heraclitus's fragment 53 as "the first and the decisively great answer to our question about what the essence of beings consists in" (GA 36/37: 89/72): "*polemos* is the father of all and the king of all; some it has shown as gods and others as men; some it has made slaves and others free." Heidegger translates *polemos* as *Kampf* in the sense of "standing against the enemy" (GA 36/37: 90/72–73).

What follows may be the most chilling passage in Heidegger's writings, and it demands to be read in full.

> An enemy is each and every person who poses an essential threat to the Dasein of the people and its individual members. The enemy does not have to be external, and the external enemy is not even always the more dangerous one. And

it can seem as if there were no enemy. Then it is a fundamental requirement to find the enemy, to expose the enemy to the light, or even first to make the enemy, so that this standing against the enemy may happen and so that Dasein may not lose its edge.

The enemy can have attached itself to the innermost roots of the Dasein of a people and can set itself against this people's own essence and act against it. The struggle is all the fiercer and harder and tougher, for the least of it consists in coming to blows with one another; it is often far more difficult and wearisome to catch sight of the enemy as such, to bring the enemy into the open, to harbor no illusions about the enemy, to keep oneself ready for attack, to cultivate and intensify a constant readiness and to prepare the attack looking far ahead with the goal of total annihilation [*Vernichtung*]. [GA 36/37: 90–91/73]

For those who wish to exonerate Heidegger, some excuses lie at hand: he cannot mean "annihilation" literally; he surely cannot be referring to the Jews; he must mean inauthenticity as the internal enemy that lies within each of us; and so on. Such readings are too quick to dismiss what he says: the *Volk* may have to "make" an internal enemy—invent one—in order to keep its "edge," and then these persons must be rooted out, eliminated with no mercy whatsoever.

One could fairly point out that just before the passage, Heidegger says that *polemos* "does not mean the outward occurrence of war and the celebration of what is 'military'" (GA 36/37: 90/72), and just afterward he says that Heraclitus's saying "does not only deal with struggling as a human activity; it deals with *all* beings" (GA 36/37: 91/73). One could also observe, correctly enough, that Heidegger is characterizing the Greeks, and that he explicitly says that the point is not "to become Greeks and Greek-like" (GA 36/37: 89/72). Nevertheless, to take up the Greek inception might very well mean to adopt the Greek insight into the necessity of enmity and make it our own. (In this connection one could ask: who are the essential enemies of the Greeks? Heidegger refers to "the Asiatic" as "the unrestrained" [GA 36/37: 92/74] and contrasts "Asiatic" fatalism with Greek fate as vocation [GA 39: 173].) Furthermore, even if struggle is not reducible to obvious human warfare, it does not exclude such warfare, either. War, including the persecution of an internal enemy, might very well be one way to put the essence of beings to work.

Let us remember the reference to *Kampf* in *Being and Time*, and consider its connection to truth as unconcealment. The term *a-letheia*, Heidegger writes, implies that truth must be wrested from unconcealment, that it is a sort of robbery (SZ 213). It takes work, struggle, to draw things into presentation. Likewise, Heidegger now says that through struggle, beings come into visibility, perceptibility, or "is"-ness (GA 36/37: 93). Thus "the essence of being is struggle" (GA 36/37: 94/75 tm), and *polemos* is crucial to unconcealment (GA 36/37: 117–18).

When Heidegger speaks in stirring but abstract language about unconceal-ment, decision, and confrontation, can he have in mind something as terrible as this: the murder of scapegoats for the sake of drawing the "truth" of the victorious group into the light? Through struggle, which can apparently mean the slaughter of innocents, a group can define who they are and thus draw the line between what is and what is not—including what is worthy of being and unworthy of being. Unconcealment has the potential, at least, to take the form of this specific, violent action. One way to draw the line between being and nonbeing, and to answer the "who" question in practice, is to exterminate those among us who "we" are not.

Perhaps Heidegger could not have known that within a decade, the "dark future" of Germany (GA 36/37: 3/3) would assume the merciless shape of the death camps or *Vernichtungslager*—but it is disingenuous or self-deceptive of him to insist defensively, in a postwar letter to Marcuse, that "the bloody terror of the Nazis in point of fact had been kept a secret from the German people" (GA 16: 431/HC 163). Terror and annihilation were essential elements of Na-zism; Heidegger knew this, and in the first year of the regime he celebrated it. When he defines evil on the day after Germany's surrender as a hidden, self-disguising "insurgency," he is evading or repressing the fact that he saw the evil at the time of the political insurgency of 1933 and explicitly endorsed it (GA 77: 208/134). But perhaps these very acts of evasion and repression confirm Hei-degger's definition: dishonesty is part of the concealment that belongs to evil.

In the passage on *polemos* as *Kampf*, Heidegger is both touching on some central themes in his thought and embracing the most sinister currents in the party that he has joined. One can fairly accuse him of having adopted and en-couraged, in this passage, the mentality of persecution that was to culminate in the so-called Final Solution. The vehemence of the passage, its rhetorical force, suggests the sort of excitement that comes with the knowledge that one has violated morality.

Heidegger's discussion of enmity suggests affinities to Carl Schmitt. In the early 1930s, Heidegger paid close attention to Schmitt's uncompromising as-sault on liberal political theory and his harsh reduction of the political to the friend-enemy distinction—and Heraclitus served as a common reference for Heidegger's and Schmitt's thoughts on struggle. In a letter to Schmitt from August 22, 1933, Heidegger thanks Schmitt for quoting the *polemos* frag-ment, presumably in a letter or in an inscription on a copy of the 1933 edition of *The Concept of the Political* (GA 16: 156/HS 132).[14] In the 1933–1934 lecture course, Heidegger does not mention Schmitt, but he seems to relish developing a somewhat Schmittian idea about enemies. However, we have seen that he criticizes Schmitt's friend-enemy theory in the 1933–1934 semi-nar (NHS 46), as he will in the following year (GA 86: 609, 655).

After suggesting that language is rooted in silence—a topic we will consider in the next section of this chapter—Heidegger claims that an insight into *polemos* as unconcealment "compels us into struggle and transposes us into decisions that grasp out into the future and prefigure it" (GA 36/37: 119/93). As an example, he cites the struggle against liberalism—"a marginal epiphenomenon, a very weak and late one at that, rooted in great and still unshaken realities" (GA 36/37: 119/94). Presumably he means that liberalism understands the subject as an atomistic individual who is free to form judgments and intentions about the objects presented to him. But truth does not arise in judgments or intentions; truth is the process whereby the objects get presented in the first place, and that process involves struggle—quite possibly a kind of struggle that runs roughshod over liberal sensibilities.

Heidegger turns to the allegory of the cave, where he claims we can witness the struggle between unconcealment and correctness. The allegory is a story of liberation. As we would expect, he rejects a merely negative conception of liberty—the removal of chains—and insists that genuine liberation requires struggle, courage, and even a certain violence that the liberator wields against the will of the benighted prisoner (GA 36/37: 140–45). He associates this thought opaquely with "this tremendous moment into which National Socialism is being driven today [. . .] the coming to be of a *new spirit of the entire earth*" (GA 36/37: 148/116). Only Nazism, we might infer, embraces struggle in the appropriate way. Liberalism rests satisfied with negative freedom, while the Marxist concept of ideology depends on Hegelian idealism, which in turn depends on an inadequate appropriation of the Platonic doctrine of ideas (GA 36/37: 147, 151).

But if freedom is not negative, what is it for? "For the light," says Heidegger: "putting oneself under the *binding obligation* of what the things in the light demand, and willing this" (GA 36/37: 160/124). In this positive freedom, man "sets his being back into the *roots* of his Dasein, into the fundamental domains into which he is thrown as a historical being" (GA 36/37: 161/125 tm). Heidegger denies that he is saying this for purposes of the *Gleichschaltung*, or the Nazi ideological "alignment" of German institutions (GA 36/37: 161/126), but we cannot miss his antimodern, antiliberal thrust. His reference to "roots" emphasizes the prerational nature of the struggle for unconcealment, which cannot be explained in terms of abstract values or norms. The abstract way of thinking draws on the Platonic forms, interpreted as moral standards. "In the Enlightenment and in liberalism, this conception achieves a definite form. Here all of the powers against which we must struggle today have their root. Opposed to this conception are the *finitude*, *temporality*, and *historicity* of human beings" (GA 36/37: 166/129). Platonist ethics, the Enlightenment, and liberalism have alienated the Germans from the historically specific, ordered sense of being that they must take up as their inheritance.

For Heidegger, then, the promise of National Socialism is that it acknowledges thrownness: no one is a human being in general, making unhampered choices and forming beliefs on the basis of pure reason; everyone begins as a member of a community with a heritage. "Each individual [. . .] is already born into a *community*; he already grows up within a quite *definite* truth, which he confronts to a greater or lesser degree" (GA 36/37: 176/136). "Openness is always limited, definite" (GA 36/37: 225/172).

But growing up within a given truth is not enough to be free: we have to *confront* truth, or struggle on the basis of our thrownness to project a vision of being. This creative "catching sight" is the true sense of the Platonic notion of the *idea* (GA 36/37: 171/133, 174/135). The ideas are not "a set of rules posted somewhere" (GA 36/37: 172/133)—objective "ideas in empty space, values in themselves" which might generate culture (GA 36/37: 172/134). But the ideas are not a subjective fantasy, either (GA 36/37: 172/133). They transcend the subjective-objective distinction—much as the act of drawing is neither arbitrary will nor passive reception.

When we accept the responsibility to catch sight of being, we decide who we are (GA 36/37: 176–78). "The human being engaged in struggle must [. . .] decide for reality in *such a way* that the truly determinative forces of Dasein will *illuminate* the history and reality of a people" (GA 36/37: 185/142).

The philosopher, then, recognizes the need to struggle for truth in this way. He is solitary, but will be ready to speak at the decisive moment, to descend into the cave in order to liberate (GA 36/37: 183). However, the liberator is threatened with death "at the hands of the powerful cave dwellers who set the standards in the cave" (GA 36/37: 182/140).

One day, Heidegger arrives late and delivers an agitated attack on one such troglodyte: Erwin Kolbenheyer. Kolbenheyer was the author of several popular historical novels who chose to support the Nazis and whom the party eventually glorified as one of the people's great artists. We can judge his success by the fact that by 1935, a book about him, *Kolbenheyer und das neue Deutschland*, was in its fifth printing, and one of his pamphlets had been lauded by a Nazi newspaper as revealing "the innermost grounds of our movement and its success, and the fundamental significance it has not just for us, but for Europe and indeed for all white humanity."[15] Kolbenheyer evidently offered an interpretation of Nazism that was easy to understand and adopt.

On January 30, 1934, the first anniversary of Hitler's appointment as chancellor, Kolbenheyer spoke in Freiburg on "The Value for Life and Effect on Life of Poetic Art in a People." This lecture was composed in 1932.

Kolbenheyer advocates "life philosophy" (3), which cuts through rationalist concepts to get in touch with deeper vital impulses. Life must "naturally" be understood with "the systematic tools of the science of life—biology" (4). Biology tells us that poetic art must have some function; it must contribute to the "self-assertion of a people" (5). Kolbenheyer defines the *Volk* as the largest human unit that we can experience directly. We cannot have an "international, supraethnic [*übervölkliches*] experience" of humanity as such (7), but at moments of crisis—such as the outbreak of the Great War—we can directly feel the *Volk* (8). The progress and preservation of the species requires "differentiation, individuation, and not amalgamation" (8): each separate people needs to form its specific "life-domain" (7). The role of poetry is to seize us as "an awakening, arousing, captivating event [*Ereignis*] . . . a deeply moving experience of real existence [*Dasein*]" (12). Poetry moves our feelings—and they, rather than our "logical consciousness," are what reveal our dependence on the communal realities that "constitute the sense and value of our existence" (16). If a poet does not work to support the "struggle for existence" of the people to whom he owes his life, "he becomes unfree"; so the poet's work must be evaluated in terms of whether it enhances or depresses the people's emotional life (20). This evaluation is not easy, for even the healthier members of a people may include elements "inherited from an earlier world of an inferior humanity [*Untermenschentum*]." In an anticipation of the 1937 "Degenerate Art" exhibit, Kolbenheyer argues that the urgent "struggle of life against inferior humanity" in this time of crisis requires us to minimize the effects of "devastating art" and to ensure that art fulfills its responsibility to the people (21).

Heidegger can hardly contain his fury when he denounces Kolbenheyer to his class the next day. He had already said earlier in the semester that "race and lineage" are to be interpreted "from *above*," from the relation to truth and being, and not "by an antiquated biology based on liberalism" (GA 36/37: 178/138). In what sense is biologism "liberal"? Presumably he means that Darwinian organisms, struggling to survive and reproduce, are like liberal individuals with private desires. This understanding of life misses the animal's relation to its environment (its impoverished world, as he had put it in 1929–1930: GA 29/30: 274). And even a sufficient understanding of animals is inadequate to human existence; our being is supported by the body, but not determined by it. Biology can never explain "the decision for a particular *will to be* and *fate*—engagement of action, responsibility in endurance and persistence, courage, confidence, faith, the strength for sacrifice" (GA 36/37: 210/160)—in short, spirit, which is based on freedom, not life. Freedom determines the sense of bodily action, not the other way around. Heidegger argues that biologism is no different from "the psychoanalysis of Freud and his ilk" or Marxism: the spiritual is reduced to a function of the subspiritual (GA 36/37: 211/162).

There could be no clearer evidence that even at the time of his greatest support for Nazism, Heidegger was opposed to biological racism; he saw it as an unphilosophical ideology that failed to do justice to human freedom. Of course, his point of view cannot be assimilated to liberal sentiments. Heideggerian freedom is the positive freedom to be bound to the power of being, rooted in our heritage, and destined to decide who we are through a struggle. He does not reject racism in the name of a universal human essence or human rights, but in the name of a less universal, more historically situated and particular community. This is why he denounces Kolbenheyer's thoughtless adoption of the categories of nineteenth-century biology. (And it is indeed thoughtless: Kolbenheyer does not reflect on the contradiction between denouncing "rationalism" and interpreting life by means of the rational science of biology.)

We should also note that Kolbenheyer's standpoint is close to Heidegger's in some ways: there is a sense of struggle and crisis, concern with defending the particularity of a people, and opposition to rationalism, liberalism, and negative freedom. There is a significant overlap in their vocabularies: *Dasein*, *Volk*, *Kampf*, *Selbstbehauptung*, and even *Ereignis.*

Nevertheless, Heidegger's approach is essentially more philosophical. For Kolbenheyer, the question "Who are we?" seems settled, and we need only draw the line in practice between *volksverantwortlich* art and art that threatens the people. For Heidegger, the very act of drawing such a line is questionable. Although his critique of Kolbenheyer can be considered a dispute between National Socialists, the basis of his critique is not Nazistic: a human being is neither a thing nor a beast, but a "who"—"a *self*," as Heidegger puts it here, "an entity that is not indifferent to its own mode and possibility of being; instead, its *being is that which is an issue* for this entity *in its own being*" (GA 36/37: 214/163 tm). Only such an entity is capable of freedom and sacrifice. The question, then, is not *what* we are, but *who* we are. This is the "condition of possibility of the political essence of man" (GA 36/37: 293/220, cf. 218/166–67). One might agree with this while rejecting Heidegger's political commitments.

The lecture course on Plato goes on to explore unconcealment as "a happening" (GA 36/37: 223/170) that calls on us to project a world. The Führer, Heidegger says, envisions a "*total transformation, a projection of a world*, on the ground of which he educates the entire people. National Socialism is not some doctrine, but the transformation from the bottom up of the German world—and, as we believe, of the European world too." He then reminds us that "truth, for the Greeks, is nothing but the *assault on untruth*" (GA 36/37: 225–26/172).

Let us pause again to consider what this "assault" might mean. Heidegger often emphasizes that the *a-* in *aletheia* is a privation, a robbery, a struggle against concealment. But what does this mean concretely? Does it simply mean a strong mental effort to remove confusions and let the phenomena speak for themselves? Or are there no phenomena except within a world, a world that is "projected" by a people that decides who it is—or by the leader, who "educates" the people? If struggle is not an innocuous intellectual effort but the actual persecution of designated enemies, then the assault on "untruth" might mean the elimination of human beings who do not fit the leader's vision of the identity of the *Volk.*

This troubling suspicion cannot be ruled out as an interpretation of how Heidegger understands truth at this juncture. We need not agree with it, though, in order to appreciate his general point that truth is a happening of unconcealment. As he puts it with reference to the aporetic nature of the *Theaetetus*, "The answer lies precisely in the *confrontation*, not in some flat proposition that gives the definition at the end" (GA 36/37: 233/179). To draw on the analogy to drawing once again: the truth of drawing lies in the experience of finding the contours of the beings one is drawing, and not in the final object, the graphite-smeared paper. A viewer might encounter that product aesthetically and be struck by its "realism" without ever appreciating the event in which the artist found her way to reality.

The question is what this act of "drawing" means in the political sphere, as an act of founding. Heidegger insists that the struggle against untruth "is always a specific struggle. Truth is always truth *for us.*" Historical man "exists in the togetherness of a historical people, with a specific, *historical mission*, and exists in the preservation of the forces that carry him forward and to which he is bound" (GA 36/37: 263/200). He asks "whether the people is strong enough—whether it, in itself, has the will to itself, to stand up to the will to its own essence," whether we will "take on as our task this knowing and will to know in their full intensity and hardness" (GA 36/37: 263/201).

The irony is that this urgent call for "specific struggle" remains completely abstract. Heidegger does not spell out what the mission is—other than to find the people's essence, whatever it may be—what the preserving forces are, or which "hard" tasks are required. The darkest interpretation, again, would see him as steeling himself and his audience against weak moral sympathies and preparing them for violence against supposedly un-German elements. The *Vernichtung* passage tends to spread its shadow on everything else that Heidegger says in this course. When his statements seem vague and indeterminate, his reference to the enemy of the people threatens to provide what we know would become an all-too-concrete content.

Logic as the Question Concerning the Essence of Language: Founding as Collective Being-There

In a November 1945 letter to the rector of the University of Freiburg, Heidegger portrayed his lecture course *Logic as the Question Concerning the Essence of Language* (Summer Semester 1934)[16] as an act of resistance against Nazism (GA 16: 401/HC 64). The truth is more complex. His lectures can be seen as engaged in an internal debate within Nazism, siding against biological reductionism but still accepting the premise that a people needs a strong state, a state that establishes an "order of rank" (GA 38: 165/137 tm) rather than a liberal society grounded on a social contract (GA 38: 143/119). His arguments are politically charged and laced with contemporary imagery, such as service in the SA (GA 38: 50/44, 73/63) and Hitler's visit to Mussolini (GA 38: 83/71). But the text rises above the level of propaganda, as Heidegger refuses to let his audience rest content with unquestioned, one-dimensional interpretations of people and race (GA 38: 60–61/53–54, 65/57).

Heidegger's train of thought in these lectures must be understood as a sequence of questions (summarized at GA 38: 78/67, 97/81–82, 114–15/95–96). First of all, what is logic?[17] It is normally understood as the science of the formal rules of assertion, and assertions confront us primarily within language (GA 38: 5/4). Language is distinctive of human beings (GA 38: 25/23). (Heidegger denies that lower animals have true language: GA 38: 139/115.) To be able to speak is to be human. But what is humanity? To be human is to be a self, an entity whose own being is at stake. A human being is thrown into the question, "Who am I?"—but also, as a member of a community, into the question, "Who are we?" (GA 38: 34/32).

We are a *Volk*, a people, he finally proposes—but what is a people? Belonging to the people is a matter of decision. We decide to testify that "We are here!" (*Wir sind da*) and we affirm the will of a state that wills that the people become its own master (GA 38: 57/50, cf. 63/55). Decision brings us into history. But what is history? There is history if, and only if, there is humanity.

Heidegger considers some objections to this proposition in a passage that has drawn fire since its publication: What about "Negroes like, for example, Kaffirs [*Kaffern*]," who are not historical (GA 38: 81/69 tm, cf. 87/74)? What about objects such as the propeller of a plane, which becomes historical when it takes the Führer to Mussolini (GA 38: 83/71)? And don't plants and animals have a history (GA 38: 81/69)? Since this last suggestion is clearly one that he does not endorse (GA 38: 88/75), it is not immediately obvious that he is making a racist or Eurocentric assertion when he entertains the objection about Africans. The term "kaffir" (from the Arabic *kafir*, "infidel") is an offensive racial insult when used in South Africa today, but he could simply mean non-Europeanized Africans, without a pejorative sense. However, in 1928 he had asserted that "the Dasein of today's Kaffirs," who are "primitive," is wholly unlike "the heroic age [*Zeit*] of the Greeks," which belonged to "early times" (*früh-zeitig*) (GA 27: 123). Heidegger may be implying that tribal people who lie outside the sphere of the West have not entered history at all, and perhaps not even ecstatic temporality. Then again, another text from 1934 affirms the essential historicity even of "unhistorical" peoples (GA 16: 328).

It is clear that, although he does not develop a consistent theory, Heidegger is experimenting with distinctions between Westerners and non-Westerners, and with the idea of degrees of historicity. Disturbing though it is, we should consider the possibility that some human beings—including Westerners—fall short of authentic historicity, or that they can fall away from history altogether at a certain point, left stranded without a future (GA 38: 84/71). We will return to this troubling question in chapter 4.

Whatever historicity may be, we can at least say that history is temporal. But what is time? Original time is the future of having-been (GA 38: 118/98), and in this deep sense we must realize that we ourselves are time's "temporalizing" (GA 38: 120/100) or "time-formation" (GA 38: 125/104).

The question of logic, then, has brought us to language, humanity, people, decision, history, and ecstatic time, with the question "Who are we ourselves?" as the crux of the whole reflection (GA 38: 97/82).

We will consider this lecture course's thoughts on language and silence in the next section of this chapter. For now, how does it contribute to Heidegger's reflections on founding a community? The question of collective selfhood certainly takes center stage here—but it seems that the question can be answered, that an identity can be established through a shared choice in which all citizens (or those who qualify as citizens) pledge allegiance to the right kind of regime. Such a moment would also be an inception, in the sense we explored in chapter 1: time would "temporalize" in this founding event, as future, past, and present would be lit up through a collective leap into being-there.

Hölderlin's Hymns "Germania" and "The Rhine": Poetic Founding

In contrast, Heidegger's first lecture course after resigning as rector, *Hölderlin's Hymns "Germania" and "The Rhine"* (GA 39, 1934–35), displays a wary distance from the Nazi conception of the "who." *Nature, History, State* suggested that the people was to be founded from the top down by the "soaring will of the leader"; the course *On the Essence of Truth* implied that the being of the *Volk* might spring from the blood of innocents; and the *Logic* course called for a collective decision that would answer the "who" question. But Heidegger now turns to poetry in search of a deeper understanding of the elusive German essence. Lecturing on Hölderlin, who muses on Germany's relation to the Greeks and the departed gods, Heidegger emphasizes the enigma of the fatherland and the challenge of discovering, or even of asking, who we are (GA 39: 4, 49, 290–94). The riddle of national selfhood calls for an elite who can participate in a hidden, poetic founding.

Heidegger's goal is to think about Hölderlin's poetry without reducing it to prose or pseudophilosophy (GA 39: 5). To this end, he casts aside various clichéd theories of poetry, including psychological interpretations and the notions of symbolism and expression (GA 39: 26–29). Instead, he tries to inhabit the language and mood of the poem, catching on to its "overarching resonance" and "fundamental attunement," in order finally to find its "metaphysical locale," the relation to being in which Hölderlin dwells (GA 39: 15/18). This is a crucial task if great poetry is not just a flimsy aesthetic diversion but language at its most intense and genuine; the poet's mission is to found a people's relation to being by withstanding the divine lightning and bringing it into words (GA 39: 31, 33, 35, 100, 251).

Hölderlin's "Germania" pictures Germany as a maiden whom a divine messenger charges to "give counsel" to "kings and peoples" (GA 39: 13/16). The poem takes place in the absence of the ancient gods, for whom the poet longs without pretending to revive them, and in anticipation of a fresh destiny for Germany. Heidegger painstakingly elucidates the mood that is at work here, characterizing it as "holy mourning in readied distress" (GA 39: 107/97). As he had insisted in *Being and Time*, such moods are not just subjective overlays, but primordially open a world and its sense (GA 39: 89). As he will say a few years later, fundamental moods create the emergencies that generate necessities (GA 45: 129).

From "Germania" Heidegger shifts to "The Rhine," where Hölderlin's aim is to limn "the beyng of the demigods" (GA 39: 245/223). Demigods, existing between gods and humans, are riven and unified by an "intimacy," or harmony of opposites. There are similarities here to Heraclitus and Hegel (GA 39: 123–34), but according to Heidegger, Hölderlin develops an understanding of "beyng" all his own that stands outside the metaphysical tradition and points to the possible new inception of a history that will decide the arrival or flight of the divine (GA 39: 1, 147, 220, 269).

Heidegger sums up the beyng of the demigods in a diagram (GA 39: 245) that might remind us of various things: the relation between thrownness and projection in *Being and Time*, the conflict between earth and world in "The Origin of the Work of Art," the mirror-play of the fourfold in the 1949 Bremen Lectures, and (the impression is irresistible) the swastika that one can easily extract from this figure.

Throughout these interpretations, he stresses the mystery of the German essence. The course begins with a reference to the fatherland as a riddlesome "origin withheld in silence" and a "forbidden fruit" (GA 39: 4/4); it ends with Hölderlin's saying that what is most difficult of all is the free use of the national (GA 39: 290–94). In the middle of the course, Heidegger uses an image reminiscent of Kafka's "Before the Law": the being of the people is a "closed door," and it will remain closed—but the poet can point us toward it (GA 39: 120/108). The mood of the lectures is a painful longing, a feeling of abandonment and forgotten possibilities endured with forbearance. Not only do we not know who we are, we have forgotten how to ask who we are (GA 39: 49–50)—and forgotten that the question "Who are we?" has to *remain* a question "throughout our entire short lifetime" (GA 39: 59/55).

This melancholy evocation of a secret Germany is an awkward fit with "patriotism full of noise" (GA 39: 120/108) and "the needs of the day" (GA 39: 4/4). The creator of a state is mentioned a few times in the abstract, but Heidegger does not name Hitler—although we could speculate about his remark that a *Führer* is not a God, but finite (GA 39: 210). Heidegger "has no need to talk about the 'political'" (GA 39: 214/195), and looks down on political maneuvers: "The crude regimentation of the all too many within a so-called organization is only a makeshift expedient, but not the essence" (GA 39: 8/7). The Germans are gifted with the ability of "setting in order to the point of organization," but their greater task is to be touched by being (GA 39: 292).

Still, these lectures concern politics in a higher sense (GA 39: 214): the question of who the German people are and can be. "We have no desire to bring Hölderlin into line with our times. On the contrary: We wish to bring ourselves, and those who are to come, under the measure of the poet" (GA 39: 4/4). The poet—like the thinker and the statesman, but more primordial than both, it would seem (GA 39: 51, 144)—stands on the "peaks of time" (GA 39: 52/50) where he insistently waits upon *"the event"* (GA 39: 56/53). The poet's primordial language founds the historical being of a people; in everydayness, this language is degraded into prose, and finally into idle talk (GA 39: 64). But at the peaks of time, time itself arises (GA 39: 109)—ecstatic, historical time that retrieves what has been for the sake of what may be. The poet, dwelling on such a peak, challenges us to attain this primordial historicity and enter a space where the divine may appear or disappear (GA 39: 111, 147).

Our being, at its highest, is "originary time" (GA 39: 109/99): human beings are challenged to retrieve what we have inherited for the sake of a vocation, as we work toward fresh revelations of being and beings (GA 39: 62), constantly dwelling on the earth (GA 39: 195–96), mindful of death (GA 39: 173). This originary time or "care" (GA 39: 58/55, 141/125, 281/255) is normally dormant, because we usually inhabit a degraded "everydayness" (GA 39: 20–22/22–24) where things simply seem to lie present before us, and the sense of being and presence is taken for granted, falling prey to idle talk (GA 39: 64).

Under the sway of this everyday mentality, we may focus on one or another domain of present entities and attempt, perversely, to explain ourselves in terms of it. We might also try to define ourselves in terms of our everyday interactions with other things—but what we do never exhausts who we are (GA 39: 57–58).[18]

Heidegger comments that race theorists have no understanding of the being of the community. Alfred Rosenberg would take poetry as expressing the experiences of the soul of the race or *Volk* (GA 39: 26); but this is no better than taking poetry as expressing the experiences of individuals, the masses, or a culture—poetry is still understood in terms of lived experience (*Erlebnis*) and not as a power that founds a people's way of being. Heidegger now quotes the speech that Kolbenheyer delivered in Freiburg: "Poetry is a biologically necessary function of the people." But this would apply just as well to digestion. Such reductionism is "so wretchedly banal that we speak of it only reluctantly" (GA 39: 27/27).

Heidegger remains concerned with the distinctive mission of Germany, but this mission is starting to seem less militaristic. He claims that both Hegel and Hölderlin stand under the power of Heraclitus, in different ways (GA 39: 129), and glosses a few Heraclitean fragments, including the *polemos* fragment (GA 39: 125–26)—but *Kampf* now seems more distant from physical violence. Heidegger dreams of a greatness that no longer needs "defense or resistance, that is victorious through Da-sein, insofar as the latter brings beings to appearance as they are" (GA 39: 289/263). It would seem that the question of who we are is not to be decided by a war against the other, but by asking who we ourselves are in a profound way—and this question requires an *encounter* with the other, at least in the form of the Greeks. The Germans and the Greeks share the *Urdrang zum Ursprung*, the "primal drive to the origin," but they have their separate paths (GA 39: 204–5/187).

In certain regards and at certain moments, one can still take these lectures as an exercise in Nazi ideology. In exploring "'politics' in the highest and authentic sense" (GA 39: 214/195), Heidegger affirms the trio of poet, thinker, and statesman—extraordinary human beings (or demigods?) who stand on high peaks and can creatively reinvigorate the nation in the domains of language, thought, and action (GA 39: 51, 184). If the first two are Hölderlin and Heidegger, it seems obvious who the third must be. One can patch to-gether a more concretely political message from several passages: reclaiming "Earth" (e.g., GA 39: 216/197) and our "endowment" (GA 39: 292/265), we will oppose the "Asiatic" (GA 39: 134/118, 173/158), not shying away from "battle" (*Kampf*, GA 39: 125/112), inciting the *Volk* to will "to be itself" (GA 39: 144/126) in a time of "threat to our spiritual and historical Dasein" (GA 39: 113/103) when "the West [is] hovering at the edge of the abyss" (GA 39: 222/202). While there are no direct references to Jews, the biting comments on Christian churches (e.g., GA 39: 222/202), together with Heidegger's focus on the "Greco-Germanic mission" (GA 39: 151/132) and his intense in-terest in the gods who have "fled" (e.g., GA 39: 80/73–74), anticipate a blunt comment in the *Black Notebooks* from the early 1940s on the importance of rediscovering the Greek inception, "which remained outside Judaism and thus outside Christianity" (GA 97: 20). Finally, although the book as we have it never directly names Nazism, a reference in the printed edition to "the inner truth of natural science" (GA 39: 195/178), an odd expression for Heidegger, should actually read "the inner truth of National Socialism."[19]

But the case is not closed with this discovery. We have to reflect on the word "inner," which implies a rejection of the "outer" manifestations of the Nazi movement. These include theories of the master race pro-pounded by ideologues such as Rosenberg and the attempt to subordinate science to the *Volk* (GA 39: 41). As we noted above, in a rather strange move for a Nazi, Heidegger imagines a "defenseless" Germany (to quote "Germania"); this is not "unilateral disarmament" (GA 39: 17/19), but the idea that a great enough nation would need no defense (GA 39: 289). If the national, or one's own, is what is most difficult to adopt and develop freely (GA 39: 292–93), then the "fatherland" remains a "forbidden fruit," supremely mysterious and challenging (GA 39: 4/4, 120/108, 294/267). Here, "fatherland" does not mean jingoistic and racist xenophobia, but the challenge of drawing on a heritage for the sake of a mission (GA 39: 139/123; cf. GA 75: 277–78).

There is no doubt that Heidegger is writing as a German who is passion-ately concerned with the future of Germany, and that he sees this future as a "singular" destiny (GA 39: 186/169, 227/207) rather than conformity to "the shallow waters of some universal world reason" (GA 39: 290/263). It is diffi-cult for us to avoid seeing this future-that-was as the gruesome nightmare that came to be. But it would be too simple to pigeonhole these lectures as a piece of political ideology. They are philosophy, which means that, as Heidegger himself suggests, they "can, and indeed must, one day also be interpreted otherwise"; they can "be discovered . . . ever anew and in an inexhaustible manner" (GA 39: 145/127).

On Hegel's *Philosophy of Right*:
Founding as Abyssal Self-Assertion

At the same time as he was teaching this course on Hölderlin (1934–1935), Heidegger conducted a seminar on Hegel's *Philosophy of Right*. His notes for the seminar are available along with student transcripts and protocols.[20]

This seminar explores the relevance of Hegel to Hitler's Germany, and Heidegger is clearly attracted to a right-Hegelian point of view: he emphasizes Hegel's critique of a liberalism divorced from community and history (e.g., GA 86: 150, 605, 650). But Heidegger's ultimate position is far from obvious. When he asserts, against Schmitt, that when National Socialism came to power, Hegel did not die but first came to life (GA 86: 85, 606), is this praise of Nazism? Is it praise of Hegel? Or is there room for reservations about them both?

We cannot simply consider this text a Nazification of Hegel or a Hegelianized Nazism, for Heidegger takes an open-ended and exploratory approach, particularly in his notes. The Hegel seminar is considerably less doctrinaire than the seminar on *Nature, History, State* one year earlier. Heidegger takes Hegel as the occasion for rethinking the phenomena of people and state. His main goal seems to be to persuade his students that (contrary to American pragmatism, he asserts) books and thoughts do matter, even in revolutionary times (GA 86: 95, 109–10, 155). No doubt, the Heidegger teaching this seminar is still a Nazi—but what that means is still indefinite for Heidegger himself. He is interested in exploring the deeper sense and potential of this revolution whose significance is still unclear.

Although Heidegger has not yet abandoned Hitler, he is asking what will come of the new order. He still insists that the people "comes to itself" in the will of a true leader (GA 86: 169/182 tm), and claims that if the revolution and the leader succeed in expressing the essence of the people, then "this binding of the state to the essential being of the people makes an arbitrary recognition or rejection by an individual citizen impossible. The citizen can reject or validate a government [*Regierung*], an institution of the state, but by no means *the state*" (GA 86: 641). The passage seems to leave a little room for the possibility of deciding that particular Nazi governmental structures or leaders have failed to embody "our German essence" (GA 86: 640). But Heidegger's sympathies remain authoritarian, as we can see in his remark that the expression "total state" is a pleonasm (GA 86: 74). Yet he wonders, "What is the 'total state,' in positive terms?" This requires "*essential* reflection of the *metaphysical* sort" (GA 86: 606).

The seminar, then, cannot simply be reduced to an unambiguous ideological position, so that we could conclude that "the aim of [Heidegger's] teaching is not philosophical, but political."[21] While we must not naively forget the political context, we should also acknowledge that the seminar considers some genuine philosophical questions.

Heidegger combines his semisympathetic appropriation of Hegel with indications of a new outlook that will decisively choose the finite over the infinite. Ultimately, he is not interested in any neo-Hegelian revival (GA 86: 85), but wishes to distinguish himself from Hegel as part of his project of overcoming the metaphysical tradition.

Here we can only mention a few facets of this new outlook in connection with the questions of self-assertion and founding. These two phenomena are closely linked: when a people asserts itself, or decides who it is, it founds a state that establishes or consolidates a world, unifying the people's way of life. Heidegger clearly believed that the National Socialist revolution might turn out to be such a self-assertion. But what raises the seminar above mere cheerleading for a regime is reflection on the meaning of these phenomena. This reflection is carried out historically, on the way from modern conceptions of self-assertion and founding to what we can label, for convenience, post-modern ones. As he works through Hegel's theory of the state, Heidegger appropriates certain aspects of the Hegelian account of political autonomy and self-consciousness while working toward a post-modern understanding of the self. This new account of selfhood will involve a new interpretation of founding—not only in the political sense, but as a facet of how being itself takes place finitely and "abyssally," riven by "fissuring."

As we saw earlier, the crux of the Hegel-Heidegger confrontation is the question of finitude (GA 32: 55–56, 209). Hegel claims to attain an in-finite or absolute standpoint. In contrast, Heidegger adopts a resolutely finite stance, and wishes to carry out the "difficult" demonstration that "the absolute position cannot be an absolute position" (GA 86: 587). This is a rebellion against eternity, understood as "equal to itself—calm—present—sated with the past—futureless essence!" (GA 86: 117/143). The effect of embracing a finite standpoint is to give philosophy historical traction and restore a sense of urgency to it. In contrast to the Greek inception, where thinking was experienced as an urgent need calling for decision, Hegel's philosophy illustrates the dying out of urgency and the reduction of truth to a hollow system—the "empty eternity of the decisionless" (GA 36/37: 77/61). To know, for Hegel, is not to venture into the future, but only "to 'cognize' dispassionately the already *enacted* reconciliation" (GA 86: 117/144).

Our own selves are at stake here: if we are not infinite spirits but ineluctably finite, then we are faced with the question "Who are we?" as a historical decision. Philosophy, like all our activities, attempts to come to grips with the destiny of a particular community and tends to move this community in the direction of some uncertain future. Without finitude, there is no destiny proper, no heritage that inspires a venture into the unknown. Such a venture draws a line between who we are and who we are not, so it is necessarily polemical; in fact, it requires an understanding of being itself as *polemos* (GA 86: 115).

Any response to the "who" question can be seen as a self-assertion—a founding of the individual or collective self. Thus, in May 1933, Heidegger had chosen to frame his rectorate as a sign of "The Self-Assertion of the German University." The academy was to find its role in the new German order by affirming its identity and fulfilling its own essence—not in isolation from the larger nation, but as a place for "knowledge service" that would harmonize with "labor service" and "military service" to empower the German spirit (GA 16: 113/HR 113–14). By doing its own, to use the Platonic phrase (*Republic* 433b), the university would help the community as a whole do its own.

These themes resonate not just with Plato, but also with crucial elements of German idealism. For Kant and his successors, freedom as self-positing is a presupposition of all coherent thought and action. Politics is then guided by the demand to actualize this freedom in a way that harmonizes the self-positing of individuals with the self-positing of collectives. The state and law exist so that the human spirit may be able to assert itself, both in private and in public.

Accordingly, as Heidegger puts it in his notes, Hegel fulfills the project of Rousseau, Kant, and Fichte by establishing the free will—the ability to assert and posit oneself—as the principle and ground of the state (GA 86: 595). The state is "the proof of the ethical, highest freedom of man" (GA 86: 639). The *Philosophy of Right* is thus essentially concerned with "*freedom as self-standing and sovereignty*" (GA 86: 60/102 tm). I translate *Selbständigkeit* very literally as "self-standing" because the usual translations (independence, autonomy, self-sufficiency) can carry unwelcome connotations. *Selbständigkeit* means taking a stand or stance of one's own, but for Hegel and Heidegger, this by no means excludes reliance on a larger community that provides one with physical maintenance, legal protection, and cultural norms. "One's own" is to be harmonized with the collective selfhood of one's people. Thus, according to Hegel, "In duty the individual acquires his substantive freedom."[22] On a smaller scale, Heidegger comments that it is *echt hegelisch* to assert that a woman can become self-standing by getting married (GA 86: 578n5).

Heidegger elucidates the Hegelian concept of sovereignty in terms of the Greek concepts of *eleutheria* and *autonomia* as characteristics of the city, the all-important center of communal life:

> This drive to the center in the essence of the *polis* was announced externally by the protective and defiant wall, as a delimitation against the external world as

its original and natural enemy. This clarifies the important role of *eleutheria* as independence with regard to the outside and *autonomia* as inner self-standing in every alliance agreement . . . The comprehensive unity of *eleutheria* and *autonomia* constitutes the essence of the *polis* and can be summed up as: *self-assertion*. [GA 86: 654–55]

Because the individual's self-assertion must be harmonized with the self-assertion of the political whole, Hegel's is not a purely negative conception of freedom, but is freedom made rational through responsibility. For Hegel, the individual citizen cannot assert himself in a rationally satisfactory way unless he also recognizes others' rights to self-assertion within an overarching system of law. This principle of recognition ensures that freedom does not devolve into caprice. Heidegger's commentary, as we might expect, emphasizes freedom as duty rather than liberty: "Every essential commitment and recognition is a necessity, an ethical compulsion, but at the same time the highest freedom" (GA 86: 641).

Mutual free commitment and self-assertion constitute the freedom of a community—"the simultaneous, common, and self-standing being of many. *Many* are self-standing only when they let each other *count as valid* [*gelten*], or recognize each other" (GA 86: 578). "I am in the right [or I exist in a system of law: *ich bin im Recht*] when I am *recognized*" (GA 86: 584). Thus, against the supposed liberal conception of freedom as the liberty of the individual as such, the Hegelian conception takes freedom as a feature of "the individual who wills himself as he is linked to the others in recognition. Thus there is freedom only where there is the simultaneous and common self-standing of many" (GA 86: 650).

The phenomena of mutual recognition and mutual self-assertion are prior to the friend-enemy dynamic that Schmitt takes as the essence of the political. Enmity must be understood as a form of "*not-recognizing* [*Nicht-anerkennen*] . . . *dis-qualifying of the mightiness of being* [*Ab-erkennen der Seinsmächtigkeit*]" (GA 86: 174/186). The latter phrase might also be translated as "denial of recognition to the power to be": that is, we refuse to acknowledge our enemy's ontological potency. Likewise, "only on the basis of the *self-assertion* of the historical Dasein of a people does the political *appear* as the friend-enemy relation" (GA 86: 655). "There are friends and enemies only where there is self-assertion. . . . Because the state is this self-assertion of the historical being of a people *and* because one can call the state the *polis*, consequently the political shows itself as the friend-enemy relation; but this relation is not = *the* political" (GA 86: 609). Heidegger is not questioning the validity of the distinction between friend and enemy, but he is denying that the nature of a community can be understood solely in these terms.

So far, his reflections are recognizably Hegelian, but he hints at his reservations by commenting that Hegel operates with "a concept of the freedom of the will of practical reason" (GA 86: 60/102). Freedom and self-assertion cannot ultimately be understood in terms of rational will. Instead, we need concepts developed in *Being and Time* such as "care" and "*being-with*," which describe the prevoluntary, prerational domain within which recognition and denial of recognition can occur (GA 86: 174/187).

Since care is fundamentally an engagement in the question of who we are, Emmanuel Faye makes a basic error when he characterizes Heidegger's concept of self-assertion as the "perfectly trivial" view "that the affirmation of existence is primary and that it is on that basis that the struggle for life ensues."[23] Heideggerian self-assertion is not a Darwinian "fight for bare existence" (GA 73.1: 847–48), but a decision regarding the sense of one's being.

This is not to deny that such a decision involves conflict and battle. Lest we forget that being-with is polemical, Heidegger writes: "Why is there right [*Recht*]? Because *being recognized*— | because *struggle for recognition*—and this because *self-standing*—i.e. freedom—and this because historical Dasein of the human—*polemos*" (GA 86: 135/155 tm). To expand on these jottings: a community must risk self-definition—decide who "we" are—by deciding between alternatives that cannot be calculated rationally. We must draw a line between who belongs and who does not. Universal concepts of humanity and its faculties contribute nothing to this act of self-assertion. Thus, while the friend-enemy relation is not the essence of the political, it seems to be implied immediately by that essence.

The Nazi regime was an absolute dictatorship: there was no separation of governmental powers, and the Führer's will was supposed to rule unimpeded. Heidegger, at this time, sees this as a feature that is full of potential: "The unification of powers in the Dasein of the leader is not a mere coupling and heaping up (quantitative), but rather in itself already the beginning of the development of an originally new—but still undeveloped—inception" (GA 86: 73/111). There is a founding at work in the revolution that goes deeper than a mere seizure of power, and whose true significance has not yet come to light. A similar distinction between beginning and inception is at work in Heidegger's notes on the "constitution of the National Socialist state," which list several dimensions of founding: "beginning," "inception," and "origin" or primal leap (*Ur-sprung*) (GA 86: 74–75/112 tm).

Hegel has his own critique of the beginning: the truth of a movement (political, economic, philosophical, religious, or artistic) is not found in the simple principles of its beginning, but in the developed "idea" as fully manifest and explicit (GA 86: 602). Only in retrospect can we understand the meaning of a movement.

However, Heidegger emphasizes the importance of a free act of founding more than Hegel can. The act is not arbitrary, nor is it the spontaneity of a self-sufficient, autonomous subject, since he insists that freedom requires binding oneself to the liberating power of being. But there is an element of creativity in the way in which we take up our bond to being and commit ourselves to originating a new order. Creative decisiveness opens a new world and makes "inception" possible.

Creativity cannot play a comparable role in Hegel. There is certainly room in Hegel's thought for freedom, creation, and personality—in fact, these elements are essential to the subjectivity without which spirit could not live at all. But for Hegel, "the person enshrines the actuality of the concept."[24] The creative individual finds his freedom in helping to actualize a rationally intelligible potential. The founder of a state, for example, is great only if he finds a way to resolve the insufficiencies of existing orders and embody a more rational order in the institutions of a government. From a Hegelian perspective, Heidegger's exaltation of a creative inception is a Romantic self-abandonment, a celebration of the arbitrary and irrational.

This brings us back to the central point in the confrontation between Hegel and Heidegger: finitude. For Hegel, the efforts of a particular statesman or of any individual gain their true significance only in the light of absolute knowing, which reviews the internal logic of a development and comprehends what the actor could only obscurely glimpse. For Heidegger, no such absolute standpoint is available. This means that the element of risk in political action, as in every human venture, cannot be transcended or softened, either now or later. The daring actor enables the birth of a new sphere of truth, a new kind of finite unconcealment that cannot be gainsaid in retrospect. This is a truth inevitably shadowed by ignorance, subject to the urgency of a particular time: "the leadership relationship . . . is *historical* and, as such, has its movement—revelation and concealment—instant" (GA 86: 169/182). This is a truth that embodies *polemos* and danger (GA 86: 177), a truth born in a moment of vision.

In this connection we can read Heidegger's distinction between two kinds of political philosophy. "A philosophy 'about' ['über'] the state—suspicious—awakens mistrust—rightly so. . . . But *where an actual philosopher*—compels to decisions—there—mistrust—reluctance—resistance—*struggle*—and actual effectiveness [or effecting] of spirit" (GA 86: 116/143). To some extent, as Heidegger knows, Hegel would agree that philosophy cannot stand "over" the politics that it judges. For Hegel, this is the case because the philosopher can only recognize the rationality embodied in existing states. But Heidegger still sees this as an untenably superior attitude, an attitude that presumes to look back and look down on what has been without being threatened by "the difficult becoming of a dark future" (GA 36/37: 3/3). Instead of rising above this temporal chiaroscuro, thought is supposed to engage in it.

Philosophy, then, is part of the self-assertion and self-founding of a people—and if philosophers may actually be the hidden leaders of a people, then philosophy can participate creatively in this founding movement. Heidegger asks in some ruminations on Schmitt, "How is the precedence of leadership as such to be grounded? What does grounding mean here? *Self-founding* [*Selbstbegründung*]? . . . As grounding back [*Rückgründung*] into the people, and that is a grounding ahead [*Vorgründung*] into its historical sending" (GA 86: 170/183). Who can carry out this grounding that reaches back into heritage and forward into destiny? Who can initiate the inception? The statesman, insofar as he is a born leader; the poet, insofar as he discerns the deeper themes in a people's world; but perhaps above all the philosopher, who can articulate the very being of the people and the state.

Because philosophy is finite—because it remains and must remain implicated in historical contingencies, drawing on a heritage for the sake of some possibility—one can argue that, for Heidegger, philosophy becomes a form of action. We should not be distracted by his defiant declaration that his seminars are "useless": "'Heidegger! Is that the one the students don't learn anything from?' . . . This would be the very best definition of my teaching activity. Here you'll learn nothing, *practically* speaking!" (GA 86: 559–60). Even though thinking yields no immediate solutions, its deeper effects in the long run can be profound: "In sixty years, our state will certainly not be led by the Führer anymore; but what happens *then* is up to *us*. *This* is why we must philosophize" (GA 86: 560).

These philosophical and political ventures take place over an abyss: they are a founding without a ground. An inception that forgoes any metaphysical necessity or secure selfsameness in favor of a historical urgency tears open the domain of selfhood. Because it lacks a ground and an identity, selfhood is neither an object nor a modern subject, neither an "I" nor a "we" (GA 82: 32, 95; GA 73.1: 170, 364), but an adventure on which we can embark by leaping creatively into "the happening of owndom [*Eigen-tum*]" (GA 65: 320/253 tm).[25] This event can be seen as a "fissuring" (*Zerklüftung*), a word Heidegger uses in connection with *polemos* (GA 86: 115/142), finitude (GA 86: 162/175), estrangement, and darkness (GA 73.1: 8). Fissuring is a rupture in being itself, a wound that cannot heal; it embraces the Hegelian themes of alienation and opposition without promising any final reconciliation. The *Contributions to Philosophy* will pursue fissuring further as a way to preserve the "uniqueness and strangeness of beyng" (GA 65: 315/249, cf. §127, §§156–59).

If we are Hegelian absolute knowers, "we have already let go what is ours in the sense of what is humanly relative" (GA 32: 71/50 tm). But if we are

Heideggerian leapers, we discover our own in an initiating event that establishes the very domain of ownness. Groundless founding initiates finite sense.

But where do we look for guidance in this venture of founding, if not to rational requirements or a logic of history? What defines the destiny of a community, if it is not just an arbitrary choice? "A people first comes about through 'theophany,' i.e. the cutting [*scheidende*] nearness of the coming god" (GA 86: 139/159). The *Contributions* will develop this suggestion into an opaque but important discussion of "the passing by of the last god" (GA 65: 406/321). The urgency of the approach or flight of the ultimate god, or gods, draws a people into decision (*Entscheidung*) and provides the essential impulse that founds their own.

From a rationalist perspective such as Hegel's, Heidegger's embrace of finitude and historicity was doomed from the start to fall prey to irrational enthusiasm and the attractions of tyranny. If we abandon the very attempt to reach nonfinite comprehension, then there is no basis for a balanced, harmonious development of the state, and we are vulnerable to dark and willful impulses dressed in the sparkling robes of a god that is no God. "The ethical world" is supposed by irrationalists "to be left to the mercy of chance and caprice, to be God-forsaken."[26]

Heideggerians will retort that totalitarianism is the triumph of the objectivizing, all-comprehending modern spirit. Openness to the divine and to poetic dwelling is precisely what we need in order to gain distance from this modern mentality.

Is the modern or post-modern view preferable? Is Heidegger's view actually post-modern at that, or is it just another permutation of the modern predicament? Is there room for a compromise, such that we abandon the Hegelian pretense that we can achieve a complete and final account, yet maintain rational concepts of rights, responsibilities, and freedoms where they are needed in the political sphere? Or would such a compromise be a mishmash of radically incompatible philosophical positions? We will postpone such questions until chapter 3.

Introduction to Metaphysics: Founding and Violence

The last public reflection on founding from Heidegger's most political period that I will consider is the 1935 course *Introduction to Metaphysics*. This text has been available since 1953 and has been discussed extensively in the secondary literature, but it deserves to be considered once again, at least in brief.[27] Here Heidegger plunges into the question of what we mean when we say that something *is*, challenges us to wonder how being can mean anything to us at all, and urges us to rethink our own existence as human beings. He also embraces the language of power and conflict in a way that blends politics with ontology. Human beings struggle to affirm their power in the face of the overpowering violence of being; in this way they take a stand on who they are and what difference it makes that there are beings instead of nothing (GA 40: 159–73/166–83). Here we will focus primarily on the political dimension of these thoughts, leaving aside many other aspects of these rich lectures, which display Heidegger's increasingly desperate hopes for a new German awakening as well as his growing disillusionment with the actual Nazi party and its policies.

Heidegger embeds the current political situation in a sweeping vision of the history of metaphysics. The Germans are "the metaphysical people" (GA 40: 41/42)—even if they do not yet possess a metaphysics of their own, as he had said in a recent semester (GA 36/37: 80). Germany, with its great potential for a new confrontation with the question of being, is caught between Russia and America, which are slaves of the technological worldview (GA 40: 40/41). While this passage aligns Heidegger with the Nazis to some extent, he also criticizes the interpretation of spirit as intelligence, made subservient to the project of organizing a race (GA 40: 50/52). The proper essence of spirit is "the empowering of the powers of beings as such and as a whole" (GA 40: 53/54–55). But this empowerment cannot happen unless we understand why being has become an empty word for us, and the original urgency of the question of being has dried up and been supplanted by the mere management and exploitation of resources.

Heidegger argues that we have forgotten the roots of our understanding of being in the Greek conception of the abundant, emergent presencing of things—*physis*. *Physis*, for Heidegger, is polemical: a world opens only through confrontation (GA 40: 66/67). In the absence of strife, being turns its back on beings (GA 40: 67/68). We are called, then, to participate in the struggle that separates being from nonbeing, truth from semblance. Heidegger discerns such a struggle in *Oedipus Rex* (GA 40: 114–16/116–19) and in *Parmenides* (GA 40: 117–21/121–25).

The struggle for truth and being is at the same time a struggle to decide who we are. The determination of the human essence "is *never* an answer, but is essentially a question. . . . The question of who the human being is must always be posed in an essential connection with the question of how it stands with being" (GA 40: 149/156 tm).

Heidegger's interpretation of Sophocles's "Ode to Man" in *Antigone* develops a conception of founding as the violent creation of a site where the creators themselves cannot belong.[28] The main theme in his reading is "the uncanny," which refers both to the "overwhelming sway" of being and to the human being, who "uses violence against the overwhelming" (GA 40: 159/167). Both being and humanity are powerful contestants whose power can be put into play only in confrontation, in the "happening of uncanniness" (GA 40: 160/169). Such a confrontation lifts the creative, authentic individuals beyond their accustomed homes and institutions. They are *apolis*, alien to their community, precisely because "they, *as* creators, must first ground" that community (GA 40: 162/170). In the clash between human knowledge and the cosmic order, humanity achieves its essential status as the site where "the violent powers of the released excessive violence of being suddenly emerge and enter the work as history" (GA 40: 172/182 tm). Humanity takes over the gathering power of being and defends unconcealment against concealment (GA 40: 183/194). In another formulation, man is "*the site . . .* that being necessitates for its opening up" (GA 40: 214/228). We are Da-sein, the "there" for the happening of being, but this "there" needs to be founded. The founders do not inhabit the accustomed realm, the world in which beings can make sense; instead, they create it.

Heidegger understands the *polis* as the ultimate place: it is "the site, the there, in which and as which being-there is as historical" (GA 40: 161/170 tm). What is lacking in America and Russia, as Heidegger sees them, is awareness of the historicity of the "there," which would require an openness to being as a transformative force. In the place of such awareness and openness is the "demonism" of technological calculation and of a reductive, unquestioned interpretation of what is (GA 40: 50/51).

Politics is hardly ever far from the surface of these lectures. Although the term "National Socialism" appears on only one page (GA 40: 208/222), Heidegger often implicitly attacks Nazism as it stands in 1935—not in the name of a return to liberal democracy, but because current Nazism is insufficiently revolutionary. He criticizes external Nazism in the name of its "inner truth and greatness" (GA 40: 208/222), praising recent developments in Germany while snatching the praise away in his next breath by claiming that they remain superficial. Various elements of Nazi ideology do not go deep enough, such as the celebration of body over spirit (GA 40: 50–51/52), the notion of the "time of the We" (GA 40: 74/77), or the "value philosophy" of supposed National Socialist thinkers (GA 40: 208/222). Nazi initiatives are also superficial, such as purges of the academy (GA 40: 51/53), language reforms (GA 40: 55/56), and reforms of the elementary curriculum (GA 40: 57/58). But Heidegger leaves little room for doubt that these are friendly criticisms when he praises Knut Hamsun, a Nazi sympathizer (GA 40: 29/29–30), and denounces *What Is the Human Being?*—a work by Catholic theologian Theodor Haecker that attacked both Nazism and Heidegger (GA 40: 151/158–59).

In short, Heidegger wants to be more revolutionary than the revolution itself—and certain themes in these lectures echo the most terrifying aspect of the Nazi movement, its eagerness to commit violence and murder against its perceived enemies. In particular, his elucidation of *Antigone* explores the idea that great human beings are uncanny and violent: they must fight against other beings and being itself until they are tragically crushed by being's overwhelming power. In this context, he deploys a variety of related words with the root *walt-*. *Gewalt* often means unjustified and willful violence, though it can also mean legitimate governmental force. He "reaches beyond the usual meaning of the expression, which generally means nothing but brutality and arbitrariness" (GA 40: 159/167), but he stresses the radically creative (and thus destructive) work of the *Gewalttat*, the "violent" deed, highlighting its danger and terror. What happens in such a deed is *walten*, or "holding sway." This sway is not simply a human affair, but a characteristic of *physis* itself—the powerful upsurge of the presence of beings.[29] Likewise, Heraclitean *polemos* may lie at the root of human warfare, but it is also a deeper, ontological confrontation that affects the very process of sense and disclosure.

Heidegger's ontological explorations of violence and war in *Introduction to Metaphysics* find resonance in other texts, such as the contemporaneous "The Origin of the Work of Art," where, as we have seen, he presents great artworks as embodying the neverending strife between world (a realm of shared sense) and earth (the basis that exceeds sense). Throughout the midthirties, he appears to celebrate creative conflicts that take place at the very border of the meaningful; he seems to believe that Nazism may find an appropriate way to spur such creativity and revive an ancient understanding of forceful and disclosive struggle.

According to *Introduction to Metaphysics*, philosophy cannot contribute directly to politics (GA 40: 12/11): the thinker and the statesman are both great creators, but they are distinct (GA 40: 66/68, 162/170). What philosophy can do is initiate a creative reconception of the basis of politics and the sense of human existence. Accordingly, we do not find any concrete political recommendations here. There is no explicit celebration of the will of the Führer, such as we saw in *Nature, History, State*, a will that would found the *Volk* from the top down. *Introduction to Metaphysics* seems closer to the notion of poetic founding in the Hölderlin lectures. Heidegger emphasizes struggle and power, and the need to shatter established conventions, but it is not clear that such shattering would take the form of persecuting internal enemies or going into battle. The struggle must be "spiritual"—although we should not imagine that this term refers to merely mental or emotional experiences. Spirit inspires the happening of history. How this might happen, though, remains an open question.

In these courses and seminars, we have seen Heidegger exploring the possibility of an inception, the emergence of a time when the people's time would arise, the awakening of a shared selfhood. Would such a founding stem from the genius of a born leader, from the voices of the *Volk*, or from the poet's "peaks of time"? Would it draw a violent line between those who belong to the people and those who do not? Would there be any room for diversity or dissent? Would founding as self-assertion ground a common identity, or keep the question "Who are we?" open, hovering over the abyss?

Heidegger clearly has difficulty articulating a political inception. In fact, as we saw in chapter 1, in his view inceptions are intrinsically elusive: they found a domain of discourse and, for that reason, resist assimilation to that domain. Can a political founding be articulate, then? Or must it remain, at its core, profoundly silent?

THE POLITICS OF SILENCE

> I keep silent in my thinking—not just since 1927, since the publication of *Being and Time*, but *in* that book itself, and constantly before then. This keeping silent is the preparing of the saying of what is to be thought, and this preparing is the journey of experience [*das Er-fahren*], and this is a doing and acting. [GA 16: 421–22]

This passage comes from a draft of a letter, written about 1946 to an unknown person, that Heidegger may never have mailed. In effect, this letter is a text for nobody, telling nobody that he does not tell all—but not telling what he does not tell, or why he does not tell it. It is simply an announcement that not all has been announced. It cryptically reveals that *Schweigen* is a crucial aspect of Heidegger's writing. In English we can say "keep quiet" or "keep silent," but these expressions sound static and passive; they do not convey as clearly as *Schweigen* that silence can be something one does, and it can be just as significant as talk.

What are some ways of keeping quiet and some reasons for doing so? First, there is a political esotericism which is a mark of caution: it may be imprudent to say everything that could be said. When living in democracies, Heidegger chafed at the liberal worldview; when living under the Hitler regime, he increasingly diverged from official doctrines. In neither situation did he fully and publicly express his political views. His posthumously published texts of the thirties contain various criticisms of the predominant Nazi ideology, and they certainly could not have been published without exposing him to danger. It is also clear that he was concerned with his political position after the war; this is why he eliminated the more political passages from his Nietzsche lectures when they were published, and specified that his interview with *Der Spiegel* could be published only after his death. However, a manuscript that is treated secretively need not be an intrinsically esoteric manuscript. I agree with Peter Trawny that the political dimension of Heidegger's texts is not the deepest root of their esotericism.[30]

Heidegger also practices an esotericism of understanding. For example, he writes in *Besinnung* that his lecture courses "come from outside" (GA 69: 173/147 tm). "The lecture courses always remain superficial. . . . Perhaps at a later time some may succeed in experiencing what is kept silent . . . and will then be able to set what is explicitly said within its limits" (GA 66: 421/372 tm). Years later, in a 1964 letter, he says that, with the exception of "The Thing," the goal of his public philosophy is "to make my thought understandable in a first attempt on the basis of the tradition . . . [this work] always still speaks the language of metaphysics to some extent, or uses its language with a different meaning."[31] The purpose of this kind of esoteric writing is to address an audience that is not yet ready to understand Heidegger's central thoughts. According to the passage with which we began, "keeping silent is the preparing of the saying of what is to be thought." He holds out hope, then, that he or someone else may find a way to communicate what so far has been kept quiet.

But the most essential esotericism in Heidegger's thought concerns the content of what he is thinking: silence may be the best and only way to respond to a necessarily self-concealing topic. This esotericism is based on the recognition that certain matters intrinsically resist being said. As Trawny puts it, "The truly esoteric communication can neither be spoken out nor written down. It *cannot* appear."[32] This is a paradox: an unutterable utterance. But Heidegger's *Schweigen* is an *Erschweigen*. This Heidegger-ism is even less translatable, but we do have the English expression "telling silence"—an absence that betrays something of import. There is a kind of silence that is meaningful, even if it cannot be translated into a set of propositions.

Keeping silent is not only voluntary, but can also be an unavoidable silence in the face of what necessarily conceals itself, but is not alien to us—instead, it is what is most our own. A telling silence is demanded by the unspoken ground of language. It might also be demanded by an inception that makes us a problem for ourselves and thus founds the realm of sense.

Silence and its political ramifications are explored in a few key texts of the thirties. As we will see, in the fall of 1933, Heidegger announces to his students that he has overturned his former understanding of language and silence. Whereas *Being and Time* described speaking and keeping silent as two modes of discourse, he now sees speech and discourse themselves as founded on a deep silence in which the world is disclosed. His next course, his first after stepping down as rector, is explicitly devoted to "logic as the question concerning the essence of language," which he links to the essence of the *Volk*. But many issues here remain implicit and unspoken. In particular, he draws no connections between his reflections on silence in the first lecture course and his reflections on community in the second. As regards the political implications of silence, Heidegger keeps silent. How telling is this silence? Can we reveal some of what he keeps concealed? Is it an accident that silence gains importance for him just when he is speaking out to support and interpret the Nazi revolution?

Let us set the stage by returning to *Being and Time* for a moment. Here Heidegger presents discourse (*Rede*) as a fundamental characteristic of Dasein. Discourse is the tendency of Dasein's being-in-the-world to get articulated, in the root sense of developing limbs and joints. Our lives and environs emerge as possessing a certain physiognomy: certain features are more rigid than others, developments tend to occur along certain lines, and a network of significance and purpose—a world—becomes apparent to us in our operations. As we do things, things become meaningful articles in an articulated whole. Discourse is the basis of language, because "to significations, words accrue" (SZ 161): language as we ordinarily think of it, a vocabulary and a grammar, responds to the exigencies of the articulation of being-in-the-world. If it is the responsibility of language to cut the world along its joints (Plato, *Phaedrus* 265e), then language is indebted to the jointure or articulation that discourse achieves.

The phenomenon of keeping silent interests Heidegger in *Being and Time* in part because, like many "deficient" phenomena, it points to a deeper structure: both language and silence are grounded in the more fundamental phenomenon of discourse. We ordinarily oppose speech to silence, but both can be significant. In fact, silence can often say more (SZ 164). Think of a refusal to answer, a discreet omission, a pregnant pause, a delayed reply. In context, these telling silences can be highly revealing—they can be appropriate ways to cut a situation along its joints. "Reticence" can be a deep form of communication with others (SZ 165) and even with oneself—for one's own conscience "discourses in the uncanny mode of *Schweigen*" (SZ 277): it does not tell me anything in particular, but draws me back from my absorption in inauthentic existence. Similarly, anxiety cannot be described in "everyday discourse" (SZ 187). Extraordinary or poetic language may suggest it; but since the experience is essentially a withdrawal of sense, an emptiness, it seems to make all language hollow.

Because Dasein is being-with, discourse and language necessarily have public and communal dimensions.[33] The interpersonal articulation of the world normally takes the form of "idle talk," everyday chatter that reinforces truisms (SZ §35). However, Heidegger hints at a deeper political role for language when he says destiny is discovered through struggle and communication (SZ 384). When he embarks on his own political venture, he returns to the relation between language and community with renewed passion.

In the course *On the Essence of Truth* (1933–1934), which we considered earlier primarily for its comments on enmity, he claims that we are open to beings as such and as a whole because we are exposed to the "superior power of being." This exposure impels us to speak, and also sets us apart from both animals and divinities—for it would be "impossible for a god to 'speak'" (GA 36/37: 101/80 tm). These remarks are implicitly political, if we recall Aristotle's statement that one who needs no *polis* is either a beast or a god (*Politics* 1.2). We might infer that, for Heidegger, just as Dasein is thrown into being, it must also be thrown into both language and community. Aristotle himself draws a connection between *logos* and the *polis*:

> That man is much more a political animal than any kind of bee or any herd animal is clear. For, as we assert, nature does nothing in vain; and man alone among the animals has speech [*logos*]. The voice indeed indicates the painful and pleasant, and hence is present in other animals as well; for their nature has come this far, that they have a perception of the painful and pleasant and signal these things to each other. But speech serves to reveal the advantageous and the harmful, and hence also the just and the unjust. For it is peculiar to man as compared to the other animals that he alone has a perception of good and bad and just and unjust . . . and community in these things is what makes a household and a city.[34]

A significant difference between Aristotle and Heidegger may lie in Aristotle's reference to justice as a theme for *logos*. When Heidegger claims in *Being and Time* that destiny is worked out through struggle and communication, he does not mention that debates over what is just are at the heart of this process.[35] We will return to this point.

As Heidegger continues his train of thought in *On the Essence of Truth*, he refers to language as political debate over justice only in passing, as part of his account of the rise of the "logical-grammatical conception of language." For the Greeks,

> speaking, discourse, is speaking with one another, public transaction, advising, assemblage of the people, judicial proceedings; speaking of this kind is having a public opinion and consulting, deliberating, and *thinking*. And in connection with the question of *what* thinking and opining and understanding and knowing are, contemplation arrives at *discourse*, speaking, as what is immediately accessible and in reach of the senses. Discourse is *given* and *is*, just as are many other things; it "is" as the Greeks understood the being of beings: the available, stamped, durable presence of something. Language is something present-at-hand. [GA 36/37: 102/81 tm]

Heidegger's story, then, is that for the Greeks, language or discourse (*logos*) was one present-at-hand entity among others that could become the object of study (cf. SZ 159). Language, however, is a distinctive present-at-hand entity, from the Greek point of view, because it has the power to attribute a present-at-hand predicate to a present-at-hand subject by forming assertions, such as "The stone is hard" (GA 36/37: 103/81). Greek logic takes such assertions as the paradigmatic expression of thinking, where thinking is understood as theorizing, or ascertaining what is present-at-hand. Greek grammar, in turn, is dominated by Greek logic. In this way, our traditional interpretations of language are pervaded by the unquestioned ancient interpretation of being as presence-at-hand (GA 36/37: 103–4/82).

This narrow interpretation of language, Heidegger protests, "is *a monstrous violation of what language accomplishes*." It cannot do justice to what happens in a conversation or poem, where much more is at work than the assertion of facts about the present-at-hand; "the tone of voice, the cadence, the melody of the sentences, the rhythm, and so on" may convey a way of being-in-the-world or an encounter with being itself, not just beings (GA 36/37: 104/82). The usual logico-grammatical prejudice would define these dimensions of sense in a way that takes assertion as the paradigm: they are connotative rather than denotative, sense rather than reference, subjective rather than objective, or artistic embellishments separable from the factual content. Even when Romanticism celebrates subjectivity and imagination, it fails to overcome these hackneyed distinctions. In contrast, Heidegger focuses on how the event of language in its entirety reveals both beings and being, without consigning any part of this event to the merely subjective domain. We might add that rhythm depends on pauses between beats, silences between sounds; Heidegger is starting, then, to approach the question of silence.

At this point he attacks the further prejudice that language is a kind of sign that expresses thought. Such notions are taken for granted by linguistics, which, as the empirical science of language as an entity, is inherently inferior to a philosophical consideration of being (GA 36/37: 105/84)—such as a reflection on the ontology of language and signs. Such ontological reflection would have to ask a number of questions (GA 36/37: 106/84): Is language in fact just one species of sign, or are there human signs only because we already exist in language? Do we speak only in order to signify things, or are things available for us to signify only because we can speak—that is, because language first allows beings to display themselves in their proper power? Do we speak in order to express thoughts, or do we speak because we can keep silent? Is silence a negation, or is it something positive and profound, whereas speaking is the negation of keeping silent? Heidegger prefers the second, less obvious alternatives.

He turns now to his proposal that *"The ability to keep silent is . . . the origin and ground of language"* (GA 36/37: 107/84). First he distinguishes silence, in his sense, from the quiet of an inanimate object, a beast, or a mute; genuinely keeping silent is the prerogative of someone who is able to speak (GA 36/37: 107–9/85–86). To avoid a misunderstanding: there is no need to assume that Heidegger favors audible speech over other forms of language. A mute person who knows sign language can speak, in a broad sense, and can keep silent by refraining from gestures; but someone so disabled that no communication is possible is incapable of keeping silent.

But so far, as Heidegger acknowledges, he simply seems to be repeating the claim in *Being and Time* that both language and silence are modes of discourse. Now he wants to go farther:

> I did not see what really has to follow from this starting point: keeping silent is not just an *ultimate* possibility of discourse, but discourse and language *arise from* keeping silent. In recent years, I have gone back over these relationships and worked them through. This obviously cannot be explained here. Not even the different manners of keeping silent, the multiplicity of its causes and grounds, and certainly not the different levels and depths of reticence. Now only as much will be communicated as is needed for the advancement of our questioning. [GA 36/37: 110/87]

As Heidegger remarks earlier, simply keeping silent about silence would be inadequate—it would leave silence unexamined and let it seem to be an emotional, inarticulate, "mystical" matter. But chattering on and on about silence would suggest that one does not understand what one is talking about (GA 36/37: 107/85). While we can grant him this point, we can only wish that he had communicated more of his thoughts on silence.

He does, however, convey an essential idea: profound silence is *"the gathered disclosedness for the overpowering surge of beings as a whole."* Disclosedness, or being opened up (*Aufgeschlossenheit*), does not mean attending to "every random attraction and incident," but being receptive to the arising of what is, as such and as a whole. "Gathering" here does not mean an egocentric domination or taciturn stubbornness, but a kind of self-discipline that keeps one wholly focused on the whole of beings: "the gathering of one's entire comportment so that this comportment holds to itself and so is bound in itself and thereby remains properly oriented and fully exposed to the beings to which it relates" (GA 36/37: 111/87).

The primordial "reticence" (*Verschwiegenheit*) of keeping silent lends sense and coherence to any words that may emerge from it (GA 36/37: 111/87–88). Words, then, "break silence"—but as long as they do not become uprooted, free-floating chatter, they still bear witness to silence and draw their power from it. The power of silence empowers us to face the superior power of being, and empowers words to reveal beings (GA 36/37: 111–12/88). The primordial gathering of silence enables words to gather beings and disclose them in their gatheredness (GA 36/37: 114–16/90–91). This gathering power of language is what the Greeks named in the word *logos*, derived from *legein* in the sense of assembling. *Legein* then depends on *sigan* (keeping silent)—hence Heidegger's talk in the *Contributions* of turning from "logic" to "sigetics" (GA 65: 62–64/78–80). Heidegger adds that for the Greeks, *logos* and philosophy retain a connection to *mythos*, the kind of language that indicates and hints rather than grasping the togetherness of beings (GA 36/37: 116/91–92). The gathering power of the word draws on the fundamental power of silence as it assists a being in coming forth.

In less Heideggerian terms, we could say that our words are most telling when we do not presume that they are completely adequate to their task. Deep speech is not self-sufficient, but must pause frequently to listen—and what we hear when we listen in the right way is not more speech, but the silent oneness of the world. We must attend to our prelinguistic sense of what things mean as we try to find the words that best reveal what is in the moment.

This process, Heidegger notes, is not captured by standard notions of the sign. A word does not signify a being, as if we encountered them separately and then established a relation between them; instead we find a unified phenomenon, *"the being in the word"* (GA 36/37: 114/90). (Consider how when English speakers hear an "s" at the end of a noun, they immediately feel the plurality of the things in question.) The distinction between signifier and signified is not illegitimate, but it is a theoretical concept that remains dependent on a more basic experience of the disclosure of beings in language.[36] Beings and words emerge together from the unspoken gatheredness of what is.

All these remarks are pregnant but undeveloped, or at least they keep many points tacit. One notable unexplained shift from *Being and Time* is that Heidegger no longer distinguishes discourse from language; he uses the terms *Rede*, *Sprache*, and *Wort* as near synonyms. The work of articulating being-in-the-world is now done by reticence, not discourse; instead of discourse as the basis for both language and meaningful silence, we have silence as the basis for discourse or language. To silence, words accrue.

It might seem that this is simply a change in terminology: one could argue that if "discourse" in *Being and Time* is prior to language, then discourse in this sense is already silent. However, Heidegger's substitution of "silence" for "discourse" may have a substantive force. The significance of the world is no longer brought out by Dasein's practical pursuits—its articulative appropriation of ready-to-hand articles for the sake of a way to be. Significance comes forth, instead, when we set things aside and listen—in a state not unrelated to the Aristotelian "leisure" that Heidegger mentions in *Being and Time* (SZ 138). There, Heidegger seems unsure whether theoretical disengagement from practice is anything more than a deficiency. Now, however, the non-practical (though not theoretical) reticence that gathers beings as a whole is a positive, founding experience—a deep attunement to being. This emphasis on our thrown exposure to being is central to Heidegger's turn to the "happening of being" after *Being and Time*: we must understand ourselves as responsive to the enigmatic event in which being is given to us. Our dependent receptivity is silent.

However, we should not exaggerate the difference between 1927 and 1933 in this regard: Heidegger's discussion of "reticence" in 1933 is akin to *Being and Time*'s account of anxiety and the call of conscience. Perhaps once we admit that these profound modes of disclosure are wordless, it "has to follow" that silence is the most fundamental phenomenon (GA 36/37: 110/87).

There is another question that Heidegger leaves unasked in these lectures: *Who* is keeping silent? It is easy to get the impression from this text that language ultimately stems from the silent experience of an individual, something akin to the radically solitary experiences of anxiety and the call of conscience. But Heidegger says it is not a matter of "isolating oneself" (GA 36/37: 112/88). Could a whole community, then, experience primordial silence? What are the political implications of silence?

Heidegger's next lecture course, *Logic as the Question Concerning the Essence of Language* (Summer Semester 1934), touches on this question by exploring the connection between language and *Volk*. As we saw when we first considered this text, Heidegger quickly makes a transition from formal logic to living language. Most logicians give little thought to so-called natural language, and focus instead on developing precise, formal rules for constructing propositions and ascertaining their implications. The enterprise proceeds under the implicit or explicit assumptions that truth is the correctness of a proposition and that thought (or at least, clear and meaningful thought) consists of arguments that derive propositions from other propositions. But Heidegger moves in the opposite direction: he shows no interest in symbolic logic, which he considers superficial (GA 38: 6/5), and instead challenges logicians' assumptions about truth, thought, and language. The question of logic is rooted in the question of language (GA 38: 13/11).

But will turning logic into an investigation of language illegitimately restrict logic's universal relevance and sense? Heidegger retorts that language appears to be a narrow topic only if one accepts the assumption that it is the sciences that make beings accessible; language is then the theme of some specialized sciences, whereas logic regulates all sciences. But beings are, in fact, accessible in a way that precedes and exceeds all science. Philosophy must attend to this revelation that is deeper than science can ever be—and (Heidegger implies) language plays a role in this revelation (GA 38: 15–16/13). Language is not a mere means, a pointer to things themselves, but is indispensable to the emergence of these things in their being (GA 38: 16/14).

Heidegger thus rejects several stock approaches to language. Language cannot be understood by the "philosophy of language" as an academic specialty; this approach subordinates the topic to an overarching conception of philosophy, whereas perhaps "philosophy originates only out of a sufficient understanding of language" (GA 38: 14–15/12–13). Grammar is another stumbling block for a deeper understanding of language. Grammar is based on Greek logic, and thus on the Greek language and on a specifically Greek way of thinking and existing (GA 38: 17/14). Language is surely not to be found in the dictionary, which is an "ossuary" holding the dead remnants of speech (GA 38: 23/21).

But actual speech is not identical to language, either: when people fall into silence, language does not cease to exist (GA 38: 24/22). Heidegger mentions silence directly in only two contexts in this lecture course: in this brief remark (repeated at GA 38: 31/29) and in the comment that a great mood is kept quiet in an individual or an artwork, while a petty mood "continually displays itself, be it in wretchedness or dull boisterousness" (GA 38: 130/108).

But the question of silence returns indirectly, in a highly political context, when Heidegger argues that no one can know with certainty whether someone else has made the decision to stand by the state, or whether his attitude is a front.

> No individual person among you can in any manner ascertain about any individual person how he has decided. Even you cannot say how I myself have held my lecture, whether decisively or simply as a report, or as stock phrases [*Redensart*]. . . . We are *properly* ourselves only in the decision, namely, each one singly. . . . In willing to be himself, [the individual] is sent out precisely beyond himself into the belongingness to which he submits himself in the decision. In the decision, each is separated from each, as only a human being can be separated. . . . Despite the fact that individuals are separated in decision, a concealed *unison* takes place here, whose concealedness is an essential one. This unison is fundamentally always a mystery. [GA 38: 58–59/51–52 tm]

There is no sure way to distinguish decisive speech (*Rede*) from a figure of speech (*Redensart*) (GA 38: 58/51) or idle talk (*Gerede*). Yet the individual decisions that lie behind speech—decisions that are necessarily secret and silent—bind a community together.

Heidegger returns explicitly to language only in the closing moments of the lecture course. After his train of thought, language has become all the more riddlesome, but he ventures this proposal: the world, as the totality of the being of beings, announces itself to us "in the mystery" and "in the primal-event [*Urgeschehnis*] of language" (GA 38: 168/140). Language is thus far more than a means of communication between subjects: it exposes its speakers to being and the world. "Language is how the world-forming and preserving center of the historical Dasein of the people holds sway" (GA 38: 169/140 tm). Genuine knowledge thus requires mature, creative language (GA 38: 169/141).

Such language, Heidegger suggests in conclusion, is not the degraded language of everyday business, but poetic language, which has "world-forming power" (GA 38: 170/141). The true poet is never contemporary, but reaches into the past and the future, alerting us to the being that has long been assigned to us, but which we have never yet reached (GA 38: 170/141–42).

There is one clear parallel between Heidegger's statements on language in the two lecture courses we have reviewed so far (GA 36/37 and GA 38): in both courses, he associates language with the primordial unconcealment of beings in their being—which is why language cannot be considered simply as one entity among others, or subordinated to some unquestioned concept of being. However, in the first course Heidegger attributes the primal event of unconcealment to silent reticence, which nourishes language; the second course says that language itself plays a role in this unconcealment. Are these views compatible? Is our basic openness to the world linguistic, or silent, or somehow both? Of course, there is no need to assume that a worked-out, systematic theory underlies his lectures; it is more likely that his views are in development.

The juxtaposition of the two courses raises other questions as well. Is there a link between the apparent solitude of silence (which is most evident in an individualizing mood such as *Angst*) and the communal dimension of language? As we asked above, can a community experience silence? Does silence have political implications? In sum, how is silence tied to the *Volk*?

One more text from this period can help us find some connecting threads: the 1933 radio talk "Why Do I Stay in the Provinces?" (GA 13: 9–13). In few words, this piece deftly, if somewhat kitschily, portrays Heidegger's existence among the peasants of the Black Forest. He faces a choice between accepting an invitation to teach in Berlin and keeping his appointment in the town of Freiburg, with its proximity to his mountain cabin at Todtnauberg. As he had in 1930 (GA 16: 61–65), he declines the invitation. He makes the case that he would be betraying his own vocation if he became a citified professor, for his "work remains embedded in the happening of the landscape" (GA 13: 10/WS 16 tm). In the course of his solitary work, he experiences the events in the countryside, not as an observer who talks about them, but as a participant.

Heidegger's life in the Black Forest circles around language and silence. His "struggle to mold something into language is like the resistance of the towering fir against the storm." This language-work is quite unlike the urban tourist's "long conversation with a peasant"; Heidegger, in fact, mostly says "nothing at all," but smokes in "silence" when he spends time with his rural neighbors (GA 13: 10/WS 17).

In the conclusion of the piece, he gets advice from a septuagenarian farmer on whether he should accept an appointment in the capital. "Slowly he fixed the sure gaze of his clear eyes on mine, and keeping his mouth tightly shut, he thoughtfully put his faithful hand on my shoulder. Ever so slightly he shook his head. That meant: absolutely no!" (GA 13: 12–13/WS 18). These gestures are language kept at a laconic minimum—language that keeps as close to silence as possible and, for this very reason, carries more weight than any extended argument could.

For Heidegger, the peasants who waste few words live close to the soil, in every sense: they literally know how to work with the earth, and they also are rooted in the unspoken sense of things that is their heritage as members of the *Volk*. There is no need to disturb this visceral feel for the whole with facile chatter that pretends to illuminate things, but actually warps them to fit rootless truisms. Since the farmers inhabit a common earth and are each tied silently to it, there is no need for them to talk their way into a mock belonging. Instead, they share in silence.

Does language play no role in opening the world, then? Is Heidegger wasting his time as he writes his manuscripts in his hut? No—he would say—because his language springs directly from the silent rootedness of the people, and questioningly articulates what is experienced in this rootedness. Everyday gossip and assertion are superficial, but the rare forms of language that can draw directly on primordial silence have a special role to play in fulfilling a people's destiny. As he puts it in a 1937 reflection on cross-cultural encounters, the "fundamental attitudes and moods of peoples, which usually cannot be spoken at all in an immediate way, gain their definitive form and their power of enticement in great poetry, in formative art, and in the essential thinking (philosophy) of a people" (GA 13: 17). Poetry and philosophy find ways to say what cannot be said in ordinary assertions; they indicate a people's basic orientation to being.

That orientation, however, remains elusive and resists all attempts at direct speech. Although Heidegger, to my knowledge, does not make this play on words, we could speak of *die heimliche Heimat*, "the secret homeland" that silently sustains a people. As he says in August 1934, "the historical vocation of the people . . . remains a secret, a mystery" (GA 16: 303).[37] No language has depth unless it pays tribute to the self-concealing mystery of the homeland, a mystery that is both *heimlich* and *unheimlich*—uncanny. Everyday language is shallow because it forgets or abjures its home. It is thus in perpetual flight from uncanniness; at the same time, it fails to dwell on the familiar.

Both language and silence, then, can participate in primal unconcealment—but this must be creative, poetic language that is capable of reticence. Such reticence is an individual's attunement, but it connects the individual to the shared silence at the roots of a community. The poetic founder of language is in tune with this shared silence and has the gift of finding the words to name a shared destiny.

Could a political movement somehow manage to maintain its connection to the secret homeland? Heidegger's reluctance to move to Berlin already indicates his doubts, which were to grow more serious over the decade of the thirties. As Germany's largest city and the seat of its government, Berlin was a center of language in two senses: a place for idle talk about everything and anything, and a place for the official use of language in legislation and orders. Heidegger himself, acting as rector of the University of Freiburg, issued his share of orders and passed on orders from higher authorities. But this uncreative, legal and organizational use of language could hardly satisfy him as a philosopher.

To choose the most inflammatory example: as rector, he faithfully implemented a government order that required all professors to fill out a questionnaire about their family background in order to identify the "non-Aryans."[38] They would, of course, be fired (GA 16: 84–85) with few exceptions (GA 16: 91–92); Heidegger himself argued against the dismissal of two Jewish colleagues (GA 16: 140–41, 144–46).

But whatever the extent of his antisemitism, as a philosopher Heidegger insisted on the ambiguity and obscurity of the *Volk* and its irreducibility to scientific or pseudoscientific notions of race. The secrets of the homeland could hardly be uncovered by the crude categories of a questionnaire, and the marshaling of human and natural resources could not constitute a primal gathering. Already in 1933–1934, then, his collaboration with the regime fit poorly with his insistence on silence, poetry, and philosophy.

In summary: Heidegger envisions a "metapolitics" (GA 94: 115/85) that springs from the fundamental silence of the people and the mystery of the homeland. At a crucial moment, the reticence of individuals might secretly combine in support of an inception, a moment when the "there" is founded and an authentic response to the question of collective selfhood becomes possible. Everyday chatter takes place only within an established "there," a *polis* whose founding can be neither accomplished nor understood by such idle talk. In chapter 3 we will consider whether this is an adequate conception of the political sphere and the role of discourse in politics.

BEYOND STRUGGLE AND POWER

So far, our review of Heidegger's political thought in the thirties has considered his attempts to imagine how an authentic German community might
be founded and his thought that such founding would depend on a primal
silence. We now turn to his mounting critique of Nazi ideology, which is
largely to be found in posthumously published texts that he kept secret for
most or all of his life. As the thirties draw to a close and the Second World
War gets under way, he turns away from typical Nazi motifs such as struggle
and power, toward play and letting-be. His account of "machination" develops into a global vision of the modern age.

Heidegger's claim in his November 1945 letter to the rector of his university that he developed a "spiritual resistance" to the Nazi regime (GA 16: 402/
HC 65) has often been received with skepticism. However, we can now recognize that, especially in his unpublished meditations, he in fact mounted an
extensive critique of totalitarian ideology. But this critique has to be judged
in light of the ambiguous stance that we will explore in the *Black Notebooks*:
actual National Socialism is a distortion of the truth, and its own account of
itself is inadequate, but it may still have to be "affirmed" as the catastrophic
destiny of the West. Heidegger certainly never accepted liberal democracy,
and he may never have abandoned his faith in the secret potential of National
Socialism—what the movement might have become, or might have made
possible. We must be clear, then, that he does not oppose the Nazi movement,
despite his deconstruction of its metaphysical presuppositions.

We will start with some general characterizations of Heidegger's growing
critique of Nazi ideology, and then consider how the critique unfolds in the
Contributions and some later texts.

Much of his growing uneasiness with actual Nazism has to do with the
centrality of the question, "Who are we?" A community must pose this question to itself in order to exist: "The question 'Who are we?' includes the question of *whether* we are" (GA 65: 51/41). If the Germans, then, suffer from
"alienation from their essence" and have been "torn away from their essential
ground" (GA 95: 181/141 tm), this is not to say that they have been estranged
from a defined identity. They must learn to embrace the very question of who
they are as part of their being. The people's destiny must be born in a process
that combines creation and discovery.

The imperative to question our selfhood implies that the nation must maintain its revolutionary spirit, rather than settling into a new everydayness. The
revolutionary, Heidegger writes in 1937, is the true relation to the inception
and thus to history (GA 45: 37).[39] The Germans must feel the emergency that
led to the change of regime in the first place. But in Heidegger's judgment,

Germany has failed to hold itself within revolutionary urgency. The new order is not overcoming tranquilized self-satisfaction. Rather than leaping into
selfhood, the nation is settling into a collective subjectivity.

In order, then, to draw the contours of what National Socialism can be, Heidegger confronts the philosophical ideas that the political movement echoes or
claims to echo. His first lecture course on Nietzsche (GA 43, 1936–37) focuses
on the question of art—the question that he wished in 1934 that Kolbenheyer
had addressed, instead of resorting to biologism (GA 36/37: 212). Heidegger's
increasingly critical readings of Nietzsche parallel his disillusionment with
the quasi-Nietzschean Nazi regime.[40] As Heidegger himself puts it, "The four
lecture courses on Nietzsche and the seminars since 1937 are a confrontation
with Nietzsche, whose metaphysics is seen as the end of philosophy hitherto,
and is critically overcome" (GA 86: 891). For Heidegger, Nietzsche's struggle
against traditional metaphysics ended up as a mere "inverted Platonism": his
thought is the ultimate metaphysical representation of beings as such and as a
whole, instead of an opening to the question of being itself. Nietzsche's "affirmation of 'becoming'" (GA 66: 26/20) and his "will to power" reduce all
beings to conditions of power, or "values" (GA 67: 48).

As for later thinkers inspired by Nietzsche, Heidegger takes Spengler
and Jünger seriously as visionaries who anticipate or express the political
dimension of the will to power. He writes in 1935: "It seems to me that Ernst
Jünger's vision is confirmed, beyond or beneath what otherwise passes for
the 'movement' and is becoming ever more petit-bourgeois. This 'simplifica-
tion' of Dasein, which is clearly something new as a whole, will be necessary
if our world is to succeed. . . . What has always pained me, and in recent years
more than ever, is the *formlessness* of our 'spiritual' Dasein."[41] At this point,
Heidegger is fascinated by Jünger's description of a total mobilization that
would forge a new human type.

Yet by the late thirties, he writes that Spengler's "Caesarism" and Jünger's
concept of the worker do not penetrate far enough into the metaphysical roots
of contemporary politics (GA 66: 27–28/21 tm). Jünger's Nietzscheanism
proves to be inadequate and one-sided, as Heidegger says in many of his
notes on *The Worker* (e.g., GA 90: 213).

Even a broader and deeper interpretation of Nietzsche is forced to conclude
that his thought is the end of metaphysics, not a new inception (e.g., GA 87:
155). In the emergency of their alienation from their essence, the Germans must
seek a new inception not through Nietzsche but through Hölderlin, who suggests poetic dwelling rather than the exercise of power as the way to selfhood.

Heidegger's confrontation with the Nietzschean will to power is part of his
own journey from a fascination with power in the earlier thirties to a renun-
ciation of both will and power in the forties. This should not be characterized

as a move from a simple "activism" to a simple "quietism." Instead, in both his earlier and his later thought he employs a language of "letting" that is neither passive nor active. (The German *lassen* is often used in a productive or imperative sense, as in the English "let's.") For example, our use and understanding of ready-to-hand equipment is a "letting-be-involved" (SZ 84–85). This is not inaction, but neither is it the imposition of human plans and efforts on a valueless material world; in our activities, each of us encounters the teleology of everyday things as a given. The essay "On the Essence of Truth" extends this notion into a general "letting-be" (*Sein-lassen*). To let be is not to detach oneself, but "to engage oneself [*sich einlassen*] with the open region and its openness" (GA 9: 188/144). (The idea of letting-be is introduced in the second version of this text, dating from October 1930: GA 80.1: 363–65.) Toward the end of the thirties, he writes that letting-be requires the highest form of "steadfastness" (*Inständigkeit*, GA 66: 103/86 tm).[42] Thus, he never simply advocates activity or passivity.

However, it is clear that his enthusiasm for action and power reaches a peak around the time of his own political activity. "Power" (*Macht*) is a relatively insignificant term in *Being and Time*, although it does appear at the climax of the text (SZ 384–85). But during his political engagement, he celebrates power, often in conjunction with struggle, as when he lectures during his rectorate on *polemos* as "confrontation with and between the *primal powers*" (GA 36/37: 92/74).

As we saw, by the time of *Introduction to Metaphysics* (1935), he is experimenting with a family of words stemming from *Macht* and *Walten* in order to express the relation between being and Dasein: faced with the overwhelming sway of being, man must use violence and unfold his own powers against the overpowering. Although this is an interpretation of *physis* in the tragic age of the Greeks, and not directly of Heidegger's own understanding of being, he seems to embrace the language of power when he says that we need to recapture the archaic sense of *physis* in the face of its "disempowerment" (GA 73.1: 121–52). But he eventually retracts this expression: it lends itself too easily to a Nietzschean reading, which itself is possible only because originary *physis* has been lost.[43] Being as power is the *Unwesen* or counter-essence of *physis* (GA 69: 62).

We must read this last thought as part of Heidegger's critical turn against the dominant Nazi ideology, a turn that often takes the form of anti-Nietzscheanism and anti-Romanism. Nietzsche writes in a late text that he admires the Romans more than the Greeks. For him, the hardness of Roman style reflects the hardness of the Roman worldview, which is matched among the Greeks only by the sophistic and Thucydidean interpretation of human action in terms of power struggles (*Twilight of the Idols*, "What I Owe to the Ancients"). By the late thirties Heidegger has soured on this standpoint, and he critiques Nietzsche's thought for being "un-Greek" in its interpretations of being, the good, truth, and humanity. Nietzsche's thought is *"the philosophy of the antiphilosophical Romans"* (GA 67: 102, cf. GA 54: 63). Of course, the Nazis borrowed from Italian Fascism and the Roman Empire in their ideology, organization, and imagery (consider Speer's plans for Berlin). When Heidegger writes in 1939, then, that with the Roman translation of *energeia* as *actus*, "with one blow the Greek world was toppled" (GA 9: 286/218; cf. GA 6.2: 374–83/EP 10–19), he is implicitly criticizing the Nazi worldview. *Energeia* is originally the same as *physis*: the emergence of what is into enduring self-display, the coming-into-being of beings as such. But *actus* misinterprets this coming-into-being in terms of *agere*, acting and leading. This understanding sinks to the level of beings and their effective behavior; at its crudest, it reduces this behavior to the mechanistic impact of an active thing on a passive thing. Being as emergence into unconcealment has been forgotten (GA 66: 187, 195–96, 289). By the same token, the Greek *lethe* (concealment) is distorted when it is reinterpreted as the *falsus*, a concept from "the Roman-imperial domain" that connotes the fall of an enemy (GA 54: 61/41) and is applied in Roman Catholicism to the persecution of heretics (GA 54: 68/46). "Rome, Judaism, and Christianity completely transformed and falsified the inceptive—i.e., Greek—philosophy" (GA 35: 1/1 tm).

This falsification includes the decline of the original sense of the *polis*. "Since the time of the *Imperium*, the Greek word 'political' has meant something Roman. What is Greek about it now is only its sound" (GA 54: 67/45). Politics has become nothing but a power struggle. As we will see, this aspect of Heidegger's anti-Romanism is reflected in the *Black Notebooks'* discussions of machination and brutality—"not accidentally" a Latin term (GA 95: 394–95/308). The Nazis' emphasis on technological superiority to other nations and their glorification of sheer force are signs that they have failed to retrieve the original Greek sense of *physis*.

In the *Contributions* Heidegger is still speaking of the "empowering" of time-space and beyng (GA 65: 386/305, 430/340), but in *Besinnung* (1938–1939) he claims that beyng lies beyond both power and powerlessness (GA 66: 83, 187–88). Although he remains interested in a kind of mastery—a "masterful thinking" that participates in an inception—he insists that "the violence that is set loose in the essence of machination always underlies power alone, and never grounds mastery" (GA 66: 16/12 tm).

Grounding as active founding is gradually deemphasized in Heidegger's thought. In the *Contributions*, the appropriating event of the grounding of the there requires us to take up the truth of beyng and build Dasein on this ground (GA 65: 307). Our role is to receive the impetus of beyng and extend it creatively into a world. But Heidegger comes to see this passion for founding as misguided. By the end of the war, he is recommending "pure waiting" (GA 77: 217/140).

He also distances himself from the will. Not long after the *Contributions'* call for a "will to the event of appropriation" (GA 65: 58/46 tm), "'willing' (?) that beyng essentially happen" no longer sounds appropriate (GA 69: 27/25 tm, Heidegger's question mark). He proposes that the essence of modern metaphysics could be understood by completing the sentence, "If being is 'will' . . ." (GA 67: 159). As an alternative to this tradition, by the mid-forties he turns to releasement. This is not a human act or attitude, but the fact that humanity primordially belongs to, or is let into, the region of truth (GA 77: 122).

As Heidegger shifts from power to releasement, he also begins to shift from struggle to play. The appearance of the word *Kampf* (struggle) in §74 of *Being and Time* is an omen of a strong polemical motif that develops in his thought. This theme reaches a peak as he assumes the rectorship: "All capacities of will and thought, all strengths of the heart, and all capabilities of the body must be developed *through* struggle, must be intensified *in* struggle, and must remain preserved *as* struggle" (GA 16: 116/HR 115). But struggle continues to exert some fascination for him for some time after his turn away from power. One of its most important developments is the idea of the conflict between the disclosive power of the world and its self-concealing ground in the earth. According to the *Contributions*, this strife is fundamental to all truth, and being itself is engaged in strife (GA 65: 269, 322, 349, 484, 497). As he develops these thoughts, Heidegger comes to understand struggle and strife in a sense that is increasingly distant from military reality.

We can trace some of these developments in terms of his readings of Heraclitus's famous fragment 53: "*Polemos* is both the father of all and the king of all; some it has shown as gods, others as men; some it has made slaves and others free."[44] Heidegger is particularly interested in this fragment at the height of his political engagement, which is also, as we have seen, the time when he takes *polemos* as "struggle" in a concrete and seemingly bloody sense (GA 36/37: 91).[45] Shortly after stepping down as rector, he speaks at his twenty-five-year school reunion about the legacy of the Great War, *polemos*, and "the power of struggle in all being of things and men" (GA 16: 283). But by 1935 he is emphasizing that *polemos* is not a human war, and translating it as *Auseinandersetzung* (confrontation or conversation) instead of *Kampf* (GA 40: 66/67, 121/125, 153/160).[46] By the time that war in the literal sense is raging, he has deemphasized *polemos* to the point that his two great lecture courses on Heraclitus include only a single note that refers to fragment 53 (GA 55: 46).

As struggle declines in Heidegger's thought, he turns to play—another Heraclitean motif (fragment 52). By the late thirties, he is writing that philosophy "puts the truth of beyng into play in the time-play-space of beyng" (GA 66: 41/32 tm). He envisions a "play in which, in the future, one must play with the 'engagement' of beyng itself" (GA 66: 45/37 tm). This development culminates in his postwar descriptions of "the fourfold." Before the war, he described the strife of earth, world, gods, and man as the "struggle of struggles" (GA 66: 15/11). By 1949, the relation of earth, sky, gods, and mortals has become a "mirror-play" (GA 79: 18–21/17–20). The polemical tension has largely been superseded by a harmonious cooperation—although it has not disappeared.[47]

Keeping in view this general sketch of Heidegger's turn away from struggle and power, let us look more closely at a few of the posthumously published manuscripts in which he develops a metaphysical critique of the basis of Nazi ideology.

The first of this series, and the most clearly structured, is the *Contributions to Philosophy* of 1936–1938.[48] As I indicated in chapter 1, in my reading, the *Contributions* are the culmination of the themes we traced in chapter 1: the inception of time, emergency, and the "who." The appropriating event is the inception that founds a world and lets being become an issue. It is the event of the grounding of the there (GA 65: 183, 247). It generates time-space as the "site of the moment" (GA 65: 323/255) where and when earth and world can clash (GA 65: 30) and a decision about the divine can take place (GA 65: 230, 264, 411). The moment is, in this sense, *"the time of being"* (GA 65: 508/399) and the origin of ecstatic time (GA 66: 114).

The appropriating event gives birth to our own being by calling it into question and urging us to decide who we are. It is an event of owning, an event that seizes us and makes it possible for our being to be our own. It is thus an emergency, and Heidegger suggests that emergency is the truth of beyng itself (GA 65: 46)—or will be, if *Ereignis* fully comes to pass. But in a time that is indifferent to crisis, the greatest danger is that beyng will fail to happen (GA 65: 11, 107, 119, 125, 234–37). Without such an event, there is no disclosure and no selfhood.

The event would thus found a site where the people's destiny can unfold—a site where "we" belong, and where the question "Who are we?" has purchase.[49] "Human beings are appropriated to themselves only if they themselves reach the open time-space wherein an appropriation can occur" (GA 65: 51/42). The event initiates us into selfhood and belonging. Through it we enter "the *domain of what is proper*" (GA 65: 320/253). This emphasis on belonging gives *Ereignis* a slant to the right—but this belonging is not grounded on a fixed identity, as invoked by nationalist and racist myths. Selfhood cannot be settled, for appropriation also involves alienation, nihilation, or expropriation (GA 66: 312). Absence, departure, denial, and longing point more genuinely to our selfhood than any easily ascertainable, present-at-hand characteristics. Sense and self hover over an "abyssal ground" (GA 65: 379/299).

Heidegger diagnoses complacent self-certainty, devoid of genuine self-hood, as the fatal trait of his time. The self-assured subject willfully plans and manipulates the world, turning itself into the center of all sense. "This (namely, such self-certainty) is the innermost essence of 'liberalism,' which precisely for that reason can apparently unfold freely" and march on in its unstoppable "progress." The predominant racial ideology is nothing but "biological liberalism" (GA 65: 53/43), and Marxism is an equally thought-less outgrowth of Judeo-Christian egalitarianism (GA 65: 54). He is coming to see all the established political and religious options as forms of bankrupt subjectivism, whether on the individual, the national, or the international scale. All the ideologies of his time posit humanity "as already known in es-sence" (GA 65: 25/22).

Heidegger insists on the problematic character of the *Volk*: "How is the essence of a people determined?" (GA 65: 48/40). He rejects the idea that we should simply decide who we are by willfully organizing the people; busy activity may or may not indicate genuine selfhood (GA 65: 49–50).

The question of what it means to be a people is essential (GA 65: 42), but Heidegger addresses it only tentatively, and for the most part negatively. He insists above all that the people's highest goal is not to maintain itself as one entity among others, but to watch over the truth of being (GA 65: 99, 321). The people cannot be an end in itself (GA 65: 98–99, 139, 319, 398). When we fail to put ourselves in question, we take ourselves as examples of a fixed essence, rather than entering a unique historical moment. Participating in history is then reduced to "occurring within a belonging-together that has already come to be" (GA 65: 61/49 tm).

Heidegger's conception of the people as ineluctably questionable distances him from official Nazi ideology. As always, he insists that race and the body are not absolutes. They enter history only as part of the earth, but the earth needs to come into conflict with the world (GA 65: 399)—so it is grotesque to try to ground history on blood and race alone (GA 65: 493). Physical traits are part of the given into which a people is thrown, but the people's leaders must find ways to project possibilities on the basis of this thrownness (GA 65: 398). Nazism turns the people into a fixed, self-centered subject, instead of recognizing its potential as Dasein. The Nazis reduce the people to "the communal, the racial, the inferior and lower, the national, the permanent" (GA 65: 117/93). If a *völkisch* principle is ever to play a role in German destiny, it will have to be handled by those who have reached the "highest rank of beyng" (GA 65: 42/35; cf. 24, 319, 479). These few thinkers, poets, and men of action are ready to sacrifice themselves in order to gain true selfhood (GA 65: 7, 397).

The many who cannot yet take part in such an event will also eventually be needed—for ultimately only a people can ground the truth of beyng (GA 65: 97). Conversely, unless the people grounds this truth, it is not yet a true people—so its pioneers, the future ones, must often seem to be its enemies (GA 65: 398). Yet these future ones, not the man on the street, are the genuine voice of the people (GA 65: 319); only they can set the people "free for its law (to be achieved through struggle)" (GA 65: 43/35). A deeper belonging could be prepared only through a happening that would bind together the few and the many—"an original gathering" (GA 65: 97/77).

As for how such a gathering might take place, Heidegger is nearly silent. He no longer has faith that political measures can bring it about—although he does not rule out the possibility (GA 65: 98). The rebirth of the people is more likely to happen through a religious awakening: the people must seek its own god, and the future ones will lead this search (GA 65: 398).

The need for a new grounding implies that contemporary humanity is inadequate and groundless. "The Resonating," the most polemical part of the *Contributions*, thus describes modernity as an age of nihilism (GA 65: 138–41). Modernity is bewitched by machination (GA 65: 124)—"an interpretation of beings in which their makeability comes to the fore, so much so that constancy and presence become the specific determinations of beingness" (GA 65: 126/100). Machination is accompanied by a craving for "lived experience"—subjective stimulation, information, and entertainment (GA 65: 109/87, 129–34/101–6). The manipulation of the "external" world thus corresponds to a manipulation of the "internal" world: as we measure and manipulate our external surroundings, we accumulate internal, subjective, shallow experiences. In both cases, we simply control and toy with our representations, instead of opening ourselves to an event greater than we are that calls for genuine decision. A related phenomenon, "the gigantic" (GA 65: 135–38/106–9), characterizes the contemporary triumph of quantity as quality. To be now means to be measurable, and there are no limits to measuring. Nothing is seen as impossible or unreachable anymore, so the possibility of "what is inexhaustibly unexhausted" (GA 65: 137/108) is eliminated. An amusement park or a movie theater provide clear examples of machination, lived experience, and the gigantic, as do mass rallies and spectacles such as the 1936 Berlin Olympics.

The *Contributions* are followed by a series of other unpublished meditations. These writings go farther along the path begun in the *Contributions*, but place a new emphasis on the critique of power and make more explicitly political observations. The concept of *Ereignis* is somewhat stabilized and formalized, as *Besinnung* develops a thought that was briefly introduced in the *Contributions* (GA 65: 310): in the event of appropriation, "the encounter of god and man crosses the strife of earth and world" (GA 66: 163/141 tm). Heidegger calls this crossing the "out-come" (*Aus-trag*)—an event of clearing in which god, man, earth, and world come out, or are drawn out, from concealment into the truth of beyng (GA 66: 84/70 tm).

Heidegger still employs the word *Kampf*: "*beyng now demands that its ownmost essence be struggled forth*" (GA 66: 85/71 tm), and we need a "*struggle for a passing* of the god" (GA 69: 219/184). Unlike the rather idyllic and pastoral "fourfold" of Heidegger's postwar writings, the out-come is "the struggle of struggles" (GA 66: 15/11). However, he distinguishes this "struggle" from modern war, which is nothing but "domination through technical power" (GA 69: 65/56 tm). He has also moved away from Heraclitus as he searches for a new inception: appropriation and out-come are not *polemos* (GA 67: 36, 77). There may be a "struggle" between the first and other inception (GA 67: 36), or a "decision between beyng and 'beings,'" but all this is "what is originally and completely other than *polemos*" (GA 95: 188/147 tm). He even suspects that the very concept of struggle is too indebted to the concept of power, as we can see in his comment that there can be no genuine struggle against power: that would just reproduce power's machinational essence (GA 69: 69).

Heidegger now develops an extensive interpretation of this essence and its implications.[50] Power has become the contemporary sense of being: beings are now essentially manifestations of power and occasions for the use of power. Power seeks to overpower itself, overcoming its current level and increasing without limit as it mobilizes everything, subjecting all beings to it (GA 66: 62–63, 176; on Nietzsche's conception of overpowering, see, e.g., GA 5: 234–35/175). The drive for overpowering creates oppression and devastation (GA 66: 20)—not the destruction of objects, but a condition in which "beings no longer enter into the decision of being" (GA 69: 48/43).

These are the metaphysical roots of contemporary phenomena such as "the *'total'* . . . the *'imperial'* . . . the *'planetary'*" (GA 66: 18/13–14). Power destroys everything inceptive and all worth (GA 69: 74). It creates a "total organization" without true "commitment" (GA 69: 83/71). Under the sway of this organization, all beings and acts are viewed as subject to calculation and planning. However, the plans bring themselves into a wasteland that they cannot control, and necessarily run into the incalculable and unforeseeable (GA 69: 84).

Power manifests itself as both "planetarism" and "idiotism," where the first is the tendency to extend the rule of power over the entire Earth, while the second is a self-centered subjectivism that is turned in upon what is peculiar to it (*idion*) yet views all individuals through the same lens of the essence of modern subjectivity (GA 69: 74/63). The planet is becoming one huge, greedy, anonymous subject. This idiotic subject is "the unconditional essence of the 'they' in the history of beyng" (GA 70: 35).

Power knows no goals or standards other than itself; as violence, it uses itself to enhance itself (GA 69: 22, 75). This violence becomes a brutality that turns not only against other brutal forces but ultimately against itself (GA 69: 76–77). To call such machination "evil" would be to evade the genuine horror of it: it dissolves the very standards of good and evil, the very concept of a final goal (GA 69: 217).

Heidegger is talking about political power, of course, but also about how being itself is manifested in terms of power, in everything from science to art. Art is reduced to propaganda and kitsch (GA 66: 31, 174–75). The ideal of manliness becomes a muscle-bound figure with an empty, brutal face (GA 66: 34).

Political phenomena must be understood from a metaphysical, not political point of view (GA 69: 66). So Heidegger attributes little responsibility to dictators; we live under the "dictatorship" of power itself (GA 69: 20/20), not of persons such as Hitler. The so-called possessors of power cannot in fact get power within their grasp—instead, power possesses us (GA 69: 63–64). Those who appear to be free because they are powerful are in fact enslaved to power and warped by an interpretation of selfhood in terms of power. Because power destroys all moral and legal standards, the age of power must include the "planetary criminals" who can be counted on the fingers of one hand (GA 69: 77–78/66). Their destructiveness bursts the bounds of ethical judgment and legal punishment; "even hell and the like is too small" for them (GA 69: 77/66).

Power does not belong to the "powerful" tyrants, then, but neither does it belong to the people. The public face of power, its propaganda and pageantry, presents the power as belonging to society at large; but this "socialism" covers up the fact that the people are actually disempowered (GA 69: 82/69). The capacity for decision is obliterated by an atmosphere of declarations and commands (GA 66: 19); these create only a fanaticism that seizes on a ready-made appearance of salvation (GA 66: 119). Political action is then nothing but the "total planning of 'life' trained to secure itself" (GA 69: 100/85). The youth is particularly used and abused by this process, because young people are sufficiently ignorant and shameless to carry out "the planned destruction" without question (GA 66: 19/14). This entire so-called struggle is only the evasion of the "questionworthiness of beyng" (GA 66: 141/120 tm).

How could the dictatorship of power be overcome? Obviously not by an attempt to overpower it—that would simply be a reaffirmation of power, and our ultimate enslavement to it. But powerlessness is also unsatisfactory—it is just weakness that thirsts for power (GA 69: 67). We must find "that which is in no need of power," a position that no longer allows power to "make" opposition to itself (GA 69: 70/60). "The one who transforms its essence is sovereign master of power. Such transformation springs from beyng alone" (GA 69: 21/20). Thus genuine mastery would be the "*charis* [grace] of beyng as beyng" (GA 69: 69/59 tm) or the inceptive worth of beyng (GA 66: 16–17). Only the mastery of beyng is "mastery in the inceptive sense," transcending hierarchy and size (GA 66: 193/170 tm) and lying beyond both power and powerlessness (GA 66: 192).

Heidegger questions the drive for "'space' and 'land'" (GA 66: 167/145), nationalism (GA 66: 174), "the 'eternal *Volk*' and other such thoughtlessnesses" (GA 66: 318/283 tm), totalitarianism (GA 66: 169, 234), and the concept of world war (GA 66: 28)—although he also attacks liberal democracy (GA 66: 39, 234) and the concept of world peace (GA 66: 28, 84).

The most dramatic political passage in all the unpublished meditations may be §47 of *Besinnung*, which begins with a sentence from a speech delivered by Hitler on January 30, 1939: "There is no attitude that cannot be ultimately justified by its ensuing usefulness for the totality." Heidegger proceeds to attack every concept in this sentence. "Who makes up this totality? . . . What is its goal? . . . Who determines the usefulness? . . . What does *attitude* mean?" (GA 66: 122/102 tm). Heidegger concludes that Hitler is promoting the oblivion of being and entanglement in beings—an obsession with domination in the name of "ideas" that alienate us from our true essence (GA 66: 123/103).

Other Nazi ideas also fare poorly in Heidegger's analysis. The irrationalist "biological world-view" is not a genuine alternative to rationalism, but simply a different way of calculating with humanity and with beings as a whole (GA 66: 250/220). The ideal of "heroic realism" propounded by ideologues such as Alfred Baeumler and Werner Best leaves no room for genuine *Angst* (GA 67: 114); instead of accepting and affirming the struggle for power as the essence of reality, we must question being once again (GA 66: 19–20). The neo-pagan life-philosophy of Ludwig Klages vulgarizes the will to power by reducing it to "vitality" (GA 67: 114). Here, "boozing and whoring have received their metaphysical justification" (GA 67: 122).

Heidegger certainly shares the Nazis' general desire to rescue the Germans as a people, but he disagrees both with their means and with their conception of salvation. "The 'ones to come' . . . are of a rugged stock that will rescue the Germans and bring them back into the emergency of their essence" (GA 66: 61/50 tm). But the way to this essence is not through control and violence, and essence cannot be found in blood and land (GA 66: 167). The notion of breeding a strong human type perpetuates the subjectivistic manipulation of what is (GA 66: 42). Racial calculation is a consequence of subjectivism, as are both nationalism and socialism (GA 69: 44): whether the goal is to save a race or to protect individual freedom, subjectivity and its drive for power are at work (GA 69: 154). Racial thinking ranks some races over others, on the basis of their achievements or expressions (GA 69: 70). This is inadequate—not because Heidegger is an egalitarian, but because the racist perspective unhistorically reduces Dasein to a substrate, an underlying thing whose power is manifested in its thoughts and acts. "Peoples and races" are not understood in terms of their relation to being when they are interpreted as "units of life" (GA 66: 282/250).

Some of these ideas are summed up in "The Age of the World Picture" (1938), where Heidegger characterizes modernity as an age that objectifies beings and represents them in terms of willfully affirmed principles. The modern subject blocks off the event that might call into question what it means to be and who we ourselves are. This is not selfhood, but insistence on the presence of a secure ground. Heidegger apparently concluded that actual Nazism was just another form of modern subjectivity that had to be transcended.

In an effort to discredit this reading, Sidonie Kellerer has documented various discrepancies between the 1938 manuscript of "The Age of the World Picture" (preserved in the Deutsches Literaturarchiv in Marbach) and its 1950 published version (in GA 5). In particular, Heidegger reworked the passage that describes the *Volk* as a type of subjectivity (GA 5: 92–93/70). The original reads:

> Only because and insofar as the human being has, absolutely and essentially, become a subject, must he arrive then at this explicit question: is it as the "I" limited to its arbitrariness and released to its caprice or as the "we" of society; is it as an individual or as a community; is it as personality within the community or as a mere group member of the body corporate; is it as a state and nation or as a *Volk* that wants [to] and must be the *subject*, that the human being *already* is *as* a modern being.[51]

Among other changes, the revised 1950 version has "state and nation and [not "or"] as a *Volk*" (GA 5: 92/70). Kellerer takes such discrepancies as evidence for a pillar of Emmanuel Faye's interpretation: Heidegger endorses modern subjectivity when it takes the form of the *Volk* and of the militaristic, racist promotion of the *Volk* by Nazism; he rejects individual subjectivism, but exalts communal subjectivism. Faye says that his "entire interpretation of

Heidegger's relationship with National Socialism depends on" his reading of this distinction.[52]

Philological work such as Kellerer's is valuable and necessary, and it often does show Heidegger trying to make his earlier texts as palatable and persuasive as he can. But Faye's reading of Heidegger on subjectivity is not clearly supported by the original version of "The Age of the World Picture," or by other texts of the period. Faye leans heavily on a passage in the 1940 Nietzsche lectures where Heidegger rejects the identification of subjectivity with egotism, and points out that "the emphasis on the community" is another form of subjectivity (GA 48: 212; cf. GA 90: 152–54). According to Faye, Heidegger "has a very positive view of the fulfillment (*Erfüllung*) of subjectivism in the affirmation of . . . the people and the nation. . . . Heidegger's intended meaning is unequivocal, and perfectly in conformity with the Nazi doctrine of the *Volksgemeinschaft* as opposed to all forms of individualism."[53] But the sense of Heidegger's text is hardly as obvious as Faye believes. Heidegger writes:

> The emphasis on the community as opposed to the selfishness of the individual is, thought metaphysically, not the overcoming of subjectivism but only its fulfillment, for man—not the separate individual, but man in his *essence*—now goes about basing everything that is, everything that is brought about and created, suffered and fought for, upon himself, and including it within his dominion. . . . [This] liberation of man to himself . . . is carried out as the awakening and furthering of all human capabilities toward the mastering and use of the "world." . . . The history of subjectivity is the history of liberation to the new essence of freedom in the sense of the unconditional self-legislation of man. [GA 48: 212–13]

An audience that was unfamiliar with Heidegger's thought might well take these statements as celebrating "liberation." But if one understands that he rejects the subjectivist conception of freedom as autonomy (e.g., GA 36/37: 161; GA 66: 48), then details such as his reference to "the overcoming of subjectivism" and his scare quotes around "world" prove to be significant: true freedom is not control over a vast number of entities, or an individual's or community's self-control, but participation in the historical unfolding of the sense of being.

Many other texts written during the Nazi regime confirm that Heidegger is critiquing the predominant ideology as a form of subjectivism. For example, when describing Dasein's displacement into beyng, he writes that "there is no room at all here for the interpretation of the human being as 'subject,' whether in the sense of the egological or communal subject" (GA 65: 488/384). "Technology is removed from the willing and unwilling of man insofar as in his essence he is decided as 'subject'; the subjectivity of humanity takes form most purely in the nations; the community of a nation drives the singularization of man in subjectivity to an extreme"; and in this subjective-technical objectification of beings, "truth is forgotten" (GA 66: 173–74/152 tm). In a letter from 1943, he complains about how "the 'egotism' of peoples, nations, races, and groups" has become "the obvious form of domination."[54] One might think that he is celebrating subjectivity nationalistically in a sentence such as this: "Only when metaphysics . . . has been founded on the essence of subjectivity and the Ego do the concepts of 'nation' and 'people' obtain that metaphysical foundation from which they might possibly have historical relevance." But he goes on to say that as long as we fail to understand "subjectivity as the modern form of selfhood, we are prey to the error of thinking that the elimination of individualism and of the domination of the individual is ipso facto an overcoming of subjectivity" (GA 54: 204/137). The point, I take it, is that subjectivity, whether individual or communal, must be transcended before an appropriate relation to truth, being, and ourselves can take place. However, as we will see in the next section, Heidegger thinks that modern subjectivity must drive to its catastrophic end before a postsubjectivist dispensation becomes possible. This is the grain of truth in Faye's interpretation.

Let us turn to the essay "*Koinon*: From the History of Beyng" and the "Draft" of this essay (GA 69: 179–214/153–80 tm), which are noteworthy efforts to think ontohistorically about the start of the Second World War (1939–1940). Heidegger begins "*Koinon*" with the "strange" character of the war, which at this stage did not have constantly visible effects on everyday German life. The strangeness, he suggests, is a distant echo of the worth of beyng—a questionability that lies beyond the coming "gigantic battles of annihilation" (GA 69: 180/153–54 tm). In this eerie new condition, the difference between war and peace evaporates: peace becomes nothing but the domination of the means and possibilities of war (GA 69: 181, cf. GA 7: 91/EP 104).

The new war is a "world war" inasmuch as the world in the Heideggerian sense—the whole of senses and purposes that orient Dasein—is now intelligible only in terms of power (GA 69: 180–81, cf. 50). Power has taken over the "play of the world" (GA 69: 182/155) or the "play of being" (GA 69: 186/159). Beings have been reduced to makeable, replaceable resources; everything is planned, calculated, producible. Our relation to beings has become "readiness for deployment": we are human resources, ready to produce and destroy (GA 69: 185/158).

It is impossible to resist power in the name of freedom, morality, values, or law; all such attempts are merely manifestations of power, as is the ideal of saving the race. All these efforts posit goals that coordinate powers; power is thereby empowered, and the particular goal that is supposedly served is in fact irrelevant. Power needs no ideal or goal to justify it; it makes all justification obsolete, as its Protean process of self-empowerment through subjection and annihilation keeps driving on (GA 69: 182–85, 188, 202).

From this perspective, world wars are only "interludes of a more essential process" (GA 69: 187/159); the essence of power far exceeds military and political categories. Heidegger's suprapolitical perspective views totalitarian and democratic systems as essentially the same. Both are based on an "idea" to which reality must conform (such as the idea of democracy or the idea of the people); both are subject to the illusion that power rests with the people (the majority, the race), when in fact, power can belong to no one (GA 69: 188–89). The competing "interests" of the world powers, which they try to defend by launching mass wars, are epiphenomena of metaphysical power (GA 69: 206–7, 210).

It may seem that dictators have power, but in fact they themselves are dominated by the process of power. This process overwhelms the current rank of the despot, as every stage of power is only a stage to be overcome; the power process also demands a uniformity of all beings, thereby destroying the distinctive status of the so-called powerful individuals (GA 69: 190). The "just-a-few" (GA 69: 193–94/164) are then not so different from the "never-too-many" (GA 69: 190/161). The elite are bound together only by their anxiety in the face of any possible obstacle to the constant growth of power (GA 69: 193–95). Heidegger sees this elite as anonymous, and proposes in his "Draft" that even Stalin is just one of the "front men" (GA 69: 203/172).

The meaning of the title "*Koinon*" emerges when Heidegger focuses on a metaphysical analysis of communism. As he had commented in a lecture course a few years earlier, the Platonic concept of essence as the universal or *koinon* is relatively superficial: the fact that a number of beings have a characteristic in common is only a possible *consequence* of their essence (GA 45: 60–61). For example, what makes a tree a tree is not its similarity to other trees—it would still be a tree even if it were the only one in the world. Yet the superficial interpretation of the essence as a universal has become dominant in Western thought, and has encouraged us to view thought itself as generalization. This metaphysical "communism" assimilates everything to the common and eliminates the incomparable. Our age is communist in this sense, and in this sense communism is the consummation of metaphysics in its meaninglessness (GA 69: 37, 191, 201).

Communism, as Heidegger understands it, is not essentially a political affair (GA 69: 195), but he does relate it to political practice: the Soviet regime reduces everything to the average and interprets Dasein in the reductive terms of work, use, and enjoyment. The Communist Party and its ideology impose a uniformity of "proletarian" attitudes and behavior (GA 69: 191–92). Ownership disappears—not only in the legal sense, and not only in regard to material property, but in regard to the self, which is plunged into anonymity (GA 69: 195). The particular destinies of peoples are ignored; the reliability of beings is destroyed (GA 69: 196).

Soviet Communism cannot be overcome by a supposedly more spiritual understanding of the human condition. Communist "materialism" is itself thoroughly spiritual, in that it is a product of Western metaphysics (GA 69: 204). The very dichotomy between spirit and body must be called into question; we can neither affirm "spirit" in an empty, unquestioned sense nor turn the body into an article of faith for a worldview (GA 69: 206).

What could defeat communism? Heidegger now seems to have little hope that National Socialism can overcome it. Race and its cultivation are just more subjectivist power-concepts determined by modernity (GA 69: 223). As for Anglo-American liberal egalitarianism, Heidegger sees it as little more than a hypocritical communism wearing the masks of Christian and bourgeois morality. Liberalism must be destroyed if modernity is to be overcome (GA 69: 208–9). Communism can be defeated only by itself: incapable of rising to the level of the history of beyng, it will destroy itself by mobilizing for total war (GA 69: 209–10).

Standing apart from this grim spectacle, Heidegger seeks a kind of knowledge that has no utility, but remains within the event of beyng (GA 69: 197) and awaits the final god (GA 69: 211–14). Expressing a similar mood in another wartime text, he sighs at the "power-based, external strengthening of the Reich" that is pursued by "fools whom defeats do not teach to meditate, any more than victories do." He resigns himself to letting such machination take its course: "all must be as it is" (GA 74: 36).

Any reader who may take heart from Heidegger's attacks on Nazi ideology and hope to see him draw closer to liberal or leftist points of view will be disappointed. All political systems demand a blind "*faith in faith*" (GA 67: 115). All ideology is a thoughtless vulgarization of the metaphysics of ideas that must ultimately be blamed on Plato's idea of the good (GA 67: 40–41)—and perhaps, in the case of liberalism and communism, on "*Judeo-Christian domination*" (GA 66: 39/30). Heidegger is never able to see liberalism as anything more than the triumph of the calculating and rapacious subject. He looks upon democratic idealism and "cultural optimism" with contempt (GA 66: 39/30), seeing the "'common sense' [Heidegger uses the English words] of the democracies" as essentially identical to "the rational conformity to plan of 'total authority'" (GA 66: 234/207 tm).

The fate of our subjectivistic age is nihilism—the happening in which being loses its sense or truth. With Nietzsche, this process has reached its philosophical end, but the consummation of nihilism is still to be carried out in culture and politics. Which peoples are destined to fulfill this fate? Heidegger speculates that the encounter between Germany and Russia—not on a military, but on a metaphysical level—will be decisive (GA 69: 120). The future mission of Russia (not of Bolshevism) is the salvation of the earth; the mission of the Germans (a mission for their thought, Heidegger emphasizes) is the salvation of the world (GA 69: 108, 119).

As for the sector of humanity that is destined to bring machination to its acme, it is neither German nor Russian. Bolshevism is capable only of "destruction," not of "devastation, for which the highest spirituality remains necessary" (GA 67: 147). The ultimate devastation, the "erection of the counter-essence of machination, is reserved for Americanism," which is more horrible than "Asiatic wildness": it is the ultimate rootless oblivion of being, dressed up in mendacious moralism (GA 67: 150; cf. GA 70: 97–98). Americanism "represents modernity in its unconditional counter-essence."[55] In these statements, the "counter-essence" (*Unwesen*) of machination and modernity is not the opposite of these phenomena, but their inner, perverse unfolding; we will soon consider the concept more closely.

Heidegger broods on the war in similarly dark terms. The ideologies of liberalism, fascism, and communism are bound to clash, even though they are metaphysically the same: they are all expressions of the overpowering essence of power, which requires "a planetary opponent" (GA 66: 18/14, cf. 20). Such war does not rise above the enemy who is to be overpowered, but sinks into "the lowest realm of opposition" (GA 69: 153/132). This new, boundless kind of war makes the entire reality of a nation subservient to it (GA 69: 44). But this is not to say that Heidegger is a pacifist. "World peace (in the Christian-Jewish-ambiguous sense)" is no less machinational than world war (GA 66: 28/22 tm). Both are attempts to dominate and order beings, to make them available as exploitable resources. In our age, the significance of even the most "peaceful" things lies in power and overpowering.

Heidegger looks to the event of appropriation for salvation, and not to human action; he now views "activism" with contempt (GA 67: 39–40) and says philosophy cannot provide a foundation for "the 'active life'" (GA 66: 52/42). He approvingly quotes Heraclitus's scorn for political activity.[56] Revolutions lead only to "deracination" and "destruction" (GA 66: 66/54 tm); by trying to reverse the inception, they get stuck unwittingly in the past. Neither conservatism nor revolution is an authentically historical relation to the inception (GA 67: 39, GA 69: 23).

In sum, what we learn from Heidegger's secret manuscripts of the thirties is that he came to see Nazism (at least in its actual and official form) as an extreme instance of the late modern metaphysics of the will to power. Where he had hoped for a founding of the *Volk* as a new inception, Nazism posited the *Volk* as a settled thing. Where he had hoped for an awakening of shared selfhood, Nazism developed a collective subjectivism. Where he had hoped for emergency, Nazism implemented imperial control.

Does he condemn Nazism, then? The answer is not so easy. We must turn to his journals, the *Black Notebooks*, to understand his attitude toward what he calls the *Un-wesen*.

A JOURNAL OF COUNTER-ESSENCE

The ominous-sounding *Black Notebooks* range from the 1930s to the 1970s. In addition to their general name, which literally refers to the color of their binding, the notebooks were divided by Heidegger into several series that bear vague titles such as *Überlegungen* (*Considerations*) and *Anmerkungen* (*Annotations*).

These texts were kept secret for decades, and they still harbor mysteries. In fact, they often speak of the need "to write out of a great reticence" (GA 94: 28/22); the very "essence of being" is "a *taciturnity that conceals*" (GA 94: 52/40). With publication comes publicity, and with publicity come superficiality and sensationalism—as is evident in some existing discussions of the notebooks. Heidegger would be indignant at this reception, but would also take it as proof of his point that "yanking everything into the public sphere means destroying all genuine Dasein" (GA 94: 158/116 tm). Still, he himself chose to preserve these notebooks and to provide for their eventual publication in the *Gesamtausgabe*. It is fortunate that he did, as they give us an intimate view of his attitudes toward the events of the thirties and beyond, including the ascendancy of Hitler, the consolidation of the Nazi regime, and the Second World War.

The Genre of the *Black Notebooks*

Before we survey the content of the *Black Notebooks*, we have to consider their genre and how they should be read. This question has become particularly pressing when it comes to Heidegger's malicious comments about Jews. It is incumbent on all readers to review these comments—which we will consider in some detail below—and to consider how deeply his thought was distorted by prejudice.[57] However, the anti-Jewish passages have sometimes been quoted out of context, with little reflection on the genre of the text in which they are situated. Some interpreters have then systematized them, articulating a doctrine that connects them through a logic that is allegedly at work in Heidegger's thought. In an extreme version of this practice, it is claimed that the *Black Notebooks*, as the final element of the *Gesamtausgabe*, represent the keystone of Heidegger's thought, and the statements about Jews constitute the essential teaching of the notebooks. Heidegger's entire philosophy is thus unmasked as systematically antisemitic.

But what kind of texts are the *Black Notebooks*? Heidegger calls them "attempts at simple naming—not statements, much less sketches for a planned system" (GA 94: 1/1 tm). As translator Richard Rojcewicz puts it, these are "notes to self" (GA 94 trans. vii). Still, it is clear that Heidegger thought they had value: he reread them, adding some cross-references and compiling partial indexes.

Inevitably, they appeal to our curiosity about the man Martin Heidegger and provide material for biographical and psychological theories. The tone is more personal than in most of his writings, and the first-person singular appears much more frequently. Still, this is not a conventional diary; one very rarely gets a sense of what he was doing on any particular day, although there are occasional descriptions of weather and landscape (e.g., GA 94: 325–26) or flashes of childhood memories (e.g., GA 94: 488). Something more is at stake than the vices or virtues of an individual, and Heidegger insists that thoughts with a philosophical dimension cannot simply be "explained through a bringing in of the 'personal'" (GA 94: 328/239, cf. 439, 475).

Are these texts works of philosophy, then? Philosophy (or "thinking") is certainly one of their main themes: what is demanded of thinking, how the contemporary world is failing to meet these demands, and how to prepare for the thinking of the future. But in general, Heidegger is not working out fundamental philosophical questions and problems, or breaking new philosophical ground; he is reflecting on philosophy as part of a more general meditation on his times. One could plausibly argue that the *Black Notebooks* are not philosophy at all, but a collection of attitudes and opinions. However, there is rarely a well-demarcated border between an individual's philosophical and unphilosophical views. For those who want to understand where Heidegger was "coming from," and how, as he saw it, his ideas related to his own times, the notebooks are indispensable reading.

The *Black Notebooks* are not just a personal diary, then—but not a philosophical treatise, either. As editor Peter Trawny suggests, they can best be called thought journals (*Denktagebücher*) (GA 94: 530). They have affinities to Kierkegaard's journals, Levinas's *Carnets de captivité*, and Wittgenstein's later texts. While it is tempting to extract statements from a thought journal out of context, particularly when they are offensive or outrageous, Heidegger fought throughout his life against readers' tendency to take thoughts as theses.

The basic presupposition of Heidegger's hardest critics, and even of some of his defenders, seems to be that a philosopher possesses a philosophy—a set of doctrines that are present in the philosopher's mind and are expressed in his texts. Every statement in the philosopher's writings must be fit together with every other statement, until his philosophy as a whole has been reconstructed; it can then be subjected to critique. But this conception, which I will call the doctrinal approach, contradicts some of Heidegger's most persistent thoughts. He has no philosophy at all, he declares in 1925 (GA 20: 417), in 1932 (GA 35: 83), and again around 1940 (GA 96: 100, 193). He repeatedly argues that propositions derive from a more fundamental unconcealment, which is always shadowed by concealment. He describes his writings as "ways, not works" (GA 1: iv)—paths through the dark forest, which often become *Holzwege*—"woodpaths" that may lead to a clearing, but also force us to backtrack. This kind of thinking is not a set of doctrines at all, but an enterprise and an experience. It is a process, not a possession.

The assumptions behind the doctrinal approach are also contradicted by familiar psychological realities and by the experience of anyone who has attempted to pursue philosophy. One is not born with a fully formed philosophy in one's head, but gradually comes to pursue questions and intimations that are transformed through the experience of dialogue, reading, and writing. Writing philosophy is a process of discovery that unfolds in the tension between what one wants to say and what one finds oneself saying. Of course, one may try to order one's views into a systematic doctrine, but that doctrine never completely obscures the process that led to it—and often the process remains thought-provoking even when the doctrine has been refuted. Around every system there lingers a haze of more or less articulated, more or less consistent thoughts that suggest a variety of dimensions and alternatives.

When one begins to write an entry in a thought journal, one rarely has a clearly developed idea that is now simply being vented. The idea takes shape as it is written, and the author may be surprised by a question, paradox, or objection that arises in the course of writing. An idea in a journal is not necessarily an affirmation: the entry may be an experiment, a hypothesis, or a *Holzweg*. And a thought journal may not be a balanced presentation of the various aspects of a philosopher's views, but rather a place where the author typically goes with certain urges that can be satisfied in this kind of writing.

These realities of the philosophical enterprise and the journal genre may be especially pertinent to the *Black Notebooks*, which are neither a methodical investigation like *Being and Time* nor tightly knit essays like Heidegger's shorter publications. How do they show their exploratory and experimental character? How did he use his notebook entries after their initial composition? What roles do various types of writing play in his thinking?

Heidegger's need for his notebooks evidently waxed and waned; he turned to them only at certain times, in certain moods. A purely numerical indication of this fact is the variable frequency of his entries. He wrote the equivalent of about 400 printed pages during 1932–1937. In 1938–1941, the volume swells to approximately 800 pages. From the most violent years of the war, 1942–1945, we have only about 50 pages. But in 1946–1948, he writes some 450 pages, and in 1948–1951, 400 more.

In the notebooks, Heidegger seems to develop thoughts as they come to him, write until he is satisfied for the moment, and turn to a new thought as needed. However, the notebooks are not a random collection of separable texts. Words and ideas ebb and flow, and currents run for a while between entries, establishing shared themes that come in waves. For a period, he will return persistently to a certain trope or word, but he often ends by rejecting that line of thought.

For example, the earlier entries return obsessively to the theme of greatness, as Heidegger evidently hopes that Germany will find its way to a spiritual rebirth in connection with its political revolution, but worries about whether greatness is being correctly understood by the regime. "What is politically right and great, to bring the people back to itself, becomes arbitrary and petty as a worldview—an idolizing of the people" (GA 94: 223/163 tm). "The sign of *greatness* . . . is never gigantism as the sheer mass of the achievements, but—the unrepeatable simplicity of decisions" (GA 94: 450/326 tm).

By 1938, however, he thinks that the hidden emergency of decision lies "outside of every appraisal of greatness" (GA 95: 121/94):

> . . . it must be asked whether even greatness and what is great . . . are not merely "historiological [*historische*] categories," hidden forms of calculation without an origination in beyng itself. At the very least, the concept of greatness is still ambiguous. Either this concept refers to something towering which is looked up to and in relation to which a distance is experienced; and then the calculative and historiological are still providing the measure. Or else greatness means the incomparable and that which does not at all admit of comparison . . . but *in this way* then what is great can no longer be named such . . . what is in this way grasped as "great" refuses to be made public and in such refusal hides its essence. [GA 95: 122/94–95 tm]

The doubts continue in later passages: "To want to *strive* for 'greatness' is a dwarfish beginning" (GA 95: 288/225 tm). The word "greatness" "mistakenly suggests evaluation and calculation" (GA 95: 430/335; cf. 195, 283, 319).

The change in Heidegger's thinking is more dramatic when it comes to "the history of beyng." The word *Seynsgeschichte* pervades his thought in the thirties, frequently in connection with the verb *geschehen*. Especially in earlier entries, he often speaks of the happening of being (GA 94: 6, 29, 57, 59, 62, 95, 97). But the concept of the history of beyng runs aground in a startling entry dating from the late forties that one could take as an attempt to hammer the final nail into the coffin of the thirties: "In appropriation, nothing happens. Here there is no happening anymore; no destiny either; for even sending still essences on the basis of opposition. In appropriation, the essence of history is abandoned. The talk of the history of beyng is an embarrassment and a euphemism. . . . In appropriation there is no sequence, no going and coming" (GA 97: 382). It would be rash to conclude that Heidegger wants to think of appropriation as an atemporal or permanent condition; instead, it operates with "suddenness" (GA 97: 391–92, 403). It is not a type of movement (*Be-wegung*), not because it is immobile but because it is waying (*Wegen*) itself (GA 97: 412). Is this not a happening, then? We cannot pursue this fundamental question about Heidegger's late thought here, but it is clear that he is at least trying to set aside a crucial concept from the thirties.[58]

We often find Heidegger trying out new concepts and expressions, only some of which reach his publications. For example, he experiments with writing *Seyn* with an X through it (e.g., GA 97: 218, 222, 238, 253). This graphic device entered his essay for Ernst Jünger, "Über 'Die Linie,'" later published as *Zur Seinsfrage* (GA 9: 411–16/310–14).

An example of a concept that, to my knowledge, does not make it past the pages of the *Black Notebooks* is "postscript" (*Nachschrift*). This word means "neither the copying and recording of something already written nor a text issued after another as its expansion"; it is "near-script" (*Nähe-Schrift*), written "from the neighborhood of the danger in appropriation" (GA 97: 344). "The simplest handiwork, which also becomes the most precious, is the handwriting of the postscript" (GA 97: 346). The meaning does not crystallize into a consistent, definable term, and he drops the word *Nachschrift* after a few attempts (GA 97: 336, 358, 376). But what is at stake in this word is the way a certain kind of writing attempts to approach a matter without either recording previously formulated thoughts or attempting to communicate, for "postscript is not for readers" (GA 97: 363). This kind of writing, whatever one may call it, is characteristic of the *Black Notebooks* as thought journals.

The ebb and flow of thoughts should inoculate us against taking particular statements as "Heidegger's philosophy," even if they are repeated. It is safer to say that the journals document phases of his interests, or paths he wished to pursue. Some are well-traveled avenues for several years, only to fall into disuse later on. Some are smaller trails to which he occasionally returns. Some are brief excursions into texts that he may never revisit, such as a quotation from *Moby-Dick* (GA 97: 431). This flux of thoughts will frustrate an interpreter who follows the doctrinal approach, so it is tempting to pick the statements that fit one's preferred conception of the supposed Heideggerian system, while disregarding those that do not. A more open-minded interpreter can consider each journal entry in its own right, turning it over to discover its meanings, reflecting on its possible truth and untruth, while not failing to neglect its connections to other entries.

How did Heidegger intend to use these journals? What role did they play in his thinking? How did they contribute to his publications?

Peter Trawny tells us that these are clean manuscripts with hardly any corrections (GA 94: 534). One possibility is that Heidegger had some initial, messier drafts that he rewrote, but Trawny reports that no such first drafts are known to exist. Another possibility is that he felt less need to perfect these journal entries than texts that he planned to read out loud or put into print. A typescript presenting a selection from the *Black Notebooks* is extant; this selection omits all comments on Jews, among other things.[59] Whether it was Martin Heidegger, Fritz Heidegger, or another who created this selection, it is in keeping with Martin's tendency after the war to edit his earlier writings to make them more acceptable. At the same time, its very existence indicates that the more complete *Black Notebooks* as we have them in the *Gesamtausgabe* are probably not edited texts, but were composed as they stand.

Although it seems unlikely that Heidegger rewrote his journals, it is clear that he reread them: there are frequent cross-references, including references to later pages. The indices he prepared for each notebook give us a clue to what topics he found most interesting or worth pursuing as he reread his texts.

Was Heidegger planning to publish any parts of the notebooks at the time when he was writing them? Were they intended as paths to public statements, as apparently is the case with Pascal's *Pensées* and Nietzsche's notes for *The Will to Power*?

It is impossible to write a journal in full confidence that it will never be seen by others, especially if the author is well known. There are signs that Heidegger imagined that the public might read his journals someday—in particular, a "note for jackasses" that insists that his thoughts on Jews have nothing to do with antisemitism (GA 97: 159). This note attempts (unsuccessfully) to forestall a future judgment that will be made by the public sphere that Heidegger so hated. That hatred must have had its limits, at least in his old age, because he did provide for the eventual publication of the *Black Notebooks* instead of destroying them. We do not know when he reached a firm decision that they should be read by posterity, but they were brought to the archives shortly before his death.

However, it is unlikely that Heidegger originally intended most of his journal entries for the public eye. Their goal is exploration, not publication:

"The real result of a text that one writes for oneself is always that one has not understood oneself. How is one supposed to dare, then, to make oneself understandable to others? So?—to *write*, yes, for it brings to light the not-yet-understanding; but not to publish" (GA 97: 466). This kind of "silence is more difficult than 'speaking' and 'printing,' for it involves bearing, enduring, what one *has* to say and yet can say only in a space that must first be prepared by the saying" (GA 97: 149). The thoughts in a journal unfold by being written; they are necessarily tentative, unready, and liable to be misinterpreted if they are published.

Nevertheless, sometimes he seems to be debating whether the eventual publication of some of his intimate thoughts might be worthwhile. The main point in favor of such publication is that, with multiple copies, some of his texts might survive a catastrophe (GA 97: 375). Of course, this presupposes that such survival is desirable.

As far as I know, the main public use that Heidegger made of the notebooks during his lifetime was to select certain sayings and publish them under the title *Aus der Erfahrung des Denkens* (in GA 13). Like Presocratic fragments, these sayings stand in the published text as enigmatic and evocative utterances—stripped of their original context and juxtaposed with other fragments. The sentences feel as if they allude to a wider, unsaid realm. In the *Black Notebooks*, this unsaid—or some of it—was said.

A particularly significant case is the entry from which Heidegger extracted the sentence, "He who thinks greatly must err greatly" (GA 13: 81/TP 9). This well-known statement is usually seen as an acknowledgment of his own missteps, but not as an apology. In fact, it would be the worst apology imaginable: it is not a personal *mea culpa*, but a generality addressed to no one in particular; it affirms Heidegger's greatness (the concept returns here, despite the doubts we have noted); it speaks of error, not fault; and it legitimates error by claiming that it is inevitable.

In the context of the *Black Notebooks*, this statement is one of many reflections on errancy that harmonize with Heidegger's published thoughts on the issue.[60] The term "errancy" is introduced in the second draft of the essay "On the Essence of Truth," from October 1930 (GA 80.1: 372–73). But its roots lie in Heidegger's thought of the twenties: "What has been uncovered and disclosed . . . has been disguised and closed off by idle talk, curiosity, and ambiguity" (SZ 222). The sense of beings gets distorted and impoverished by our "falling" way of being. Even when we get our facts straight, we tend to interpret them in superficial ways. And errancy is not just an everyday temptation; it is insurmountable, because truth itself is finite and thus requires untruth. "Complete opening—*would be no opening any more (pure openness—nothing)*."[61]

In the *Black Notebooks*, the statement on erring "greatly" appears within a long postwar entry (GA 97: 174–79). Heidegger begins the entry by drawing a contrast between being "old" by staying true to one's original thought and fruitlessly attempting to stay young by keeping up with the times. His single thought is "being and time," and he has gotten no further than the book by that title. "Yes, Heidegger has remained standing," he writes in the third person.[62] He stayed true to his thought even "when he tried in 1933 to grasp a historical moment directly as an opportunity for a possible total meditation of the West. Because Heidegger keeps standing where he stood, he had to err. As a consequence of the error, and not the other way around, he had to deceive himself for a few months about the superficial and contemporary" (GA 97: 174). The ground of the error lies in *Being and Time. Being and Time* thinks the truth of being as Da-sein, which, as the "there," sustains the clearing of being. Da-sein's belonging to being is what *Being and Time* calls "thrownness." The truth of being sets Da-sein free by throwing it, but also holds itself back (GA 97: 175). Readers wrongly take "thrownness" as an anthropological or crypto-theological concept. The throw of being brings about a clearing toward which Dasein is authentically open and resolved. Appropriation is "this throwing-temporalizing essence of being, in which the own [*das Eigenhafte*] in every form rests" (GA 97: 176). The thought of appropriation is where Heidegger's thinking must remain (GA 97: 177). This does not mean settling down in a doctrine, but developing the same thought in its concealed sameness. This requires attention to history, which is how the throw of being holds sway. Thinking must converse with the history of being, including metaphysics. He refers to his 1934 *Logic* course as evidence for his "complete withdrawal from *every* sort of 'political' and quasi-political activity" (GA 97: 178). He now reflects on retrospection itself: as he thinks over his way, what he says seems firmer than the various stages of the way, which are full of possibilities for progress, regress, and straying. The path now seems clearer and easier than it actually was. True persistence requires taking a risk and embarking on the unsustainable as a necessary transition, so it would be petty to take everything he has attempted as something enduring. The didactic responsibilities of a professor have their advantages, but can also block one's own thinking (GA 97: 178). "Whoever *thinks* greatly must err greatly" (GA 97: 179). The erring thinker has to expect that misguided and ambiguous elements in his thought will be identified with the essence at which he is aiming, and the entirety of his thinking will be discarded. The basis of this danger is the absolute solitude of ontohistorical thinking. Heidegger concludes with the thought that this solitude stands beyond moral good and evil, but must not become arrogant.

How was this entry composed? It seems that it originated, as many philosophical reflections do, in a paradox. Heidegger wants to explore the idea that he has remained standing at the same place only by wandering. In doing so, he develops interpretations of his philosophical work and his political behavior. Near the end of the entry, the pithy statement that he was later to publish emerges. In its erratic course, the text illustrates the point he wants to make about errancy. But the texts that he published during his lifetime are typically much more artful than this one—because they are, as he puts it here, didactic rather than solitary.

In selecting one sentence from this entry for publication (GA 13: 81/TP 9), Heidegger removed the emphasis from *denkt* and prefaced the sentence with a brief description of a butterfly swaying on a flower in the summer breeze and three other sayings. The juxtaposed sentences create echoes that are not present in the entry we have reviewed: *Mut—Anmutung—Denken—Großmut—groß denkt*. New trains of thought are fostered, and the seasonal setting suggests that thinking has its times, its ebbs and flows. The retrospective aspect of the original entry nearly disappears. The original emphasis on standing and staying true to the origin is faintly echoed in the image of the butterfly. This is an experiment in bringing out new facets of a sentence by putting it in a different light. By recovering the original context we can confirm that, as readers have long suspected, the phrase originated in a moment when Heidegger was defensively reflecting on his own political error.

We can venture some guesses now about the role of the various genres of Heidegger's writing in the ecology of his thought.

The texts that he published during his life are his most polished creations, showing careful attention to the choice of words and sequence of thoughts. They are intended for an educated but indeterminate public, so they are exoteric. Heidegger quotes Leibniz: *Quis me non nisi editis novit, non novit.* "Whoever knows me only from my publications does *not* know me" (GA 97: 325). To be sure, such a reader would have only a partial understanding; but Heidegger published texts only if he thought they were useful for grasping some aspect of his philosophical project.

As for the lecture courses, he refers to them as a "mask" (GA 94: 243/178, cf. 257). Their "'interpretations' can easily be shown to be 'historiologically' false"; "in each case, the interpretation is an overinterpretation, for it goes beyond the limits of what 'lies there'" in order to "say the unsaid" (GA 96: 211/166 tm). The lectures are exoteric, as they are intended for a student audience and express Heidegger's own thoughts primarily by way of interpretations of other writers. However, most of the courses are rich in analyses and comments that suggest his more esoteric thoughts, so there is no need to assume that they are systematically deceptive. For example, GA 45 includes various passages that are taken almost verbatim from the contemporaneous, esoteric *Contributions to Philosophy*.

The editors of the *Gesamtausgabe* use the term "unpublished treatises [*Abhandlungen*]" for writings such as the *Contributions*. I prefer "unpublished meditations," since "treatises" wrongly suggests that these texts fall into the same genre as *Being and Time*. Here Heidegger returns obsessively to certain clusters of words and ideas, sketching connections and experimenting with phrases that he hopes will express a basic experience. He attempts to spark better thoughts from the friction among a set of core words that he brings together. "Thinking must think anew, fifty or a hundred times, the Same, and attempt to arrive at the place of the Same, until something simple once succeeds" (GA 69: 30/28). Although these texts were withheld from the public during Heidegger's life, he would reject the idea that they are "private"; that word suggests a subjective and idiosyncratic realm, when what is at stake in these texts is a dedicated dwelling with being (GA 96: 220; GA 97: 65–66).

Something similar is at work in his verses (GA 81), where conceptual resonances are brought out by rhythms and rhymes, and his dialogues (GA 77), where thoughts emerge from the back-and-forth of friendly interlocutors.

Heidegger's extensive correspondence, much of which is yet to be published, is still another genre. Here, one must judge the rhetoric and content of each document with reference to its intended reader.

Finally, the *Black Notebooks* are akin to the unpublished meditations: they are exploratory spaces where words and thoughts are generated. But they also partake of the more personal and occasional character of the journal genre. Thus, they include analyses of the times from the perspective of Heidegger's thought—attempts at critical dissection of the zeitgeist or of the metaphysical underpinnings of contemporary movements. There are also reflections on Heidegger's own course of thought, way of thinking, and situation in the world. He had little interest in making such things public during his lifetime, and we can easily see why: he distrusted public discourse, felt unjustly persecuted, and did not want to invite the world into his house. But he needed to write these journals for himself, in order to develop his thoughts and feelings.

The doctrinal approach to reading a philosopher aims at enabling the reader to master a system and pass judgment on it. An appropriate reading of the *Black Notebooks* makes a more strenuous demand: that we learn to wander, to shift our thoughts as the writer shifts his, yet to keep in view the persistence that coexists with the erring, the simplicity that emerges from the pattern of paths—all while remembering to keep blazing our own trails. "Paths must be *gone along* if they are original; only conventional paths can be followed. Every portrayal of an original path, if it is justified at all, becomes yet another path, and in this way it abandons portraying and reporting" (GA 95: 214/166 tm).

Tarrying with the Negative

What, then, is the content of the *Black Notebooks*? What does Heidegger think in them—not as a system or doctrine, but as a series of explorations? As we answer these questions, we have to consider the tonality of his thoughts—his stance toward the phenomena he is describing.

The predominant mood of the notebooks could be called sour. These journals were a place where Heidegger went to vent his spleen—characterizing everything from the movies to hostile readings of his own work as manifestations of an age devoid of thought. He never tires of exposing what he sees as the pettiness, blindness, and bankruptcy of every phenomenon around him, from the "banality of . . . American pragmatism" (GA 94: 191/140) to "the ascendancy of Catholicism" (GA 94: 186/136). On this last point, Heidegger sees any turn to Christianity as a deluded "escape" from the modern predicament (GA 94: 40/31); Western history is unthinkable without Christianity, but its creative power is long gone and "the great decisions do not occur there" (GA 94: 523/380).[63] The picture is bleak: "The world is now out of joint; the earth is a field of destruction" (GA 94: 218/160). The only hope is "to learn great joy in little things" (GA 94: 321/233) while we await the dawn: the world "is no longer a world, or, said more truly—it never was a world. We are standing only in its preparation" (GA 94: 210/154).

This sourness sometimes becomes misanthropy. "What does it signify that the human masses are worth so little they could be annihilated in *one* stroke?" (GA 94: 282/207, cf. GA 65: 113). Once the war is under way, he writes that "the final chapter [of technology] will consist in the earth itself blowing up and the current humanity disappearing. That will be no misfortune but, instead, the first purification *of being* from its most profound deformation on account of the supremacy of beings" (GA 96: 238/187; cf. GA 71: 101–2).

Only two groups emerge in the notebooks as having the potential for something other than machination: the Germans, who Heidegger hopes will someday recognize their true vocation as the people of poets and thinkers, and the Russians, whom he distinguishes from Bolshevism, a mere Western import (GA 96: 47–48, 56–57, 109–10, 124, 134, 139, 148, 235, 237, 241; cf. GA 69: 108). Some of these thoughts on Russia may have been inspired by the Hitler-Stalin pact, but Heidegger takes care to note that his interest in Russia goes back to 1908 (GA 96: 148).[64]

It is easy to tally up the many things Heidegger criticizes, and the few that he favors. But there are two caveats here. First, we must be clear that his standard for judgment is not a moral one, even though it is difficult not to read some of his observations as so-called value judgments. Morality, he insists, is a superficial criterion, based on a bankrupt metaphysics (GA 95: 13). The Christianity that sustained it for so long is now a pathetic remnant, "the loudest possible screaming about the long-since-dead God" (GA 95: 396/309). Nonreligious but suprahistorical moral ideals of a Platonic or Kantian sort are also dead for a thinker who insists on the historicity of being itself. As for the moral pretension of Anglo-American democracies, Heidegger sees it as a hypocritical ideology, a veneer for the profit motive (GA 96: 114–15). Heidegger refers to American hypocrisy as part of his rejection of the moral stance in general. He attempts to think beyond supposedly childish categories such as moral good and evil, or optimism and pessimism. Such categories are myopic: they focus on the benefit or harm of one, a few, or many without reflecting on the deeper currents of being and Dasein. "What is *'good'* is not the 'pleasant,' nor what brings 'happiness,' nor the beneficial, nor the useful, nor the obligatory, nor a mere value; instead, it is the steadfastness of Dasein in freedom on the basis of an affiliation with beyng" (GA 96: 159/123).

The second caveat is that Heidegger denies that his criticisms are simply negative. This means that despite his numerous critiques of Nazi ideology, it is untenable to say that he resists Nazism.[65] However, by the late 1930s he is hardly a straightforward supporter of Nazism either. His position is more complicated than any "simple calculation of yes or no";[66] in order to understand him and to develop an accurate critique of his political views, we must grasp his two-sided relation to National Socialism as an *Un-wesen*—a counter-essence.

We can begin with some facts on which every decent judge will agree: The Nazi regime was a reign of terror that operated with massive brutality. Hitler's willful rampage through Europe demonstrated his criminal madness. The atrocities of the Nazis embodied a nationalism gone wild. Nothing can justify this ideology that despised the mind itself.

Do these truths immediately damn Heidegger? Not at all. In fact, I take these characterizations of Hitler and the Nazis from postwar entries in the *Black Notebooks*. They are his own judgments on Nazism.[67]

So does he condemn Nazism? That would be a rash conclusion, first of all because we must attend to the context of these phrases. They were largely written during the Allied occupation and partition of Germany, which involved purges and reorganizations of various sorts, including Heidegger's own denazification hearings and forced retirement. His attitude in this period is never contrite, but rather indignant and bitter. He pushes back against the talk of German guilt, rejecting calls for morality and justice as nothing but the spirit of revenge, disguised in the remnants of a bankrupt Christianity

(GA 97: 64, 99, 117, 129, 134–35, 146–47). All his comments on the Nazis are embedded in denunciations of postwar developments, which he often portrays as worse than Nazism. One hyperbolic passage claims that contemporary "thoughtlessness . . . exceeds by many thousands of degrees the irresponsible misdeeds with which Hitler raged around Europe" (GA 97: 250).

In short, Heidegger is unapologetic, and many entries in his journals exemplify the denial, evasion, and defensiveness that is typical of people who are doing their best to avoid the unpleasant sensation of a bad conscience. There is no apologizing for the unapologetic, and none of my interpretation should be understood as an apologia. The complexities of his positions should not be abused to construct excuses for his behavior or thought. His attitudes toward both the essence and the counter-essence involve an appalling indifference to concrete victims, whose suffering he disregards as merely inessential. The point is not to exonerate him, but to understand his ambiguous attitude.

Still, it is a fact that he describes Nazism as brutal and criminal. But could these descriptions just be a sop thrown to public opinion? Are they an attempt at posthumous public relations? This possibility is not to be rejected out of hand. In many of his voluminous notebook entries from the late 1940s, he is clearly trying to defend himself—either in his own mind or to posterity. He looks back over his acts and thoughts, doing his best to minimize the extent of his support for Nazism. Many of these self-interpretations made their way into other accounts and became the "official" Heideggerian exculpation. We now know that the story that he, sincerely or insincerely, told to himself and to others was at best one-sided. At least through the mid-1930s, he forcefully attempted to influence the direction of Nazism, clinging to a belief in its "inner truth and greatness," and he never sympathized with the enemies of the regime.

However, it would be inadequate to take the postwar *Black Notebooks* as a whitewashing operation, because as much as Heidegger criticizes Nazi ideology there, he also makes his rejection of liberalism, Christianity, and morality quite clear. His disgust with the postwar order of Europe is obvious. His contempt for the public—which would include us today—is boundless, and he surely knew that many remarks in these notebooks would be considered unacceptable by the victors of World War II. So if the purpose of his postwar entries were to make himself palatable to the postwar world, they would be a complete failure. It is more reasonable to take them as genuine expressions of his self-perception and his perception of the world at that time, even though those perceptions involve selective remembering and distortions.

There is another, and more fundamental, reason to take Heidegger's postwar characterizations of Nazism seriously: in entries of the thirties, he attempts to give concepts such as "criminality" and "brutality" ontological content. He does not just adopt these terms after the war and give lip service to anti-Nazi discourse; years before, he gave them specifically Heideggerian interpretations and applied them to Nazism at length. We will soon look at these concepts more closely.

For now, let us return to the postwar comments on Nazism and focus on another word that has some philosophical depth. Heidegger speaks of "the irresponsible misdeeds" of Hitler (GA 97: 250). "Misdeeds" is my attempt to translate *Unwesen*, which in its everyday use means something like "malicious mischief," "disorder," or "disturbance." But *Unwesen* is an ontological word, based on *Wesen* (which can mean "essence" or "entity" depending on the context). The German prefix *un-* is not simply a negation, like the English "un-," but connotes malignancy, deformity, or perversity. The *Un-wesen* is not the inessential, but the distorted essence or counter-essence—the degenerate genus, the deformed form. Heidegger, who chose his words carefully when being was at stake, is referring to the malignant essence of Adolf Hitler.

So does he reject this counter-essence? We cannot say simply that he does or does not—and at this point we have to take our leave once and for all from black-and-white, pro-or-con readings. The matter hinges on Heidegger's attitude toward the negative and perverse—or to put it in a word, *Un-wesen*. As early as 1930, in the second draft of "On the Essence of Truth," he writes, with reference to untruth: "Must we not retrieve what has been left aside until now, that is, *let in the counter-essence of the essence? . . . Letting in the counter-essence* is not an extra, dispensable addition to the knowledge of essence, but belongs to the innermost substance of the empowerment of essence" (GA 80.1: 367). The epigraph for the seventh volume of the *Überlegungen*, composed around 1938, states that "one who encounters the distorted essence [*Unwesen*] only negatively will also not ever be equal to the essence" (GA 95: 1/3). In a note to "The Age of the World Picture" from the same period, he writes that "the shadow is the manifest, though impenetrable, testimony of hidden illumination" (GA 5: 112/85).

In a crucial passage in the notebooks, dating from 1939, he applies this thought to Nazism:

> Thinking purely "metaphysically" (that is, in terms of the history of beyng), during the years 1930–1934 I saw in National Socialism the possibility of a transition into another inception and gave it this interpretation. Thereby I mistook and underestimated this "movement" in its authentic forces and inner necessities as also in the extent and kind of its greatness. Instead, what begins here is the consummation of modernity as regards the humanization of the human being in self-certain rationality—in a much more profound, that is, more encompassing and gripping way than in fascism. . . . The consummation required the decidedness of the historiological-technical in the sense of the Complete "Mobilization"

of all capacities of a humanity that has based itself upon itself. . . . On the basis of the full insight into the earlier deception about the essence and historical essential force of National Socialism, there results the necessity of its affirmation, and indeed on *thoughtful* grounds. This also means that this "movement" remains independent of its contemporary shape in each case, and of the duration of these directly visible forms. Yet how is it that such an essential affirmation is appreciated less, or not at all, in contrast to mere agreement, which is mostly superficial, clueless, or just blind? [GA 95: 408–9/318–19 tm]

This text makes it clear that although Nazism represents a modernity that Heidegger longs to transcend, his philosophical critique of modernity does not translate into resistance—to the contrary.

The words "consummation" (*Vollendung*) and "greatness" play key roles in this passage. Elsewhere, Heidegger associates both concepts with counter-essence. "'*Consummation*' of metaphysics—means fulfillment of its essence; consummation here does not mean perfection in the sense of the exclusion of the counter-essence, but precisely the developing inclusion of the counter-essence," which consists in the absence of questioning concerning being (GA 67: 15). "Greatness is the grounding of something inceptive, or since it also has its counter-essence, the extreme ossification of something already elapsed" (GA 96: 171/135).

Now we have to ask in what sense, on what level, Heidegger said yes to Nazism even after recognizing it as a counter-essence. Why did he affirm its monstrous "greatness" as the "consummation" of modernity? Just how thoroughly did he tarry with the negative, to use the Hegelian phrase?

The question of negativity in Heidegger could be the object of a voluminous study. As Gregory Fried has shown, confrontation as *Auseinandersetzung* or *polemos*, at its best in Heidegger's work, can be a form of deep respect for the opponent.[68] In one text where Heidegger takes Hegel as his opponent, it is precisely the question of negativity that is a main focus of the confrontation (GA 68). *Das Nichts* is, of course, a recurring theme in Heidegger's thought, and he constantly insists that being cannot be understood without a profound encounter with nothingness.[69] Similarly, truth is constantly shadowed by *lethe* or untruth.

The *Black Notebooks* include various thoughts on negation. Since Heidegger's critiques of an age in decline serve the purpose of preparing for a new inception (GA 94: 384–85), his negations are "the battle over the most essential affirmation of the full essence of beyng" (GA 95: 21/16). His descriptions of contemporary phenomena appear pessimistic only because the counter-essence "is taken negatively . . . since we are too small and too poor in resistance to experience . . . the self-refusal and to grasp this itself as beyng" (GA 95: 37/29). Ontohistorical thinking understands the deeper roots of the counter-essence: it "recognizes the ground of the necessity of the imminent era and its uncanny consistency" (GA 95: 221/172 tm). "If the *Un-wesen* in beyng fulfills the essence in case after case" (GA 97: 46), a confrontation with the counter-essence is a path to truth. In sum: "It is petty to think that what is brought to confrontation in an essential opposition, and in this confrontation is first set into the essence, is thereby merely rejected and becomes the object of mere negation—an object that then haunts us like an evil specter, which is never understood because it is never thought through, and cannot be" (GA 97: 180).

As we are about to see in some detail, the *Black Notebooks* describe the world of the thirties as a realm of the oblivion of being, dominated by brutality, machination, and criminality—all in special, Heideggerian senses. Those who work for the future must "stand amid the gigantic machination of a complete mobilization and at the same time harbor a passion for the great silence" (GA 96: 174–75/138). What does it mean to "stand amid" machination? It cannot be either indifferent objectivity or unadulterated rejection. Instead, Heidegger expresses a sort of horrified fascination. He cannot stop looking at the spectacle, which involves a certain suspense: "Which convulsion is essential enough to let a meditation arise? Or does the *brutalitas* have the last word? Has it perhaps already spoken this word, such that everything is still only an empty tottering on into the long ending?" (GA 95: 397/310).

Certainly, the language he uses often suggests that he abhors or disdains the phenomena of the times, but his attitude is not simply negative. For instance, he speaks with irritation of "*existentiell literati*" whose writing yields only "a disfigurement of the spirit of the age [that] tones down the '*brutalitas*' of the age and thereby impedes the great decisions" (GA 96: 18/15). In order for the age to reach a clear climax and crisis, its metaphysical brutality should not be disguised or retarded; it has to be faced and, as we have seen, "affirmed."

Heidegger thinks that humanity faces "an originary decision between the grounding of a truth of beyng and the raising up of the machination of beings to a definitive predominance" (GA 95: 278/217). This is the decision between "*the supremacy of machination and the sovereignty of the event*" (GA 96: 59/46). But the decision is not as simple as saying yes to one and no to the other, since "we will never *immediately* liberate 'beings' from machination" (GA 94: 425/309). Machination should not simply be represented as bad, either: "machination fosters the *Unwesen* of being. But the *Un-wesen* itself, since it is essential to the essence, is never to be depreciated" (GA 65: 126/99 tm).

By the same token, "saying no" as "the most essential yes" (GA 95: 20–21/16 tm) is not a wholehearted embrace, a sheer plunge into the *Un-wesen*. That would mean submitting to the machinational system and simply assuming one's role within it. Even if one attained great skill within that role, it would come at the cost of enslavement. As Heidegger says in a 1941 lecture course, "Technology is mastered only where it is affirmed from the outset and without reservation. That means the practical mastery of technology . . . already presupposes a metaphysical subjugation to technology" (GA 51: 17–18/14). (On the small scale, consider a video game "master": in order to become a top-scoring player, one has to accept the premises of the game and inhabit its world, developing reflexes that reflect its mechanisms, incorporating the game's parameters into one's own body and mind. One has to submit to the game in order to win.) Heidegger follows this comment with a clear allusion to the Third Reich as one of the regimes that are "knowingly planned to last millennia." The source of such phenomena is "metaphysical will," not individual dictators. While he is impressed with the depth of this will, his distance from it can be seen in his comment that the Greeks, far from fortifying themselves against downfall (*Untergang*), saw greatness in it (GA 51: 18/15).

For Heidegger, the will to power determines the character of action today. Two types, "the worker" and "the soldier," are the faces of the actual. Together, they are the kind of humanity that is called to carry out today's "world-convulsion" and direct our relation to beings (GA 51: 36/32). A clear source for his thoughts here is Jünger's *The Worker*, which portrays a world of "total mobilization" that empowers a new form of subjectivity. Heidegger takes Jünger to have painted a strikingly accurate picture of the metaphysical vision underlying the contemporary world, but the experience of being a worker and soldier does not necessarily bring insight into being (GA 51: 39/34). Absorption in the metaphysical game is not an understanding of the deeper ontohistorical currents.

Machination, Brutality, and Criminality

Having considered the genre of the *Black Notebooks* and Heidegger's ambiguous stance toward the "counter-essence" that he is describing, we can turn to three major concepts that he deploys: machination, brutality, and criminality. Again, these are not ethical or political concepts, but "ontohistorical" descriptions of how entities are revealed in our age. Such phenomena cannot simply be rejected or condemned, but must be acknowledged as essential to the way beings present themselves to us. It is also important to remember that these concepts are not intended as distinguishing characteristics of Nazism per se, but characterize late modernity in general and apply to left, right, and center. "National Socialism is not Bolshevism, which is not a Fascism—but both [right and left?] are machinational victories of machination—gigantic forms of the consummation of modernity—a calculated depletion of nationalities" (GA 96: 127/99).

We have already repeatedly encountered the word "machination" (*Ma-chenschaft*). It normally refers to scheming, but Heidegger does not mean it in this "superficial and derived" sense, and denies that it is a human creation (GA 96: 111/87). He takes it in an ontohistorical sense, drawing on its root *machen* or "making." It is a productive and manipulative understanding of beings as such, so that they appear as objects to be calculated, controlled, and transformed.[70] Machination is "the makeability of what is, which makes everything and makes up [i.e., constitutes] everything" (GA 66: 16/11 tm). Under the sway of machination, to be means to be a computable construction. This is the culmination of the subjectivism and objectivism of the modern age: we represent ourselves as self-conscious and willful subjects who stand against objects to be overpowered.

Machination fulfills the nihilistic destiny of Western metaphysics. In machination, "beings, as the effective and operative, 'have' the priority over 'being,' which gives itself out as the last vapor of mere thinking" (GA 95: 382/299). "The highest sovereignty of being as machination spreads round about itself a complete forgottenness of being" (GA 95: 385/301). Our obsession with the calculable and malleable blocks out any question about what else it may mean to be, or how we come to understand being in the first place; yet it was precisely a certain understanding of being that led us to interpret beings as calculable and malleable resources to begin with.

Heidegger tends to see machination as the inevitable outcome of the "first inception" of philosophy among the Greeks, who received the gift of being as presence but were not able to preserve the mystery of the giving, falling instead into the project of ascertaining correct claims about present *beings*. (For a compact genealogy of machination, see GA 65: 126–27.) Thus, "*What is now happening* is the *ending* of the history of the great inception of Western humanity; in this inception, the human being was called to the stewardship of beyng, although this calling was immediately transformed into the claim of representing beings in their machinational counter-essence" (GA 95: 96/75 tm).

The *Black Notebooks* portray machination as a fate that envelops the West, turning individuals into agents and spokesmen for the machinational understanding of what is. War and politics are merely the implementation of this metaphysics; there can be no winners and losers, but "all become the slaves of the history of beyng" (GA 96: 141/110). The "unconditional empowerment of makeability [*Machsamkeit*]" is not the work of individual personalities who "make" it; to the contrary, "unconditional power creates concurrently its own holders of that power. . . . The service toward the essence of power also enables the unchecked and unrestricted enlistment of everything and thus the transformation of each thing into the character of power" (GA 96: 186–87/146–47 tm).

In passage after passage, Heidegger portrays machination as a global counter-essence, an understanding of being that dominates all contemporary systems and events, leaving us little or no hope for extrication. "The power of machination . . . has reached its final stage; distinctions of peoples, nations, and cultures are now mere facades. No measures could be taken to impede or check machination . . . Everything is still entangled in the machinationally overfilled emptiness of the abandonment by being" (GA 96: 53/41–42). "The current world war is the extreme overturning of all beings into the unconditionality of machination" (GA 96: 173/136).

Heidegger's feelings about the Second World War as machination can best be gleaned from a selection of his letters. They combine a sense of doom in the face of the massive deployment of systems of domination with a persistent hope that, once the juggernaut has rolled on to its consummation, a thoughtful alternative can emerge.

Once again, the terrible specter of war looms on the horizon. But I still hope that it will be turned aside once more, and that meditation [*Besinnung*] will master the blind forces.[71]

What has long been decided, namely, the essence of modernity and the predominance of machination, is now driving toward its consummation. For those who think ahead, the present, despite its obtrusive grief and confusion, is already something past. Spiritual impulses and necessities for meditation will not arise from this world war, any more than they did from the first.[72]

As hard as things are . . . we can't just sink into empty brooding, but must work for the future; one way or the other, one day meditation will be needful, and through it, a turnabout [*Umdrehung*] will come into the world, compared to which the Copernican revolution was just a game.[73]

The complete mastery of technology has in advance produced a quite different kind of strategic thought. . . . The ruthless 'operation' is in itself also an unconditional commitment to the inner lawfulness of the unconditional mechanization of warfare. . . . Even so, yet other forces are necessary [which can] find their way out . . . to another inception. Yet these forces are still without space & without shape; but I believe *that they* are there.[74]

The question is not which "hemisphere" will predominate, for the whole sphere of the earth has entered the process of devastation. . . . But for some time, something else has found its inception [*angefangen*]. This is why I am publishing the Hölderlin lecture.[75]

What is now taking place over the entire planet is of such a kind that an essential event must be concealed within, even if we cannot yet see it & cannot yet speak of it. . . . Over everything there now lies a rubble of incongruity and strangeness, which is all the more disconcerting because it was heaped by one's own people over the hidden striving of its own essence to grope its way to its truth.[76]

Of course, after the war Heidegger does not think that machination has reached its end. He continues to reflect on the essence of modern technology, which he calls the *Ge-stell* in the 1949 Bremen Lectures (GA 79). The term has been translated in several ways; I like Gianni Vattimo's suggestion "im-position." In the light of im-position, beings are disclosed as what can be posited or ascertained through rational calculation, and then put in position so that they can serve the functions imposed on them by human will. Entities get broken into "pieces" that can mesh into a global system of production and exploitation. They become "standing reserve" or resources, which can yield energy for our projects—and we ourselves become "human resources."

In addition to machination, a second ontohistorical concept that stands out in the notebooks is "brutality." Sometimes Heidegger seems to use this word in its everyday sense, as when he distinguishes heroism from "purely physical virility (brutality)" (GA 94: 183/134) or speaks of "the mere brutality of a street fight" (GA 95: 438/341). There is also a somewhat more ontological concept of the brutal as the brute facts (cf. GA 95: 396): under the domination of machination, what *is* is "that which is effective and real, effectuated and effectuatable, the so-called 'facts' and the 'real'" (GA 96: 105/82).

But Heidegger's primary concept of brutality alludes to the "brute" as the subhuman animal. He portrays *brutalitas* as the necessary counterpart of *rationalitas* (GA 95: 402; GA 96: 18)—its *Un-wesen*, as it were. He rejects the simple valorization of the rational over the brutal, and attempts to see them as two sides of the same coin. (Similarly, several passages put culture on a par with barbarism: GA 95: 280, 294, 322; GA 96: 201; cf. GA 54: 103.) To view ourselves as *rational* animals is, at the same time, to assert our animality. Conversely, the "abandonment of the human being to animality does not exclude, but rather includes, the fostering of the 'spirit' and of 'psychic' assets, because 'spirit' and 'psyche' present interpretations of the human being only in terms of animality" (GA 96: 14/12). The modern form of the "rational animal" is split in two: we develop logical calculation to its extreme while indulging our bestial impulses. Thus, "The mark of the reality of everything real at the end of metaphysics is the *capacity for brutality*. This is what the 'mastering' of technology consists in" (GA 96: 253–54/201 tm).

That which in the future will have to called by the (not accidentally Latin) term *brutalitas*, namely, the unconditional machination of being . . . is a *reflection* of the essence of the human being, a reflection of the *animalitas* of the *animal rationale*—thus also and precisely a reflection of *rationalitas*. . . . *that* the human being had to be defined as *animal rationale* and *that* the *brutalitas* of beings will one day drive forth to its consummation—these have one and the same single ground in the *metaphysics* of being. [GA 95: 394–95/308]

Brutality is essential to machination, as Heidegger sees it: "to the consummation of machination in being, there corresponds and must correspond the unconditional *brutalitas* of humanity" (GA 95: 402/313). The "motorizing of humanity," most clearly implemented in the Soviet system, fulfills the brutalization of modern man (GA 96: 256/203).

Brutality and machination are tied to violence. We are entering the consummation of modernity as "the unconditional empowerment of power for unrestricted violence" (GA 96: 12/10). "The stupid obstinacy of sheer violence becomes the instrument of inner destruction" (GA 96: 176/139). "The *gigantic disruption* of all human constructs that is spreading over the planet . . . can only be the spasms of a machination that no longer has power over itself, and thus . . . must impress . . . empty violence into the essence of the actual" (GA 96: 104/82 tm). Violence is "the constantly annihilating essence of machination" (GA 66: 16/12 tm).

Calculating brutality and controlled violence are summed up in the figure of the predator. "It is not an accident" that "animality is emerging in the consummation of the predatory nature of the roving beast. The predatory animal, covetous of victory and power" is now the "'ideal' of humanity" (GA 95: 422–23/329). Heidegger credits Nietzsche with foreseeing this development (GA 96: 14; GA 46: 216–18). The beast of prey becomes "the primal form of the '*hero*'—for in the predator all the instincts are left unfalsified by 'knowledge'—and at the same time are tamed by the predator's ever racially bound urge. But the predatory animal endowed with the means of highest technology—completes the actualization of the *brutalitas* of being" (GA 95: 397/310). Man has become the predatory subject (GA 96: 21). (In a first-person shooter game of our own day, one becomes the technological predator who fulfills the brutality of machination.) Modern metaphysics culminates in "world-war thinking on the basis of the highest will to power of the predator and the unconditionality of armament" (GA 66: 28/22 tm). True thought and action are replaced by the logistics of bestiality. This striking analysis does seem to capture something of the horror of Nazism—what Heidegger was to call after the war "the production of corpses" in annihilation camps (GA 79: 27/27).

We live in a time of "criminality" (*Verbrechen*)—a third ontohistorical concept that describes the age. Heidegger thinks of criminality in a more or less ordinary sense when he writes that robbery and banditry take various forms in the age of the complete domination of all the means of veiling and deceiving. The Treaty of Versailles, he says, was a preliminary form of such robbery

(GA 96: 40). We have heard him speak of a handful of unnamed "planetary criminals" (GA 69: 77–78/66). In a line that Peter Trawny reports from the manuscript of this passage, which was omitted from the published version, Heidegger writes: "The question remains . . . what is the basis for the peculiar predetermination [*Vorbestimmung*] of Jewry for planetary criminality."[77]

But what sense can this make in Heideggerian terms? Criminality would seem to be a legal and moral concept—perspectives that Heidegger rejects. However, an important passage in the *Black Notebooks* gives criminality ontohistorical depth:

> The genuine experience which has been allotted to the current generation, but which this generation was unable to take up, see through, and place back into its essential inception, is the untrammeled outbreak of the unconditional criminality of the modern human essence, in accordance with its role in the empowerment of power into machination. Criminality [*Verbrechen*] is not mere breakage [*Zerbrechen*]; instead, it is the devastation of everything into what is broken. The broken is broken off from the inception and dispersed into the domain of the breakable. Here, there remains only one possibility of being—in the mode of order. Ordering is only the counterpart of criminality, understood in terms of the history of beyng (not juridically-morally). [GA 96: 266/211 tm]

Brokenness is not the obvious shattering of things and bodies in "the catastrophes of war and wars of catastrophe" (GA 96: 45/36), but an insidious desertification of sense. Heidegger is more concerned about this "invisible devastation" than about "visible destructions" (GA 96: 147/114, 159/123). Destruction could even be "the precursor of a concealed inception," whereas "devastation is the aftereffect of an already decided end" (GA 96: 3/3 tm).

When Heidegger refers to "criminals," then, he means those who contribute to depriving the world of sense. Here we must not forget the "Semitic nomads," who supposedly turn everything they touch into a wasteland (NHS 56)—but they are hardly the only group that embodies the process of desertification, in Heidegger's opinion. He does not attribute creative agency to any of the "planetary criminals," but sees them as creatures of a deeper ontohistorical trend that runs throughout modernity.

In the broken world, ordering is merely "the reverse of criminality." In a narrow sense, lawbreaking and policing are the two sides of crime. In a broader sense, what has been smashed into pieces can be picked up and artificially stuck back together. In a world without meaningful connections among beings, the only solution seems to be a forced consolidation or arrangement, a willed and planned order. When worldhood in the Heideggerian sense has faded away—when there is no organic, felt, meaningful coherence to life—it remains possible, and even urgent, to coordinate the remnants. We thus seem to be faced with the choice between "complete destruction and disintegration" or "the constraint of a total compulsion" (GA 95: 70/53). Modern man thus becomes "the organizer of nihilism" (GA 94: 452/328). "The consummation of modernity" is that "in the age of unconditional machination, the gigantism of criminality becomes public under the title of the 'true'" (GA 96: 115/90 tm).

Which world could serve as a model of wholeness? Sometimes Heidegger looks to the Greek *polis* as the pole of a people (GA 40: 161–62). Or, in his 1933–1934 seminar, as we have seen, he shows a certain nostalgia for the Middle Ages—not in their doctrines or their specific social arrangements, but in the unity that he imagines obtained before modern dualisms broke it apart (NHS 64).

Inception and Downfall

This brings us to the broader vision of history that sustains Heidegger's onto-historical concepts and pervades his ambivalent stance toward the *Un-wesen* of late modernity. His vision draws on the concept of inception that we considered in chapter 1 and pairs it with that of downfall.

Again, an inception, in contrast to a mere beginning, is the time when time arises—the mysterious origin of a world with its own understanding of being. "The inceptions withdraw from every will to seize hold of them; in withdrawing, they merely leave behind the beginning as their mask" (GA 94: 283/208 tm). "We never grasp the *inceptive*; in order not to become a bygone given [*ein vorhandenes Gewordenes*] and thereby forfeit itself, the inceptive must constantly withdraw. This is why the inception can never be presented [*darstellen*]; it can only be carried out, namely, in the downfall of stepping back, so that the withdrawal may truly *remain*" (GA 94: 334/243 tm).

In texts such as the *Contributions*, Heidegger understands himself as standing between the Greek "first inception" and the possibility of "the other inception" (GA 65: 5/7, 75–76/60–61, 171/135 tm). The first, Greek inception asked the question: What are beings as such? The answer was *physis*, the burgeoning and enduring presence of things. But this experience degenerated into the categorizing of various sorts of presence, and ultimately into the scientific and technological description and manipulation of what is taken as present. The first inception seems to have lost its force: being was "once the *lightning* that suddenly bursts and draws all things into its light," but is "now a weary semblance . . . an exhausted possession, an object of prattle, a bore, a name—the end" (GA 94: 89/67).

The other inception would "recollectively internalize" (*er-innern*) *physis*, yet no longer take *physis* as its point of departure (GA 94: 241/176). It would turn from what is, or beings, to being itself (or "beyng"), and ask how it essentially happens. The first inception was "an immediate Yes that took a stand for continuance and constancy" (GA 94: 49/37 tm)—it affirmed presence as the central sense of being. In contrast, the other inception is open to "the full essence of being—in which presence (the 'is') is positively incorporated . . . Not the 'it is,' but the 'so be it' (thrown projection)" is the primary clue (GA 94: 51/39 tm). No longer can we stand before the given as what is present; that stance has long degenerated from awe and wonder to mere objectification. Instead, we have to become alive to history, to the way in which any givenness of entities draws on a heritage for the sake of a destiny.

What difference would that make? Another entry from this period is cryptic but suggestive: "Here is the original limit of history—not empty, supratemporal eternity, but the stability of rootedness. *Time becomes space*" (GA 94: 38/29 tm). The passage seems to express the desire to belong, to stand, to inhabit a meaningful place—a *there*. Such a place would be founded in a transformative, transfiguring event: "the world-event" (GA 94: 93/70), the event of the grounding of the there, the appropriating event. This founding would be a liberation, but not negative freedom as the dissolution of bonds; it would be a kind of binding (GA 94: 126–27, 140; cf. GA 16: 96, 281).

As the notebooks continue, Heidegger loses his faith that the new inception can be provoked by a nationalist revolution; it becomes a more elusive possibility to be explored by poets and thinkers. But the relation between the first and the other inception continues to serve as a potent organizing scheme. We stand before a decision between these two, for which futural thinkers can perhaps prepare the way. Only a very few can be admitted to the "decisive domains," and many are excluded. In particular, "The more original and inceptive the future decisions and questions become, all the more inaccessible will they remain to [the Jewish] 'race'" (GA 96: 46/37 tm).

If the first inception is to be superseded by the other inception, then the first must, somehow, come to an end. This brings us to the theme of *Untergang*. Literally the term means "going under"; it is often translated as "decline." Both translations fail to capture the enormity of the event as Heidegger thinks of it. I will translate *Untergang* as "downfall" and the verb *untergehen* as "collapse."[78]

An inception, if it is great, ends in a great downfall. "What is great collapses, what is small remains forever" (GA 95: 427/333 tm). "Only those who can never know the inception are afraid of the downfall" (GA 97: 17). Or as Heidegger puts it in *Introduction to Metaphysics*, "The great begins great, sustains itself only through the free recurrence of greatness, and if it is great, also comes to an end in greatness. . . . Only the everyday understanding and the small man imagine that the great must endure forever, a duration which he then goes on to equate with the eternal" (GA 40: 18/17). A collapse that is "necessary and is affiliated to the history of being" (GA 94: 481/349) may make a new inception possible (GA 94: 277).

Inception and downfall are linked in "the *storm* which blows within beyng itself"; downfall is a sign of beyng (GA 94: 429/312), "the supreme victory of beyng," "the highest testimony to, and history of, the uniqueness of beyng" (GA 95: 403/315). The granting of sense is a powerful upheaval that lasts only until its eventual collapse. Thus, "*beyng* itself is 'tragic'—that is, it has its inception in downfall as an abyssal ground" (GA 95: 417/325 tm). "Beyng itself brings itself into the 'catastrophic' course of its history, it becomes manifest in and through it; and 'metaphysics' proves to be the prelude to it" (GA 95: 50/38 tm). What we need is "a *katastrophe* into the abyss of beyng" (GA 95: 417/325 tm).

But what if the greatness of an inception fails to eventuate in a great downfall? "The age of the consummation of modernity faces two possibilities: either violent and swift demise (which looks like 'catastrophe,' but in its already decided and distorted essence is too lowly to *be* such) or else the degeneration of the current state of unconditional machination into the endless" (GA 96: 138–39/108 tm). The latter is more insidious: "The great doom everywhere threatening modern humanity and its history is that a *downfall* is denied to humans, since only the inceptive can collapse. Other things merely perish, and do so in the endlessness that offers the possibilities of its own kind of 'infinities'" (GA 96: 251/199 tm). We can continue indefinitely increasing the stock of information we possess about beings, and developing ourselves as "the masters and possessors of nature," without questioning the understanding of being that underlies this condition. "The more gigantic the human being becomes, all the smaller must his essence contract, until he, no longer seeing himself, confuses himself with his machinations and thus 'outlives' his own end" (GA 94: 282/207 tm).

Heidegger fears the indefinite continuation of a tradition whose essential possibilities have been played out. "The procreative succession of generations can keep going on for centuries . . . but that does not at all mean there will be a history of a people—for the most intrinsic configurative law of a historical people is in each case temporally restricted to a short span of ages" (GA 94: 286–87/210). A long, well-populated pseudo-future can mask the disappearance of destiny. This seems to be how he views China (GA 94: 302, 432; GA 96: 183). "A people can have its 'time' in which it is too late for its very downfall, for it lacks the essential *height* from which it would have to plunge."[79] "The greatest danger is not barbarity and decay [*Verfall*], for these conditions can drive us into an extreme and thus bring forth an emergency. The greatest danger is averageness and the uniform management of everything" (GA 94: 330/240 tm).

This means that critiques of dictatorship are misguided. Totalitarian systems, as "effective forms of machination," cannot be judged in moral terms or condemned from a democratic point of view; dictators are "the executors of the consummation of modernity" who bring modernity "to its highest essence." Their "greatness consists in their capacity to be 'dictatorial'—in their sensing the concealed necessity of the machination of being and not letting themselves be drawn off course by any temptation" (GA 95: 404/315–16 tm).

> The talk of "dictatorship" is idle talk arising out of the horizon of a "freedom" which has forgotten—or rather never knew—to what its freedom frees, namely, to the self-assurance of the human being as *subjectum*. . . . The alleged "dictatorships" are not a *dictans*, but . . . the *dictatum* of that essence of being from which modern humans cannot withdraw, because in order to become themselves they must affirm that essence, even in all its essential consequences. [GA 95: 431/336 tm]

The struggle between liberal individualism and totalitarianism is a conflict between two forms of aggressive, closed-minded modern subjectivity—and totalitarianism has an advantage in that it recognizes the naked, absolute claim of total machination, thus accelerating the salutary catastrophe. Here Heidegger is strikingly similar to Hegel, who sees certain transformative forces and individuals as embodiments of a historical dialectic that operates on a higher level than morality (thus Napoleon is "the world spirit on horseback").

If being is essentially "catastrophic" or "tragic," then we should not fear the collapse of modernity but accelerate it. Downfall can become a transition to the other inception (GA 94: 277). "Before being can take place [*sich ereignen*] in its inceptive truth, being as the will must be broken, the world must be driven to implode, the earth driven to desolation, and man driven to mere labor. Only after this downfall, over a long time, the sudden while of the inception takes place" (GA 7: 71/EP 86 tm). Heidegger links this idea to the fate of Germany in a troubling question: "If a truth lies in the power of 'race' (the innate), will and should the Germans then lose their historical essence—abandon it—organize it away—or will they not have to bring it to the highest tragic outcome?" (GA 94: 168/123 tm).

No compromises will be adequate to overcoming modernity; the modern will to power must be played out to its extremity before the new inception can take place. "Only when the consummation of the modern age affirms the ruthlessness of its own greatness is future history being prepared" (GA 5: 112/85 tm). "Before the downfall, man must rise up to become the overman" (GA 97: 367). Only the overman is capable of being completely ruled by the essence of technology, so that he can direct particular technological processes (GA 48: 205). The "highest possession of power" may be capable of passing beyond power itself to prepare a "new truth of being" (GA 90: 222). After the war, Heidegger writes that "a few" (including himself) realized in 1932—"in a genuine and completely non-destructive sense"—"that the technical world of today's humanity cannot be overcome with half measures—but only by passing through its complete essence" (GA 97: 250). The claim about the "non-destructive sense" is revisionism, but the rest of the thought is in line with his position in the thirties.

In his late thought, he views "planetary" technology as embodying the will to power. His attitude continues to be one of grim fascination, as he waits for modernity to culminate in a convulsion. He also pursues Hölderlin's thought that where the danger is, salvation also grows (GA 7: 29–30; GA 79: 72–73); the key is to experience technology as a given destiny, a gift, and then to recollect what gives it.

It is presumably in this sense that he writes in a 1968 letter to Shlomo Zemach, an Israeli writer and translator of "The Origin of the Work of Art," that "it is a great error to say that I am against technology." But the same letter claims that by 1935 "my position toward National Socialism . . . was already unambiguously hostile" (GA 40: 233/251). We have seen that this is not the case. In fact, if Nazism was a form of technology, then Heidegger could not simply be "against" it. As a counter-essence, it was a gift of the essence, and it would have to be "affirmed."

In Heidegger's vision, then, we stand between the first inception and the possibility of the other inception, awaiting a great downfall, or a sudden destruction that fails to attain the rank of a downfall, or the worst—a dreary, indefinite prolongation of machination, brutality, and criminality.

Nazis and Jews in the *Black Notebooks*

With this conception of history in place, we can take a closer look at the notebooks' account of Heidegger's plunge into politics and at their characterizations of Nazism and "world Jewry." Some have claimed that the notebooks certify Heidegger as a convinced Nazi.[80] It is more accurate to say that he comes across as an initially excited, yet apprehensive participant in the Nazi movement; then as an embittered observer; and always as a nonconformist whose conception of the potential greatness of the revolution is abstruse and elusive.

The entries from Heidegger's fateful year as rector (GA 94: 110–62) are required reading on Heidegger's political engagement. However, those who are hoping for concrete explanations of his behavior at the time will be disappointed. He offers us nebulous moods that are rarely tied to particular events, and ambiguous and abstract reflections that can play into the hands of both his enemies and his defenders, without settling the controversy one way or the other. The notebooks express his emotions as he assumes the rectorate—first with hesitation, then with steely determination—and becomes increasingly frustrated as his year as rector draws to an end.

An atmosphere of tense, unspecified anticipation begins before the rectorate. Convinced that his times lack a sense of emergency (e.g., GA 94: 88), Heidegger writes that *"what matters* [is] *to open up the world-place"* (GA 94: 94/71). He longs for the "strength for *world-formation"* (GA 94: 31/24 tm) and "the *empowerment of being"* (GA 94: 36/27) by way of "liberat[ing] the Da-sein in today's humanity" (GA 94: 45/34). He imagines "a decisive attitude that does not remain empty and formal but [grounds] the truth of beings in quite determinate horizons of vision and spheres of action" (GA 94: 24/19)—but he names no particulars.

The mood is also nationalist: German heritage can provide resoluteness with a content. "Only someone who is German [*der Deutsche*] can . . . poetize being" (GA 94: 27/21). The Germans should dare to get involved in "the happening of being" (GA 94: 95/72). Heidegger fancies himself *boden-ständig,* "as if I went over the fields guiding a plow, or over lonely field-paths . . . which kept Mother's blood, and that of her ancestors, circulating and pulsing" (GA 94: 38/29 tm).

The excitement mounts: "The world is in reconstruction; mankind is awakening" (GA 94: 63/48). "A marvelously awakening communal [*volklich*] will is standing up into a great darkness of the world" (GA 94: 109/80 tm). However, Heidegger has his reservations: rootedness does not guarantee a new empowerment of being, and individuality should not be absorbed into community (GA 94: 40). True community requires *"aloneness"* (GA 94: 59/45).

He seems to have a presentiment of risk and even of disaster, but he bucks himself up: "Only if we . . . actually *go* into errancy, can we strike up against 'truth'"; the philosopher is essentially an errant figure (*Irrgänger*) (GA 94: 13/11 tm). *"Unflinchingly* [*unbeirrbar*] *into the ineluctable!"* (GA 94: 34/26 tm). The authentic, historical "so be it" (GA 94: 51/39 tm) requires one to choose a particular option that is necessarily limited and partially opaque; it must be chosen with bold daring, *tolma* (GA 94: 3, 95, 96, 323). Heidegger begins to think that there is a role for him to play in history: a philosopher can contribute indirectly to "the grounding of humans in soil—work—struggle and collapse" (GA 94: 82/63).

When he accepts the position of rector, he worries that he is "acting for the first time *against* my innermost voice" (GA 94: 110/81). We can only wonder how Heidegger's life and thought would have evolved if, like Socrates, he had obeyed his *daimonion,* as when he declined an invitation to Berlin in 1930.[81] Instead, he takes the plunge, steels himself, reminds himself of his determination, and fights all the harder—as if he is determined to dive into a denial of errancy. "The Führer [gives] our thinking the correct course and impetus"; we must be "relentless in the hard goal" (GA 94: 111/81).

But what exactly is this goal? Heidegger is unwilling to articulate it in terms of the prevalent slogans and programs. "*National Socialism* is a genuine nascent power only if it still has something to withhold behind all its activity and talk . . . if the present were already that which is to be attained and striven for, then only a dread of the downfall would be left over." "*National Socialism* [is] not a ready-made eternal truth come down from heaven—taken in that way, it is an aberration and foolishness" (GA 94: 114–15/84). The ascendant Nazi "'ideology'" (GA 94: 142/104) or "'phraseology'" (GA 94: 153/112) is "a confused worldview" based on "the most problematic means of the nineteenth century" (GA 94: 129/94), such as "a *dismal biologism*" (GA 94: 143/105, cf. 157). This is just "cheap dogmatics" and "semblant philosophy" (GA 94: 129/95), "*merely a Marxism set on its head*" (GA 94: 159/116).

Instead, Heidegger seeks what in 1935 he will notoriously call "the inner truth and greatness" of Nazism, as opposed to its external trappings (GA 40: 208/222). This secret potential or "metapolitics" (GA 94: 115/85) aims at "a completely other being" (GA 94: 120/88), "a transformation of being" (GA 94: 125/92), or "the historical greatness of the people in the effectuation and configuration of the powers of being" (GA 94: 136/100). Such a transformation requires a "spiritual nobility" (GA 94: 121/89) that will foster "the people's knowledge" (GA 94: 123/90). (One must remember here that *geistig* or "spiritual" is not a specifically religious term, but refers to the entire range of human thought and creativity.) This project is tied to Heidegger's philosophy: "the projection of being qua time" can indicate a "mission" that "first opens and binds blood and soil to a preparedness for action and to a capacity for work and for *effectivity*" (GA 94: 127/93).

It is important to identify the enemy (GA 94: 125, 141, 145–47), which must be confronted on the "spiritual" level. Heidegger singles out "the worlds of Christianity, of socialism as communism, and . . . modern Enlightenment-science" (GA 94: 131/96).

He repeatedly writes that what is needed is "knowledge cultivation" (*Wissenserziehung*, e.g., 125/92). However, "what dominates . . . is an aversion to all spirit, which one has previously misinterpreted as intellectualism" (GA 94: 131/96 tm). Even though a "spiritual National Socialism [is] necessary" (GA 94: 135/99), there is little or no room for thinking within the Nazi movement. Before the rectorate, Heidegger had sneered at "the writing of the thickest possible books" (GA 94: 54/41) and opined that "it bodes well for the future that German youths deeply reject 'philosophy' and 'science'" (GA 94: 54/42). But in the face of the crude reality of anti-intellectualism, he sours on the student movement: the students "are *essentially not* at the age of creative maturity with regard to the spirit and worldview" (GA 94: 159/117).[82]

By the end of Heidegger's term as rector, his mood is bitter, as he gives up on the idea that he can work within a dogmatic and authoritarian system. "We will remain in the invisible front of the secret spiritual Germany" (GA 94: 155/114). He pens a resignation speech (surely never delivered) in which he admits he has failed, but consoles himself with the idea that "*foundering is the highest form of human experience*" (GA 94: 161/118).[83]

This all makes for absorbing reading, yet it remains disappointingly vague, and the journals are opaque as regards any philosophical basis for Heidegger's actions. The content of his political thinking is, for the most part, left unsaid or expressed so diffusely that it is difficult to understand, on the basis of the *Black Notebooks*, why he would see National Socialism in particular as worthy of support. Was there a specific result that he wanted to achieve? Or was he excited by the revolutionary upheaval and the possibility of creative transformation, without any concrete sense of what might come about? Earlier in this chapter we have seen that his reflections on founding are just as wavering and abstract.

The *Black Notebooks* reflect the moods of Heidegger's rectorate; the public documents from 1933–1934 consist of bureaucratic directives and exhortatory speeches. We are left wanting specific analyses and rationales that might link the moods and the pronouncements to a more clearly articulated long-term goal. In short, true deliberations (*Überlegungen*) are lacking.

As we have seen, Heidegger does tell us that in 1930–1934 he viewed Nazism as a step toward a new inception (GA 95: 408). This passage is consistent with his statement in the *Der Spiegel* interview that "I believed at the time that, in engagement [*Auseinandersetzung*] with National Socialism, a new path could open itself up—one that was the only remaining possibility of a renewal" (GA 16: 658/HR 317). Nazism might reestablish a quasi-medieval or *polis*-like harmony that would unify the modern broken world, and maybe disclose new possibilities for an inception. Near the beginning of his rectorate he writes, "If the dawning German Dasein is great, then it bears millennia ahead of it—and we are obliged to think correspondingly far out in advance—that is, to anticipate the arising of a completely other being" (GA 94: 119–20/88 tm).

To put this in terms of the distinctive concepts that led Heidegger into the thirties: the National Socialist revolution was, in his view, an emergency from which a new temporality might originate, along with a fresh response to the question, "Who are we?" The revolution was an opportunity to draw a new line between being and nonbeing.

But after his initial period of enthusiasm, which is not devoid of apprehension and disagreements, Heidegger increasingly sees that the only unity the Nazis can provide is a coerced, calculated order, a totality held together by the exploitation and "mobilization" of the populace and resources of the territory. He criticizes particular facets of the new regime, and then—in conjunction with an intense study of Nietzsche and Jünger—tries to identify its metaphysical underpinnings. Here, his views are more philosophical and original than in his scattered remarks on other groups and ideologies. If there is something of lasting philosophical value in the *Black Notebooks*, it may well be his critique of Nazi metaphysics. But as we turn to the details of this critique, we should remember that he continues to "affirm" the movement, fatalistically viewing it as the essential counter-essence that is destined to bring modernity to its collapse.

Heidegger's growing distance from the predominant Nazi ideology develops misgivings that he had expressed early on. Even before his rectorate, he is suspicious of mythmaking (GA 94: 88) and "the *fabrication of a . . . 'world-view'*" (GA 94: 77/58). Successful Nazi ideologues such as Ernst Krieck are "mouthers of mediocrity" (GA 94: 179/131 tm) who are cooking up a "witches' cauldron" of "political worldview, concocted paganism, perplexity, idolization of technology, idolization of race, worship of Wagner, etc, etc." (GA 94: 261/191). "Political science," i.e., research that is subordinated to the Nazi program, is harming Germany externally and internally (GA 94: 191/140). "Where a people posits itself as its own goal, egoism has expanded into the gigantic. . . . All this is radically un-German" (GA 94: 233/171). Nazism, as "the machinational organization of the people," is essentially technological, which means that it can never freely command technology itself (GA 94: 472/342).

From the start, Heidegger is eager to distinguish his own conception of the potential of the movement from its more stupid forms. These baser, cruder versions of the ideology, for Heidegger, always included biological racism, which he increasingly sees as a form of subjectivism and will to power. Race, as part of "thrownness," is a real condition of existence, but it is "elevated to the unconditioned" (GA 94: 189/139) by biological racism. "Those who want to breed the people 'biologically'" (GA 94: 364/266) are carrying out an "animalization and mechanization of the people" (GA 94: 223/163). This program is "a *consequence* of the machinational power which must subjugate beings, in all their domains, to planning and calculation" (GA 96: 56/44). By the late thirties he writes that "all glorification of 'blood' [is just] a facade and a pretext" to distract the masses from "what properly and only *is*, the unconditional sovereignty of the machination [*Machschaft*] of destruction" (GA 95: 381–82/298 tm).

Commentators have rightly observed that Heidegger himself sometimes adopts the language of race, and that race does not have to be understood in reductive biological terms.[84] There is a concern for the ethnic in his reflections, a call to root the *Volk* in its soil. The following passage, which dates from around 1939, clarifies the matter to some extent:

> *With their marked gift for calculation*, the Jews have for the longest time been "living" in accord with the principle of race, which is why they are also offering the most vehement resistance to its unrestricted application. The instituting of racial breeding stems not from "life" itself, but from the overpowering of life by machination. What machination pursues with such planning is a *complete deracializing [Entrassung]* of peoples by clamping them into a uniformly constructed, uniformly tailored instituting of all beings. Deracializing goes hand in hand with a self-alienation of peoples—the loss of history—that is, of the domains of decision regarding beyng. [GA 96: 56/44 tm]

Here Heidegger indulges in his favorite trope of finding sameness in apparent opposites: both Nazi eugenics and Jewish attention to who counts as a member of the chosen people supposedly reflect a calculative management of genetic resources.[85] When National Socialism becomes "*Rational Socialism*" (GA 96: 195/153 tm), it prevents a people from digging deeper into its heritage to find its distinctive destiny.

We must also note that he gives some credit to concern with "race" as a necessary though not sufficient condition for a people, as in this passage from around 1938: "Of what use—if indeed usefulness is at issue here—is the best race, if that is merely a race of dogs, while the decision is avoided as to *who* then are supposed to be the ones for whom, and even justifiably, a good race must be required?" (GA 94: 465/337). The question "Who are we?" always exceeds race, but that does not necessarily mean that racial cultivation is not needed at all. After all, during his rectorate, Heidegger promptly and vigorously instituted the pro-"Aryan" measures decreed by the new regime.

Nonetheless, the question "Who are we?" should provoke a people to look for its destiny beyond its merely given facts. Thus, he objects to crude nationalism (GA 95: 31)—the idea that a people is an object that can simply be found and fostered as an end in itself, as a mass of millions of genetically related human beings whose strength and survival are unquestionably good.

Many more aspects of Nazi ideology come in for critique in the notebooks. For one, the Nazis' anti-intellectualism leaves no room for genuine philosophy. Heidegger sums up this mentality as "*ego **non** cogito, ergo sum*" (GA 95: 300/234).

The Nazis' extreme hostility to their designated enemies is another error. For Heidegger, the surface enmity of modern states and peoples is based on a fundamental sameness in their goals and means (GA 95: 39), a shared subjectivist machination. There can be no creative confrontation as long as one is unfreely fighting for a political dogma (GA 95: 83) and making one-self dependent on one's opponent (GA 95: 326). "If the opponent is made immediately into an enemy, and the enemy is already made into the 'devil,' then all opposition is deprived not only of anything creative but even of the space for a struggle" (GA 95: 56/43). Heidegger distinguishes greatness from domination and denigration:

> What is small betrays its smallness most visibly in its choice of an opponent, for it chooses as an opponent only what it already believes it can surmount, because it can count on getting applause for making it an object of contempt. But whoever feels contempt always makes himself smaller by what he despises. Only one who is able to overcome contempt has no more need of superiority in order to be great; i.e. to *be* and to let the other lie where and how it lies. [GA 94: 507/368–69 tm]

For the Nazis, enmity was, of course, a matter of potential and actual violence—a power struggle. But as the notebooks unfold, Heidegger increasingly associates this point of view with the Nietzschean will to power as the last stage of modern metaphysics. According to one passage in the notebooks (GA 94: 429) force or violence is a trait of being itself, much as he claimed in *Introduction to Metaphysics*. But soon after, he writes that "futureless violence" is an example of *"complete lack of questioning"* (GA 94: 455/330 tm). He even speaks of the "mildness" of the thinking of being (GA 96: 22/19, 24/20). As the world around him becomes more violent and brutal, Heidegger draws back.

His other targets include the quest for *Lebensraum* (GA 96: 131) and propaganda as *"the art of telling lies"* (GA 96: 229/180, cf. 274).[86] He claims that Nazi ideology appropriates the principles of Germany's enemies: power politics, cultural politics, authoritarianism, totalitarianism, imperialism. None of these ideas are properly German, but rather English, Jewish, French, Russian, Italian, or generally modern (GA 95: 326; GA 96: 197). The Nazi image of proper Germanness is nothing but a confused Wagnerism (GA 95: 52, 60, 108–9, 256, 333, 383).

It may be gratifying to see Heidegger, even before the war, condemning feature after feature of the National Socialist worldview. It seems safe to say that by the late thirties, he was no Nazi anymore. But we should remember that he does not criticize Nazism as morally inferior to any other contemporary political movement. His criticism is not ethical at all, but purely *seynsgeschichtlich*. His refrain is that Nazism is machination—but so is all else. There is no nonmachinational alternative. And as we have seen, he thinks that Nazism must be "affirmed" because it will accelerate the necessary apocalypse.

Heidegger wavers on which modern movement is the worst, but at no point does he wish Nazism to be defeated by a rival, such as liberal democracy. The moderation and moralism of Anglo-American liberalism only forestall the total catastrophe that is necessary to clear the way for the other inception. All that liberal democracy promises is a half-hearted, prolonged diminution. Democracy lacks the strength for "the step into the consummation . . . from here, no decisions are made." Democracy is "a barricade that can delay but is incapable of stopping the essential consummation of modernity"; it is modern, "but without the courage for the unfolded essence and for the extreme essential consequences" (GA 95: 406/316–17). These consequences must be brought out in order for modernity to collapse, and totalitarianism is a necessary part of this process.

Although his criticisms of Nazism are substantial, these are the grumblings of a disappointed lover. In 1934, after stepping down as rector, he takes Nazism to be essentially a "*barbaric principle*," but claims that this is precisely where "its possible greatness" lies (GA 94: 194/142). Later he writes that although the *völkisch* worldview is superficial, it also has its necessity for "the task of a historical gathering" (GA 94: 446/324 tm). To "affirm" National Socialism is a sort of *amor fati*: "*The new politics is an inner essential consequence of 'technology'*. . . 'technology' can never be mastered by the ethno-political [*völkisch-politische*] world view. What is already essentially a servant can never be a master. Nevertheless, this birth of the new politics from the essence of technology . . . is *necessary*, and thus is not the possible object of a shortsighted 'opposition'" (GA 94: 472/342–43). In such statements, Heidegger edges toward the submission to "fatality" that he had formerly denounced as "Asiatic" (GA 39: 173/158).

Passages such as these shed light on the notion of the "inner truth and greatness" of National Socialism—its hidden potential that only Heidegger could have properly articulated—which infamously appears in *Introduction to Metaphysics* (GA 40: 208/222) but is echoed in other texts as well. We can now understand that he was not only distinguishing this "inner truth" from external, superficial manifestations of the "movement," but also developing a peculiar conception of greatness. In 1953, in a letter to *Die Zeit*, he endorsed Christian Lewalter's interpretation of the phrase as "accurate in every respect" (GA 40: 232/250). In Lewalter's reading, "the Nazi movement is a symptom for the tragic collision of man and technology, and as such a symptom it has its 'greatness,' because it affects the entirety of the West and threatens to pull it into destruction."[87] This has always had the ring of a dubious exercise in apologetics, but the *Black Notebooks* support the claim that it was precisely the global destructiveness of Nazi "machination" that made it "great" and "true," in a sense: it was the unvarnished expression of modern metaphysics (cf. GA 5: 112 on modern "greatness"). However, what is misleading in Lewalter's reading is the unspoken assumption that the West should *not* be destroyed—whereas, at least in the increasingly desperate times of the thirties and forties, Heidegger often seems to have wished for a complete collapse.

There is no resistance to any concrete Nazi actions in Heidegger's ambiguous reflections. At the same time, though, it is clear that he does not accept Nazi rhetoric: he critiques (not morally but in ontohistorical terms) racism, domination, brutality, violence, and the demonization of opponents. By the late thirties, he does not expect Nazism to heal the broken world, although he does hope that it will accelerate the coming of a new inception.

Is Heidegger a Nazi philosopher? "'Philosophy' must never demean itself to the task and demand of either erecting a 'worldview' or 'grounding' and 'configuring' one that already prevails" (GA 94: 300/219). "To say a philosophy is 'National Socialist,' or is not so, means the same as to say a triangle is courageous, or is not so—and therefore is cowardly" (GA 94: 348/254, cf. 509).

We close our look at the *Black Notebooks* with an examination of their anti-Jewish passages. These lines have received a great deal of attention, and deserve it; they raise disturbing questions about Heidegger's character and the character of his thought. But some of the more irresponsible discussions have created the impression that the *Black Notebooks* as a whole are an antisemitic screed. This is simply a distortion. The first four volumes (GA 94–97) comprise 1,753 pages by Heidegger. Twenty-seven passages in these volumes refer to Jews or Judaism, and these references along with their context easily fit on ten pages. I consider around half of these passages to be obviously and overtly anti-Jewish: that is, they express hostility to Jews as a group or to supposedly Jewish traits, drawing on stereotypes and conspiracy theories. Of course, it is possible to interpret other passages in these and other texts as alluding to anti-Jewish stereotypes.[88]

Most of Heidegger's statements on Jews and Judaism are directed against a supposed powerful, global Jewish elite, and against the Judeo-Christian worldview. The following references are *prima facie* anti-Jewish by my definition: Jewry's "groundlessness" and "worldlessness" (GA 95: 97/75–76); its power and calculation (GA 96: 46; GA 97: 20); its exploitation of both pacifism and bellicosity (GA 96: 133); its "uprooting of all beings" (GA 96: 243/191); its destructive metaphysical role (GA 97: 20). The reference to an "intangible" Jewry that avoids having to fight while the Germans must sacrifice (GA 96: 262) is almost surely anti-Jewish, although one should note that it is an item in a list of "'facts' [which] are always only half true and therefore are erroneous" (GA 96: 261/207). There is an animus in the reference to "the Jew Litvinov" (GA 96: 242/191). Heidegger's references to Jewish anthropology (GA 94: 475; GA 95: 322), the "Hellenistic-Jewish 'world'"

(GA 95: 339/264, cf. GA 97: 20), Phariseeism (GA 95: 396), Jewish prophecy (GA 97: 159), and Judeo-Christian monotheism (GA 97: 357, 369, 409,
438) are generally negative. He compares Nazis to Jews, often appearing
to be hostile to both, in his references to sociology (GA 95: 161); anti-
Cartesianism (GA 95: 168); psychoanalysis (GA 95: 258; GA 96: 218); cultural politics (GA 95: 326); racism (GA 96: 56); Barmat and Kutisker, Jewish
swindlers denounced by Nazis in the 1920s (GA 96: 234); and the supposed
"Jewishness" of the very persecution of Jews (GA 97: 20). Opposition to Nazi
dogma, he comments, does not imply agreement with Jews (GA 95: 325).

However we may interpret these texts, it is clear that Jews are not the main
focus of Heidegger's journals; they are treated almost incidentally, mostly in
passing comments, and Heidegger did not even list Jews or Judaism as a topic
in the indices he prepared for his own notebooks. This fact militates against
the notion that antisemitism is the culmination of his thought, although one
might take it as a telling omission that reflects his indifference to the destiny
of the Jews, an indifference communicated in that most Heideggerian of
forms—silence. Evidently, such indifference can be very culpable. But it is
fair to say that although Heidegger had persistent anti-Jewish attitudes, he
was not obsessed with the topic. His comments on Jews are generally brief
and poorly developed. They are often telling and troubling, but it is clear that
Heidegger did not think it was worth his time to research Jewish life or tradition in any depth, or to explain and justify his ontohistorical judgments on
the Jews.[89] The familiarity of the stereotypes in which Heidegger is dealing is
not to his credit as a thinker. As Jean-Luc Nancy puts it, "He let himself be
carried away and stupefied in the worst of heinous banalities."[90] We are left
to resolve various opaque hermeneutic situations created by remarks that are,
philosophically speaking, rudimentary and unsatisfactory.

Heidegger himself would reject the label "antisemitic": "Note for jackasses: this comment [a postwar reflection on Jewish prophecy and the will to
power] has nothing to do with 'antisemitism,' which is as foolish and despica-
ble as Christianity's bloody and, above all, non-bloody attacks on 'heathens.'
The fact that Christianity even brands antisemitism as 'un-Christian' is part
of its highly developed and refined power technique" (GA 97: 159). By "antisemitism," Heidegger appears to have meant the racist ideology invoked by
most Nazis to justify the persecution and murder of Jews. Since he claims that
this ideology is itself an example of "Jewish" manipulation and machination
(GA 97: 20), and since Christianity is an outgrowth of Judaism, Heidegger's
rejection of antisemitism is hardly a defense of the Jews.[91]

In any case, his own views are distinct from racist ideology. Most of
them do not fit under the label "anti-Judaism" either, if this is understood as
enmity to Jewish religion. Nevertheless, the most repellent passages in the

Black Notebooks certainly express a general antipathy to Jews, mixed with Heidegger's antimodernist worldview. Peter Trawny's term "being-historical anti-Semitism" is not inappropriate.[92] One could also refer to "metaphysical anti-Semitism,"[93] which can be very hostile at the same time as it washes its hands of racism: "The question of the role of *world Jewry* is not a racial question but a metaphysical one, a question that concerns the kind of humanity which *in an utterly unrestrained* way can undertake as a world-historical 'task' the uprooting of all beings from being" (GA 96: 243/191).

What is clear is that Heidegger sees "world Jewry" as a carrier of machination and criminality, in his senses. The Jews, as rootless cosmopolitans, are destructive and devastating. He does not attribute brutality to the Jews, but rather, a spectral, sly, conspiratorial manipulation. This is all consistent with standard antisemitic tropes. His concept of machination fits all too neatly with the stereotypes that Nazism took to a new extreme. Jews are represented in the *Black Notebooks* as scheming and rootless; Heidegger refers to their "tenacious facility in calculating, manipulating, and interfering" (GA 95: 97/76) and to their "empty rationality" (GA 96: 46/37, cf. GA 96: 56). Of course, as we have seen, the Jews are hardly alone in embodying machination, according to him. America, England, Catholicism, Bolshevism, fascism, and National Socialism all come in for similar criticisms. In fact, he emphasizes that the Nazis show the same mentality as their supposed enemies, the Jews; they are metaphysically equivalent (GA 95: 161, 258, 326; GA 96: 56, 218).

The paradox of a "world Jewry" that is "worldless" (cf. GA 95: 97) is not hard to explain: the idea is that a cosmopolitan, global entity is precisely what lacks a Heideggerian "world," a historically grounded unity of senses and purposes. As Heidegger puts it in a notorious 1933 letter denouncing Jewish neo-Kantian Richard Hönigswald, when the human essence is "dissolved into a free-floating consciousness in general" and "thinned down into a universally logical world reason," one forgets about "historical rootedness and the *Volk*-based tradition of its heritage from soil and blood" (GA 16: 132). In modernity, the world becomes an *Unwelt* (GA 7: 91/EP 104).[94] Heidegger's notion of "worldlessness" thus connects to the familiar right-wing canard that Jews are devoid of place and culture. (The Jews, of course, cannot win, since from the cosmopolitan, rationalist point of view of philosophers such as Kant, their problem is precisely that they are too bound to tradition and particularity.)

Heidegger rarely picked up his journal during the most intense phase of the Second World War; there are only a few pages dating from 1942 to 1945, when the Shoah was in full force. But these pages include three comments in a row on Jews. The most striking one reads: "When what is 'Jewish' in the metaphysical sense combats what is Jewish, the high point of self-annihilation in history has been attained—supposing that the

'Jewish' has everywhere completely seized mastery, so that even the fight against 'the Jewish,' and it above all, becomes subject to it" (GA 97: 20). The passage can certainly be read as blaming the victim. It seems to say that European Jews have brought their own annihilation upon themselves, that they themselves are responsible for the Holocaust. But Heidegger is also saying that the Nazis are unwittingly lashing out against their own ideological source: they are futilely fighting against a "Jewish" viewpoint without understanding that they themselves exemplify the same mentality. The thought gains some clarity from his previous entry, which claims that anti-Christianity must, like Christianity, stem from Judaism, which is "the principle of destruction" in the West. Heidegger cites Marx's destructive reduction of "spirit" to a superstructure of "life" as economics, which is essentially the same as "the 'people'" (GA 97: 20). Nazism's positing of the *Volk* as a ground thus mirrors Marxism—as well as the theories of "the Jew 'Freud'" (GA 96: 218/171 tm). Hence, "Jewish" thinking is reflected in the supposedly anti-Judeo-Christian Nazi ideology. (Heidegger already made this point about Marx, Freud, and Nazi racism during his rectorate: GA 36/37: 211/162.) Nazism is "Jewish" in that it insists on a given substrate that underlies spirit, and advances by way of manipulation and calculation.

Of course, this entire discourse operates on the level of ideas rather than paying any attention to the actual persecution and killing of human beings. There is no hint of sympathy here for the victims; Heidegger seems to be distantly and ironically observing the events of the time. This is an ice-cold analysis of a program of mass murder.[95]

It is helpful to compare the passage at GA 97: 20 to remarks on other forms of self-destruction, which proves to be a recurring theme in Heidegger's reflections. Two pages before these comments, he writes, "The highest stage of technology is reached when, as consumption, it has nothing more to consume—than itself" (GA 97: 18). Elsewhere he writes that the Soviet onslaught against the West is really a form of the West's self-destruction, since communism is Western (GA 96: 276; GA 97: 37, 53). Or, he writes after the war, since the Americans are destroying Europe and they are essentially Europeans, Europe is destroying itself (GA 97: 230).

On the one hand, Heidegger hardly seems to be celebrating these events. His expressions "high point" and "highest stage" should not be taken naively as some sort of praise. "Neither annihilation nor ordering nor new ordering can essentially satisfy a historical determination; what can do so is only the poetizing of the essence of being and the constructing of a grounded affiliation to being" (GA 96: 260/207). Although he is no pacifist or moralist, then, he could hardly have agreed that the Holocaust was a solution, final or otherwise, to any real problem. If both war and peace are merely ontic affairs (GA 95: 189, 192, 235), the same would be true of genocide.

On the other hand, the dynamic of self-destruction may be precisely how Heidegger imagines that machination, taken to an extreme, may lead to its own downfall, making way for a new inception. This malignancy turned against itself, this self-canceling *Un-wesen*, would then have to be "affirmed." As always in the *Black Notebooks*, Heidegger's distance from the phenomena he describes coexists with a continuing attachment to the Nazi movement as a catalyst for catastrophe, and with anti-Jewish fantasies that are morally and philosophically appalling.

*   *   *

Chapters 1 and 2 have traced how Heidegger entered the phase of his thinking I call the thirties, and how his political thought developed during that period. To sum up: *Being and Time* thinks of Dasein's ecstatic temporality as the transcendental horizon for the sense of being. He then develops the concept of an inception as the moment when ecstatic temporality emerges. Such an inception would be an emergency and the origin of selfhood. When he leaps into politics, he envisions a founding inception that would arise from the silent ground of the *Volk* with the aid of an absolute leader, or through philosophy and poetry. But eventually, he comes to see all contemporary politics as variants of the will to power, with Nazism as its most extreme form. Nazism promotes a communal subjectivity, the counter-essence of selfhood; it tries to establish a secure ground, the counter-essence of inception; it launches a program of global conquest and destruction, but insulates the Germans from true emergency. In Heidegger's view, there is no point in resisting this movement; to prepare the way for a post-modern essence, one must affirm the counter-essence within modernity. Before a new inception can become possible, the metaphysical destiny of the West must grind on to its catastrophic conclusion.

Chapter Three

Recovering Politics

As Heidegger remarks, not only is there is no "Sophocles in himself," but Sophocles would find our attempts to formulate the essential Sophocles insufferably dull (GA 39: 145/127). His point is not that we can assign any meaning we like to a text, but that our inherited meanings keep appealing to us to draw new possibilities from them. Likewise, there is no Heidegger in himself; there is the letter of what he said, but the sense, truth, and falsehood of the words operate within a range of darker and brighter possibilities that his texts make available. The question is which of these possibilities remain worth pursuing, and which are dead ends.

Heidegger's sympathies for Nazism are certainly a dead end from a moral point of view, and so is his increasingly ambiguous attitude toward Nazi ideology as "counter-essence." When it comes to tyranny and genocide, ambiguity is no virtue. But a phenomenological critique may get us farther than a moral one: we can learn by thinking through his visions of political founding, language, power, and the political, deciding where these visions have some validity and where they fall short. For Heidegger's most dedicated enemies, even considering that there may be some truth in his political thought of the thirties amounts to crypto-fascism, but this attitude is unfair. No matter how misguided a political decision may be, it is not normally undertaken in sheer blindness; those who support tyrants do so in reaction to some tension or problem that is not mere illusion, even if they misinterpret this problem or propose a false solution to it. As Heidegger rightly argues, even a false appearance is an appearance, a case of something showing itself—as something that it is not (SZ 28–29). If we cannot accept a point of view, the question is what phenomena were glimpsed, but misinterpreted, in that view.

As for the anti-Jewish passages in the *Black Notebooks*, it would be a mistake to minimize them—to emphasize their ambiguities, their relative mildness for the times, and finally to be left with a handful of assertions that we can dismiss as part of a personal journal that has nothing to do with Heidegger's "real philosophy." This would be an error because his comments on Jews (and Americans, Englishmen, and Christians) are part of a whole. It is not a mathematically deductive system, but more like an ecosystem: it may well survive if one element is removed, but only in a changed form. In Heidegger's thinking, suspicion of rootless, calculating, nomadic, cosmopolitan, "Jewish" ways of life goes hand in hand with his emphasis on thrownness, rootedness, and historicity. His hostility to rationalism, universalism, and all things global— such as "world Jewry"—fits with his attempt to think of Dasein and being as radically finite. As Robert Bernasconi puts it, "ideas hunt in packs."[1]

But it would also be a mistake to maximize the anti-Jewish passages by representing them as the capstone or cornerstone of a Heideggerian edifice, or assuming that it is impossible from the start to find fruitful insights in his thinking that can contribute to our own philosophical ecosystems. "The strength of a work is measured by the extent to which it refutes its creator— i.e., grounds something altogether different from that in which its creator himself stood and had to stand" (GA 94: 438–39/318 tm).

The time for childlike admiration of Heidegger is long gone. No part of his thinking stands as a settled, proven body of assertions, but it all endures as a provocation that can inspire us to think more attentively. For a mature appropriation of his thought, we need a different kind of maximization of its disturbing elements. We must take them as welcome opportunities to think as hard as we can about his limitations and our own—about errancy, finitude, and responsibility. If we find these elements morally unacceptable, we can take this as an invitation to reflect on his hostility to moral points of view and on the basis of our own moral positions. If we find them politically obtuse, we can take this as a chance to rethink politics in a productive struggle with him, the kind of struggle he called an *Auseinandersetzung*—a confrontation that sets the opponents apart and clarifies their positions as they learn from each other.

This is just what Heidegger, at his best, would have us do. He wants a fight, not followers. "I still do not have enough enemies" (GA 94: 9/8 tm). "Perhaps even my *errors* still have a power to provoke in a time overloaded with correctnesses that have long lacked truth" (GA 94: 404/295 tm).

REASON AND ITS CONDITIONS

Heidegger's anti-Enlightenment, antirationalistic political thought is one key issue to consider. Is there a way to acknowledge whatever insights he achieves while also defending reason, and rational politics in particular? Can we articulate the most promising insights of modern rationality while appreciating his critique of the principles and concepts in terms of which those insights have often been couched? My purpose in this section is not to settle these questions, but to sharpen them by bringing out some of their implications.

The great thinkers and movements of the Enlightenment place their faith in the ability of the human mind to rise above its particular surroundings, understand them, and improve them. Daring to know (as Kant puts it in "What Is Enlightenment?"), with courage and work, we can transcend superstition, authority, and tradition in order to understand the principles of the universe and the mind, put them to use, and choose reasonable courses of action. Not only can we comprehend and control nature, but we can develop codes of conduct for individuals and communities that are based on mutual recognition and respect among rational beings. The citizens of a liberal democracy—the most successful type of regime founded on Enlightenment principles—are presumed to be at least capable of rational action, and the fundamental laws of such a regime are (in theory) designed to achieve a harmonious maximization of human freedom. Politics can thus be founded on the conditions of possibility for free, rational action.

This rationalistic approach seems incompatible with the situated, historical point of view that Heidegger espouses. We have seen him contrast "the *finitude, temporality,* and *historicity* of human beings" with the ahistorical rationalism of Platonism and the Enlightenment. "Here all of the powers against which we must struggle today have their root" (GA 36/37: 166/129). The French Revolution and liberalism erect an ideal of reason and are *therefore* proto-nihilistic.[2] In some texts we have considered, he presents Heraclitean struggle, the endless fight against concealment, as the finite counterpart to the in-finity of Hegelian truth; despite Hegel's aim to incorporate the finite rationally within the infinite, Heidegger sees Hegel's system as the apotheosis of deracinated logic.

Two more key ideas that led Heidegger into the thirties seem to run contrary to rational politics: the time when time arises and the event of emergency. Such moments are unpredictable, unique junctures that seem to escape any rational order. They reveal a situation and make discourse possible, but they themselves elude rational scrutiny and discussion. In some texts, as we have seen, Heidegger suggests that all discourse, all reasoning in the broadest sense, rests on a fundamental silence. Such events also seem to burst the boundaries of law: a state of emergency is typically invoked to authorize extraordinary powers and suspend normal rights.[3] The sovereign is the one who decides in an emergency, and such a decision exceeds the normal limits of law and justice. From a liberal or rationalistic point of view, the attempt to base a regime on apocalyptic revelations or the special gifts of a supreme leader is bound to be ruinous (not to mention the idea of turning for guidance to fragments penned by a mentally ill Romantic poet).

Two decades into the twenty-first century, liberal democracy is once again under pressure from authoritarian, nationalist, and religious movements that are reacting nonphilosophically against trends that Heidegger scrutinized philosophically: an economic and cultural globalization that shows no respect for place and history; an anomie that haunts people cut off from their roots; the empty seductions of technology. These problems are real—but how do we address them without plunging into the tyranny and bloodshed unleashed by the anti-Enlightenment movements of the last century? Heidegger's reflections remain highly pertinent, but we must guard against abandoning the moral, political, and scientific ideals of the Enlightenment without articulating a responsible alternative.

Is Heidegger's rejection of rationalism, then, an abandonment of thought itself, even an invitation to irrational violence? Or is it a more limited critique? What does he offer instead of reason as an essential characteristic of human beings?

"Reason," he writes, "is the most stubborn adversary of thinking" (GA 5: 267/199). His fiercest critics, from Carnap to Faye, have long denounced his denigration of reason. Does it not make him illogical and unphilosophical? Does it not turn him into a mystic, a poet, a sophist—anything but a thinker?

In its crudest form, this line of criticism is not hard to answer. The logical positivism advocated by critics such as Carnap has long been recognized by most philosophers as narrow and dogmatic. Furthermore, Heidegger himself writes that "irrationalism, as the counterpart to rationalism, speaks only with a squint about matters to which rationalism is blind" (SZ 136). One line of interpretation has drawn on Heidegger's work of the twenties to emphasize that Heideggerians can retain an important role for reason and "norms," even as they explore the existential conditions of possibility for giving grounds.[4] Even in the thirties, the *Black Notebooks* reject "Aryan" ideology with its celebrations of passionate "life experience"; "against the semblant depth of the [irrationalist] bog," we must seek "clarity" and "light" (GA 95: 60–61/45–46).

So even though Heidegger denies that thought must be guided by reason, he leaves room for the proper operation of reason in its legitimate domain, and insists on thinking, not just feeling or acting. If this sort of thought is no longer "philosophy," so be it—the Heideggerian may concede—but at the end of philosophy, we must still pursue the task of thinking.

However, the question of Heidegger and reason deserves to be investigated further. For one thing, even if we might be quite ready in principle to accept the nonlogical course of his reflections—their circles, their shifting significations, their sudden twists—we may suspect there are moments when he simply injects dubious claims, tenets disguised as questions, and relies on the force of his rhetoric to secure our assent. At such moments he verges on sophistry, and one wishes for a debate and dialogue that one cannot find on the pages of his text.

These concerns are important—one could reply—but no philosophers have anticipated every objection or been fully aware of their own unwarranted assumptions. Heidegger's way of thinking may be no more essentially irrational than anyone else's; it is a matter of degree. Nothing hinders a responsible and intelligent reader of Heidegger from questioning this or that assertion in his writings, just as one should with any other philosopher.

But there is a deeper issue, having to do with the overall thrust of his thought over the decades and the challenge that it poses to modernity. When we look past the particular problematic claims that he makes in one text or another, we find a cogent and consistent critique of the place of reason in human existence that is neither arbitrary nor unsupported. The implications of this critique are significant for both theory and practice.

Heidegger has affinities to some other critics of Enlightenment rationalism. Like the Romantics, he seeks revelations in moods and in the particularity of land and language. Like Kierkegaard, he rejects totalizing systems and, in *Being and Time*, emphasizes commitment to a possibility in the face of anxiety. Kierkegaard mercilessly mocks the notion that we can cogitate our way into authenticity or give reasons that will fully ground our own way of existing; the very attempt to live by reason alone is, first and foremost, an attempt to live, a way of seizing one's own being.[5]

But Heidegger goes farther than these modern antimodernists. His reflections extend past the Enlightenment to modernity at large, and farther back to the origins of Western philosophy itself. He identifies presence as the root sense of being that has sustained Western inquiry and practice for millennia. In order to overturn that tradition, he even pushes back to a question that precedes presence itself: what enables us to understand being at all, to recognize any distinction between something and nothing? If being were not at issue, the activities of giving reasons and seeking principles would not even be possible. This thought demotes reason from its traditional philosophical role as the supreme guide to theory and practice. How, then, is being at issue for us, if not through reason?

Let us briefly recall three major phases of Heidegger's response to that question. His answer in the twenties is that our understanding of being is made possible by time—a conjunction of situated thrownness, projected possibilities, and engagement in the world. We are able to reason, or give grounds, only because we exist in a significant "there." This significance is fragile: it is subject to dissolution in nonrational experiences such as anxiety.

In the thirties, he tries to understand time more radically, not as a structure but as an appropriating event, an emergency that thrusts us into being-there and impels us to ask who we are. In such an event, we are assigned our own problematic site and moment. This line of thought focuses on the inception, the elusive origin of our condition, as well as on the particular destinies of the West and the Germans.

In the forties and beyond, he meditates on the "open region" into which we have been "released." This region is not a structure either, but a permeable, vulnerable clearing. He encourages us to encounter the things that emerge in the clearing with a new simplicity and appreciation. He continues to stress that we depend on our involuntary exposure to a realm that we did not make, cannot control, and cannot exhaust. We have been granted unconcealment by a source we cannot fathom. At most, we can be attuned to how we find ourselves in the clearing and stay open to new possibilities.

In all these phases, Heidegger undermines the Enlightenment's confidence in reason by pointing to at least two forms of dependence that reason cannot eliminate. First, we depend on our nonrational familiarity with the standards and practices of our community—so much so that one's default identity is simply to be the "they," a typical participant in a group. All possibilities are drawn from a "heritage" (SZ 383). We do not have to take this word as referring to a narrowly bounded ethnic or national culture; the point is that possibilities do not come from nowhere, but are made available to us by some shared world in which we are enmeshed. We inevitably depend on our historical "thrownness." One cannot shed one's deep belonging to history as simply as Descartes suggested, by traveling abroad and learning to let go of one's prejudices (*Discourse on Method*, I)—or through multiculturalism, which, according to Heidegger, is just rootless curiosity and confusion (SZ 21, 178, 396).

Secondly, we depend on unpredictable moments of illumination. The banalities and truisms of the "they" can be transcended, but not through reason, and only in order to appropriate our own heritage more deeply. According to *Being and Time*, we awaken at moments when we hear the call of conscience, feel anxiety, or stare our own mortality in the face. These experiences give us no concrete guidance or values; they face us with "the nothing," the absence of any objective ground. In the thirties, the arrival of a deep emergency, a poetic "peak of time," or a new inception are also incalculable events.

Any reasoning in which we may engage, then—any fact-gathering, explaining, discussion, or deliberate choice—takes place on the basis of nonrational thrownness and nonrational moments of insight that expose us to the abysses of the happening of being. "Philosophy is not autonomous, but ontonomous" (GA 73.1: 688)—as is all of our existence. The shadowy preconditions of unconcealment sustain all our reflections and plans. We could not be sure of any principles or calculate any outcomes if we were not already "there"—and our way of being-there is not a matter of calculation. Rationalism thus fails to acknowledge our indebtedness to the hidden process of presentation. It takes this process for granted, as if things were simply, automatically available for our use and inspection.

When modernity forgets its roots, it distorts the human condition and destroys the richness and mystery of things. The result, for Heidegger, is a growing wasteland—a world where all beings, including humans, are reduced in both theory and practice to mere objects present for measurement and resources present for exploitation by a blindly arrogant subject.

This antirationalistic direction of Heidegger's thought is both promising and dangerous. One of its promises is its resistance to reductionism. This resistance continues to be necessary as the undeniable achievements of modern natural science and technology keep tempting us to believe that all human phenomena can be explained and understood through techniques that measure, predict, and control the nonhuman. Heidegger opposes "humanism," understood as the view that we human beings can judge and master all beings, including ourselves, through propositional and calculative thought. But he leaves open the possibility of a deeper humanism that understands us as distinctive beings whose selves are always in question, who are blessed and burdened with the task of interpreting the whole, and who exist as clearings where beings can reveal themselves, albeit never absolutely. For Heidegger, human beings are historical—not in the sense that they are hemmed in by conventional constructs, but as the recipients of a partial disclosure that has been entrusted to them and that they have the opportunity to develop. "Humanization becomes proportionately less destructive of truth as human beings relate themselves more originally to the location of their essential corner, that is to say, as they recognize and ground Da-sein as such" (GA 44: 129/119). This tentative, nonreductive approach to understanding ourselves and our world is a welcome corrective to the positivistic dogmatisms of our times.

But these promising aspects of Heidegger's antirationalism obviously coexist with its dangers. When antirationalist views enter the political sphere, they tend to undermine efforts at prudent decision and respectful debate, and to promote an unthinking attachment to a supposed collective destiny. Heidegger chose to align himself with an authoritarian and violent regime, hoping that it would bring a new inception of Western history. He develops a critique of the machination, brutality, and criminality of Nazism, but this critique has no moral dimension, and he applies it to all forms of modern politics. We have also seen that the universalism of the Enlightenment is linked all too easily in his discourse with antisemitic motifs.

Heidegger's concept of the moment of vision can be accused of emptiness: he does no more than hint at which phenomena in particular it illuminates. It simply reveals that our task is *"to be there"* (GA 29/30: 246/165). Furthermore, he offers no criteria for deciding whether a momentary vision is genuine or illusory. To these difficulties is added his personal lack of judgment: in 1934, the "moment" of being-there takes the form "We are here! We are ready! Let it happen!" (GA 38: 57/50), where the "we" is a *Volk* that affirms an authoritarian state. Yet despite this communal impulse, the moment of vision is an essentially secret and incommunicable decision on which authentic relations with others are subsequently grounded (GA 24: 408; cf. GA 38: 19/16). One could well object that a more universal and rational concept of insight is required, a kind of insight that involves articulate discussion and deliberation about particulars in the light of intelligible principles.

Heidegger might retort that since the moment of vision reveals a concrete and unique situation, it is not possible to specify its content philosophically; he could add that rational communication may well unfold within superficial everydayness, with no connection to the deeper sources of the concepts that it deploys. Such sources are revealed in moments that are necessarily rare (GA 29/30: 428/295), sudden (GA 66: 114), and granted only to a few. "One forgets to ask whether the genuine essence of truth does not consist in the fact that it is not valid for everyone—and that the truths of everyone are the most trifling of what can be gleaned from the domain of truth" (GA 33: 198/170). Heidegger has a point that is perfectly compatible with an appreciation for reason; Andrew Wiles's proof of Fermat's last theorem is no less true or rational for the fact that very few people can grasp it.

However, in his most chauvinistic thoughts of the thirties, the exclusivity of truth is taken to an extreme: the ecstatic existence of Dasein is not even available to human beings who lie outside the domain founded in the inception of Greek philosophy (GA 35: 84, 92). For both ethical and theoretical reasons, we should prefer the view that Heidegger seemed to hold in *Being and Time*: philosophy becomes possible only on the basis of an implicit understanding of being that is proper to all human beings. In this sense, "To be human *already means* to philosophize."[6] Ethically, this view encourages us to respect and learn from a broad variety of people (and perhaps some nonhumans as well). Theoretically, it gives philosophy a source and a subject matter in life, and acknowledges the indebtedness of concepts to practice and experience.

A proper appreciation of our finitude and historicity does not have to rule out all universal claims about the human condition; after all, Heidegger himself often tried to glean such insights. A universal assault on universality would soon become incoherent.[7] We do not have to pretend to a divine point of view in order to affirm the universal point that human beings are not gods—that we depend on diverse others as we make our incomplete efforts to define ourselves. We can recognize the universal truth that humanity has no right to declare, "I am that I am," but only to ask, "Who am I?" and "Who are we?"

The danger of Heidegger's political attitudes is evident to anyone who still finds truth in a morality of universal respect and in political liberty. But for those who wish to defend this ethical and political vision on philosophical grounds, he remains unavoidable, because his work brings us face to face with a series of essential questions.

What are the conditions for rational thought? Can we preserve an awareness of these conditions while we continue to analyze and explain the beings around us? Then we would develop our legitimate ability to seek grounds and make inferences, without presuming that our entire existence can be rationally grounded.

What are the conditions for rational action? Can we preserve an awareness of them while we continue to try to act in ways that are rationally justifiable, and to show respect for other rational actors? Then we would conduct ourselves reasonably, as far as we can, while recognizing that nonrational elements need to be in place before reason is possible.

If we are to develop a more thoughtful Enlightenment and cultivate reason without rigid rationalism, we should take to heart Heidegger's insight that only finite entities whose being is at issue are able to engage in reasoning. The political question is whether a pluralistic public sphere is compatible with this insight into our condition.

RAMIFICATIONS OF THE "WHO"

We need to draw the line between Heidegger's insights and his errors, between the elements of his thought that appropriately uncover the phenomena and those that go too far—or not far enough. As he repeatedly says in the thirties, to draw such a line between truth and untruth, or being and nonbeing, is also to delineate who we are and who we are not.

The questions "Who am I?" and "Who are we?" are crucial ones, and Heidegger is right to say that human beings cannot be reduced to a "what," an objective identity. As we have seen, against the prevailing ideology of the Nazi period, he insists that the mission of the people is a question, not an answer. A community is always becoming itself, without ever completing that journey; its members ought to remain alive to the problematic significance of all things, including themselves. Even during his year of greatest complicity with the Hitler regime, he insists that a people is continuously faced with its own being as an issue. The persistence of the question "Who are we?" is a "condition of possibility of the political essence of man" (GA 36/37: 293/220). As he puts it in some later texts, "We cannot wholly belong to any thing, not even to ourselves" (GA 40: 31/32). "We will not be permitted to believe that we simply have being-there and securely subsist; for this would run up against the innermost essence of being-there" (GA 73.1: 75).

But if Heidegger understood national destiny as an open question, why did he go so wrong in politics? How could he have lent his support to a dictatorship that tried to settle the "who" question in the worst possible way: by murdering those who "we" are not? The most troubling passage we have considered envisions answering the question by drawing a line with a sword: in order to keep its "edge," a people needs to identify an internal other who must be sacrificed (GA 36/37: 91/73). Are persecution and violence necessary to define who "we" are? Do we have to exclude some of "us" in order to define the rest? Heidegger was right to ask "Who are we?" but all too ready to lend a hand to a movement that tried to answer this question by inventing enemies of the people.

His approach starts to become more cautious after his rectorate. He seeks a subtler understanding of communal existence—a sense of shared self-hood that looks primarily to poetry and thought. But eventually he distances himself so far from all political movements and ideologies that he becomes incapable of making any distinctions between a politics that might allow for the free exploration of selfhood and a politics that would shut the question down. Even worse, he imagines that a new inception can come about only after a catastrophe brought about by the most extreme form of machination.

In his postwar thought, the "we" becomes more diffuse—he looks beyond Germany to the West at large, and even to the whole planet—and human beings cannot answer the question "Who are we?" even by drawing a tentative line. The human condition becomes an impressionist painting, as it were, rather than a drawing: what matters is less the outline of our selfhood than the color of it, and we must learn to appreciate that tone—even if it is a drab gray, dominated by the technological understanding of being—as the work of a painter greater than ourselves.

Despite Heidegger's promising beginning with the question "Who are we?" he ignored or disdained several fundamental political problems. Regardless of any moral judgment we may pass on his behavior, he failed to consider these basic issues, and instead became increasingly bitter and alienated from the entire political realm. The absence of any serious reflection on these problems means that he does not engage in political philosophy as such, which should not limit itself to ontological reflections on the essence of the political but must also consider more concrete ways in which political conflicts develop and may be temporarily resolved. The question of "who" leads to a wealth of issues in the political realm that have no final solution, but are always potentially at stake in a genuine political space, a space where emergencies and inceptions are allowed to take place, a space electrified by the "who."

First, to what communities does an individual belong, and how are they related? How do conflicts among them arise, and how might such conflicts be negotiated? For example, members of a minority linguistic or cultural community may find themselves at odds with their state, and may have things in common with citizens of another state. This was the case with the German-speaking inhabitants of the Sudetenland in Czechoslovakia, who according to Heidegger were denied "being," since they were not part of the Reich (NHS 56). Many non-Jewish Sudeten Germans welcomed Hitler's invasion in 1938. But for the Jews within the Reich, of course, being both Jewish and German became a crucial problem, and often a matter of life and death. The establishment of Israel created a Jewish homeland, but Israel includes an Arab Muslim minority as well as a Christian minority, ethnic Jewish minorities, and Jewish sects.

These are just a few familiar examples of how human beings combine a number of "identities." The term is a poor one, since it suggests that one could be "identified" if all of one's affiliations and lineages were named, or that one is "identical" to the intersection of all those groups. "Identity politics" at its crudest becomes a struggle for power among factions who wrestle against each other, but fail to wrestle with who they are. In reality, what it means to be, say, German, Arab, or Jewish is always in question, and so is what it means for an individual to "belong" to a series of groups. Judaism, with its history of debating interpretations of scripture, may be more sensitive to the permanence of such questions than some other religions. In a classic Jewish joke, a man asks his rabbi whether it is the tradition of their synagogue to stand during a certain prayer. "No." Is it our tradition to sit? "No." Then what is our tradition? "To argue over whether to stand or sit."

If every individual participates in a range of communities, each of which has its own constitutive debates about "standing or sitting," then a perfectly homogeneous community is impossible. Every group necessarily has differences and minorities. Heidegger mentions this issue, but does not pursue it: "The 'folkish' first attains its proper—which always means *conditioned*—truth when the essence of a people is itself recognized in its manifold inner contrariness" (GA 94: 521/379). How far should a state go in recognizing its subgroups—linguistic, racial, ethnic, cultural, or political? Should they have specific rights? Spain, for example, has consisted since 1492 of a combination of regions that differ in dialect, language, and even language group

(Basque is not Indo-European). During some periods in Spanish history, such as the Franco regime, linguistic minorities were repressed and Castilian Spanish was imposed on them. But even a liberal Spanish state that granted Catalonia a measure of autonomy and gave its blessing to Catalan-Castilian bilingualism was unable to prevent a declaration of Catalan independence in 2017. Of course, an independent Catalonia would have its own problems with a non-Catalan-speaking minority.

A perfectly unified community is impossible. As Aristotle observes, an excess of unity destroys a *polis* as such, reducing it to a household or an organism (*Politics* 2.5). But of course, a community of people who have nothing in common would not be a community at all. Divisions can become so intense that a society breaks down in civil war. The question, then, is how much division, diversity, and dissent a community should tolerate, or even encourage. Although the Moorish regime in southern Spain before 1492 was no liberal democracy, it tolerated Christians and Jews. After the defeat of the Moors, the rulers of Spain and Portugal chose to expel all Jews who would not convert to Catholicism. Today, Muslim immigration to European countries has led to passionate debates about how much cultural diversity and change a country can stand before it ceases to be itself.

To take a different tack: the question "Who are we?" is an excellent question, but one must also consider who gets invited to ask it. Who is asking "who are we" in the first place? Heidegger asks what "we Germans" connotes, but rarely considers whom it denotes. Were German Jews called to ask the question? What about Turkish or Syrian Germans today? How about South Tyroleans in Italy, or German-Americans? At one point in the *Contributions*, he does recognize that the reference or extension of "we" is problematic. "*Which ones* do we mean in speaking of 'we'?" (GA 65: 48/40). Unfortunately, he does not develop this question in any detail.

Who, then, gets to count as a member of a community? Can membership be established simply by legal status? Does it require participation in certain practices or allegiance to certain norms? Is it a matter of ancestry or language? Can individuals voluntarily join or leave the community? In recent American history, controversies over illegal immigration have brought these issues to a head. Most Americans feel that those who were brought to the United States illegally as children should have the right to become American citizens. But why, exactly, is that the case? And are these "Dreamers" more American than a person who entered the country illegally at age eighteen, but has learned English and participated gladly in American traditions and institutions?

Once the "who" question has been asked, who has the right or responsibility to respond to it? In one sense, this is the task of everyone in the community, who will respond to the question at least implicitly through their choices and habits. But Heidegger holds that some individuals are particularly qualified to articulate a community's destiny: Hölderlin, for instance, is the preeminent poet of the German mission. How would we recognize such individuals and deal with conflicts between them?

We are always faced with competing articulations of destiny—"sitting or standing." How can we tell which is preferable? Do we choose arbitrarily? Is the question decided through rhetorical force? Are these issues subject to debate and discussion? Americans, for example, have inherited both a tradition of individualism and self-discovery and a tradition of social responsibility. They have a tradition of industry and entrepreneurship, as well as a tradition of respect for wilderness. How can they do justice to the variety of their traditions while at the same time staking out their own answers to the questions embedded in those traditions?[8]

Perhaps "the people" can decide who they are, and which side in a traditional conflict will win. But is there such a thing as the will of the people? Is it to be decided by one or a few prophetic leaders? Or by a majority vote? Heidegger reportedly made the lame remark that the will of the people is "a complicated structure that is hard to grasp" (NHS 60). This is another crucial weak point in his reflections. If we have no account of how the so-called will of the people is to be ascertained, how disagreements are to be expressed and resolved, and when a leader's will transgresses its proper limits, then we have no philosophical bulwark against tyranny and demagoguery. His attitude in the 1933–1934 seminar seems all too typical of the times, when too many were ready to abandon the unruly pluralism of the Weimar Republic and submit to a dictator. But such a temptation is understandable when one contemplates the constant back-and-forth of democracies, where the political "pendulum" swings left and right without ever uniting the country.

One issue that can divide a people, and that often marks the difference between regimes, is the question of individual rights. Is a certain respect for our fellow human beings crucial to acknowledging them as "whos"? *Being and Time* suggests that teaching a man how to fish is more authentic than giving him a fish; it respects him as a being who projects possibilities (SZ 122). But should this kind of respect entail certain liberties and laws? Does it mean that a community should establish individual rights that recognize that each member is an issue for him or herself? Citizens might be guaranteed the right to assemble, to speak openly, and to practice their own religions—on the assumption that even though they will often make errors, beings faced with the question of who they are should be granted the freedom to explore their selfhood. Heidegger's attacks on liberalism portray it as an ideology that codifies thoughtless will to power, a system of atomistic subjectivities pursuing their own interests. His own account of Dasein is meant to shake up the subject and challenge the notion of individual autonomy. But does a liberal regime have to rest on a subjectivistic concept of self-determination? Could it also be founded on the very idea that our own being is at issue for us?[9]

Finally, let us turn briefly to international politics. If there is some gathering into a national unity (which, again, cannot be total), is there always a complementary diaspora, in which members of a nation explore other communities, learn from them, and even live abroad as expatriates or exiles? Heidegger's 1933–1934 seminar briefly asserts a fruitful tension between rootedness in the homeland and interaction with the exterior (NHS 55–56), but this is another theme that he leaves underdeveloped. One could argue that great cities—Berlin, New York, London—are great not because of their size or property, but on account of their openness to what lies beyond them, their restless curiosity about the alien. By incorporating the alien without assimilating it, by continuing to look past themselves, these cities develop their own dynamic character. The same open spirit may characterize entire nations.

Can different communities find their way to mutual understanding? How can members of one group learn from those of another? Heidegger reflects on such issues as regards the relations between the Germans and the ancient Greeks, Germany and France, and East and West.[10] Unfortunately, his thoughts never reach the level of concrete political problems. For instance, today many are asking whether the European Union promotes healthy international relations, or dissolves the culture and independence of European countries. Relations between countries with and without Muslim majorities are particularly fraught, and are exacerbated by acts of terrorism and military responses to them.

All of these issues are as familiar as the daily news, but they need to be explored well beyond what Heidegger's writings can offer us. He never thought through the problem of the internal multiplicity and multivalence of every community, not to mention its diaspora and its interactions with other communities. A nuanced understanding of these phenomena is indispensable to any grasp of actual politics. His insight that Dasein's own being is at issue for it provides an ontological starting point for basic questions of political philosophy, but his own political errors are examples of inadequate and unacceptable responses. If we stay alert to these questions, and do all we can to encourage public debate about them, we erect the strongest obstacles to an authoritarianism that attempts to settle them by establishing a collective identity through violence. The questions cannot genuinely be settled—they can at most be silenced. Contests over these questions—contests that engage both passion and reason—are a permanent part of authentic political life. No matter how firmly one may adhere to certain answers, either in philosophy or in practice, one should recognize that individuals and communities will continue to be faced with the challenge of the questions, for they are intrinsic to the burden of being.

ABOVE THE SEA OF FOG

Why does Heidegger fail to consider these implications of the fact that our own being is at issue for us? Why are his reflections limited to broad, often simplistic considerations of *the political* as such, without considering the *politics* of conflicting allegiances, minorities, rights, and other concrete issues? If he had thought about these complications, it is imaginable that he would have been more reluctant to serve as a functionary of the Hitler regime, and better able to make political distinctions after his disenchantment with the Nazi party. Even if ontological errancy is inevitable, perhaps he should have paid more attention to ontic error; then he would have been wary of presuming to understand the political situation in 1933. But such speculations do not take us far. We need to take a closer look at a certain abstract and disengaged point of view that characterizes his writings of the thirties.

Let us start with the *Black Notebooks*, which I have presented as a series of thought experiments—an incubator for ideas that Heidegger then used, very selectively, for publication. Many of the ideas developed in these journals are dropped sooner or later, and they cannot be summed up in a logical system. But we should not lose sight of the forest for the trees, or the overall *Denk-weg* for the individual *Holzwege*. Despite various contradictions one may find in a thinker's statements over the years, an overall tendency—not a set of consistent tenets, but a cast of mind—emerges from the whole. Heidegger himself, as we saw, claims that he has remained standing. "What one ferrets out as contradictions is in truth the essential unfolding of the simple that has come to language" (GA 97: 195). What cast of mind, then, is disclosed in the *Black Notebooks*?

An overriding tendency is the typical philosopher's thirst for essence, even if it is a historical essential unfolding (*geschichtliche Wesung*), at the expense of historiological facts (*das Historische*). For instance, when we want to learn about concrete incidents in Rector Heidegger's experiences in 1933–1934, we are disappointed; the pages from the rectorate (GA 94: 81–119) consist of vague expressions of determination and dissatisfaction. A reference to a particular change in Soviet leadership is the exception among sweeping speculations about the Russian soul (GA 96: 242). The metaphysics of power as the basis of Nazi ideology gets many pages of discussion, but specific Nazi actions go without comment. In a letter from 1939, he affirms "what the philosopher must always already know": "the invisible is more in being [*seiender*] than the visible."[11]

This is not a simple disregard for the concrete, but outright hostility: Heidegger dismisses facts, which he calls "the most superficial gray scum of a concealed history [*Geschichte*]" (GA 95: 96/75 tm). He despises *Historie*, which "compares everything to everything"[12] and never can reach the level of *Geschichte*. *Geschichte* has no need of *Historie* (GA 54: 94/64—but cf. GA 45: 50/46). "The occurrences of war . . . have nothing to do with *Geschichte*."[13] "All references [in the *Black Notebooks*] to what is historiologically graspable and to incidents and to what is contemporary are made only in passing, leaving behind all this stuff devoid of history [*dieses Geschichtslosen*]. But these frayed threads of the fluttering semblance of concealed history must at times be named" (GA 96: 250/198 tm). But is he not flying too fast into abstractions? He retorts: "The thinking which is heedful of the history of beyng is without 'content' and gives the impression of something 'abstract' and empty. Yet what looks like emptiness is only the falling away of beings in the determination of beyng" (GA 96: 26/21 tm). "Genuine experiencing has no need of the 'empirical.' It consists in being thoroughly attuned by being. . . . there is a phantasy of concepts that draws all beings together into what is essential in being, and precisely does not 'abstract'" (GA 96: 253/201 tm; cf. GA 96: 225, GA 95: 118).

Attuned by being or not, Heideggerian "phantasy" certainly runs the risk of falling into the purely fantastic, and of losing all perspective on everyday reality. Consider his statement that the Antichrist "would remain a harmless lad, over and against what is 'happening.'" What provokes this statement in the year 1940? The fact that the world looks like an American humor magazine (GA 96: 194/153).

Heidegger's hostility toward the empirical also excludes any feeling for victims of war and tyranny. In one of the more embarrassing entries in the *Black Notebooks*, he writes that the Gs in his name stand for the goals of *Güte und Geduld*, benevolence and patience. After *benevolence* he adds: "(not pity)" (GA 94: 273/200). That is a notable understatement in a journal packed with overstatements. Heidegger appears wholly unempathetic. We have seen misanthropy creep into the *Black Notebooks*, sometimes venting itself in extreme statements: it does not matter who gets "pulverized" by the war (GA 96: 133/104 tm); the self-destruction of humankind would be no tragedy, but the purification of being (GA 96: 238). In such passages he comes across as a bitter "Platonist," obsessed with essences at the expense of particulars.

His thirst for essence often takes the form of finding the unity of opposites. The *Un-wesen* must be understood as integral to the *Wesen*, and seeming opponents must be reduced to the metaphysical ground that they share.

"Metaphysics . . . provides [an] age with the ground of its essential shape. This ground comprehensively governs all phenomena distinctive of the age" (GA 5: 75/57 tm). Thus fascism, liberalism, and communism are all variations on a theme. Heidegger hunts for ironic twists that supposedly illustrate this common essence—such as the notion that the persecution of Jews is itself "Jewish" (GA 97: 20).

While he lays no claim to absolute truth, he often seems convinced of his superior insights, and despite his hostility to "an egoism of the private" (GA 97: 66) he sometimes comes across as a supreme egotist. In the postwar entries, his narrowness and coldness lead to a grotesque indifference to the victims of the Nazi regime. As we have seen, he does refer to Nazism as a "reign of terror" (GA 97: 84) under Hitler's "criminal madness" (GA 97: 444). But at the same time, he rejects the victors' claims to morality and justice, which he sees as mere masks for the spirit of revenge (GA 97: 50, 64, 117, 134–35). In a typical passage, he refers almost with contempt to "the broadly visible devastation and the horrors that can be graphically portrayed on posters," which showed photographs of concentration camps (GA 97: 84–85); these crude, ontic facts pale in comparison to the "self-annihilation that now threatens Dasein in the form of a betrayal of thinking" (GA 97: 83; cf. GA 97: 59, 63, 99–100). What is the prime example of this betrayal? Heidegger's own forced retirement.

Heidegger's scorn for morality, his lack of empathy, and his egotism should not simply be condemned from a moral point of view. He challenges us to ask ourselves: Is our moral indignation based on a bankrupt philosophy, religion, or political ideology? Is it myopic and hypocritical? In response I would suggest that the readiness to respect and care about other individuals is always something deeper than the fumbling, simplistic words and concepts in which we may try to express and justify it; ultimately, openness to the other goes deeper than any metaphysics or worldview, or any narrative about the fate of the globe.

This openness has something in common with the phenomenological attentiveness that Heidegger showed in his writings of the twenties, which faded away in the thirties, along with signs of concern for individual human beings. In the twenties he scrutinized not just texts, but experience, and was able to show that the usual metaphysical concepts were inadequate to that experience. He was able to build new, subtle concepts that were flexible enough to point to the richness of human life. In the thirties, he often sees life itself as determined by metaphysics; the alternative lies not in experience, but in a new inception that would establish a relation to being itself. He falls into the illusion, then, that his ability to critique the metaphysical concepts is also the ability to grasp human existence, what is happening on the ground.

One of the *Black Notebooks*' little surprises is Heidegger's praise for the painter Caspar David Friedrich, whom he calls "a peak towering into the godforsaken spaces of the divinity of the onetime God," a figure on a par with Hölderlin (GA 95: 364/285 tm). Heidegger must have known what is today Friedrich's most famous painting, *The Wanderer Above the Sea of Fog*. A man adopts a bold stance on a craggy peak, and we look out with him over a breathtaking landscape where the lower elevations are shrouded in mist. Heidegger must have felt that exhilaration when thinking of himself as one of the rare dwellers on mountaintops. But did he reflect on the mist? The wanderer in the painting has a magnificent view, but he does not see all: the clouds obscure the valleys below. Maybe he does not care—maybe that is part of his triumphant mood. So be it. But at least he should realize that he does not know what lies under the mist.

The heights are heights of both knowledge and ignorance. In his Olympian pose, Heidegger not only fails to see through the mist, but fails to see the mist itself. He not only has no sympathy for real, suffering individuals, but also thinks that he knows them when he does not. The dismissive statements in the notebooks—such as the repeated claim that he is living in the age of the total lack of questioning and thought—are themselves thoughtless, because the fact is that he does not know whether others are questioning.

Zarathustra must go down in the beginning of Nietzsche's book, and the philosopher-rulers must return to the cave in the *Republic*. Heidegger, who blames Platonism for so much, failed to learn the lesson of Plato's allegory. The philosophers return to the cave not only in order to save the *polis*, but also in order to understand the political realm in its particularity after spending time in the light of the intelligible forms. When they first return, they are unable to see in the relative darkness (*Republic* 516e, 518a). Knowledge of essences, then, does not suffice to grasp politics; we must both ascend and descend, and take the time to adjust our understanding to both realms. Heidegger's interpretations of the allegory of the cave exemplify blindness instead of recognizing it: he wrongly asserts that "with his view of essence [the philosopher] can now see what happens in the cave for what it is" (GA 34: 89/65). He takes the returning philosopher simply as an enlightened liberator who may be the victim of the deluded masses' stupidity and resentment, rather than understanding that the philosopher himself needs to relearn to see in the dimness (GA 34: 80–94; GA 36/37: 180–85).

Despite Heidegger's supposedly non-Platonist philosophy, then, he is a consummate "Platonist": he spends too much time in a Platonic realm "outside the cave" where he meditates on "being itself," without managing to do what Plato himself demanded: go back down and readjust his vision so he can see entities again. Plato's own dialogues express a cautious sensitivity to particulars. At his most "Platonist," then, Heidegger is actually least Platonic.[14] In his blindness, he resembles Plato's caricature of the "philosopher": "his next-door neighbor has been concealed from him—not only what his neighbor is doing, but almost whether he is a man or some other creature. Instead, the question [the philosopher] investigates is: what is man?" (*Theaetetus* 174b). This passage is often read as Plato's sincere praise of the philosophical life. Heidegger likes to quote the anecdote recounted there that Thales fell into a well and was mocked by a maid, which he uses as an occasion for defending philosophy (GA 35: 160; GA 41: 2–3; GA 73.1: 432). But a little reflection shows that the portrait of "the philosopher" in this portion of the *Theaetetus* contradicts Socrates's own behavior in this very dialogue: Socrates is not oblivious to particulars, but finely attuned to individual human beings. The passage satirizes abstract theorists such as Theodorus, the clueless astronomer and mathematician who is Socrates's interlocutor here. Heidegger plays the Theodorus in the most irresponsible possible way: he laments "the annihilation of the human essence" (GA 77: 207/133), but fails to face up to the "total annihilation" of particular human beings that he himself had legitimated in 1933 (GA 36/37: 91/73).

After his own brief venture in the cave of politics, Heidegger comes running back into the light. The events that the public considers significant are only a "shadow" of the history of beyng (GA 69: 205/174). To vary the metaphor, we can say that beyng casts the dice, which fall according to the "incline into which beyng appropriates itself to beings. Only those who are climbing know the incline" (GA 69: 213/180 tm). To anyone who may object that Heidegger is ascending only toward abstractions—that he is turning his back on real power relations, for example, as he focuses on the essence of the will to power—he replies that power is not an abstraction at all, and that we will know this when the apparently concrete is revealed as fleeting and "spectral" (GA 69: 182/155 tm).

There is a Hegelian flavor in this turn of phrase, which appropriately warns us that if we focus on the particular while neglecting the essence, we will lose ourselves in a domain that is ephemeral, unintelligible, and more "abstract" than any philosophical concept. But for Hegel, the essence too is abstract, until it is actualized in the concrete. In Heidegger, there is no comparable mutual dependence between being and beings. For all his criticisms of the traditional concept of essence as the abstract *koinon*, he directs his attention to generalities and disregards the particular. It is true that in the *Contributions* he insists on the importance of "turning back" from beyng to beings (GA 65: 453/356–57); he speaks of the "simultaneity" of beyng and beings (GA 65: 13/13, 223/174, 349/276) and the "sheltering" of the truth of beyng in beings (GA 65: 389–92/307–10). Yet all this remains an *abstract* tribute to particular beings: the particular is barely described or appreciated, and Heidegger strives almost exclusively to think beyng without beings (GA 65: 75–76).

There are certainly questions about being (or "beyng") that are relevant to politics but are ignored by ordinary political analysis. Heidegger's metaphysical genealogies of the key elements of political worldviews help us reflect more deeply on ideologies that tend to cover up their own roots. Sometimes he seems prescient: his concept of peace as the domination of the means of war anticipates the Cold War, and some of his insights can also be applied to twenty-first-century phenomena with little effort. In North Korea, "total mobilization" has been instituted in every aspect of life, keeping the population in a constant state of readiness for war in the name of national survival and an abstract idea that affirms collective subjectivity (*juche* or "self-reliance"). Attempting to resist the West, Islamic radicals have borrowed Western technology and ideas, creating a religious form of this subjectivist "self-reliance." The American reaction has been marked by a hubristic confidence in the self-evidence of the American worldview. Meanwhile, the Earth suffers the effects of being treated as a supply of "natural resources," while the most influential discussions of our environment continue to assume that we face a technical question—a problem of resource management—and not a question about the very being of nature.[15]

The error in Heidegger's thinking does not lie in his ambition to think on the level of being, but in his view that truth lies only on that level. In consequence, his drawings of humanity are too schematic and his paintings too monochromatic.[16] There is a leveling and oversimplification in his political thought, both early and late.

In particular, he eliminates the reality of human action when he insists that being is the root of political events. For him, "self-reliance" is an illusion that ignores our dependence on the happening of being. Once he loses faith in Nazism, he holds that choices cannot affect politics; they occur on the surface of the impersonal movement of being as power. He comes to see the entire thematic of choice and will as fatally indebted to modern subjectivism. His entire interpretation of his times is then focused not on action but on being. Current events are to be grasped not in practical terms, but in relation to the metaphysical essence of modernity (GA 66: 46–47). To the objection that "history has to go on, after all; something, after all, has to happen with man," he replies that history will go on in any case, no matter what the philosopher does, and that "knowledge of beyng" is a rich enough source of nobility, sacrifice, and inceptiveness (GA 70: 137–38). "The desire to battle politically against political worldviews . . . means to misunderstand that in them something is happening of which they themselves are not the master": "the abandonment by being" (GA 95: 317–18/248).

When Heidegger tries to give a narrative account of the history of being, the simplistic confines of his story get in the way of a fuller appreciation of political phenomena.[17] Even though he denounces "the age of the world picture," and is often at pains to distinguish worldviews from philosophy, it is obvious that in texts such as the *Black Notebooks* he is a man with a worldview. He is enmeshed in his narrative of the Greek inception that must be played out to its end—including the "catastrophe" of Nazism—before another inception can dawn. In these terms he sketches his caricatures of nationalities and ideologies—images that are constantly at work, shifting places but always playing menacing roles in the drama. We certainly need stories, but his master narrative is too restrictive and too closed to experience.

There are moments of lucidity when Heidegger sees through the crudity and hypocrisy of Nazi propaganda. He is also relentless in his criticisms of journalism and historiology—that is, *Historie* as the investigation of supposed facts about present or bygone states of affairs. But these criticisms come with a glaring blindness: for where is he getting his opinions about foreign countries and ethnicities (the English, the Romans, the Russians) except from historians, journalists, and propagandists? There is little evidence of firsthand observation of these groups. His comments, particularly on Jews, are appalling, but also philosophically disappointing in that, for the most part, they are nothing but clichés.

The essence of politics is by no means anything political, as Heidegger might rightly say (cf. GA 7: 7/QCT 4). For this very reason, when he focuses on the essence of politics, he turns away from politics itself—the realm of actual parties, policies, lawmaking, debate, and political power. In his view, this is no loss, because such phenomena are nothing but shadows on the wall of the cave. "One believes that everything that concerns 'the fatherland' must be 'political.' But 'the fatherland' can be approached and touched in its essence only when it itself is open to its essential ground . . . everything 'political' is the incarceration of the fatherland in its counter-essence" (GA 74: 38).

But this posture prevents him from recognizing crucial practical questions. It is not that he should be expected to have an answer to every concrete problem, but to deny that such problems exist as such, to reduce them to metaphysics and the history of being, is to obliterate a genuine domain of experience. Without an appreciation for this domain, it is impossible to judge events such as wars and revolutions appropriately.[18]

One of Heidegger's greatest failures as a political thinker is his indifference to liberty—his inability to see that political freedom is not reducible to the sometimes crude ideologies that support it. The metaphysical basis of modern liberalism is questionable, but the liberties that it provides are crucial if individuals and peoples are to find their way into the questioning thinking that Heidegger desires.

To Heidegger's credit, he saw through and passed beyond Nazi ideology and the metaphysics of struggle and power. But in doing so, he also overlooked all concrete struggles and powers. He passed through the political—and never returned.

THE SPHERE OF ACTION

Our critical discussion so far has identified several defects in Heidegger's political thought of the thirties: he identifies certain dependencies of rationality, but does not do enough to explore an appropriate role for reasoning within political life, and instead bases communal existence on a common silence; he sees that shared selfhood is permanently at issue, but does not fully appreciate the ramifications and conflicts that necessarily accompany the question "Who are we?"; and he develops penetrating analyses of the metaphysical presuppositions of political ideologies, but does not attend to the concrete situations in which actual politics are played out. As he turns away from politics, he discounts will and decision so much that action itself seems to become impossible or irrelevant. In order to recover politics while retaining what is illuminating in Heidegger's reflections on the political, we need a richer account of the sphere of politics that does not downgrade action, that attends to the multiple ways in which we develop our selves, and that gives rational discourse a part in this process.

Hannah Arendt's reflections in *The Human Condition* can contribute to this project. Her antitotalitarian argument draws on Heidegger's early insights into the truth in practical engagement and his phenomenological reading of Aristotle in the twenties; she develops a concept of action that is obviously at odds with the dictatorship that Heidegger supported in 1933, but also calls into question his late attempt to transcend power and the will. Arendt sent Heidegger a copy of *The Human Condition*, which was published in German under the title *Vita Activa* in 1960—but it arrived too late. Whereas she insists on the importance of rescuing *praxis*, he had already thrown the very concept of "the 'active life'" into scare quotes in the late thirties (GA 66: 52/42), and had turned toward an abstract analysis of the functioning of machination. If we are dissatisfied with his Olympian point of view, Arendt can help us see through the "fog" and turn back toward the "cave" where actual politics unfolds.[19]

In *The Human Condition*, Arendt rehabilitates the classical and medieval distinction between the life of the mind and the *vita activa*. She further divides the active life (in a broad sense) into labor, work, and action (in a specific sense).[20]

"Labor" consists of our cyclical efforts to sustain and promote our biological existence. The prototypical labor is farming, a necessary bodily effort that must constantly be renewed in order to keep us fed. Arendt associates this sphere with the household, which is also centered on biological life—procreation and family. For Aristotle, we might add, the household is also the scene of slavery; his model slave is primarily a servant who assists the master with the daily details of life (*Politics* 1.4). Although Aristotle argues that some are slaves by nature and thus slavery is sometimes just, he is at pains throughout the *Politics* to distinguish rule over slaves from other sorts of rule. Governing free citizens is a noble pursuit that calls for virtue; ruling a city despotically (as a master rules slaves) is nothing but vicious tyranny. Rule over slaves may be necessary within the household, but it is nothing to be admired (*Politics* 1.1, 1.7, 7.2, 7.3). This Aristotelian thought lies in the background of Arendt's arguments that the modern world risks becoming a field of labor and nothing else; labor is a sphere of necessity where despotism can easily take hold.

"Work" transcends the daily cycle of labor; it is the production of lasting things amidst which we dwell. In work we escape the realm of necessity and family, and generate a shared human "world." The prototypical work is architecture, which aims to produce an enduring scene for human activities. Work can also be less tangible: legislation or poetry can also produce a lasting context for our lives. But as a rule, work is physical fabrication, and fabrication transforms: it does violence to the existing form of things and uses them as raw material to produce new things. The original material becomes a means to a new end. The risk here is that the mentality of fabrication, the worldview of *homo faber*, may end up degrading the universe, viewing it as a collection of resources and judging everything in terms of utility. What this mentality overlooks is that the "in order to," or utility, is not the same as the "for the sake of"—the sense of who we are and can be (SZ §18). We must also note that although it generates a shared world, work itself is not necessarily shared with others; sometimes the worker can best concentrate on fabrication in solitude.

In contrast, "action," the most elusive and fragile domain of the *vita activa*, requires plurality as its very condition: action happens between people. The prototypical act is the response of a newcomer who is asked, "Who are you?" (HC 178). The response introduces the stranger to the community, reveals him as a player in the drama, and may start a new chapter. It is almost impossible to reply appropriately without using words, and these words are themselves an action. They partially display the stranger's self, and by the same token do something to connect him to the others: "I'm a friend of so-and-so," "I bring a warning from so-and-so," "I've come to help." These words are neither labor nor work: they produce nothing directly, their immediate efficiency is zero—but their revelatory and initiatory power may be immense. Reasoning, in a broad sense that includes all discourse and articulation of goals, is crucial to human interaction.

Arendt takes the newcomer's response as a paradigmatic act because human beings as such are newcomers: "We are all the same, that is, human, in such a way that nobody is ever the same as anyone else who ever lived, lives, or will live" (HC 8). She does not mean the triviality that there will always be discernible points of difference between the present-at-hand qualities of two individuals; this point remains external, and could even be applied (with Leibniz) to all beings as such. Her point concerns the "who": we have each been given our own being as a burden that only we, as individuals, can bear—or fail to bear. Because we live in a world that we share with other such beings, we must deal with our own being by initiating events within that world. In short, we must act, and thereby emerge as who we are. Thus to act, for Arendt, is essentially to come into appearance—to disclose oneself and become oneself in a public space, "to make articulate [one's own being] and call [it] into full existence" (HC 208).[21] *What* we are is generic: organisms with a human genome. But *who* we are is revealed and comes to be only if we distinguish ourselves from and in front of the others by freely undertaking some action. This thought offers us a fresh concept of inception, or to use Arendt's well-known word, "natality."

The significance of action, then, has more to do with the character and biography of the actor than with the desired result. Of course one acts with the hope of achieving something, but "if nothing more were at stake here than to use action as a means to an end, it is obvious that the same end could be much more easily attained in mute violence, so that action seems a not very efficient substitute for violence" (HC 179).

It would also be naive to hope for too much from any act, because several "disabilities" inhere in action (HC §32). In principle, labor can be automated and work can be mastered technically, but action, as an interpersonal intervention, exceeds anyone's control. Every agent's action invites the participation of other agents, who will take it in unexpected directions. Because of this dependence on others, and because of our limited understanding of our situation and ourselves, we cannot be sure where our actions will lead, or what their sense will be in retrospect. Since we cannot undo what we have done, we inevitably get entangled in the unintended consequences of our initiatives. These difficulties can be ameliorated, but never eliminated, by forgiving and promising (HC §§33–34). If these sobering truths lead us to retreat from action altogether, the shared future will wither away. But if we act while pretending that the disabilities do not apply, we fall prey to a foolish hubris.

As an interpersonal event, action will always involve the possibility of resistance, misunderstanding, and abuse. There is no "final solution" to these conditions; they are essential to the process. The very concept of a solution is appropriate to the domain of making, not acting. There can be an optimum solution to the problem of designing the most aerodynamically efficient aileron, but there can be no solution to the problem of friction in human action; to eliminate the possibility of friction would be to eliminate action itself. Inequality, injustice, and unfreedom cannot be purged from human relationships without abolishing those relationships themselves—which usually means abolishing human beings. We may combat these obstacles in case after case, but they exist and will always recur because of human freedom itself.

Arendt also draws a useful distinction among strength, force, violence, and power, reserving the last term for a phenomenon specific to action (HC §28). By "strength" she means an individual's natural physical and mental ability; it is possessed by one person, can in principle be measured, and is needed for both labor and work. "Force" can be controlled either by an individual or by a group, and may rely on man-made objects (such as weapons). Force is a means of "violence," which can be "stored up and kept in reserve" (HC 200). Force and violence, like strength, can be used in labor and work.

This is all straightforward enough, but when we come to Arendt's notion of "power" we encounter a cryptic concept that has nothing to do with our usual notions. Physics conceives of power (energy) as the capacity to do "work," that is, change the velocity of a mass; in the human sphere, power (as we all too often think of it) is the capacity to make something or someone bend to our will. Power is always an event of overpowering, as Nietzsche might say—and as Heidegger puts it in his analysis of machination. But for Arendt, "Power is actualized only where word and deed have not parted company, where words are not empty and deeds not brutal, where words are not used to veil intentions but to disclose realities, and deeds are not used to violate and destroy but to establish relations and create new realities" (HC 200). Power, in her sense, is essentially interpersonal and political; unlike strength and force, it cannot belong to one person alone. It cannot be measured or stored up. Violence can overcome power, but cannot substitute for it. Arendt thus describes tyranny as a combination of force and powerlessness (HC 202).

Here again, Arendt follows Aristotle's lead. For Aristotle, there is no such thing as "power" in general, but only potentials to perform qualitatively different activities.[22] The concept of power as overpowering other human beings and bending them to one's will is only one kind of power, modeled on slavery. The relation of master and slave differs qualitatively from that of husband and wife, parent and child, or political leader and fellow citizens (*Politics* 1.13). The differences lie in the purposes of the relationships and the capacities of the people involved. There is no single phenomenon of ruling common to all human relationships; ruling takes on different characteristics in accordance with the function that it performs. On the despotic extreme, the master uses the natural slave as a living tool who has brawn, but not brains—or has reason enough to understand commands, but not to make prudent decisions for himself. The natural slave essentially belongs to another, because his highest fulfillment lies only in making the good life possible for someone else. Although the natural slave benefits from slavery, according to Aristotle, this benefit is incidental; the inherent purpose of the relationship is to assist the master. On the other extreme we find specifically "political" rule, rule over fellow citizens for the sake of the common good. Here the ruler should be first among equals, one who has learned how to rule by being ruled and is now taking his turn as leader (*Politics* 3.4). Only the ruling that occurs in this political sphere is inherently noble and great, whereas the art of ruling slaves has nothing admirable about it. Political rule is free activity in relation to free human beings, and its essential element is *logos*, which is necessary to reveal the just and unjust (*Politics* 1.2).

Aristotle's politics are aristocratic, but his insights into political power are not limited to a highly hierarchical situation. Whenever individuals motivate and inspire others in a community, setting in motion revelations and creations, political power—what Arendt calls "power" simply—is at work. This dynamic cannot be captured by despotic models of politics, the physics of forces, or the metaphysics of overpowering. Political power is unpredictable and may well seem miraculous. (Weber has to use an originally religious concept, "charisma," to describe it.) It can spring up in situations that seem hopeless and from agents who seem insignificant, given the right conditions for political *logos* to stir and transform us.

Arendt's distinctions among labor, work, and action help us clarify the purpose of politics. Politics is often confused with economics: it is seen as the job of all jobs, the task of maintaining the whole system of labor. "Economics" is Greek for household management, and on this model of politics, a nation is a vast household that has to be kept running. But if we reduce politics to labor, we strip it of its ability to set goals. The human good is determined in advance: to survive and thrive by producing and consuming. Politics is then just a means of perpetuating this cycle. If this is all there is to human life, we become no better than ants or bees—healthy, industrious animals that satisfy their wants. As the ancients put it, higher than mere life is the good life, and labor serves mere life.

One could argue, instead, that the goal of politics is nationbuilding—creating a physical infrastructure and legal superstructure. Law enforcement and national security are included in this project, for defending a nation is a corollary of building it. Politics can then do more than housekeeping: it can construct and protect the house itself. This concept makes politics a kind of work, in Arendt's terms. Such a notion makes us impatient with the political process, since debating, campaigning, and haggling are obstacles to the implementation of any plan. If politics is work, it may even be the case that violence is inevitable.

But from an Arendtian point of view, politics is neither labor nor work, but a kind of action whose purpose is to keep the possibility of action itself alive—to foster further action by citizens. The impulse to act is universal, but the opportunity is not; action thrives only if there is a space for it, an atmosphere that encourages us to speak out and intervene. Good politics continually reopens a shared future by provoking debates about who we are and where we should go, and inviting citizens to participate in these debates. What appears as an obstacle from the architectonic point of view—the messy business of compromise and persuasion—is the lifeblood of politics as action.

In an apolitical environment freedom cannot flourish, even if individual liberties are legally guaranteed. A world in which we spend all our time in our houses, our vehicles, our workplaces, and our shopping malls is a world defined by the private realm of family and the economic realm of the marketplace. In such a world we are not free in the full sense, because no truly public space exists; we are not encouraged to reach beyond the familiar, disclose ourselves to other citizens, and start something new together. Inceptions and emergencies are kept to a minimum—and the question "Who are we?" is kept quiet.

With these points in place, we can make some tentative distinctions among types of revolutions and types of regimes.

All changes of regime require some action and power, in Arendt's senses. What may seem like brute force—a military coup or the triumph of one side in a civil war—could not come to pass without the exercise of authority and persuasion, speech as action. Sometimes revolutionary action has the effect, intended or not, of establishing a repressive regime that sets up obstacles to action—but that is no reason to deny that action took place. Furthermore, since all action is undertaken in uncertainty, the retrospective judgment that a revolution was essentially and inexorably closed to action is always somewhat unfair.

However, sometimes obstacles to action are an explicit part of the program of the revolutionary leaders—betraying the very meaning of revolution, if Arendt is right to claim that "the aim of revolution was, and always has been, freedom."[23] If we prize the freedom that is exemplified in all action, we should be loath to lend our support to a leader who expresses contempt for individual liberty and thinks of politics in despotic terms. If conversation and argument are essential parts of opening the future, then no dictator, no matter how rhetorically gifted, is able to engage the people in a political project. Such a project is not marching or building in unison, but coming together to argue and converse. What we share are the issues and the urgency, the care for the future of the community, and not any particular answer.

To use one's own freedom to support an attack on freedom disregards the value of one's act as such by subordinating action to a "higher end" that may end up denying the essence of the human condition. If our being is an issue for us, and we can appropriate our being only by acting, then a system that leaves no room for action smothers human existence itself. When we try to judge a revolution, we must ask whether its leadership and its program value free action as such, or subordinate it to an architectonic program that aims to "remake" a community in accordance with a single vision.

The revolutions of 1989 would seem to be prime examples of genuine action that promoted further action. The ground was prepared by individuals such as Mikhail Gorbachev and Lech Wałęsa, but the revolutions themselves seemed to spring up through an interpersonal dynamic that could not be localized or attributed to a few ringleaders. They swept through the communist bloc unpredictably yet irresistibly, showing how "force" can sometimes melt away in the face of "power." And the predominant view among those who participated in and witnessed these revolutions was that their goal was not a particular arrangement of society, but liberty itself—the freedom to act freely.

For Arendt, the "attempt to replace acting with making is manifest in the whole body of argument against 'democracy,' which, the more consistently and better reasoned it is will turn into an argument against the essentials of politics" (HC 220). The ancient antidemocratic argument is summed up efficiently in *Republic* 557e–558c: democratic freedom amounts to anarchy, democratic majority rule elects popular but not virtuous leaders, and democratic equality is sheer injustice—because unequals should not be treated equally. But this line of thought undermines political action itself. If we are unwilling to hand our destinies over to a group that claims to possess knowledge of "the good," then the authority of the "superiors" has to give way to debate, pluralism, and broad access to political power. Freedom, majority rule, and equality before the law promote the widespread action and discussion that are the alternative to submitting to "wise" political architects.

How often does a good democratic regime, a regime that fosters action, come about? Arendt looks back with heavy nostalgia to Periclean Athens, whose culture was supposedly devoted to the glory and remembrance of individuals' great words and deeds, in all their extraordinary uniqueness (HC 197–98, 205–6). *The Human Condition* is so short on references to "power" in the present day that it is easy to get the impression that for Arendt, the present is hopeless. This view would do the present an injustice. Spontaneous actions still take place every day in countless meetings and forums. (Some are cyberforums, which are ambiguous and problematic, but better than nothing.) Still, there must have been something extraordinary about fifth-century BC Athens, a small town by our standards, where so many memorable individuals came on the stage. The character of a regime and its worldview certainly affect the likelihood that political power and action will arise.

It is true that no institution or constitution can guarantee the frequent flowering of action, and action may manifest itself anywhere. What will always tend to drag action down is the weight of its everyday requirements and antecedents: the ensuring of physical survival and comfort, the construction and maintenance of the world. Most of us, most of the time, are left with little initiative for action. No matter where action occurs, and precisely because moments of action are unique and extraordinary, they tend to be reabsorbed into the ordinary and generic. Action is born from its everyday antecedents, dies back into them, and is reborn. No political system can make this rebirth come about. Action cannot be made—it can only be taken.

But even though no system can bring about action, some systems leave room for it or even encourage it, while others try to minimize its possibility, seeing it as a threat to the social machine. A culture or regime may focus its attention on work and labor, forgetting that these exist for the sake of the action that they enable.

This line of thought also enables Arendt to develop a critique of the modern age. Modernity first destroys the notion of a superior and independent *vita contemplativa*; the *vita activa* is then conceived in terms of work; finally, the entire human enterprise devolves to the level of labor. Modern culture, according to Arendt, has tended to obliterate action as the highest realm of the *vita activa*; instead, the strongest force in our culture is the mentality of the *animal laborans* (HC 134).

This is a provocative, sweeping, and surely problematic diagnosis, but all we need consider at the moment is a narrower point: action is not work, and political philosophers have all too often tried to substitute work for action (HC §31). The notion of "making" a good society is unpolitical at its heart, because it leaps over the words and deeds from which political life is woven; instead, political philosophy tends to adopt the solitary perspective of the craftsman in his workshop, "where one man, isolated from all others, remains master of his doings from beginning to end" (HC 220). Dictatorship misconstrues action in terms of production, as if it were a process that could be guided by a solitary technician, when instead action is an interpersonal, public initiative. The notion of "sovereignty," which is "contradictory to the very condition of plurality," brings violence in its train (HC 234). Violence, as we saw, is inevitable when work transforms raw material into a finished product—so when we view politics in terms of production, we inevitably condone and even glorify violence (HC 228). We could think here of the paradigmatic reduction of politics to making in the *Republic*, where Socrates uses a metaphor that may initially seem innocuous (if we think the fine arts are harmless entertainment): philosopher-rulers would be like painters who look toward the forms of the just and good as models, and paint the most beautiful possible constitution and citizen using practices as their palette. Then Socrates adds the chilling remark that in order to paint, one needs a clean, white surface. When human beings are your canvas, what does it mean to wipe the canvas clean?[24] The extreme architectonic politics of the twentieth century give us an answer: gas chambers and killing fields.

The "beautiful city" of the *Republic* is a regime founded by philosophers, who tend to interpret founding as work. Questions of constitutions, laws, institutions, and structures, including the arrangement of the means of production, are easily viewed as architectonic issues, questions of how best to build a world. These issues can obviously make an immense difference in the conditions of our lives: Do we live in a situation that allows freedom and flourishing, or are we oppressed and exploited? But the construction of the conditions of our lives is not living itself. Distinctively human living, Arendt argues with Aristotle, takes place in action and thought. We could say that world-building is a means to an end, if this language were not already the language of work and production. It is better to put it this way: world-building gains its sense, its *raison d'être*, from the "action and speech" that it enables (HC 173, 204).

We can now apply these Arendtian insights in a critique of Heidegger's thought in the thirties.

In the early years of the Nazi regime, Heidegger hoped for a new founding of the German people. We have seen him waver among several conceptions of founding, none of which is particularly satisfactory and some of which betray serious misunderstandings of the sphere of action. For instance, the *Nature, History, State* seminar indulges in a crude fantasy about the unity of leader and people; he insists on the absolute authority of the Führer without recognizing that in action, the initiator is not a lone technician, but depends on others to interpret his message, take up his initiative, and develop a new chapter in the story.

Heidegger's celebration of violence in texts such as *Introduction to Metaphysics* is another sign of his fascination with the figure of the founder as creative worker, the constructor of the *polis* who is *apolis* precisely because he establishes it (GA 40: 161–62). Such images make sense only if we assume that the function of a leader is to create, to make—a kind of work that, like all work, employs violence.

In 1937, a telling reference to "the architect" joins Heidegger's usual triumvirate of poet, thinker, and statesman (GA 45: 43/40). The model of the "ultimate politician" as "the final builder of the total building"[25] has entranced fascists, communists, and capitalists alike (see Howard Rourke in Ayn Rand's *The Fountainhead*). The architect of a community stands above the existing community in order to destroy and rebuild it. But as Arendt shows us, genuine action is interpersonal initiation, a deployment of "power" on a level essentially different from violence, a power that cannot be concentrated in the hands of a lone despot.

Heidegger did eventually distance himself from Hitler, but his continuing fascination with the "maker"—now the supreme maker, the *poietes*—betrays his continuing difficulty in conceiving of action. What are we to do in the "there" once it has been poetically founded? His answer in the *Contributions* is that we should "shelter" the truth of being in beings, where the prime example of sheltering is the work of art. But as for how we are to get along with each other or speak to each other, he has nothing to say.

Being emerges in *Ereignis*, the event of the grounding of the there; a shared space rips open at a critical juncture, the "site of the moment." Being, then, happens as inception. But Arendt would surely point out that inception or "natality" is embodied in specific actions between individuals, actions that involve discourse and generate life stories. Heidegger's postpolitical ruminations on inceptivity (e.g., GA 70) tell no stories about anyone's life—they only sketch a simplistic arc for Western thought.

The founding of a system, whether such founding happens through violence, art, or Arendtian "power," is not the supreme act, but gets its *raison d'être* from what it enables: action, which cannot be understood in terms of work (founding, building, breaking, making). The deepest inception, the true natality, lies in citizens' interactions—not in the ground-laying and world-building that makes them possible.

As we have seen, Heidegger also fails to think through the "will of the people," fascinated as he is by the "soaring will of the leader" (NHS 62). In this way, he lent his hand to a revolution that aimed at constricting the German world and asphyxiating genuine action. He eventually tried to find a way beyond willfulness itself, seeing it as a symptom of modern devastation; but Arendt is closer to the mark when she accepts will and action as part of the human condition, yet emphasizes the interpersonal character of action and its irreducibility to a single actor's will or plan. The initiative may stem from an individual, but the course of the action and even its meaning are shared and unpredictable, as long as we are talking about true *praxis* rather than technical production.

The problem of plurality raises its head again in connection with language and silence. As we have seen, the 1934 *Logic* course bases belonging to the *Volk* on a mysterious unison among secret individual choices. "Each must himself venture the leap, if he wants to be a member of a community" (GA 38: 19/16). The idea echoes a comment on authentic being-with in *Being and Time* (SZ 122) and also appears in the 1933–1934 seminar: "The true implementation of the will [of the state] is not based on coercion, but on awakening the same will in another, that is [. . .] a decision of the individual" (NHS 62). Heidegger envisions complete unanimity as the ideal: "Only where the leader and the led bind themselves together to *one* fate and fight to realize *one* idea does true order arise" (NHS 49). So although community depends on individual decisions, any such decision that contradicts the will of the state, which is identical with the will of the leader, is out of order and amounts to a betrayal of the people. Heidegger wishes for a shared national mood that unites secret choices in a shared silence, not unlike the taciturn rootedness of his pipe-smoking peasant neighbors. His authoritarianism at this time is allied to a quasi-Kierkegaardian inwardness: public utterances and behavior are genuine only if they are supported by the individual's secret, inner decision to support the new state.

This totalitarian individualism, so to speak, may seem bizarre, but it is a logical consequence of tyranny: when public discourse does not tolerate dissent, inner consciousness becomes a matter of intense interest both to citizens and to authorities. What has been lost in this situation is a genuine public sphere—neither a private mind nor a governmental system, but an arena where individuals can display themselves.

Such a display should not be understood simply as the expression of a preexisting inner resolution; in a vital public sphere, individuals discover themselves and become themselves *in* their public acts. They respond to the "who?" in practice. As Arendt argues, the specifically political realm is this public arena of free initiative and self-revelation. Take a simple example: the vote of a legislator. Whatever hidden motives may lie behind this vote, it would be wrong to insist that the real decision is hidden: the political decision consists in the public act of casting a vote. The choice to vote a certain way is fully actual if and only if one votes. The same can be said of speech: to take a certain stand in language on the issues of the day is to be, and not merely seem to be, a political actor. Whatever the speaker's silent experiences or unspoken thoughts may be, they are subpolitical or suprapolitical; politics proper happens in public, between people.

If a healthy public sphere and public discourse are essential to political existence, we cannot agree that a community is ultimately bound together by reticence, or by the creations of solitary thinkers and poets. A "metapolitics" based on a secret confluence of silences is not politics. The political sphere is essentially a public sphere: it requires as much explicit communication as possible, precisely because the "who" of the people is always a contested self-hood that calls for debate. The peasants smoking silently around the hearth certainly share a world, and without a shared world, there is no *polis*. But we cannot conclude that silent coexistence is more authentic than discourse. If a dispute arises among the peasants about whether someone's cattle have the right to graze on a certain pasture, words will become necessary in order, as Aristotle says, to discover the just and the unjust (*Politics* 1.2). Such speech sets the truly political animal apart from pseudopolitical animals such as bees. A hive needs the transfer of information, but it does not need—in fact, it must exclude—*logos* as political debate (not to mention *logos* as poetry and philosophy). The specifically political being of a community does not consist in what goes without saying, but on its members' readiness to define themselves through speech in the public realm. This speech is often a kind of reasoning; it is driven by claims to justice, which come with justifications. But such reasoning need not be rationalistic; it can acknowledge that it is finite and fallible. The practice of political reasoning binds people more fully into a community. That does not mean unanimity, or common devotion to a single idea, but participation in a plurality, with all its friction and faction.

This line of thought is essentially antitotalitarian: freedom of speech and association are necessary for us to have opportunities to take up our own being as an issue. When unanimity is enforced, it excludes all genuine debate and imposes silence by raising the specter of punishment for those who express politically incorrect views. In the absence of free speech, thought and questioning are driven into hiding. For a philosopher to support totalitarianism is thus a practical contradiction. Heidegger does assert in his rectoral address that "All following carries resistance within it" (GA 16: 116/116), but he does not do justice to this insight.

Heidegger did not develop true political discourse, which is never simply a matter of deploying rhetoric but requires listening. In his passion to decide and act, he insisted that nothing less than a unanimous "yes" to the leader's will could constitute the Germans as a community. But unanimity is not community. Even if there were no dissenters, the unanimous citizens would be deprived of the possibility of acting. A political community is not *una anima*, one soul, but a plurality. Heidegger was right in *Being and Time*: a people can find itself only through communication and struggle—but as he should have understood, the *Führerprinzip* destroys both. A community can thrive only when it has a healthy space for dialogue, interaction, and competition, a space that separates and unites us at once—a world.

In Nazi Germany, such a realm was supplanted ever more forcefully by orders and propaganda; any public discussion of political matters was tightly restricted. Nazism would supposedly bring the Germans into their own, allowing the people to be itself in full. However, by destroying any sphere for genuine plurality and self-expression, Nazism in fact prevented the Germans from thriving and finding themselves. Heidegger failed egregiously to recognize this destruction of the public sphere in 1933–1934.

At the war's end, he interprets evil as a self-concealing darkness (GA 77: 208). If this thought has merit, could it follow that evil lurks in the silent core of the speech of every people? Is the secret homeland also the heart of darkness? If so, then the way to fight the evil within a people is not to appeal to silence, but to speak out. Speech—and the institution of *free* speech—is a fallible weapon against evil, but it is the deepest weapon, because it counters mute brutality with articulate humanity.

To defend the existence of a public sphere is not to deny the finite, historical, and qualitatively diverse character of humanity; to the contrary, it provides the space in which this character can be articulated and developed. The most essential space of a people is constituted by the cultural and political fora in which individuals and groups can ask, "Who are we?"

To be clear, the point is not to insist on communication at the expense of all silence. Life would be shallow without intimate and enigmatic experiences that resist public expression. Philosophy itself requires some solitary reflection, and often brushes up against the limits of language. However, Heidegger's dim view of political discussion is a philosopher's prejudice rather than a satisfactory philosophical investigation of the public sphere.

Finally, let us reflect from an Arendtian point of view on Heidegger's postpolitical disengagement in the late thirties and thereafter. In this period he rejects his earlier celebration of will and action as a subjectivist illusion. It matters little whether the subject is an individual out for profit, a race, or an economic class; in all these cases, the subject is in the grip of its own world picture and enslaved to the will to power.

Heidegger's shift of focus from individual will to larger, impersonal power structures is not without merit. He can be said to have anticipated Arendt's insight into "the banality of evil" within the mechanisms of totalitarian regimes: murderous functionaries may be driven less by personal malice or sadism than by abstractions and power relations that they leave unquestioned.[26]

But in his late thought, Heidegger is unable to think of the initiating power of will and action apart from the metaphysics of the will to power, exemplified above all in Nazi ideology. His response to subjectivism is to wait and listen for the call of being. This is a solitary thinker's response, perhaps even a response that is necessary in order to recover the *vita contemplativa*. The disdain for the life of action may be a typical attitude of philosophers, whose semidivine solitude makes their life alien to the city, *xenikos* (Aristotle, *Politics* 7.2). But in the *vita activa*, subjectivity can be transcended only through intersubjectivity. What we need in action is not the abandonment of will, but a different kind of will: the flexible determination to take part in the public world. Only by acting with and against each other—primarily by speaking and listening to each other—can we elude the tyrannical temptation in our condition.

Lack of initiative implies the impoverishment of the world and the dimming of temporality. If I project only minimal possibilities for myself, the future constricts; the past has no relevance, since I have no need to explore it for my projects; and the present, instead of enticing me as a field of interesting opportunities, becomes nothing but a static collection of purposeless objects, trapped in a "blind mirror" (GA 40: 49/50). In the utter absence of action there would be no ecstatic time, no being, and no thought. Time comes to be when we come to act.[27]

* * *

For all the complexity of his thought, some of Heidegger's failings are quite simple. As we have seen, he himself acknowledged his "errancy," but fell far short of an apology. He frankly states that his thinking lies "beyond good and evil" (GA 97: 179) and often insists that moral categories are far too superficial to grasp the meaning of machination (e.g., GA 69: 80). If we ourselves are unwilling to set morality aside, then a negative moral judgment on his stance is inevitable. He is morally indefensible. What, then, is to be gained by working through his ambiguities, if we are quite clear on the evil of Nazism? Is there anything of philosophical value today in Heidegger's political thought?

It is clear that, even if Heidegger never set aside his sympathies for the Nazi movement, he held that its predominant ideology was superficial and that it was oblivious to its own metaphysical presuppositions. His analyses of those presuppositions may have cogency independently of whether he was pro-Nazi, anti-Nazi, or (as I have argued) affirmed Nazism precisely as a catastrophic counter-essence. His metaphysical diagnosis of Nazism is certainly debatable, but that is a debate worth having, and perhaps a necessary one if today's racist and neofascist movements are to be combatted intellectually.

However, Heidegger insists that all political and historical events are to be judged *exclusively* in terms of their metaphysical presuppositions. For instance, he asserts in the 1940 Nietzsche lectures that "'totality' is not the invention of supposed 'demagogues and dictators,' but the essential trait of a metaphysical process" (GA 48: 168). We have seen other scornful dismissals of the concept of dictatorship (GA 69: 20, 190; GA 95: 404, 431). For Heidegger, liberalism has no superiority to fascism or communism, but is only the half-hearted continuation of a metaphysics that liberalism itself initiated, but is incapable of bringing to its culmination.

Thus, by dismissing all political and ethical judgments in favor of metaphysical ones, Heidegger eliminates any grounds for opposing totalitarianism. Here is where a primary danger of his way of thinking lies. We must not follow him in his utter abandonment of specifically moral and political ideas, such as the concepts of demagogues and dictators. Those concepts describe real and all too important phenomena—human beings whose behavior has ruinous effects.

Heidegger elides crucial distinctions—between justice and injustice, tyranny and freedom—in his eagerness to find the "essential" unity that underlies apparent oppositions. For him, all phenomena become instances of an overpowering essence. The counter-essence cannot be rejected because it, too, is part of the essence to which we and the whole world belong. This line of thought can serve as a cautionary example of the damage that an extreme passion for essences can inflict on good judgment.

It is questionable whether anyone is, ultimately, driven by a metaphysical ideology. There are deeper, universally human passions and vices—resentment, ambition, malice, cruelty, conformism—that go farther to explain pernicious social and political phenomena. Some human beings feel a need to enlist their reason in the service of such impulses, and to ascribe their own behavior to some set of tenets—religious, mythical, or metaphysical. These people will, sometimes with great passion and sincerity, rationalize their actions in terms of the "ism" that they espouse. To critique that "ism" philosophically is a necessary project, and some of Heidegger's analyses can help us in the task. But when that task is done, the real work of justice has hardly begun.

Heidegger cannot contribute to that work, because he overlooks and misunderstands crucial features of the political world. His own attempt at a politics of inception, emergency, and collective selfhood was misconceived and grotesque. But what of the thoughts that initially brought him into the thirties? Do they still hold any philosophical promise? What are we to make of them?

Chapter Four

Toward Traumatic Ontology

Anyone who wants to think today while remaining mindful of Heidegger's legacy has to sort through the tangle of explorations, obsessions, and dead ends that sprawl through the hundred-some volumes of his writings, trying to decide which of these strands lead to insight. Chapter 1 selected three motifs that characterize Heidegger's shift into the thirties: the inception of temporality, emergency, and shared selfhood. In chapter 2, we watched him attempt to apply these ideas to a new founding of the German people, and then develop a view of National Socialism as a form of modern, willful subjectivism that posits the people as a ground and an identity. Chapter 3 turned to Arendt's account of action in order to resist Heidegger's reduction of politics either to the work of founding or to the essences and counter-essences of the history of being; the sphere of action includes inceptions as new initiatives, emergencies as interpersonal predicaments, and the question "Who are we?" as an interminable challenge that constantly requires new acts and words. In order to appreciate this realm we must pluralize Heidegger's concepts of emergency and inception and recognize that they take place in countless encounters, not only at rare, epochal junctures in history. This approach can also extend past politics to illuminate our existence as a whole, allowing us to return to broader reflections on time and being. In this final chapter, I revisit the position of *Being and Time* that our being is at issue for us and that ecstatic temporality is the horizon for being; I then supplement this temporal ontology with the basics of a "traumatic ontology" that takes up the promise of the themes of the thirties.

SELFHOOD, BEING, AND TIME

Even if we decide that we should condemn Heidegger for supporting Hitler, this is a decision not only about him but about ourselves—and in this way we testify that he was at least right to insist on the question, "Who are we?" That question continues to face each and all of us. To have a problematic relation to our own being is to exist temporally—to pursue possible ways to be as we take up who we have been and operate in a present world. The fact that we can ask who we are is thus crucial to ecstatic temporality, and to our understanding of being as such. We should take a fresh look at the "who," both individual and collective, as the prerequisite for a temporal ontology.

If we adopt the insight that our being is at issue, we should avoid some false steps that can spoil it. First, it does not follow that our being is a sheer abyss, void of sense—a void that can then be filled by the arbitrary decision to pursue any project whatsoever. We find ourselves indebted to a tradition and community, and thrown into a world that is the only place where we can be anyone. This means that not every answer to the "who" is equally promising, viable, or coherent. If I set out to create a private language and a completely new culture, I will end in madness—or in a dated, clichéd fantasy that I fail to recognize as such.

Secondly, authentic existence does not have to avoid all stable personality. It may be appropriate to commit oneself to pursuing a single way of being in depth—as long as one remains aware that this pursuit is an ongoing response to a live question. Even though identity cannot displace the issue of being, I can build an open and evolving personality for myself. I might authentically participate in a religious community, for example, as long as this participation is not a matter of dogma and inertia but a constantly renewed commitment to become who I am. If I avoid all responsibilities or try to reinvent myself *ex nihilo* every day, I will just develop a shallow character, and my supposed freedom will be nothing but a cul-de-sac.

Furthermore, against some of Heidegger's own tendencies, there is no need to insist that only Dasein has the privilege of a problematic relation to its own being—much less that only some human beings attain Dasein. Humans are able to raise the "who" question explicitly, but maybe other animals, or even all living things, are also in the process of becoming themselves without ever settling into an essence or "species." Maybe all matter emerges from fields of potential that assume concrete forms under specific circumstances, but cannot be limited to those forms. Perhaps the ontology of presence-at-hand, where entities are objects in definite states, was never anything but a construct, not just when it comes to ourselves but as regards everything that is.

Heidegger's position may exaggerate human uniqueness, then—but it is a virtue of his approach that it militates against all objectification of humanity. This is still a battle that needs to be fought. The biologism that he denounced in the thirties has its counterparts in the "neurophilosophy" and evolutionary reductionism of today.[1] Biology legitimately uncovers a wealth of interesting facts, but interpretations of these facts often assume that in order to understand the essence of human beings, we simply have to explain the origin and structure of our bodies as present-at-hand entities. As long as the body (including the brain) is grasped as something present-at-hand—an object, no matter how complex, that is not at issue for itself—then the deeper dimensions of our existence remain obscure.

Biological reductionism is often accompanied by an informational reductionism that represents "the mind" as hardware, software, algorithmic operations, or data. Partially valid analogies between humans and computers can distract us from our own existence. If and when a machine can become an explicit problem for itself—can experience anxiety, have an identity crisis, and care about being—then it will begin to make sense to speak of artificial intelligence. Computers as we know them cannot think about entities in their being because their own being is not a live issue for them. Information processing is not a relation to entities as such because information-processing devices are not exposed to emergencies (as far as we can tell). Faced with no issues, they meet no entities. They cannot even add 1+1 as we can, with an understanding of the numerical as a kind of being, a dimension of sense.

Again, the point is not to insist on a permanent quantum leap between humanity and all other beings; there seems to be an evolutionary continuum, and we cannot know *a priori* that it is impossible to build a silicon-based Dasein. But our sciences and technologies often assume that all the entities they handle are simply present-at-hand objects, disregarding the possibility that they could be an issue for themselves. This is to exclude Dasein's way of being in advance.

Let us turn to the collective, political dimension of selfhood. For Heidegger, asking "Who are we?" impels a community to enter properly historical existence. We have seen that in the thirties, his explorations of this idea are entangled with his misjudgment of the German situation and his lasting blindness to the sphere of action. But the questions he raises, whether or not he found his way to satisfactory answers, can arise in situations far distant from Germany under the Third Reich. It remains legitimate to ask how a community deals with its being as an issue, and how its understandings of being are incorporated in both silence and language.

As a case in point, consider the small Amazonian tribe known as the Pirahã, who have been a focus of controversy in linguistics and anthropology because of their tightly restricted culture and their extremely challenging language. Is this group an exception to the problem of selfhood? Is being not an issue for them?

The tribe seems to do happily without a number of cultural elements that one might assume to be universal: a mythology or tradition of fiction, well-defined rituals, recognized authority, a collective memory that extends back more than a couple of generations, a counting system, and more. In the absence of any long-lasting material constructions, the tribe's culture is invested heavily in its language, which uses a small set of phonemes and tones and can be expressed in four different "channels" (normal conversation, humming, whistling, and shouting). The Pirahã language is highly sophisticated in some ways, with sixteen different verbal suffixes that express nuances of meaning, but it does not involve recursion: there are no subordinate clauses, no possibility of nesting one thought inside another ad infinitum.

According to Daniel L. Everett, who lived for decades with the group, the absence of recursion in Pirahã is tied to the tribe's fundamental ontological orientation: the principle of the "immediacy of experience," or a focus on what is present here and now.[2] As Everett sees it, a recursive sentence, such as "The dog with three legs is sleeping," involves a subordinate clause ("dog with three legs") that is not explicitly tied to a present fact, but creates a new abstraction. It is far better, from the Pirahã perspective, to make explicit statements about what is currently apparent: "The dog has three legs. The dog is sleeping." The Pirahã's focus on what is present is expressed in the frequent word *xibipíio*, meaning roughly "appearing or disappearing," which the Pirahã apply with pleasure and fascination whenever something new comes into view or someone leaves their territory.[3] The principle of the immediacy of experience has made for a remarkably resilient culture that has resisted linguistic and religious incursions for over two centuries. Reports from outsiders about spatially or temporally distant figures, such as Jesus, are received by the Pirahã with at most passing curiosity, and all interest evaporates when the tribe returns to its habitual, local pursuits. Everett himself began as a missionary, but ultimately lost his own faith in the face of the Pirahã's contented indifference to his efforts.[4]

To introduce some Heideggerian questions: Can the Pirahã language be understood formally, in terms of Western logic and linguistics, or do these ultimately depend on the Greek understanding of being? Must the Pirahã language then be understood, as Everett proposes, in terms of this people's own sense of being? What, then, does being mean for the Pirahã? They seem to have a keen sense of the boundary between the concealed and the unconcealed; whatever passes into concealment soon becomes a matter of indifference, a nonbeing. Do the Pirahã put this understanding of being into language? The word *xibipíio* may embody it, but there seems to be no Pirahã philosophy or poetry, no concerted attempt to find words for being as such. Instead, the Pirahã have developed delicate ways to illuminate the present beings that confront them, employing, as Heidegger puts it, "the tone of voice, the cadence, the melody of the sentences, the rhythm, and so on" (GA 36/37: 104/82). The Pirahã language richly uncovers the beings in the Pirahã world, but the people do not think about being itself—the original gift that makes their experiences of beings possible. In the absence of philosophical or poetic discourse on being and truth, has this people failed to enter fully into the understanding of being that is given to it?

We should also ask whether the Pirahã are historical. Of course, they have a long past—but they are ignorant of it, they have no creation myths or chronicles, and they simply take their situation for granted. With no care for their heritage, they have no care for their future, but take care only of their current needs, planning for one or two days at a time. Are they capable, then, of coming to grips with their own being as a historical issue? What would it take for them to become explicitly historical? Would that require forming a state and developing a new political language—a language of authority and law, in addition to the everyday discussion of their shared concerns in which they already engage? Would this development of historical and political existence be tied to the development of poetic and philosophical language? And would an attempt to initiate all this be desirable at all—or would it simply destroy the tribe, more surely than modernity destroyed the world of Heidegger's peasants?

The Pirahã do not embrace their own historicity, or even attend to it. They have not embarked on a voyage of self-alienation and self-creation, but feel that they have always already arrived at their destination. Their silent sense of being as immediate presence sustains the subtle language in which they care for the beings in their world—but they do not speak in a way that draws creatively on silence to achieve "world-forming power" (GA 38: 170/141), a power that could revolutionize their time, their space, and their sense of being.

Would Heidegger's description of people who do not exist as Dasein apply to the Pirahã? "They move in the highest simplicity and in the harmony of their needs and abilities with the powers that shelter humans and re-attune them. By way of such harmony and such shelter, nothing breaks open as regards beings as such" (GA 35: 92/70).

It is true that the Pirahã do not seem to raise the question of being, but surely they deal with beings in an open region that involves an implicit understanding of being as such. They are temporal, despite the narrow scope of their concern with future and past. They exist as being-there: they transcend the limits of their bodies to care about their place. They have a culture and a world—but they persist in remaining within that world, rather than exposing it to any crisis that would challenge it. All their emergencies lie in a forgotten past, it seems; they live among sedimented emergencies, operating within their established world, without wondering about its inception.

The Pirahã are an illuminating case because they are the seeming exception that in fact proves the rule. To an outsider it is evident that they have their own way of existing, speaking, and understanding being. They provide a definite answer to the question "Who are we?" in everything they do. From the fact of this response we can infer that their being is at issue, even if they do not explicitly question it.

The way of existence of tribal, oral cultures deserves far more attention than Heidegger gives it, or that I can give it here, but a few more comments are in order. *Being and Time* introduces the undeveloped idea of *Indifferenz* as a third possibility beyond authenticity and inauthenticity (SZ 53, 232). If one combined this idea with Heidegger's refusal to focus on "primitive Dasein" (SZ §11), one could speculate that "primitives" have not truly entered the condition of being-there, and thus can be neither authentic nor inauthentic, but only "indifferent." Heidegger may not have held any such view in 1927, but *Being and Time* makes the line of thought available, and it bursts out in the thirties, in texts such as GA 35.

There is a certain top-down phenomenology in Heidegger (as in Aristotle): we must begin with the full-fledged version of a phenomenon, and interpret the less-developed versions as privations of it (e.g., SZ 50; GA 27: 123–24). So he almost completely ignores children (aside from GA 27: 125–26, 310–11), pays only glancing attention to tribal communities and the disabled, and looks closely at nonhuman animals only to draw a sharp line between them and human beings (GA 29/30). The virtue of his approach is that it tries to understand "our" condition in its own right, instead of reducing it to simpler components or origins. Its vice is that it may obscure "our" indebtedness to and kinship with beings that are in fact far from simple, and whose intricate way of being we ought to understand.

Despite Heidegger's Eurocentric tendencies, one must recognize that he denies civilized, adult Westerners the right to rest satisfied in an identity, or to assume that sense is exhausted by what they understand and control. Lest we see the Pirahã too readily as a special case, a band of a few hundred "savages," let us remember that, in Heidegger's view, Westerners do not fully "exist" either. He asks, "Are we historical?" (GA 38: 109–110/91–92)—and answers that no age has been less historical than our own (GA 38: 114). Although the boundaries of presence are broader for us than for the Pirahã, we too, according to him, have fallen into our busy concern with present beings and failed to confront being. We too look for truth in assertions about what is present-at-hand, and have not learned to experience the event of unconcealment itself. If we can open ourselves to that experience and to the ongoing voyage of selfhood, we will perhaps be less tempted to provide simplistic answers to the question, "Who are we?"

At his most apocalyptic, Heidegger goes so far as to write that "the 'world' . . . never was a world" (GA 94: 210/154), and the human being "*was* never historical" (GA 65: 492/387). We can take these extreme statements as healthy antidotes against any complacent assumption that we ourselves are authentically awake to the issue of being. However, it is not ultimately viable to say that we (or the Pirahã) are not yet being-there. The very statement presupposes some understanding of what it is to be there, and where should this understanding come from except from our prephilosophical, implicit sense of things, our "inauthentic" experience? As I argued in chapter 3, instead of holding that Dasein's inception occurs at a unique juncture in history, and only for those people who explicitly ask about being, it is more humane and plausible to hold that the explicit question of being is just a particularly prominent example of how the issue of being pervades the human condition. It remains legitimate to ask, with Heidegger in the thirties, how this condition arises, and to investigate the inceptions that bring it to life, but to say that such inceptions have never yet taken place, or have done so only at breakthrough moments of philosophy or poetry, is not feasible. All recognizably human beings have already been thrust into the condition of being-there; their being has already become an issue for them.

If the individual and collective being of all human beings is at issue, then Heidegger's fundamental claim about human existence in *Being and Time* is on the right track: we are ecstatically temporal beings, and above all, futural ones. We constantly interpret ourselves and our surroundings in terms of some possible way in which we can be, some "for-the-sake-of-which," even if we are normally oblivious to this process of interpretation. This implies that our understanding of being—not just our own, but the being of all entities in our world—is made possible by time.

Heidegger planned to support this thesis in Part One, Division III. Recreating what he actually would have published is hopeless, but we can at least take up his project and sketch some suggestions for a temporal ontology—some ways in which the various modes of being might be interpreted and unified temporally. Then we can supplement this sketch with a traumatic ontology— a reflection on the inceptive moments that generate ecstatic temporality.

We must begin with the future.

Futurity yields possibility. Through futurity, we are challenged to find a possible way to exist, to come to grips with our own being as a problem and a task, to address the question of who we are—in short, to act.

The future allures us, beckons us, invites us. It introduces us to the imagined, envisioned, and anticipated—while also making it possible for us to be disappointed or surprised.

The future also threatens, oppresses, and burdens us, since the question of who we are can never be settled, and possibility can always be blocked and extinguished. Futurity introduces us to failure, claustrophobia, despair, and mortality—the constant possibility of running out of possibilities.

These are nothing but platitudes as long as we remain within an understanding of being that pictures the future as the not-yet-present. We represent it as a section of the timeline that lies ahead of the section we inhabit. The statements above would then mean nothing except that we know little about what has not yet happened, that we try to affect what will happen, and that at some point our own presence will cease.

But this picture of the future would fail to grasp futurity altogether. A possible way to exist cannot be reduced to a set of present-at-hand qualities—features that are given either now or in some coming moment. One's self-understanding, one's ecstatic projection of who one is, is not a list of facts; it is a guiding interpretation in terms of which one approaches life. If I interpret myself, for instance, as a parent, that possible way of being is irreducible to the fact that I have offspring, or to the sum total of my interactions with them; it is part of the difference it makes that I am who I am, instead of no one. And since the question of who one is cannot be settled as if it were a question about present-at-hand characteristics, it is always possible for my self-interpretation as parent to be shaken, superseded, or transformed, regardless of what the facts about my relation to my children may be.

Futurity does not only disclose our own being. It intersects, as we will see, with the other ecstases; and as it joins with what has been to illuminate our present situation, we can attend to how other beings involve possibility (SZ 144–45). In many cases, this possibility takes the form of potentiality—the capacity to become a certain kind of thing or take on certain characteristics. The tree in my garden has the potential to bear oranges; I understand this because I understand myself, for instance, as a parent who takes care to feed himself and his children. By the same token, I understand manmade entities, such as a knife I use to peel an orange. The potential of these things is disclosed with reference to the goals and practices that are involved in my own self-understanding. By understanding myself, I understand the purposes of things—along with the concomitant phenomena of the purposeless and purpose-free (GA 24: 418). (In general, the temporal ecstases disclose both the positive and the negative—the various senses of both being and nonbeing.)

We need not reduce all potentiality to utility for our own interests. We can notice that other trees bear fruit that we will never eat. Plants are disclosed not just as edible, but also as knowable. With Aristotle, we can even view the whole cosmos as consisting of potentials in the process of being actualized. Note, however, that this vision cannot comprise Dasein itself, whose actuality is exceeded by its potential and whose identity can never come to full fruition.

In addition to Dasein's possibilities and the potentials of natural and artificial things, there are derivative types of possible being. There is epistemic possibility, or probability, and there is logical possibility, the fact that some state of affairs involves no contradiction. Both of these types of possibility are defined in relation to assertions or propositions (we establish propositions about the weather and draw inferences, or we find that we cannot coherently assert both that a figure is circular and that it is rectangular). Propositions are an important and legitimate way of grasping certain features of beings, but they are made possible by a more basic, broader, and temporal way of encountering beings in the first place. For instance, I interpret myself as an amateur meteorologist, an informed citizen, or a commuter; thanks to such possibilities of my being, I can comprehend the epistemic possibility of a 70 percent chance of rain.

The derivative types of possibility cannot explain the futurity that makes them accessible. My ability to understand myself as a parent is quite different from (though not unrelated to) a statistical likelihood that I have reproduced or will reproduce. My inability to understand myself as a brahmin is due not to a logical contradiction, but to my pastness.

Pastness is the domain of the *factum*—of what has been done and cannot be undone. What is completely past has been finished; it admits of no appeal. Our own former acts, the acts of others, the totality of the circumstances into which we have been thrown: all this presents itself as inalterable, to the extent that it has already happened. The "it was" stares us down as mercilessly as death itself, to which pastness is akin, insofar as it lacks possibility. Just as mortality can be experienced as an alienating and troubling condition, we can also be shocked by our own thrownness into existence, the contingency of our being here at all.

As the realm of what cannot be undone, pastness gives us access to facticity and factuality (SZ 56). Facticity is the givenness of our own situation, which cannot be gotten around or replaced. Factuality is the givenness not just of ourselves, but of all the things we encounter as ingredients of our facticity. Thinghood involves this factual, settled element. To know is to grasp this factuality, to have factically seen the character that beings already have.

But the inalterable, the no longer possible, is simultaneously the basis of new possibilities: it is the ground on which we can build. In this way, pastness serves as a resource for futurity. For although the past cannot be undone, it demands to be redone. To redo the past is not to erase or overwrite it, but to retrieve it creatively, to appropriate it as a model of what can be achieved or should be avoided. Redoing the past means extending it, so that the sense and purpose of the "it was" has not yet been exhausted. Pastness serves as a provocation, an irritation, a challenge. This challenge can be ignored; we can fail to redo the past by denying or repressing it. But these failures are indirect acknowledgments of the challenge.

As the realm of what can be redone, pastness discloses heritage, tradition, and models of virtue and vice. Pastness is the basis of law, of loyalty, and of normative conventions and habits. Pastness reveals justice and injustice, since it allows us to experience what has been done as calling for redress, reward, or repeal. Pastness also discloses the "ought" in the form of a promise one has made—a freely adopted and reiterated commitment. The fact that I have chosen to undertake some project cannot be undone; if I am to carry my choice forward, to extend my freedom, I now ought to continue this undertaking.[5]

In pastness we also encounter the memorable and forgettable. In redoing the past, we distinguish between the notable and irrelevant as we pursue monumental, antiquarian, or critical ways of interpreting what has been (GA 46). The first question about any historical research is why its topic has emerged as worthy of remembrance, and such emergence is possible only if we exist as having-a-past.

Again, these are not simply anthropological facts, but conditions that enable us to approach the domain of the factual as such. Like futurity, pastness is irreducible to the present-at-hand, including what one ascertains as present-at-hand points on a timeline prior to the current moment. A graph of data that includes a "t" axis cannot substitute for an understanding of how we ecstatically reach back into our own pastness, draw on it, and wrestle with it. Pastness is more than a set of facts that can be ascertained and dated; it is the dimension in which facts can face us as what has happened. The traces of past events cannot reveal the past except to an entity open to pastness.

Presence opens at the intersection of futurity and pastness. As we pursue possible ways of existing, we redo the past, thus disclosing the present. I interpret myself as a builder by appropriating factual things and factical models of builders. Futurity in conjunction with pastness reveals potentials: I can build, and things can be handled as tools and building materials. A practical situation unfolds, and the being of the things in it emerges as readiness-to-hand. Or I may interpret myself as an astronomer by appropriating factual scientific equipment and factical models of scientists, disclosing the present situation as one in which I can study stars; the being of stars emerges for me as presence-at-hand.

Both readiness-to-hand and presence-at-hand thus involve a certain past-ness or settled givenness, in combination with possibilities that are disclosed thanks to futurity. At this juncture, entities emerge as what can be dealt with or handled in the broadest sense—either theoretically or practically. They emerge as knowable or usable—or as currently unknowable or unusable, which are deficient modes of the same phenomena.

Through their knowability and usability, entities disclose their spatial relations. They appear as already situated in certain locations that can be visited and revisited, and as susceptible to various interactions and motions. These locations, interactions, and motions cohere in a space, either as a practical environment or as measurable extension. Although space may seem to be a timeless set of relations, it is made intelligible by temporality.

Presence, then, is the third dimension of temporality. It cannot define the other ecstases and cannot, by itself, make being meaningful. Without futurity or pastness, no situation would disclose itself to us, and things would be un-available and unintelligible. They would interact with us causally, but could not emerge as present. Thus, temporality makes possible all intentional relations to what is present.

Nevertheless, presence tends to push to the fore as if it were the primary horizon for being. We "fall" into presence, since that is the ecstasis in which beings come forth as directly appealing or repellent, enticing or alarming. It is the ecstasis in which we engage with things. The present is, so to speak, where the rubber meets the road, and human existence is inconceivable without it. All the same, it cannot stand on its own.

The traditional priority of *theoria* tends to privilege presence. When we attempt to disengage in order to grasp how things are, we theorize and reveal things as present-at-hand. Yet theorizing is itself only a particular form of engagement in the present; its effect is to narrow down the sense of being and to obscure the importance of the ecstatic past and future.[6]

For instance, one can map brain activity as a set of characteristics that have been present-at-hand at various moments. Such a map disregards past-ness and possibility as dimensions of ecstatic temporality, replacing them with a distribution of facts in spacetime. As correct as such a map may be, it still fails to represent the mind—not because the mind is an elusive present entity, but because minding means being exposed to possibility, pastness, and presence.

Likewise, our temporality is irreducible to change and persistence. The present qualities of entities we meet may alter or endure, but our own being is more than a present quality. We do not consist of factual characteristics that last for short or long periods of time; we consist of our exposure to the three ecstases.

Presence may be understood in a rich Greek sense as the emergence and enduring of beings, or *physis*. It can also be narrowed down to quantifiable objectivity, or other restricted forms of presence-at-hand. But no matter how rich presence is, in a temporal ontology it must be subordinated to the other ecstases of time.[7]

This sketch of futurity, pastness, and presence may be enough to suggest the temporal coherence of the various modes of being—our own being and that of all entities.

One notable implication of a temporal ontology is that we cannot understand ourselves solely within one of the many senses of being. We must not take ourselves simply as collections of data, simply as potentials in the process of actualization, or simply as systems of norms. All of these senses of being illuminate aspects of human beings, but none can stand on its own. And even the sum total of ontological interpretations of humanity will fail to grasp us if we do not see that we are, first and foremost, those who are granted such interpreting by our own temporal condition, which exposes us to the questions "Who am I?" and "Who are we?" This insight remains crucial at a time when the continuing success of natural science and technology can easily tempt us into reductive assumptions.

TRAUMA, SENSE, AND EXCESS

These descriptions of how the temporal ecstases disclose senses of being have been suggested primarily by *Being and Time*. But to take up the impulses that led Heidegger into the thirties, we need to ask further questions about inception, emergency, and selfhood. These themes can come together in what can be called a traumatic ontology. Traumatic ontology is a way of thinking of the time when time arises—the origin of the temporal ecstases themselves. That does not mean explaining this origin, but remaining mindful of it: attending to the transformative moments (emergencies or "traumas") when futurity, pastness, and presence light up. We do not need to take this line of thought to the extreme of imagining a single event in which human time emerges from nothing; instead, we can consider the many events in which, to various degrees, our temporality is enhanced or intensified. These are moments of awakening or realization, moments of "temporalization" as the more intense and fertile occurrence of ecstatic time.

Such events are turning points—critical junctures in the life of an individual or group, events that call the protagonists' selves into question in a moment of greater or lesser trauma. Such moments make a difference not only to who we are, but to being itself: at traumatic turning points, being is refreshed and transformed in what I will call the clash between sense and excess. Neither transcendental philosophy nor simple empiricism can do justice to this clash; it calls for a traumatic empiricism, an understanding of experience as driven by and centered on challenging and disturbing events. Traumatic empiricism implies a traumatic ontology—not a system of concepts categorizing all possible beings, but provisional names and questions that draw our attention to the paradoxical relations between sense and excess.

Because traumatic ontology attends to transformative events, it leaves open the possibility of reinterpreting the ecstases themselves and what they disclose. The temporal ontology I sketched above is not *a priori* synthetic knowledge of time and being, known to be necessarily and universally true, but the way things appear for the time being. Further transformations may shift or shatter this view. Thinking on the traumatic level keeps this possibility open and avoids foundationalism, dogmatism, or a transcendental point of view that pretends to be immune to change.

The word "trauma" should not be taken as an invitation to victimology or as denying that there are illuminating and transforming moments that we experience as joyful and pleasurable. What I mean by "trauma" is not necessarily an extreme physical or emotional injury.[8] The Greek *trauma* means a wound, but wounds come in various degrees and are not always unwelcome. A life-changing injury can certainly be a turning point, but so can lesser disruptions and positive ones. Such events are not necessarily threatening; they can bring pleasure and delight. Sense can be unsettled by an experience of wonder or rapture. Such moments have often been symbolized as wounds. Bernini sculpts St. Teresa as swooning in ecstasy while a smiling angel aims an arrow at her heart—and Cupid, as we all know, is also an archer.

I propose to define this extended concept of trauma or emergency in terms of *sense and excess*. Thanks to our temporality, we inhabit a meaningful world, a world that "makes sense" in a way that often seems secure and comfortable. But in fact, our world is permeable, vulnerable: it exposes us to encounters with what exceeds sense and challenges it. These challenging, transformative clashes between sense and excess are traumas or emergencies, broadly speaking.[9]

What is most often called an emergency, the irruption of a threat that demands an immediate response, does not necessarily challenge sense, since the interpretation of the irruption may follow well-worn paths. But such an irruption always has the potential to shake our world, so it can become an emergency or trauma as defined here.

Sense and excess themselves are too fundamental to be defined precisely: sense is presupposed in every effort to define things, and excess resists all sense, including definition. But we can go some way toward elucidating sense and excess and showing how they crop up in the history of philosophy, including several of Heidegger's texts.

"Sense" is that in terms of which something can be understood (SZ 151).[10] "What is understood is never *itself* sense; we do not understand something *as* sense, but always only 'in the sense of.' Sense is never the *topic* of understanding" (GA 34: 18/12–13). Here "understanding" does not primarily mean a cognitive representation, but an ability to discover the possibilities of things in terms of our own possible ways to be (SZ 143–45). Asking about the sense of something, then, is the same as trying to discover it in its own proper possibility. For example, the sense of a shoe as such is its specific kind of equipmentality, its usability for the protection of our feet. This usability makes it possible for the shoe to show itself to us as a shoe.

Everything that we recognize as an entity, then, has sense for us. There could be no encounter at all if there were no interpretation, no meaningful context for what we notice as other-than-nothing. Beings are significant for us not only in particular contexts but also as broad categories (tools, people, forces, qualities) and even as "something" in general (what is, as such). These interpretations can be embodied not only in concepts and discursive consciousness, but in practices and habits; the term "sense" does not have to be interpreted mentalistically. We feel the sense of a mountain trail by hiking it before we ever think about it; we first appreciate the sense of a new scarf by wearing it, not by describing it. In short, whether practically or theoretically, beings make sense. There is a sense or senses of being, then, that we can try to elucidate in a philosophical ontology.[11]

But we are also frequently invited to recognize that entities exceed their own sense and are distinct from it: again, "What is understood is never *itself* sense" (GA 34: 18/12). Beings are given over and above our interpretations of them, and this "over and above" is in fact what we are especially indicating when we call a thing "real," attribute "being" to it, or acknowledge its otherness-than-nothing in practice (say, by stepping over a tree root rather than stumbling against it). "Being" points beyond any determinate sense, indicating what surpasses interpretation.

This excess is implied in the concept of being itself: something deserves to be recognized as what *is*, rather than what is *not*, when it proves to be more than just our own interpretation. There is something "there" that is not reducible to its significance for us. To be, then, is to be more than an interpretation. This is a paradox: the content of our interpretation of being is precisely that it exceeds interpretation. What it means to be is to exceed meaning. It would be rash to dismiss this paradox as a mere trick; it is a fact that "being," as we understand it, points beyond our understanding. Being is then subject to a dichotomy, a split between sense and excess.

But sense and excess are not held hygienically apart; they bleed into each other. First, although excess is not sense, it presents itself to us in terms of sense: there are senses of excess. There is always some meaningful way in which something is "there" for us or "given" to us. What is other than sense *is* for us in a way that makes some sense. For example, I find a shoe I was looking for: "Here it is!" Even though the shoe is not a sense, and the sense of shoeness in no way guarantees that I will find a shoe, when I find that there is a shoe there, this "is" has a sense (something like lying there available and ready). In short, it makes a variety of meaningful differences to us that there are beings instead of nothing.

But conversely, the sense of being always points past itself to what exceeds sense, what cannot be exhausted by sense. The differences it makes that there is something instead of nothing point us back to excess. When I say, "Here it is!" I mean not only that the shoe lies ready, but also that something other than sense is showing up now—something that is available for me to wear it, name it, and talk about it, but is not reducible to the sense it has for me. "Is" carries sense, but part of its sense is precisely that what *is* cannot be exhausted by any sense, but exceeds it. If I say "the hammer is heavy," to use one of Heidegger's favorite examples, I am affirming that something other than the mere senses of hammerness and heaviness, something that exceeds sense—an actual something that I can call a heavy hammer—is here. Note that this is not simply a point about explicit assertions; in nonlinguistic action, when I simply pick up the hammer and feel its heft, I am also recognizing excess.

In short, an entity has sense for us, yet simultaneously presents itself as exceeding sense, and this excess is itself part of its sense as an entity. Beings show themselves as being more than how they show themselves.[12] They are meaningfully given as other than meaning.

The question of being must then involve both sense and excess. This is not to say that sense and excess are both instances of some overarching category of "being," but that the problematic of being ought to consider both sense and excess, in their various relations. Treating the question of being solely as a matter of sense runs the risk of operating in a conceptual realm that is insulated from real experience and encounters. This is a risk that Heidegger did not manage to avoid in the thirties. His posture "above the sea of fog" tends to keep him in a world of texts and ideas, apart from the historical happening that he wants to experience.

Furthermore, if we forget that sense is entangled with excess and treat it as a self-contained domain of its own, we run the risk of letting it stagnate.

Although sense will still serve to let things display themselves, this display is likely to be a stereotyped semblance. An intimation of excess keeps sense sharp and nimble. We should allow sense to be challenged and altered by encounters with excess—events that I am calling emergencies or traumas.

If it seems rather abstract and bloodless to define trauma in terms of sense and excess, one should consider that sense is not just intellectual, but includes all the contours of one's lived world: emotions, desires, bodily efforts, sensations, and aspirations are all part of how we establish who we are and what everything is. Likewise, excess is not just some factual data point or neutral "given"; it can challenge sense in the form of violence, pain, pleasure, rapture, or crushing disappointment. "Unyielding antagonism and stinging rebuke have a more abysmal source than the measured negation of thought. Galling failure and merciless prohibition require some deeper answer. Bitter privation is more burdensome" (GA 9: 117/92–93).

The complexity and depth of the relations between sense and excess should become clearer if we review a few ways in which they play a role in the history of philosophy and in Heidegger's writings, and then consider some ways in which sense and excess can clash more or less drastically.

Although the terminology "sense and excess" is a little unusual, the distinction is not new, but has been drawn in various guises in the history of Western philosophy. This history seems to culminate in the clarity of symbolic logic, where sense and excess are no longer seen as connected aspects of "being" at all, but are kept rigorously distinct. The paradox of being, it would seem, tormented philosophy until logic finally untied the knot. Let us glance at a few moments in this history.

Parmenides (on one reading) presents the paradox starkly: being as intelligible sense—being as completely one with thought itself—completely excludes becoming and plurality; but this realm of "nonbeing" is given nonetheless. It exceeds being as sense—strictly speaking, it "is" senseless nothing—yet it still calls for its own account in the second half of Parmenides's poem.[13]

Later Greek philosophy looks for compromises and connections between these two domains—being as rational intelligibility and the givenness of plural becoming, which threatens to exceed intelligibility. Plato and Aristotle rethink "nonbeing" so that, under rubrics such as difference or potentiality, it can be thought in connection with the privileged sense of being as identity and actuality. Even nonbeing, then, can be said to be.

There continues to be an implicit distinction between the sense of being and the excessive factuality of what is, but in Greek, words such as *einai* and *ousia* are used in both contexts. For example, in a crucial passage in the *Theaetetus*, Socrates argues that the soul does not use the sense organs to grasp "the being [of the hard and the soft] and that they are" (*ousian kai hoti eston*, 186b). Does the "and" mark a distinction or an elucidation? In anachronistic terms, it is not clear whether *ousia* here means essence as contrasted with existence, or whether it embraces existence as one of its dimensions. Heidegger's commentary on this passage favors the more inclusive option and renders the phrase as "being, the what-being and that-being and so-being" (GA 34: 228/163).

The distinction is made explicit in the medieval concepts of *essentia* and *existentia*. To explore the essence or sense of a thing is one project; to determine whether it exists is another. This distinction has become part of our everyday vocabulary.

But both medieval and early modern thinkers refuse to keep the two sides of being wholly separate. They are attracted to conjunctions of essence and existence, particularly when it comes to the ultimate ontological knot—the supreme being. God is his own being; it is essential to him to exist.

This argument for the existence of God is coldly disarmed by Kant, who pronounces that "being is not a real predicate." In other words, to affirm that something exists is not to think anything about its essence or what it means for it to be, but rather to posit that something is given to which our concepts apply. Existence is pure "position"—the givenness of something, and not its nature as conceptually understood (*Critique of Pure Reason*, A598–99/B626–27; GA 9: 445–80/337–63). This doctrine corresponds to Kant's founding distinction between intuitions, which give us objects, and concepts, by which we understand them. Understanding grasps sense; sensibility detects excess.

It falls to Frege, a century later, to apply such distinctions to formal logic.[14] Today, symbolic logic makes confusions between essence and existence inexpressible, since it treats predicates quite differently from the existential quantifier. (The proposition that every prime number *is* divisible only by itself and 1 is symbolized quite differently from the proposition that for every prime, there *is* a larger prime.) The murky, muddled discussions of "being" in traditional philosophy are supposedly exposed as the unfortunate symptoms of an Indo-European accident: the use of a single word to indicate the logically separate functions of predication and the affirmation of existence. (Identification is a third distinct function traditionally expressed with "is," as in "Aristocles is Plato.") It seems that the distinction between being as sense and being as excess has been thought through to its end and purged of paradox: there is no split within being, there are just separate acts of thought that were seemingly connected in everyday language. Our concepts or predicates stand on one side, and on the other stands excess; the excess can apparently be summed up in a single well-regulated symbol: ∃x, or "there is something such that . . ."[15]

Heidegger, of course, rejects this conclusion—much to the consternation of logicians. As we saw in chapter 1, he objects to a strict division between "what-being" and "that-being." He also explores not just the sense of being, but its unavoidable entanglement with excess or non-sense. He recognizes that beings are more than just sense, and that the threat of senselessness lurks just around the corner. Sense is exceeded by the difference of beings from interpretation and by the possibility of interpretive collapse—and these issues, too, are part of the question of being. The project of making sense of being needs to be aware of the limits and fragility of sense—and in fact, the breakdown of sense may be a particularly valuable stimulant to thought. When sense is revealed as contingent and vulnerable, excess hits us and makes us capable of fresher philosophical insight. At such moments, excess shines through within sense, calling that very sense into question.[16]

Accordingly, Heidegger is interested in a variety of situations where sense falters in the face of excess. In 1919, for instance, he considers experiences of unfamiliar things. A Senegalese tribesman faced with a lectern might take it as a magical thing, a shield, or simply something he doesn't know what to make of (GA 56/57: 72). This raw experience of "something" is never a sheer absence of interpretation; some sense must always be operative in order for us to encounter "something" at all. But in these limit situations, when sense struggles and totters, the sheer "there is"—the difference between something and nothing—comes alive. The *es gibt* is at its most powerful, and life is at its most intense, when we shift from one world to another or experience a moment passionately, rather than settling firmly and comfortably within a world (GA 56/57: 115).

Being and Time is also concerned with such experiences. It begins by examining how Dasein exists "first and foremost" (*zunächst und zumeist*)—by looking at normal life, which finds itself already inhabiting a meaningful world. Dasein, in this condition, already has its being as an issue for it—an issue that it has resolved to some degree—and already has an understanding of the being of all the beings in its world—an understanding that is tacitly implied in its practices.

However, as the text proceeds, we find that this condition is fragile and contingent. The excess of our own existence, of beings as a whole, or of natural phenomena can overwhelm our understanding. Such events reveal an uncanniness that underlies our tranquility: the "not-at-home" is the more primordial phenomenon (SZ 189). These events, which could fairly be called traumatic, bring us back to the temporality of our being and allow us to be reborn, as it were—reawakened to the fact that our being and our world are in question.

This is especially the case in regard to the sense of one's own being. In anxiety, the excess of my being is disclosed, the naked fact that Dasein "is and has to be" (SZ 134). Anxiety allows me to encounter my thrownness, which is stubbornly resistant to sense (SZ 135). All the possibilities I have for interpreting my thrownness (such as a religious interpretation in terms of creation and fall, or a scientific interpretation in terms of evolution) are possibilities that I project on the *basis* of thrownness, and must remain indebted to the raw experience that "here I am."

Nature's being as excess can also strike us, in a way that provides a deeper glimpse into the nonhuman than we are usually afforded. In *Being and Time*, nature is primarily considered as material for ready-to-hand entities (timber, leather, etc.) or as a present-at-hand object of scientific fact-gathering. But Heidegger alludes to a further, more poetic sense of "the *power of nature*" (SZ 70), and proposes that nature can be contrary to sense (*widersinnig*): natural catastrophes can intrude absurdly into Dasein's sphere of significance (SZ 152).

He also wants us to wonder at the excess of what is, as such and as a whole—its difference from nothing (GA 9: 122/96, GA 40: 3/1, GA 52: 64). This astonishment at the existence of beings is essential to keeping being as sense in question, to challenging the very boundary between what counts as something and what counts as nothing.

As we have seen, texts such as "The Origin of the Work of Art" address excess in terms of the strife between earth and world. Sense or illumination (world) always depends on and refers to an uninterpreted excess (earth)—a *lethe* that shadows *aletheia*. This is why truth is a robbery or struggle (SZ 222; GA 36/37: 118). In the artwork, and at other privileged sites, truth takes place as the clash of earth and world. It is difficult to define earth precisely, but that is the point: earth is resistance to definition, to discovery, to sense and essence. It conceals itself at the same time as it sustains the world of sense that tries, yet inevitably fails, to interpret it. Sense always has its points of friction with the non-sense on which it is based. Only when that friction enters our awareness—when the world struggles against the earth and recognizes that it fails—is a culture alive and creative.

For Heidegger in the thirties, emergency and unease are needed in order to keep us vulnerable to excess rather than ensconced in sense. "Our being consists in the original exposure to what is" (GA 38: 155/128 tm). But without "essential affliction," or at least an experience of its lack, there is no "exposure to beings as a whole—one is not led to what is" (GA 94: 62/47 tm).

Finally, *Ereignis* itself is a special sort of excess. "The excess [*Über-maß*] is . . . the self-withdrawing from all appraisal and measurement. But in this self-withdrawing (*self-concealing*), beyng has its nearest nearness in the clearing of the there, in that it appropriates being-*there*" (GA 65: 249/196 tm).

Peter Trawny has made the suggestive proposal that in *Ereignis*, an "excess of sense," sense at high intensity, runs up against its limits and rebounds upon itself.[17] From the pressurized core of sense, jets of significance shoot out, as it were, but we cannot look directly into the core itself—just as we cannot stare directly at the sun, or as in the Bible, a man cannot gaze on the face of God without being destroyed. The ultimate intensity of sense cannot be articulated or captured within a limited vision or statement. This interpretation develops Heidegger's word *Über-maß*. The word expresses resistance to measurability, and suggests to Trawny that in *Ereignis*, sense is overflowing volcanically and intensely, blinding us with its very abundance.

However, instead of abounding in sense, the *Über-maß* may exceed sense itself. Since sense is what enables understanding, it is hard to conceive of an abundance of sense that blocks revelation; and as we have seen, Heidegger is consistently interested in experiences where sense is shaken or is absent. The inception of sense, then, is a kind of non-sense, which exceeds the realm of sense precisely because it is the source of illumination. The event of emergence is not itself something that has emerged; the source of openness is not itself open. The inception of illumination, interpretation, articulation, and sense must itself be un-illuminated, un-interpreted, in-articulate, and non-sensical. The giving of the sense of givenness cannot itself be given, as it is not subject to that sense. That may be as far as we can get in an attempt to think of the ultimate emergency, the primal emergence of self and world. (Some further thoughts on the riddle of the ultimate founding event can be found in the appendix to this book.)

Heidegger sometimes describes the opacity of the inception in the language of emergency or trauma. "All inceptions . . . elude the historian, not because they are supra-temporally eternal, but rather because they are greater than eternity: *the shocks* [*Stöße*] of time" (GA 65: 17/16 tm; on shocks, cf. 247, 432, 463, 464, 485, 486). "Dasein itself essentially happens as *emergency*, authentically initiates [*setzt*] emergency itself and thus first founds the 'where' of the 'there'" (GA 82: 505). "The essential happening of being [is] emergency" (GA 73.1: 209).

Following to some extent in Heidegger's footsteps, Jean-Luc Marion makes good use of the term "excess" in his analyses of rich, intense experience.[18] In contrast, Alain Badiou draws on symbolic logic and set theory rather than phenomenology in his theory of transformative, revolutionary events.[19] Badiou's apparatus is a dubious tool for grasping the dynamics of sense and excess, since set theory and symbolic logic have their origins and limits in particular theoretical projects. Nevertheless, he provides suggestive material for a traumatic ontology, particularly in his account of "fidelity" to a singular event.

Let us turn from these historical and textual notes to a phenomenology of ten ways in which sense and excess can interact.

1. In mathematical reasoning, being as sense is paramount: we aim at maximum clarity in our concepts so that we can discover their relations and implications. Yet this is discovery, not invention. At least, most mathematicians feel that there is an excess even in this most conceptual of fields: mathematical truths are not purely a function of our interpretations, but are foisted upon us when we think clearly. We do not arbitrarily determine how a mathematical problem will turn out, but are brought to see that something is or is not the case. This is the kind of excess that $\exists x$ is best suited to indicate, and in this area symbolic logic has yielded its most impressive results.

2. Our familiar perceptual experiences often involve a wholly unsurprising excess. To take one of Husserl's favorite examples, when we perceive an opaque object as a cube, we intend its unseen sides as well as the visible sides. Having a back is part of the sense of the cube's being. When we then turn the object around and actually see its back, our intention is fulfilled with the expected sensible intuition. There is an excess here: the givenness of the back of the cube does not depend on my interpretation of it, as it could very well have turned out that the object was not a cube at all. But in this case, being as excess fits being as sense in a harmonious, expected way. Our comfortable routines and everyday recognitions illustrate this harmony between sense and excess. Sense is not usually frustrated by experience: a stop sign means that one is supposed to stop, and there is no mystery about it. Still, even in these situations, the entity exceeds the sense of its being: the stop sign is not itself the sense "stop," but is other than our interpretation of it. This is what makes it a real stop sign rather than nothing, and this is why we in fact have a legal obligation to stop here. A shoe is not the sense of a shoe; the sense of a shoe permits the shoe to show itself both as significant and as exceeding sense. If there were no shoe to be found, then the horizons within which we interpret shoes would be, in Husserlian terms, unfulfilled intentions—senses without anything that showed up in their light.

3. In other cases, sense can point to an uncertain or indistinct excess, in a way that creates fear or excitement. If I hear a noise in my house in the middle of the night, I think of a burglar and try to determine whether I just heard a real intruder, an actual entity who is more than my interpretation. It may be hard to tell where interpretation ends and the real begins; my imagination and habits can play tricks on me. In such situations, the distinction between sense and excess not only still obtains, but becomes an urgent issue. Doubts about where the boundary between sense and excess lies do not invalidate the distinction; the more urgently we struggle to distinguish the real, the more we affirm the importance of the difference.

4. When we do have a harmony between sense and excess in our everyday activities, it is broken all too easily in what Lawrence Hatab calls

"contraventions."[20] Our dealings are disrupted when the things we need are unavailable, when they malfunction, or when other things get in the way. In *Being and Time* (§16) Heidegger takes these moments as occasions for noticing the sense of ready-to-hand things and of the environment: we become particularly aware of the structure of functionality when things cease to function—when they turn against us, as it were. Such moments can also be occasions for a switch in attitudes, a shift to a theoretical intentionality that approaches things as present-at-hand objects, interpreting them in terms of a different sense of being (§69b). So when we experience friction between sense and excess, the sense can be highlighted as such, or it can be shunted onto a different path.

5. Creative endeavors can deliberately keep themselves open to excess: the creator can develop images, sounds, or words that stay alert to their own limits and to the way they keep being challenged by the obscurities of experience. This is the practice Heidegger describes as setting up a work that incorporates the strife between world and earth. The paintings of Anselm Kiefer, for instance, allude to the great myths and themes of German history while simultaneously conveying the chaotic materiality of nature. Dürer's drawing of a hare is sensitive to the concreteness of the animal, instead of reducing it to an interpretive scheme.

6. Excess can surprise us. I turn a cube around, flinch, and recoil at that thing on the back of the cube—a centipede! The insect in its excessive being affects me, my body reacts to it, and I feel its sense corporeally before its conceptual sense has clearly emerged. Its givenness in the hazy interpretation as "that thing" gets the jump on my more detailed interpretation. Such experiences need not be unpleasant, and we may even seek them out: nature lovers hike a mountain trail because they expect it to bring them to wilderness—places they do not yet know. One can also embark on a similar exploration in the life of the mind, and be surprised by thoughts that come upon us before we quite know what to call them.

7. In the case of my encounter with the centipede, I face the surprising excess directly; it crops up in the middle of my visual field. But a more powerful form of excess denies us this position as spectator: it blindsides us. It can surprise us so thoroughly that we are swept off our feet before we can consider formulating any plan of resistance. If one is caught in a sudden, unexpected car accident, amnesia or simple ignorance may even prevent one from ever recalling the event. Only its consequences are evident, leaving the victim trying to piece together what occurred.

8. In some cases, even if we "know" quite well that the event is imminent, it can still strike a blow that leaves us reeling. We are then blindsided not by an event that we did not see coming, but by the force of its excess over

all vision and all comprehension. Jean Améry describes his experience of a rough interrogation:

> I knew what was coming . . . But does one really know? Only in part. "Rien n'arrive ni comme on l'espère, ni comme on le craint," Proust writes somewhere. Nothing really happens as we hope it will, nor as we fear it will. But not because the occurrence, as one says, perhaps "goes beyond the imagination" (it is not a quantitative question), but because it is reality and not phantasy. . . . When an event places the most extreme demands on us . . . there is no longer any abstraction and never an imaginative power that could even approach its reality. . . . Only in rare moments of life do we truly stand face to face with the event and, with it, reality. It does not have to be something as extreme as torture. Arrest is enough and, if need be, the first blow one receives. . . . At the first blow . . . trust in the world breaks down.[21]

The experience of violent assault, of passive subjection, forces us to remember that being as sense—the realm in which we make sense of things, or things make sense to us—is not all. Being as excess collides with sense-making and shoves it around. We should note Améry's point that the distinction between sense and excess is not quantitative, but qualitative. It is not as if we could grasp the reality of assault if we simply thought harder or imagined more vividly; the reality breaks in on us brutally, regardless of how detailed or correct our images and interpretations may be. Idealism is best refuted not by kicking a stone, but by being kicked.

9. We can train ourselves to suffer blows with Stoic discipline, which firms up being as sense and tries to subject excess to interpretation in advance. For most of us, however, there is a moment when Stoicism collapses. We are not just hit, but shattered. This is the kind of event usually called a trauma in the narrow sense. For Améry, it came when Gestapo torturers dislocated his arms. "Whoever is overcome by pain through torture experiences his body as never before. In self-negation, his flesh becomes a total reality. . . . Frail in the face of violence, yelling out in pain, awaiting no help, capable of no resistance, the tortured person is only a body, and nothing else beside that."[22] When Améry says he was "only a body," I take him to be pointing to an eclipse of sense during severe bodily trauma. Someone undergoing such trauma simply does not have the resources at the time to interpret it. What we call the mind—the ability to find sense in experience by minding (caring, attending, ordering)—is put out of commission, and there is only the overwhelming force of sensation. Only afterward can the survivor try to interpret the event that still echoes in his body, by seeking rituals, narratives, or judgments that can mind the trauma.

10. One could also posit a peculiar kind of excess that I will call an ultra-event—an event that cannot ever become an object of experience, but that

we nevertheless recognize as more than just an interpretation. This definition may sound speculative and distant, but I commonly acknowledge at least two intimate ultraevents: my birth and my death. I cannot experience the beginning or end of my own being. (Religious questions about where these limits lie, and even whether there are any such limits, do not affect the fundamental point: *if* my being has a beginning or an end, I cannot experience them.) Countless indicators suggest that I once was not and that I will not be; I can observe the birth and death of others; I can elaborate interpretations in response to my own birth and death as limits of my experience; I can experience my own growing or declining vitality; but I cannot experience my own nonbeing. In this way my experience points toward, and is even structured by, two excessive ultraevents that cannot be presented directly as given phenomena. I cannot experience this excess, but I can suspect it, accept it, deny it, or embrace it; in any case, it serves to stimulate or irritate me despite its nonphenomenality.

And then there are the countless encounters with other persons, which are too diverse to fit into a single category: others can behave in ways that fit smoothly into the sense of our familiar routines, but often enough they surprise us, shock us, sweep us off our feet, assail us, challenge us, or delight us. Others must be experienced as exceeding our sense of them if we are to avoid solipsism. Deeper interactions with others are often the most transformative events in our lives. One place where such interactions can happen is the political arena described by Arendt, where we expose our own initiatives to the transformative interventions of fellow actors. To act is to alter oneself by encountering excess in the form of others.

Excess surpasses sense in all these ways, which we could call "turns." Excess turns out right or wrong, for better or worse, often turning against us; it blindsides us, it breaks us, it overturns us. Can all these turns be captured with a laconic, unambiguous symbol, $\exists x$? Or is there an irreducible variety of turns, a wealth of different relations between excess and sense, so that the question of being cannot be neatly disentangled into separate strands? We cannot capitulate to symbolic logic and simply break apart the paradox of being into existence and predication. The well-regulated consistency of the logical symbol $\exists x$ is unsuited to the whole range of excess and to its entanglements with sense.

The logician may respond that the turns of excess we have described are nothing but various subjective experiences and reactions. When we cut through the reactions and think soberly about what is the case, we again find nothing but the simple $\exists x$ or "there is," in combination with a variety of predicates that express the variety in what is given: there is a number n, there is a cube, there is a blow, there is a birth, and so on.

But philosophy has an obligation to address the "subjective" experience of things, precisely because it is an experience *of things*, and thus is not purely subjective. In other words—and this is an essential insight of phenomenology—our various attitudes are various ways in which things are *given* or presented to us. There is no univocal "there is": what it means for a centipede to be given is not what it means for a number to be given.[23] As I argued in chapter 1, that-being and what-being are connected. Understanding the varieties of being requires close attention to the texture and flavor of our experiences. The seeming clarity of logic is in fact an obfuscation, because it imposes a reductive simplicity on the variety of turns that excess can take.

If this line of thought is right, it also teaches us that the distinction between sense and excess is not as clear-cut as logic would have it. As we noted earlier, there are various senses of excess, and various ways in which excess and sense bleed into each other. The living, alien excess of the centipede on the back of the cube gets the jump on my interpretation and makes me jump; in contrast, the uncircumventable, timeless excess of a geometrical relation may come into view only when sense has been set up and prepared carefully in advance. What it means for the centipede and the geometrical relation to exceed sense is not the same: they exceed and affect sense differently. All the variety of excess, and all the diversity of its interactions with sense, deserve to be considered in an ontology—an exploration of the paradox of being, both as sense and as excess.

Situations in which sense and excess collide (as in cases 4–9 above) can be called traumas—in the broad sense that includes minor conflicts and positive surprises. We could also call these events emergencies, again in an extended sense: they are disruptions or crises, great and small, in which being emerges as an issue. Emergencies or traumas scratch or lacerate the established system of sense. In such an event, the way we are open is potentially altered by something that we encounter within our opening—something that, at an extreme, may shake the very heart of our understanding because it cannot be accommodated to it. As Pascal says, "Not all that is incomprehensible fails to exist."[24] As we put it today, an encounter with the incomprehensible can rock our world.

We now need to consider how such traumas or emergencies work as inceptions of selfhood and temporality.

EMERGENCIES AS INCEPTIONS

If our being is at issue, how does it become an issue? How do we first enter selfhood? It seems that there must be a founding event of disruption, in which a formerly unproblematic identity erupts into discord and becomes a problem for itself. In a rare comment on early childhood, Heidegger writes that a new-born often experiences "shock and fright"; "a disquiet enters," and the infant begins to become itself by opening to what is other than itself (GA 27: 125). Regardless of whether we can tie such a process to particular developmental stages, we must be indebted to events of estrangement—disquieting events in which we are distanced from ourselves, so that we are faced with the intermi-nable task of becoming ourselves. We then become a "who," a problematic and historical being. We normally think of a trauma as a psychological wound inflicted on an already existing person. The ultimate trauma, however, would bring personality itself into existence by making an entity's being a problem for it in the first place. It would do more than reveal an already operative uncanniness: it would generate uncanniness itself.

In his more speculative texts of the thirties, Heidegger is concerned with just such an ultimate inception, the founding of a world—a wrenching event that establishes time-space and the realm of selfhood (GA 65: 311, 319–20; GA 74: 28). This inception (*Anfang*) literally *takes* place, or seizes the "site of the moment." The birth of a new world would be a radical emergency: "Emergency as what besieges and first necessitates the decision and scis-sion of man as one being from beings, in their midst, and back to them. . . . Where this emergency mounts to its highest, it necessitates *being-there* and its grounding" (GA 65: 46/38 tm).

As we have seen, it is difficult, if not impossible, to give an account of this primordial emergency—at least, not without falling into arbitrary mythmak-ing. Speculative accounts of the theme include Lacan's theory of the "mirror stage" as the inception of individual selfhood and Julian Jaynes's theory of the "breakdown of the bicameral mind" as the inception of self-consciousness in the species. Heidegger toys with the no less fantastic idea that Dasein be-gan at the inception of Greek philosophy (GA 35: 95). In texts such as the *Contributions*, the ultimate event remains nebulous and elusive—necessarily so, he would say (GA 65: 57–58, 188, 460). We can, at best, experience the movement of its withdrawal, and in this way combat our oblivion of it.

In my reading, then, *Ereignis* is the ultimate excess, a traumatic event that makes us a problem for ourselves, generating sense. But Heidegger makes this founding event too unique and too distant. His continuing transcendental-ist inclinations are evident in his desire to think of *Ereignis* independently of all concrete beings (GA 65: 75–76) and in his assumption, in all of his later thought, that ordinary human life is dominated by a particular sense of being, which functions in effect as an *a priori* framework.[25]

Against this eschatological speculation, we need to recognize that trau-matic inceptions take place at many junctures in each of our lives. As we bring Heidegger's insights to bear on concrete experience, his sweeping account of the history of being must be replaced with a more modest position similar to the view in *Being and Time:* we inherently tend to misconstrue and objectify ourselves, to fail to recognize our own, ineluctably problematic being. We fall and forget. This tendency can be exacerbated by certain elements in the philosophical tradition as well as in modern culture. But the response should not be to hope for an apocalypse, but to keep opening our eyes to how we actually exist, how we keep being faced with smaller and larger traumas that found and refound our "theres."

If we set aside the question of how an entire world is founded, we can still discern moments when its sense is challenged by excess. Sense develops through experiences of resistance—events in which excess expands or confounds our interpretations. As long as there is no new clash between sense and excess, no issue urgently demands to be resolved. Everything we meet can then be readily, smoothly subsumed under established senses. The everyday system functions (as it does so durably for the Pirahã). But that system, with all its senses, is the cumulative result of countless emergencies.

The project of interpreting ultraevents may be hopeless when it comes to the absolute birth and death of being as sense—here we can only gesture in the direction of sheer excess. But there are lesser, though still dramatic, births and deaths: moments when sense is not generated *ex nihilo* or annihilated, but is transformed and reawakened, retaining a connection to its earlier shape yet becoming something new that would be unintelligible from the earlier perspective. These crucial moments alter and frustrate our experience, but do not completely elude interpretation. At these turning points, a configuration of sense undergoes a traumatic quasi-death so that the new configuration can be born.

Apart from the ultimate emergency, then, which can be grasped, if at all, only in a highly speculative vein, there are a range of lesser emergencies that remind us of our being as an issue and impel us to question it again. Clashes between sense and excess sustain and refresh our selfhood as a problem. For example, *Being and Time* describes the experience of anxiety as an event in which sense is shaken. What was formerly taken for granted as an all-encompassing sphere of significance is revealed as contingent and alterable. In the grip of *Angst*, one must come to grips in a new way with who one is in the midst of the world. There are also lesser and minor traumas, such as the ordinary contraventions of losing an object or failing to achieve the day's goals. Heidegger's work of the twenties includes analyses of many of these more familiar emergencies.

At every level, every conflict between sense and excess poses some challenge to selfhood. We are provoked to ask who we are. This question is normally answered quickly—we reassure ourselves of our identities, or ignore the disturbance until it fades away—but even a small trauma is an opportunity for greater self-awareness. If traffic makes me late for an appointment, I can take a moment to reflect on how that meeting forms part of my project of being someone in the world—or does not. If a colleague in the meeting takes my words in an unexpected and unwelcome direction, I am challenged to rethink my own position.

The sense of things does not stand separate from the sense of self: we *are* our world, and when its rhythms and courses are disturbed, we are as well. When we need to find new ways of making sense of things, we also need to make sense of ourselves anew. Conversely, a challenge to the self also shakes the world. Traumas, then, are not only occasions for reconsidering who we are; they challenge and potentially rejuvenate our world, our time, and our space.

Individuals in the midst of a deep religious, political, or romantic conversion are cast into doubt, painfully unsure of their selves and of the sense of the world. They emerge from these traumas with a new understanding of who they are. A manager backs down in the face of hostility from her coworkers and becomes a coward in her eyes and their own. A heartbroken young man dedicates himself to his religion as never before.

Collective life, history, religion, and culture also circle around traumas and responses.[26] Encounters with excess can develop into crisis points, historical events in which sense is refreshed or transformed; such events open new realms of sense that, in turn, make it possible for us to encounter excess afresh. From the inconspicuous tremors that make small adjustments in our world to cultural upheavals and political revolutions, the happening of history cannot be understood purely in terms of sense, but requires our exposure to the excess of what is. "Emergency . . . besieges humanity within beings, and first brings it before beings as a whole and into their midst, and thus in each case allows the inception or decline of history" (GA 65: 45/37 tm). The revolutions of 1989 in Central and Eastern Europe, or of 2011 in North Africa and the Middle East, were moments of collective self-reinterpretation and political conversion. The history of Christianity can be read as the interminable process of retrieving and reinterpreting the trauma of the Crucifixion. The beating heart of every myth is an emergency that cries out to be retold, but cannot be exhausted by any narrative: a birth, a death, a passion, a transgression, a loss, a gift. The still-living excess in the emergency inexhaustibly yields imagery and mystery.

The history of colonialism and its aftermath offers many examples of the traumatic unfolding of collective selfhood and a common world. For colonized people, excess intrudes in the shape of invaders. The colonists, too, encounter excess in the form of the natives. Both worlds of sense are transformed in the encounter, and can never be the same again. In a city such as

London one can see the effects of colonialism rebounding on the colonizers: confluent and colliding senses create a polyphonic world where emergencies take unpredictable forms.

Spaces are reshaped as they are transformed by emergencies, including encounters with new architectural practices and habits of life. The interior of Westminster Abbey is encrusted with statues, plaques, and tombs—small places that commemorate people and events that have transformed the British world. Elsewhere in London, that inherited world is juxtaposed with modern and foreign spaces that are becoming part of a new British world, a new mix of possibilities.

A shared world is at least potentially political—an arena for action, in Arendt's sense. Then a truly public sphere arises: a place where we can risk immersion in a shared project, where we must entrust our acts to others so that our initiatives may turn into some unpredictable development. Here there are new occasions for excess and emergency: the senses of our acts are exposed to the interventions and assistance of others, and inevitably, they will be transformed in the process. Through this exposure to excess, we are bound to be challenged and thus to experience inceptions, births in which our "who" is developed and grows. The public sphere allows complex selfhood to arise through surprises and ventures.

In contrast, the technical sphere is ruled as far as possible by a method that allows surprise only within narrowly defined parameters. This technique ensures reliable and efficient production, but when it is extended past the technical realm, it hampers the arising of selves and spaces. Technocratic politics stifles action by minimizing trauma: conflicts and friction are supposed to be replaced with impersonal rules and processes. But it is precisely in political debates, with all their tension and passion, that we become engaged in the question, "Who are we?" This engagement is more fundamental than any outcome. Political conflict is not just a means to the end of some state of comfort or peace, but an opportunity to discover ourselves in a shared space. When our frustration with "the system" breaks out, we feel once again that politics can be a realm of freedom and self-discovery, where we can genuinely ask, "Who are we?" Such moments inevitably fade away, and disappointment returns, but we should take this as a challenge to keep reinvigorating the political realm as a place for inceptions.

Likewise, when buying and selling are reduced to a technical process, economic exchange becomes an alienating condition in which we cannot become ourselves. A commercial website or a tightly managed shopping mall offer superficial choices and small surprises, but rarely admit any excess that might transform the sense of the space or of ourselves. When poet Brian Sonia-Wallace spent five days in the Mall of America typing poetry for shoppers on topics of their choice, he found that about a fifth of the people he met broke down in tears when they received their poems.[27] They were surrounded by others, but they were unused to any intimate interaction with another human being who could speak to the sense of their lives, to who they were. The presence of the poet shifted the sense of the space, changing it from a realm of managed exchange to a place for unexpected and moving encounters. What were once familiar confines gained unsuspected possibilities.

Time, too, is transformed by emergencies. They are the times when time arises—even if not from nothing. At these times, established temporal ecstases are heightened, broadened, intensified, or strained. Whenever individual or collective selfhood comes into question, the future is lit up from a new perspective, becoming more urgent and vivid. The past becomes newly problematic, appearing as a legacy that needs to be rejected or renewed, instead of a basis that is taken for granted. The present gains heightened importance as a scene of opportunities, conflicts, and encounters.

In short, selfhood, time, and space are renewed in emergencies, the traumatic moments when sense and excess come into conflict.

Let us recall that since our understanding of being is temporal, being, too, originates in emergencies. "Emergency, this besieging that essentially happens—what if it were the truth of beyng itself?" (GA 65: 46/38 tm). In traumatic happenings the sense of our own being, and of all being, is challenged and revitalized. An encounter with a poet at a shopping mall might shift one's sense of what it is to shop: not just a chance to acquire new resources, but an opportunity to meet strangers and exchange significant words. Any experience in which sense meets excess can potentially alter the sense.

This is especially apparent in the rare experience of being shocked at the very existence of anything. In astonishment, the familiar loses its self-evidence and becomes surprising—not as something new, but in the very wonder of its original givenness. This experience may be provoked most effectively by a crisis in self-understanding. Then the "being of Dasein can burst forth as a naked 'that it is and has to be'" (SZ 134). Things stop making sense smoothly, and we are plunged into an insight into our own ignorance. "Celebration . . . is self-restraint, is attentiveness, is questioning, is meditating, is awaiting, is the step over into the more wakeful glimpse of the wonder—the wonder that a world is worlding around us at all, that there are beings rather than nothing, that things are and we ourselves are in their midst, that we ourselves are and yet barely know who we are, and barely know that we do not know all this" (GA 52: 64). This too is a trauma, though it may be a joyful one—a key moment in which we stand in awe at the excess of beings, including ourselves, even as the sense of these beings is eclipsed.

EMERGENT THINKING

Examples of emergency or trauma could be multiplied indefinitely; such things happen to us, on some scale, nearly every day. Traumatic ontology would understand these moments as inceptions of self, world, history, space, time, and being. Despite the frequency of such events, understanding and speaking of them is a challenge, and we have to tread carefully.

Even if these emergencies do not completely escape the realm of sense, they do reconfigure it, so the project of making sense of them is challenging. The event of reconfiguring sense exceeds and eludes both earlier and later senses. At this moment, we are held in suspense; there is a tension, a gap. The most delicate task here is to let the gap speak for itself—to find words that are not just a subset of some established configuration of sense, but are capable of bringing us back, insofar as this is possible, to the moment of reconfiguring.[28] This would mean letting the transformation of self and world come into language. We must think not merely about emergencies, but in them. To think in emergency would be to dwell in it and dwell on it. Emergent thinking must be able to stand emergency itself—stay with it, endure it, speak from it.

This project goes against our normal tendency, our impulse to reestablish a norm. We ordinarily try to get over emergencies as soon as possible and race to interpret them retrospectively, from a position of reestablished identity. We try to anticipate them, categorize them, and tell their story as quickly as we can. Even in the case of profound personal conversions, once they are complete, the transition is liable to be forgotten, dismissed, or reinterpreted from the perspective of the newfound sense; its only trace may be a certain vehemence that, one suspects, is needed to cover up the abyss of doubt and ward off any recurrence of the conversion trauma.

The methodological problems philosophy faces here are akin to those faced by people who have to deal with severe disruptions in their own lives. It is time to look more closely at how the term "trauma" is understood in psychology and at the challenges that confront traumatized individuals. Psychological trauma theory and traumatic ontology prove to share questions about the constraints on thought, language, and representation.

While there is no universally accepted definition, trauma is generally understood by psychologists and psychiatrists as an overwhelming event, often involving terror and the threat of imminent death. The trauma typically cannot be interpreted and felt fully at the time when it is happening; it is undergone and perceived, but not appropriated or "claimed" psychologically.[29] The undigested trauma typically recurs in post-traumatic stress disorder. The traumatized individual, who may have no direct memory of the trauma or may successfully avoid thinking of it in everyday waking life, may exhibit compulsive behavior that is conditioned by the trauma (acting out), and may experience vivid flashbacks, including terrifying dreams. The trauma returns, then, in habits and in visions, urging the survivor to try to come to grips with what has happened to him or her—to try to make sense of it.

Much of the debate among trauma theorists has focused on this process of making sense of the initially uninterpreted traumatic event. One common human attitude, which is shared by a few theorists that give it a Nietzschean touch, sees trauma as senseless and prefers to forget it for the sake of getting on with life.[30] Some therapists, in contrast, argue that the process of making sense is essential to healing: without incorporating the event into a forward-looking personal narrative, the survivor will forever be scarred and dominated by the trauma. Of course, this project of incorporation may never be complete.[31] Other theorists are concerned that the representation of trauma is a falsification: trauma is essentially opaque, and we have a responsibility—particularly when it comes to massive collective traumas such as the Holocaust—to avoid the glib comforts of explanations and interpretations, while never failing to remember the trauma. The horror of the trauma demands that we face it in all its senselessness. One can also put a twist on this argument: to "claim" a sense for the Holocaust would be to reproduce the totalizing, controlling mentality that unleashed the horror in the first place.[32]

Heidegger's position in the thirties resembles the view of those who would acknowledge trauma by facing its opacity, not by turning away or trying to illuminate it. The traumatized life of an individual or culture, as well as the traumatized life of thought, is an irresolvable history of remembrance and endurance. (See his reflections on the mood of "holy mourning" in Hölderlin, GA 39: 78–103.) We have become a problem for ourselves that is not to be solved, a question—"Who are we?"—that is not to be answered. Who we are is precisely those who are faced with this question in a particular historical form, with its particular losses and tensions. An attempt to impose a fully satisfying answer is nothing but the violent destruction of the question; it would reduce us to things with stable identities, rather than beings whose own being has been forced to remain at issue. To represent the inception would be to represent ourselves, when we are fundamentally unrepresentable, unpresent beings.

Some trauma theorists' hostility to narrative resembles Plato's suspicion of "telling a tale" (*Sophist* 242c) when it comes to being, a suspicion that Heidegger shares (SZ 6). We must not reduce being to an entity by treating it as if it were just another fact, just another given—by applying ontic concepts to it or tracing it back to some ontic occurrence. This is a classic transcendental line of thought. But in the thirties, Heidegger does tell tales—compulsively rehearsing his variations on the history of Western metaphysics. The story of our responses to the unrepresentable gift of being can be told, just as one can tell the tale of a survivor's responses to the unrepresentable moment of trauma. Heidegger would dislike this comparison, however, because none of his account is supposed to be ontic: he is not describing events within beings, he would argue—such as the effects of one entity's wounding another—but a "history of beyng" that calls for a very different sort of thought and language.

This position is unnecessarily idealist: it divorces ontological traumas from every ontic trauma. In Heidegger's postwar texts, this trend becomes a grotesque denigration of actual suffering. Material poverty is subordinate to an essential, ontological poverty; actual homelessness is subordinate to an essential lack of home; and most disturbingly, the murder of existing human beings matters little in comparison to the annihilation of the essence of the human, a supposed destruction that occurs on the level of being as sense, not being as excess.[33] There is no need to develop a narrowly materialist theory to counter Heidegger's, but we do need to appreciate the fact that ontological traumas—disruptive clashes between sense and excess—happen to concrete individuals dealing with concrete situations, not to a vague "man" who responds to a still more nebulous "being."

On this point, Hegel is significantly more connected to empirical reality than Heidegger. For Hegel, philosophy must trace the ways in which the human spirit—not only philosophical texts and ideas, but art, technology, religion, economy, politics, and individual behavior—suffers conflicts and breaks through to fuller self-understanding. Spirit is engaged in a series of crises in which the subject develops in tandem with its understanding of its object, heading for a culminating insight in which the subject fully recognizes itself in its object. Although Hegel himself does not favor the word "being" (the simplest and crudest of concepts according to his logic), we could say that through the traumatic experience of spirit, being as sense becomes fully articulated and harmonized with being as excess.

According to Hegel's *Phenomenology of Spirit* (¶¶85–86), every form of spirit establishes its own criterion of truth—or in my terms, a configuration of sense that attempts to determine what types of excess it will accept. But each form thereby implies its own supersession: it finds itself admitting an excess that overturns its criterion, precipitating a crisis that results in a transformation.[34] Hegel readily describes this process in terms suited to the course of a human life: despair, sacrifice, reconciliation, loss, recovery, death. Even if we do not follow his account of the necessary unfolding of ever more complex forms of selfhood, his approach has the advantage that it is not bound to particular psychological or historical claims, but can suggest ways of interpreting a variety of experiences at many scales.

For Hegel, spirit finds itself driven to evolve not by an external imposition, but by its inner logic. The actual moment of overturning may be provoked by some contingent event or by an arbitrary movement, but the possibility for this moment has been opened in advance and is awaiting the impulse that sooner or later is bound to come. Every such turning point is the death of a form of spirit and the birth of a new one. The death cannot be conceived by the old form, but only intimated in despair; the birth can be remembered by the new form, but only in terms of its new consciousness. Thus, the complete logic of this process is incomprehensible to any finite stage within the process, and can be understood only in retrospect, from the vantage point of the absolute. However, the evolutionary logic is not foreign to the finite stages, but intrinsic to them: by virtue of a self-alienation required by freedom itself, spirit sets itself at odds with itself and embarks on a journey of reintegration by which it will become itself more truly, more fully than it was before. In this process, to use some Heideggerian language, spirit's own being becomes an issue for it, and by virtue of dealing with its own being, it develops ways of making sense of all beings.

Hegel's account is so appealing because it finds rationality and freedom in what might seem to be a senseless history. The excess that drives human events is not mere contingency, but a sense-generated and sense-generating excess. Free consciousness can come to recognize itself even in the history of its confusions and alienations.

But is this desire for self-recognition, in the end, the unrealistic wish for a triumph of sense over excess? Excess has an element of contingency that cannot be erased retrospectively: we cannot reconstruct a fully sufficient reason for the centipede's presence on the back side of the cube, the accident that blindsides us, or the fact of our own birth. Hegel appears to acknowledge contingency, but by a sleight of hand he turns it into something necessary: spirit demands contingency as the medium for its own externalization, which in turn is necessary in order to achieve reconciliation (*Phenomenology*, ¶¶807–8). Every excessive event thus gains a patina of intelligibility, but the price is that no genuinely new truth can appear. In a sense, no genuine event is possible in Hegel—no assault and no gift. (This is a broadly Kierkegaardian critique.)[35] If every finite form of consciousness fails to establish an impregnable criterion of truth—a fixed sense of excess—perhaps we should accept excess *as excess*. Excess exceeds every sense, despite its constant interaction with sense.

Furthermore, given the variety of crises and responses in human experience, any rigid theory of a necessary sequence of traumas is highly dubious. Such accounts—whether Christian, Hegelian, Marxist, or Freudian—seem determined to consolidate a configuration of sense rather than doing justice to the disruptive force of turning points.

Heidegger argues that Hegel's thought is the ultimate in subjectivistic self-presence, or "unconditional subjectity" (GA 5: 153–54/115). In contrast, as we have seen, he wants to revive some of the original trauma and creative tension of thinking: the *"deepest urgency of questionworthiness* in the struggle with the unmastered powers of truth and errancy" (GA 36/37: 77/61 tm). Heidegger leaves room for excess—at least, so he says. But we have seen that he tends toward an abstract, Olympian way of thinking that has some obvious defects, such as his lack of appreciation for politics and his insensitivity to concrete suffering.

A more empirical approach seems to be called for, but this must be an empiricism that does justice to the entanglement of sense and excess in emergencies—a traumatic empiricism. This concept can be juxtaposed with transcendentalism and empiricism of the simpler, nontraumatic sort. These will be ideal types that may help us move on to a more adequate view if we consider them in the light of birth and death as ultraevents.

For the empiricist of the simple type, excess always generates sense. The sum of our exposure to beings is ultimately responsible for our interpretations of them. Knowledge grows from our reactions to the real. Our interpretations may often be far off the mark, and may improve only over the course of many generations. Nevertheless, for empiricists, all our interpretations can in principle be traced to encounters with beings themselves—and over the long run, there is a tendency for our interpretations to become more adequate, in response to the pressure of the real.

We could say that for empiricism, the ultraevent of birth acts as a stimulant. Birth is an ultraevent not only for biological life, but for interpretive life—our conversance with being as sense. "Birth" can mean not only the beginning of my own being, but the broader fact that our interpretations have an origin, that they point back to their source and are not self-created. This type of excess urges us to admit that the real surpasses us—that the universe preceded us, and we are forever beholden to its impact on us. Every arrival of an infant—seemingly unformed and innocent of interpretations, awaiting stimuli from which it will build its habits and concepts—appears to confirm empiricism, to strengthen it as the most natural, commonsensical, and honest position.

Perhaps we can develop an extended concept of the ultraevent of death, as we have with birth. My death is the extinction of my being, and thus the end of my capacity for experience; this ultraevent cannot be experienced, since it extinguishes the possibility of any encounter at all. In the extended sense, death means that our interpretive life is finite: our meanings have limits beyond which they cannot pass. There may be an excess that, given their limits, our interpretations are simply incapable of admitting.[36]

The empiricist is likely to admit freely that we are all subject to death in the narrow sense, but will not see anything philosophically profound in the fact. And death in the broader sense is an irritant that the empiricist will avoid: empiricism (in the simple form we are considering) understands us as open to all reality, as malleable to all influences, so that truth is always around the next corner and is never denied us from the outset. The simple empiricist refuses to concede that we have a definite way of experiencing—a finite or mortal way of meaning.

The transcendentalist, meanwhile, can be said to build an entire philosophy around the ultraevent of death. To dwell on the impossibility of experiencing one's own extinction is to run up against the limits of experience—ways of constituting the whole that can become the topic of philosophical investigation and that provide an *a priori* structure for phenomena. For the transcendentalist, then, sense precedes excess and makes it possible for excess to be recognized. The advance framework of what being means allows certain types of stimuli to register as meaningful, to show up as "real" within set parameters. The particular facts about the real can never determine the framework that makes those facts accessible in the first place; the transcendental cannot be reduced to the empirical.

From a subjectivist point of view, transcendental insights confront us with the necessary presence of the subject in any possible experience. Subjectivity must synthesize (Kant) or constitute (Husserl) sense in advance in order for things to become accessible to the subject. But what about the process of maturation and the origination of the subject? The transcendental ego must be distanced again and again from the empirical ego, whose history indicates its contingency. The birth of the empirical ego bars it from enjoying a constitutive role, the power to determine the sense of excess in advance. Man, then, becomes a "empirico-transcendental doublet," as Foucault puts it—an intrinsically unstable and anxious subject.[37]

The irritant for transcendentalism, then, is the ultraevent of birth. This is the case even for Heidegger's transcendentalism in *Being and Time*, which, as we saw in chapter 1, is not subjectivistic: Dasein is not self-determining, but finds itself swept up in the temporal ecstases that happen to it. Nevertheless, Heidegger's transcendental thought is incapable of dealing with a more radical happening: the inception of ecstatic temporality itself, the birth of sense. In his transition to the thirties, this ultraevent becomes ever more irritating to his thought, until he abandons the transcendental standpoint.

If both birth and death are types of excess, then neither simple empiricism nor transcendentalism fully acknowledges excess. Neither of these positions, then, provides a satisfactory approach to the relation between sense and excess. We need to think of this relation in a way that leaves room for the ultraevents—the inception and end not only of our own being, but also of our interpretations, our ways of finding sense in beings. Being as sense has been born (it is indebted to an uninterpreted excess, which we can try to interpret only in retrospect) and it is mortal (there are limits beyond which being as sense cannot pass, unless it is transformed into some unthinkably different configuration).[38]

What can we say, then, that would do justice to the ultraevents of birth and death—our own birth and death, and with them, the birth and death of being as sense? Are these events intelligible at all? Or is the attempt to make sense of them a hopeless project, since all sense is bounded by these ultraevents?

The process in which sense is transformed by emergencies is experience, and we need to think of it empirically. But this cannot be a simple empiricism that supposes that sense is the direct result of all our encounters with the real. An encounter may or may not have the potential to reconfigure sense, depending on its particular excess and impact in the context of our lives. Configurations of sense can resist change, can limit what sorts of excess we will recognize, and may be mortal—that is, their limits may have to be shattered in an unimaginable, inconceivable quasi-death before we can become responsive to excess in a new way. Traumatic empiricism attends to experience, but without misinterpreting it as the simple givenness of present-at-hand phenomena—be they sense-data, objects, or essences. Experience is *Erfahrung*, a wayfaring in which the traveler is transformed by the passage. The most crucial experiences challenge the identities of those who experience them by breaking through the current bounds of sense.

To suggest what is distinctive about traumatic empiricism, we could distinguish empiricisms by way of their preferred metaphors. Locke and others famously characterize the newborn mind as a blank slate. But a slate is never strictly blank, since it is already characterized by its nature as slate; likewise (as the transcendentalist will point out), the mind must already have certain characteristics that give it the potential to be affected by perceptions. More importantly, for our purposes, a slate cannot be troubled, cannot become a problem for itself, and thus is incapable of traumatic experience.

In a Peircean vein, we could compare the long-term effect of experience to a cable woven from many strands; the cumulative effect of countless uncertain observations and reasonings is a very strong belief.[39] This image, however, leaves little room for a paradigm shift—a transformation in sense that sheds new light on all the existing strands. Such a transformation cannot be provoked simply by new observations, but requires a more fundamental and more mysterious tremor that affects our basic presuppositions.

Perhaps surprisingly, it is Aristotle who provides one of the best metaphors for traumatic empiricism when he compares induction to a shift in a battle, when a retreat is converted into resistance (*Post. An.* II.19). At a certain moment, the actions of a few brave soldiers can become the general action of the army. This unpredictable tipping point changes the whole sense and direction of the battle, as if everything were given a new polarity. But perhaps it is not so surprising that Aristotle would find an appropriate metaphor, since he develops a theory of tragedy that emphasizes transformative, disclosive turning points (*Poetics* XI)—a theory that has little in common with his substantialist metaphysics but blazes a different ontological path, one that suggests that our being must be understood in terms of crises.

What does traumatic empiricism look like now? What form would its ontology take? With Hegel, we would find deaths and births of sense at traumatic moments in which disjunctions between being as sense and being as excess drive us into new configurations; but we would not insist that this process is ruled by an internal logic, lest we reduce excess to sense. With Heidegger, we would ask how it is that our own being becomes a problem for us at traumatic moments, and show how our ways of responding to this problem affect our understanding of all being—but we would seek these moments in particular situations rather than in a remote and mythical inception.

How would traumatic ontology speak? Philosophy lives in language, and speaking of traumas is essential to thinking of them. But this cannot just mean speaking *about* such turning points from the vantage point of some system of sense that stands apart from them. Hegel, for instance, purports to let each point of view he explores express its own truth, but he does so through a vocabulary that is highly restricted and repetitive; his favored terms, such as "in itself" and "for itself," are often obstacles to comprehending what is happening at each stage in the development of spirit. Traumatic events must be allowed to speak for themselves, then, and our vocabulary must consist of tentative names, not fixed terms. But where do we look for these names?

Often enough, traumatic experience is inarticulate: we have no idea what to say, or no chance to say anything. We may be struck dumb by what we are undergoing. All language draws on a reservoir of established sense, and if the trauma is disruptive enough, it is simply impossible at the time to make this connection.

Sometimes, however, words emerge in an emergency—words that are unique expressions of the experience. Under traumatic conditions, concepts can liquefy under pressure, and words can find their way into new possibilities. This event that takes place at "the peaks of time" is poetry. Every successful poem is an event of emergence.

Poetic emergence can also take place as recollection. Since we have all undergone traumatic transformations and retain marks of them, a certain remembering can bring us closer to understanding them. As we recall former senses of self and world and shift back and forth between them and our current senses, taking care not to impose one configuration on the other, we may recollect a moment of transition. Poetic words may emerge from this recollected moment.

However, a collection of poetic expressions of inceptive experiences—an assemblage of "escent—issant pre-personae"[40]—would be thought-provoking, but it could hardly be called philosophy. A philosophy, an ontology, must make connections and look for essences, not just -escences. We have to try to find patterns that persist for a while, even if they are unprecedented and fragile. We need paths along which one transformative moment can be connected to others, instead of remaining isolated.

Traumas always have the potential to form such connections, if they strike deep enough to shake self and world. While they can never simply be reproduced or represented, they call on us to retrieve and remember them. Individually and collectively, then, we develop histories of post-traumatic interpretations, none of which settles perfectly into an identity; every interpretation of a trauma bears within it an unsolved riddle that can provoke a reinterpretation.

As we trace such histories, we must draw on another essential form of language, perhaps underestimated by Heidegger: narrative.[41] Without emergencies, there are no life stories, no human existence. So stories will always appeal to us when they skillfully tell of traumatic experiences and encounters with the question of who we are—whether tragic or trivial, factual or fictional. Examples could come from nearly any engaging story. Stories revolve around challenges—moments of crisis, loss, confusion, suffering—and around the characters' attempts to resolve the challenges and reestablish a stable sense.

By tracing these challenges and their satisfactory or unsatisfactory resolutions, stories illuminate the human condition without objectifying it and reducing it to a case of some universal law. They certainly call for philosophical reflection, but such reflection should not crowd out narrative. Our search for essences should keep returning to stories in order to be challenged and refreshed—to encounter unreproducible happenings that may be compared but not duplicated.

Consider a few examples: one narrative of individual trauma, another of collective trauma, and a third that combines both.

Clarice Lispector's *The Passion According to G. H.* is the expression of an encounter that shocks the narrator out of her comfortable, noncommittal life.[42] Lispector plumbs this event as a vision of an alien truth, a rupture in the known world. From the first page, the narrator is acutely aware that what she

has undergone cannot be assimilated to her former way of existing and her established sense of the world, and that putting it into words risks falsification:

> I don't know what to do with what I lived, I'm afraid of that profound disorder.
> . . . Did something happen to me that I, because I didn't know how to live it,
> lived as something else? . . . I don't want to confirm myself in what I lived—in
> the confirmation of me I would lose the world as I had it, and I know I don't
> have the fortitude for another.
>
> If I confirm my self and consider myself truthful, I'll be lost because I won't
> know where to inlay my new way of being—if I go ahead with my fragmen-
> tary visions, the whole world will have to be transformed in order for me to fit
> within it.[43]

The particular emergency that the narrator experiences could be described in
a sentence and reduced to a triviality or an aberrant moment. I prefer to withhold such a sentence and let those who are unfamiliar with this extraordinary
novel discover it for themselves. Prescinding from the concrete description of
the narrator's experience and the content of the interpretation she gives to it,
we can simply consider Lispector's text as an exemplar of emergency, and of
a kind of language that stays with emergency instead of dominating it.

Lispector's achievement is to sustain the mood and language of emergency
for the duration of an entire novel, so that words build and resonate without
crystallizing into a teaching or theory. She often refers to the limitations of
language in the face of a truly new experience: "Is love when you don't give
a name to the identity of things?"[44] "Pain is not the true name for whatever
people call pain."[45] "How could I speak without the word lying for me?"[46]
She also stretches language into new syntax and diction: "its existence was
existing me,"[47] "the world independed on me."[48] Repetitions of certain images
and words in the novel indicate a persistent effort to find language, rather than
a doctrine. The narrator speaks not about, but in response to, or even *as* the
trauma that she narrates.

This trauma is a break, a rupture, an opening. The opening opens onto an
overwhelming, excessive reality that has always been awaiting us, but which
we normally dismiss as insignificant or mistaken. We recoil from the breach:
"The time to live is a slow uninterrupted creaking of doors continuously
opening wide. Two gates were opening and had never stopped opening. But
they were continuously opening onto—onto the nothing?"[49]

> Every time something I was thinking or feeling didn't work out—was because
> finally there was a breach, and, if I'd had courage before, I'd have already gone
> through it. But I'd always been afraid of delirium and error. My error, however,
> must be the path of a truth: since only when I err do I step out of what I know

and what I understand. If "truth" were whatever I could understand—it would end up being just a small truth, one my size.[50]

A larger truth, a truth of errancy and excess, is demanded by the apocalyptic breach of opening.

Lispector's novel discloses certain essences, certain patterns that are shared among many traumatic turns. But instead of formalizing them into abstract philosophical categories, the narrator keeps being set on edge by the trauma, returning to the happening of the breach. Such a story is invaluable for traumatic ontology, if we let it provoke us into further reflection instead of incorporating it into a finished system.

What happens when not just an individual, but a community is confronted by an apocalypse—is pushed to ask "Who are we?" while "peering through a flashing breach in the national memory"?[51] This is the theme of Steve Erickson's novel *Shadowbahn*, which explores the American soul through a series of contradictory pairings. The Twin Towers of the World Trade Center reappear twenty years after their destruction in the Badlands of South Dakota. Their sole occupant is Jesse Presley, Elvis's stillborn twin, who is launched into an alternate history in which Elvis was stillborn and Jesse dedicates himself to eradicating American music—a quest that also alters American political history and even averts 9/11, at a terrible cost.

This dreamlike plot, which makes a half-sense on the symbolic level, is the occasion for Erickson to pose the question of American selfhood and leave it hanging as a question. The first person to witness the reappearance of the Twin Towers is a trucker whose bumper sticker reads, "Save America from Itself." "When he first put on the sticker, he thought he knew what it meant. The more he's thought about it since, the less sure he is."[52] Rather than providing a clear interpretation of the saying, Erickson leaves us wondering what the two sides of America may be, and which one needs saving from the other.

Erickson heightens these questions through commentaries on a playlist consisting of pairs of songs. As he writes of one pair, released in 2000 and 2003: "On opposite sides of a chasm, are these two songs infused with the spirit of a stillborn nation that wanders its own landscape trying to make sense of destiny, trying to make sense of survival, trying to make sense of which twin country is really left? Which is the corporeal and which is the ectoplasm? Which is the reflected and which the reflection? Which is the sun and which is the shadow?"[53]

Any definitive answers to such questions would have to identify an American destiny to which "un-American" Americans are unfaithful. For instance, one side of the American divide would take a certain Christianity as essential to the soul of the country, while the other would insist on a certain equality.

But Erickson complicates any such move through the difficult idea that the destiny of the United States was sullied in the very moment when it was born: "the spirit of America takes off . . . for one last jaunt around all the possibilities that the country once imagined for itself, even as those possibilities were betrayed before the country began."[54] Twentieth-century music

> was the expression of and then rebuttal to America's self-betrayal—when the music was about America regardless of whether it came from America, whether it believed in America, whether it thought of America, whether it spurned or rejected America. The previous century's music knew of America whether anyone knew that it did. At the previous century's root was a blues sung at the moment when America defiled its own great idea, which was the moment that idea was born. . . . its own moment was the expression of and then rebuttal to the future's self-betrayal, the future's defilement of its own possibilities at the instant they became possible.[55]

This may be the case for every community: as soon as its founding ideals are envisioned and formulated, they enable dissent, falling away, secession, rebellion—and alternative interpretations of the ideals themselves. A contest over who counts as a "true" member of the community begins.

But what if the true destiny of the community is characterized not by one side or the other, but by the conflict itself? What makes American music American is not some uniformity of style or content, but a constellation of conflicts and questions. To abjure half a country as ungenuine makes no more sense than counting only half of a country's musical tradition. There is no simple duality between the life of a community, its true identity, and its dead, false alter ego. Every historical inception is both birth and death, a stillbirth that is still a birth. *Shadowbahn* works through the history of American still-births without ever working its way out.

Our third example of traumatic narrative is Tommy Orange's novel *There There*, which follows several Native American characters as they converge on a powwow in Oakland. Their individual lives are all scarred by particular traumas and debilities—violence, abandonment, addiction—but they also bear the burden of the collective trauma of genocide and dispossession.

These characters are faced with the need to adopt positions toward themselves, to take stances on their own being—a need that faces all of us, but which those of us who live in comfort and privilege may be able to ignore. Orange's individuals do not have the luxury of simply being what they are, but are forced to decide *who* they are. They cannot simply be there, but must take up the burden of being-there. Maybe "the only way to be Indian in this world is to look and act like an Indian,"[56] but what that means remains in question.

This ever-pressing need keeps requiring self-relations and reduplications. "We are the memories we don't remember" but must learn to recall.[57] "You have to believe that believing will work, you have to believe in belief."[58] These relations to personal and shared futures, pasts, and presents do not reduce any of these dimensions of time to a simple viewpoint, identity, or rule; they maintain time as an issue.

Orange does not hold out any definitive answer or final solution, any more than Lispector and Erickson do. The only escape from the burdens of existence—not a solution—is oblivion or suicide, that is, abandoning existence altogether by "jumping out the windows of burning buildings."[59] As Binswanger puts it, madness can take the form of seeking "a *way out*" of the traumas of existence—"the longing [for] a final *ad acta* laying aside of things, and in a 'definitely final effort,' the laying aside of one's *self.*"[60] Through exploring how individuals either try to escape or avoid the temptation to escape, Orange fleshes out the idea that our being is ineluctably at issue.

Binswanger also proposes that although there is no solution to the emergency of existing, "An individual turns from mere self-identity to selfhood . . . when he decides not only to seek to know 'what hit him,' but seeks also to strike into and take hold of the dynamics in these events, 'himself'—the moment, that is, when he resolves to bring continuity or consistency into a life that rises and falls, falls and rises."[61] A certain temporary integrity can be achieved in action and art. Stories, song, and dance can be ways of participating in the breach, responding to the fractured opening. These are ways of being there (there) where, for the moment, "your whole being [is] a kind of flight"[62]—not fleeing, but soaring.

By telling stories and listening to them, we put flesh on the bones of ontology and open our eyes to the endless variety of traumatic experience.

* * *

Drawing on the thoughts of Heidegger in the thirties, I have done no more than lay out the rudiments of a philosophical orientation that can be labeled traumatic ontology. Such an ontology would draw on narrative and poetic explorations of fractured experience. It would not try to dissolve the tension between being as sense and being as excess, but would follow the many turns this tension takes: how our individual and collective stories reach critical moments; how excess turns out as we did or did not expect; how excess turns up with or without our intervention; how excess overturns sense and enriches it. Responsive to excess in its many possibilities, including the ultraevents of birth and death, traumatic ontology would do justice to the turning points when sense is reconfigured. It would attend to endings and inceptions not by reducing them to a particular configuration of sense, but by tracing how the tension between sense and excess plays itself out at these junctures, each of which has its unique character. Traumatic ontology would push the edges of phenomenology, dwelling in the breach—the opening where sense meets what exceeds it. It would explore political questions by attending to the originations of contested configurations of sense and the fragile sphere where we act in response to the issue of the "who." It would promote individual and shared self-knowledge by staying with the emergency of the self.

Traumatic ontology would be faced with a number of difficult questions. We can end by mentioning just a few.

To return to the question of the limits of reason and the destiny of the Enlightenment: If Hegelian rationalism represents an unacceptable triumph of sense over excess, does it follow that reason has no place in ontology? Or does this insight rather make it possible to return to Kant, in the very general sense that reason can come into its own by understanding its proper limits? Where would those theoretical and practical limits lie, then? Does reason have to shrink back from the turmoil of an emergency, or is there a traumatic logic—a logic of coming to be an issue for oneself? Can reason be flexible enough to build bridges of discourse across paradigms, to understand transitions, to avoid speaking only from within a constituted identity?

If we admit that traumatic inception cannot be reduced to the terms of an established regime of sense, are we forced into a relativism whereby every representational regime is as valid as any other? Is it possible to judge one configuration of sense as richer, truer, or deeper than another? Can we say that some emergencies are more insightful and disclosive than others?

How are beings whose being explicitly becomes an issue for them—who are exposed to trauma and can experience being as such as a question—related to beings whose being apparently does not concern them? How should we understand the differences and continuities between the beings who are exposed to the tension between sense and excess, and the beings that are not?

Why are some traumas, in the broad sense, harmful while others are uplifting? Why are some reconfigurations transfigurations? If a life that has found harmonious sense is crowned with happiness, can a life transfigured by excess achieve joy?

Can a community be nourished and strengthened not through a founding identity, but by sustaining and enhancing a public sphere in which responses to the question "Who are we?" can be contested?

How do we become the ones we are? Do we keep drawing lines of selfhood that are erased and redrawn? Are our selves elicited by exposure to the interventions of others? Do we keep becoming ourselves without arriving? Is our unfinished arrival impelled by inceptions when ecstatic time unfolds, when sense is lit up by the turns of excess, when the peaks of time call for interminable retrievals?

Appendix

Propositions on Emergency

PREDEFINABLES

sense: Things can be held or beheld, defined or dealt with, because they inhabit a sense-dimension. To see things is to see past them. The here and now are meaningful only in a distance and a span. The apparently immediate needs a medium in which to appear.

excess: Things surpass their sense. They are more than the mediating dimension in which they are met. Their excess can elude definition, resist visibility, and solicit reinterpretation.

DEFINITIONS

being: the sense of excess and the excess over sense. The concept of being indicates nonconceptuality: to grasp a thing as something that *is* (an **entity**) is to acknowledge that it surpasses the grasping. To recognize something as an entity is to experience it, within a sense-dimension, as exceeding that dimension.

being as such pertains to any entity that can be met in any way. Particular ways of being pertain to particular kinds of entities, with their characteristic senses and ways of exceeding sense.

emergency: a clash between sense and excess. An event in which excess challenges sense and resists being interpreted, so that sense has trouble getting a purchase on it. The event can also be called a trauma.

the Emergency: when used with a definite article and capitalized, let this word mean the primordial clash between sense and excess, the contest that generates the contenders as such, first establishing sense with excess as its counterpart. The Emergency can be defined in terms of sense and excess, as their origin; but it itself would be neither sense nor excess. To define it is not to understand it, nor to reduce it to the terms of the definition.

emergencies: when used in the plural, let this word mean nonprimordial emergencies, events in which some settled sense is unsettled by some excess. These unsettling emergencies range from a passing confusion to a conceptual revolution to the shattering of a world. The degree to which an emergency can be understood within established sense-dimensions is a matter for judgment. Mature judgment develops through experiences of emergencies of various scopes.

to emerge as **emergent:** to originate in a clash between sense and excess and call for an interpretation; to issue from an emergency and become an issue, unresolved and dissonant, demanding to be addressed. An emergent issue may hover in the background, even though it seems to have been resolved. The emergent is pacified when it takes the form of an answered question. It is dormant when it is not even recognized as a question.

POSTULATES

1. There are entities whose own being emerges for them. Call them "we."

1.1. Our excess over sense emerges for us. That we are here, that we are and may not be—regardless of how we may interpret ourselves—has become an issue for us. We are faced with death as the ultimate excess, the extreme withdrawal from the sphere of sense. This issue can fade into the background as we take our lives for granted.

1.2. The sense of our excess emerges for us. We are faced with the question of who we are, the demand to interpret ourselves as entities. This question normally presents itself in the guise of an answer. Even though the issue has always been resolved in both theory and practice, it can always be reignited.

2. We are ourselves by facing what we are not. Our own sense is the sum of the senses all entities have for us. Who we are is what things mean to us. Complete self-enclosure would be the lack of self.

3. We encounter all entities thanks to the emergent. We do not notice or deal with an entity at all unless it has become relevant to us in terms of some emergent issue, even a minimal one. Once the initial issue has been resolved, the entities that became relevant in that issue may continue to be accessible.

Scholium: Postulate 3 is not a subjectivism or idealism. Our issues are not a subjective sphere of representation that separates us from entities themselves. Issues allow entities themselves to show up for us—and entities are never exhausted by that display, but retain an irreducible excess. We meet the real, finitely.

PROPOSITIONS

1. Emergency makes entities accessible. All entities are accessed thanks to the emergent (Post. 3), which emerges from an emergency (Def.).

1.1. Emergency enables us to be who we are. Emergency makes entities accessible (Prop. 1), and only by interpreting entities can we be ourselves (Post. 2). We are the whole of how we encounter what emergency has enabled us to encounter.

2. Being emerges from the Emergency. The primordial clash between sense and excess, which generates them both (Def.), would be the source of being as the sense of excess and the excess over sense (Def.).

Scholium: Being is emergent: it arises as an issue calling for interpretation. But normally this issue lies dormant, unrecognized as a question.

2.1. We cannot grasp the Emergency as an entity. Entities appear within sense, as exceeding sense. Their appearance presupposes the Emergency, the event in which being emerges (Prop. 2). We can speculate that an entity (such as a biological or cultural development) generated sense and excess, possibly on repeated occasions, but such speculations occur within an established sense-dimension and cannot grasp the primordial clash as such.

3. Being as such emerges for us. Our own being emerges for us (Post. 1) and every entity we meet is relevant to our own being (Post. 2). Thus the being of all these entities, being as such, also emerges for us. Because our own being is at stake, being as such is at stake. We are faced with questions about the being of entities, both as a whole and in particular.

3.1. Being as such emerges only for us. "We" is not necessarily limited to *Homo sapiens*; it may include other species, terrestrial and extraterrestrial, as long as they are exposed to emergencies (Prop. 1.1). But if an entity's own being does not emerge for it, being as such cannot emerge for it either. If something feels neither the urgency of being nor the need to ask who it is, it cannot be faced with any issue that needs resolution, including the issue of being. Thus being emerges for us (Prop. 3), but not for any other entity.

4. We emerge from the Emergency. Being emerges from the Emergency (Prop. 2), and we are those for whom being is at issue (Prop. 3). Thus, without the Emergency we could not be who we are. We are the offspring of the Emergency.

5. We are temporal. We are exposed to three temporal sense-dimensions. Since our excess is at issue (Post. 1.1), we must understand that we have been, we are, and we can cease to be. Since our sense is at issue (Post. 1.2), the question of who we are must already have been resolved, but it must be possible to resolve it again, and to do so now. We are exposed to pastness, possibility, and presence all together.

5.1. We are exposed to possibility. Our being is subject to possibilities: our excess is vulnerable and our sense is open to reinterpretation. In the dimension of possibility, we find ourselves laid open to these risks. In this dimension we meet the imaginary, the willed, the desired, and the feared; these encounters help to define us (Post. 2).

5.2. We are exposed to pastness. We find that we have already been and already interpreted ourselves. In the dimension of pastness we can face the memorable, the forgettable, the inherited, the debt that can be paid, neglected, or forgiven; these encounters also define us.

5.3. We are exposed to presence. We find ourselves exposed to pastness and possibility, so we are here, now, as those who have been and may be.

Scholium: Possibility and pastness are not inferior or alternate modes of presence; presence originates at their confluence. But possibility and pastness are not prior to presence, either; they need presence as the dimension in which they can meet.

5.3.1. The emergent emerges in presence. In emergencies, excess intrudes as an unanticipated possibility. In the intrusion, the possibility becomes something that has happened. This becoming takes place in presence, the confluence of pastness and possibility (Prop. 5.3). Thus, emergencies and the emergent occur in presence.

5.3.1.1. All entities first become accessible in presence. We encounter all entities in terms of the emergent (Post. 3) and the emergent emerges in presence (Prop. 5.3.1), so it is in presence that entities become accessible.

Scholium: Prop. 5.3.1.1 does not say that all entities are present; within presence, they may show up as past or possible. Possibility and pastness must intersect in presence, which lets all entities, including possible and past entities, appear.

5.3.1.1.1. The distinction between temporary and timeless entities occurs within presence. Among the entities we meet, we can distinguish between those that are susceptible to change and those that are not (e.g., mathematical relations). Both become accessible within presence as a dimension of our temporality (Prop. 5.3.1.1).

5.3.1.1.2. Propositions are asserted within presence. All entities become accessible in presence (Prop. 5.3.1.1), and asserting propositions is one way to notice, communicate, and develop this accessibility.

5.3.2. The sense-dimensions of possibility and pastness are prior to logical possibility and impossibility. Presence is the confluence of the sense-dimensions of pastness and possibility (Prop. 5.3), and propositions are asserted within presence (Prop. 5.3.1.1.2). Logical possibility and impossibility are, respectively, the absence and presence of contradictions within a set of propositions.

5.4. Only we are temporal. If an entity's being emerges for it, it is exposed to the three temporal sense-dimensions (Prop. 5). Conversely, if an entity is exposed to the possible, the past, and the present, it is exposed to the possibility that it could cease to be, or change its sense; thus, its own being emerges for it. An entity whose own being does not emerge for it is nontemporal.

Scholium: Being temporal is not the same as being temporary (Prop. 5.3.1.1.1). The qualities of a temporary but not temporal entity may alter, it may interact with other entities, it may be destroyed, but it cannot interpret anything as possible, past, or present.

6. Temporality emerges from the Emergency. We emerge from the Emergency (Prop. 4), we are temporal (Prop. 5), and no other entity is temporal (Prop. 5.4), so the Emergency would be the inception of temporality.

6.1. Possibility emerges from the Emergency. Without the primordial clash of sense and excess, there would be no interpretive space to explore, and no threat or promise of irruption into that space.

6.1.1. The Emergency would be nonpossible. It cannot be grasped as an entity (Prop. 2.1), either possible or impossible; it would be the nonentity that generates the realm of possibility (Prop. 6.1). The Emergency has the jump on every attempt to encompass it. It cannot be willed, desired, feared, or imagined (Prop. 5.1). It can be conceived only as a limit: as that which we cannot interpret because it enables all interpretation.

6.2. Pastness emerges from the Emergency. Without the primordial clash of sense and excess, there would be no already given entities calling for interpretation, and no established interpretation inviting entities to be interpreted.

6.2.1. The Emergency would be immemorial. It cannot be grasped as a past entity (Prop. 2.1) but would be the source of pastness itself (Prop. 6.2). An account of the Emergency as a thing of the past is a myth—an approach to the immemorial through remembrance.

6.3. Presence emerges from the Emergency. Without the primordial clash of sense and excess, there would be no context in which things could be faced, approached, or appropriated.

6.3.1. The Emergency would be unpresentable. The Emergency is not an emergent issue, which can emerge only within the dimension of presence (Prop. 5.3.1), which is generated by the Emergency (Prop. 6.3). The Emergency cannot be grasped as any entity that becomes available thanks to such issues (Prop. 2.1). Never itself emergent, the Emergency remains submerged.

6.3.2. The Emergency is neither temporary nor timeless. These categories apply only to entities that become accessible within presence (Prop. 5.3.1.1.1). Neither within time nor without it, the Emergency would be the founding temporalization of time itself.

7. Emergencies emerge from the Emergency. As the origin of all sense and excess, the Emergency would enable every clash between unsettling excess and settled sense.

7.1. Emergencies indicate the Emergency. As events that can, to some degree, be understood and absorbed, emergencies serve as semipresentable tokens and derivatives of the Emergency from which they emerge (Prop. 7), which would itself be unpresentable (Prop. 6.3.1).

7.2. Emergencies reshape the possible. The Emergency generates the sense-dimension of possibility (Prop. 6.1) and makes emergencies possible (Prop. 7). These emergencies, then, cannot generate possibility itself, but they can alter the range and character of particular possibilities. The experience of an emergency alerts us that it is possible for this particular clash between sense and excess to take place.

7.2.1. Emergencies cannot be fully imagined, willed, desired, or feared. The imagined, willed, desired, and feared are encountered within the possible (Prop. 5.1). But inasmuch as an event is an emergency, it reshapes the possible (Prop. 7.2). Insofar as an emergency is anticipated within an established dimension of possibility, it is necessarily misrepresented. The element of emergency is the element of surprise. Emergencies cannot be predicted or excluded.

7.3. Emergencies reconfigure the past. Emergencies do not generate pastness itself, as the Emergency does (Prop. 6.2), but they reveal the past in retrospect as having been vulnerable to the particular clash between sense and excess that is now taking place.

7.3.1. Emergencies cannot be fully remembered. The remembered appears within the past (Prop. 5.2), but the past is reconfigured by emergencies (Prop. 7.3), and a surprising emergency can never be ruled out (Prop. 7.2.1). Thus, every emergency remains open to a new emergency that would reconfigure the past again, and reinterpret all previous emergencies. There is no definitive account of an emergency. In every emergency, there is a transformation that eludes retrospection.

7.3.2. Emergencies are reminders of the immemorial Emergency. The Emergency itself would be immemorial (Prop. 6.2.1), but as indications of the Emergency (Prop. 7.1), emergencies bring us analogically closer to it. If emergencies reconfigure the past, the Emergency would configure it. If emergencies are reinterpretive events, the Emergency would be the interpretive event.

7.4. Emergencies reorient the present. Emergencies take place in presence (Prop. 5.3.1), where they reshape the possible (Prop. 7.2) and reconfigure the past (Prop. 7.3), thus reorienting the present as the confluence of pastness and possibility. From a small epiphany that gives us pause to a transfiguration that gives us the world anew, emergencies cast the present in a new light.

7.4.1. Emergencies cannot be fully presented. Emergencies reorient the present as a sense-dimension (Prop. 7.4), so they cannot themselves be fully interpreted within that dimension. They are clashes between sense and excess, so they cannot be smoothly presented within a stable order of sense.

7.4.2. Emergencies make both grief and joy possible. Whereas satisfaction and dissatisfaction are based on continuing desires, joy and grief both recognize the irruption of an unanticipated and transformative excess. Emergencies exceed the realm of the desired (Prop. 7.2.1), bringing devastation or delight. Such an event reorients the present (Prop. 7.4) and marks the moment as one of grief or joy.

7.4.3. The sense of our being is not our creation. Emergencies cannot be fully willed, but come to us as surprises (Prop. 7.2.1) that grant grief and joy (Prop. 7.4.2). Our lives are responses to what we are not (Post. 2), and above all to what delights or wounds us. Who we are cannot be willed, but is a collaboration between our own initiatives and the emergencies we encounter.

8. Emergencies call for emergent thinking.

8.1. The Emergency calls for emergent thinking. All propositions are asserted within presence (Prop. 5.3.1.1.2), but presence emerges from the Emergency (Prop. 6.3), which would be unpresentable (Prop. 6.3.1), so the Emergency cannot be captured in propositions. It can be conceived only as a limit (Prop. 6.1.1). The act of thinking the Emergency has to run up against the origin of the predefinables themselves, sense and excess. Emerging from the realm of sense to confront its origin, this act is itself an emergency, an event of emergent thinking.

Scholia: Statements of how the Emergency "is" tend to represent the Emergency as a present entity. Expressions such as "would be" may indicate the

Emergency's elusive status as the theme of a thinking that runs up against the origin of the predefinables, a thought that is not thetical but hypothetical.

The Emergency would not be emergent, but submerged (Prop. 6.3.1). It could not call for thought in the way emergent issues do. It would have to have its own way of calling.

8.2. Emergencies call for emergent thinking. In emergencies, some established sense is challenged by some excess. This challenge cannot be smoothly incorporated in the established sense-dimension, and it has not yet been interpreted in a new sense-dimension. An anticipatory account of an emergency is a contradiction in terms (Prop. 7.2.1), and an account after the fact has to speak from within a new order of sense, so that it cannot fully recall the transformation itself (Prop. 7.3.1). Emergencies call for a form of thinking that is itself undergoing the emergency.

8.3. All propositions on emergency are rooted in emergent thinking. If we disregard the call for emergent thinking, our statements must fail to speak of the Emergency and emergencies (Props. 8.1, 8.2). At most, an arrangement of propositions can only be the precipitate of emergencies—an assembly of statements generated by emergent thinking and inviting it.

Notes

INTRODUCTION

1. "Wie werden wir, die wir sind?": Heidegger (GA 82: 170); Martin Buber, "Judentum und Kultur" (1951), in *Der Jude und sein Judentum: Gesammelte Aufsätze und Reden*, intro. Robert Weltsch (Cologne: Joseph Melzer Verlag, 1963), 163. For Buber, "we" (Jews) are "the protectors of the roots." For Heidegger, "we" are "*the ones who become*, [who] comply with the *law of becoming oneself.*"

2. Other translations of *Dasein* have been proposed, but in my view, "being-there" is suitably close to the German and suitably open-ended. The specific meaning of the term depends on how it is used and explained. I will often leave it untranslated.

3. Letter to Karl Löwith, November 17, 1929, in Martin Heidegger and Karl Löwith, *Briefwechsel 1919–1973*, Martin Heidegger Briefausgabe II.2., ed. Alfred Denker (Freiburg: Karl Alber, 2016), 170.

4. The lecture course GA 29/30 was held on Mondays, Tuesdays, Thursdays, and Fridays from 5 to 6 p.m.: *Ankündigung der Vorlesungen der Badischen Albert-Ludwigs-Universität Freiburg im Breisgau für das Winterhalbjahr 1929/30* (Freiburg im Breisgau: C. A. Wagner Buchdruckerei, 1929), 18. The semester began on October 15, 1929 (ibid., 1), a Tuesday. Heidegger's crucial question, "*Has man in the end become boring to himself?*" (GA 29/30: 241/161) was asked shortly before the Christmas break (GA 29/30: 268).

5. The archaic "beyng" has become the predominant way of rendering Heidegger's old-fashioned spelling *Seyn* in English. This device is meant to distinguish his sense of being from an account of the general characteristics of entities, which he calls "the being of beings" (*das Sein des Seienden*) or "beingness" (*Seiendheit*).

6. Andrew J. Mitchell, *The Fourfold: Reading the Late Heidegger* (Evanston: Northwestern University Press, 2015), 18–23.

7. For a particularly thorough unifying interpretation see Thomas Sheehan, *Making Sense of Heidegger: A Paradigm Shift* (London: Rowman & Littlefield International, 2014).

8. Karl Löwith, *My Life in Germany Before and After 1933: A Report*, tr. Elizabeth King (Urbana: University of Illinois Press, 1994), 30.

9. See Peter Trawny's reservations about the language of contamination, which he himself formerly used, in the preface to his *Heidegger and the Myth of a Jewish World Conspiracy*, tr. Andrew J. Mitchell (Chicago: University of Chicago Press, 2016).

10. Heidegger was well aware of the charge that the "late Heidegger" was "unethical," but told himself to "*calmly let it pass*," observing that "behind" his work there was "a decided questioning" for the sake of a "transformation of thinking" (GA 73.2: 1440). One can concede that such a transformation is important and may eventually affect practice, yet still wish for an appreciation of the practical realm that is not offered by Heidegger's late thought.

11. Robert Bernasconi, "Being Is Evil: Boehme's Strife and Schelling's Rage in Heidegger's 'Letter on "Humanism,"'" *Gatherings: The Heidegger Circle Annual* 7 (2017): 164–81.

12. Bret W. Davis, *Heidegger and the Will: On the Way to Gelassenheit* (Evanston: Northwestern University Press, 2007), 297.

13. See François Raffoul and David Pettigrew, eds., *Heidegger and Practical Philosophy* (Albany: State University of New York Press, 2002).

14. Richard Polt, *The Emergency of Being: On Heidegger's "Contributions to Philosophy"* (Ithaca: Cornell University Press, 2006), 248–53.

15. Heidegger is a popular figure on counter-currents.com, home of Counter-Currents Publishing, purveyor of books by racists and neofascists. In Russia, political theorist Alexander Dugin has enlisted Heidegger in his project of a "Eurasianism" that is profoundly antiliberal, although he denies that it is fascist: see, e.g., Dugin, "Plural Anthropology—the Fundamental-Ontological Analysis of Peoples," in *Heidegger in Russia and Eastern Europe*, ed. Jeff Love (London: Rowman & Littlefield International, 2017). On this issue, see Ronald Beiner, *Dangerous Minds: Nietzsche, Heidegger, and the Return of the Far Right* (Philadelphia: University of Pennsylvania Press, 2018).

CHAPTER ONE: INTO THE HAPPENING OF BEING

1. For a rich yet concise study of the years immediately following *Being and Time* see Theodore Kisiel, "The Drafts of 'Time and Being': Division III of Part One of *Being and Time* and Beyond," in *Division III of Heidegger's "Being and Time": The Unanswered Question of Being*, ed. Lee Braver (Cambridge: MIT Press, 2015).

2. See Jean Grondin, "Why Reawaken the Question of Being?" in *Heidegger's "Being and Time": Critical Essays*, ed. Richard Polt (Lanham, MD: Rowman & Littlefield, 2005); Sheehan, *Making Sense of Heidegger*, Prologue.

3. See John Haugeland, *Dasein Disclosed: John Haugeland's Heidegger*, ed. Joseph Rouse (Cambridge: Harvard University Press, 2013), 21–22, 52, 62, 105, 191, 226.

4. *Sinn* is translated as "meaning" in the English versions of *Being and Time*. Despite the slight risk of confusing "sense" with a kind of sensory perception (which is also a liability of the German word *Sinn*), "sense" avoids any suggestion that *Sinn* is equivalent to a conscious, focused, mental or verbal act in which one "means" something, or that *Sinn* is only the object of such an act. Any such act presupposes a more fundamental *Sinn*.

5. The phrase *das Sein überhaupt*, which first appears on SZ 11, is rendered in the English translations as "being in general." In order to avoid the suggestion that being is a genus, I prefer the expression "being as such."

6. For recent studies of the theme see David Farrell Krell, *Ecstasy, Catastrophe: Heidegger from "Being and Time" to the "Black Notebooks"* (Albany: State University of New York Press, 2015), Part One; James Luchte, *Heidegger's Early Philosophy: The Phenomenology of Ecstatic Temporality* (London: Continuum, 2008).

7. Martin Heidegger, *Übungen für Anfänger: Schillers Briefe über die ästhetische Erziehung des Menschen: Winter-Semester 1936/37: Seminar-Mitschrift von Wilhelm Hallwachs*, ed. Ulrich von Bülow (Marbach am Neckar: Deutsche Schillergesellschaft, 2005), 94.

8. Edmund Husserl, *The Phenomenology of Internal Time Consciousness*, ed. Martin Heidegger, tr. James S. Churchill (Bloomington: Indiana University Press, 1964).

9. Heidegger pays tribute to Kierkegaard's concept of the moment both at the beginning and around the end of the "thirties." It makes a new epoch in philosophy possible (GA 29/30: 225). "Kierkegaard's recognition that the 'moment' is 'eternity' touched, in this Christian form, on a truth that has not yet been taken up": letter to Fritz Heidegger, January 4, 1944, in *Heidegger und der Antisemitismus: Positionen im Widerstreit*, ed. Walter Homolka and Arnulf Heidegger (Freiburg: Herder, 2016), 94.

10. On the moment in Heidegger's thought of the twenties and thirties, see William McNeill, *The Glance of the Eye: Heidegger, Aristotle, and the Ends of Theory* (Albany: State University of New York Press, 1999); Katharina von Falkenhayn, *Augenblick und Kairos: Zeitlichkeit im Frühwerk Martin Heideggers* (Berlin: Duncker & Humblot, 2003); Felix Ó Murchadha, *The Time of Revolution: Kairos and Chronos in Heidegger* (London: Bloomsbury, 2013).

11. Aristotle, *Physics* 4.10; Augustine, *Confessions* 11.14. McTaggart's argument for the nonbeing of time, much discussed in the analytic tradition, is a more complex paradox that also cries out for a Heideggerian analysis.

12. Plotinus, *Enneads* 3.7.11. Heidegger "learned" from this passage (GA 82: 298).

13. Heidegger, "Aufzeichnungen zur Temporalität (Aus den Jahren 1925 bis 1927)," *Heidegger Studies* 14 (1998), 17.

14. Kisiel, "The Drafts of 'Time and Being,'" in Braver, *Division III*, 156.

15. On the projected contents of Division III see Kisiel, "The Drafts of 'Time and Being,'" and Sheehan, *Making Sense of Heidegger*, Chapter 6. We will learn more about the contents of the lost text when certain manuscripts are published. In particular, some two hundred handwritten pages of notes relating to Division III exist among

Heidegger's papers in Marbach. Their topics include the ontological difference (between being and beings), the varieties of temporal modes (such as expectative, presentative, and perfective), and time as a "self-projection upon itself": Kisiel, "The Drafts of 'Time and Being,'" 151–52. "Aufzeichnungen zur Temporalität" includes roughly 15 percent of this text.

16. For an argument that all forms of being, for Heidegger, ultimately have the same sense—"meaningful presence"—see Philip Tonner, *Heidegger, Metaphysics and the Univocity of Being* (London: Continuum, 2010). The issue is difficult because Heidegger uses "presence" in broader and narrower senses and because, especially in his later work, it is often difficult to tell when he is expressing his own conception of being and when he is elucidating the tradition. For an ambitious investigation of the theme, see Jussi Backman, *Complicated Presence: Heidegger and the Postmetaphysical Unity of Being* (Albany: State University of New York Press, 2015); according to Backman, Heidegger comes to think of being as "an instantaneous folding together of complicated and contextual presence" (243).

17. For explorations of the transcendental element in *Being and Time* and beyond see Steven Crowell and Jeff Malpas, eds., *Transcendental Heidegger* (Stanford: Stanford University Press, 2007); Chad Engelland, *Heidegger's Shadow: Kant, Husserl, and the Transcendental Turn* (New York: Routledge, 2017).

18. The similarity to Kant is emphasized by Heidegger's term "horizonal schema," which echoes the Schematism of the Pure Concepts of the Understanding in the *Critique of Pure Reason*. The Schematism, which interprets the categories in temporal terms, was the focus of Heidegger's studies of Kant in the 1920s.

19. William Blattner, *Heidegger's Temporal Idealism* (Cambridge: Cambridge University Press, 1999), 181–82.

20. Von Falkenhayn, *Augenblick und Kairos*, 225.

21. In 1927, Heidegger says that a return "to the subject in its broadest sense" is necessary (GA 24: 103/73, cf. 220). But this means reinterpreting the "subject" as Dasein and understanding it appropriately, as openness rather than as a self-determined domain. This is the very opposite of "subjectivism." See François Raffoul, "The Incompletion of *Being and Time* and the Question of Subjectivity," in Braver, *Division III*, 246–49; Raffoul, *Heidegger and the Subject*, tr. David Pettigrew and Gregory Recco (Atlantic Highlands, NJ: Humanity Books, 1998).

22. In general, we can avoid an infinite regress of horizons of understanding only if we reach a condition for understanding that is not itself understood. The same issue is raised in the 1945 "Triadic Conversation on a Country Path" (GA 77: 93–95). Again, the problem points to a ground for all horizons—here, the "region" that enables all representation but resists being represented.

23. Heidegger, "Aufzeichnungen zur Temporalität," 21.

24. Along these lines, Quentin Meillasoux's *After Finitude: An Essay on the Necessity of Contingency*, tr. Ray Brassier (London: Bloomsbury, 2010) appeals to "ancestrality" in order to undercut phenomenology in general (10–27).

25. "Temporal idealism" means that "time requires Dasein": Blattner, *Heidegger's Temporal Idealism*, 231. Likewise, for "ontological idealism," "being depends on Dasein" (246). We could add that truth, too, depends on Dasein (SZ 226–27).

26. For related reasons, Steven Crowell sees Heidegger's turn away from transcendental philosophy after *Being and Time* as a "dialectical illusion": *Husserl, Heidegger, and the Space of Meaning: Paths toward Transcendental Phenomenology* (Evanston: Northwestern University Press, 2001), 242. For Husserl, *Being and Time* itself was a betrayal of transcendental phenomenology in favor of an empirical account of "human being's concrete worldly Dasein": "Phenomenology and Anthropology," in *Psychological and Transcendental Phenomenology and the Confrontation with Heidegger (1927–1931)*, ed. and tr. Thomas Sheehan and Richard E. Palmer (Dordrecht: Kluwer, 1997), 485. But Heidegger himself also tries to distinguish his project from anthropology (GA 31: 122; GA 80.1: 213–51).

27. Polt, *Emergency of Being*, 107.

28. Heidegger, "Unbenutzte Vorarbeiten zur Vorlesung vom Wintersemester 1929/1930: *Die Grundbegriffe der Metaphysik: Welt, Endlichkeit, Einsamkeit,*" *Heidegger Studies* 7 (1991), 7.

29. Ibid., 8.

30. Ibid., 9.

31. Ibid., 10.

32. Heidegger, "Vom Ursprung des Kunstwerks: Erste Ausarbeitung," *Heidegger Studies* 5 (1989): 21 = "On the Origin of the Work of Art: First Vision," tr. Jerome Veith, in *The Heidegger Reader*, ed. Günter Figal (Bloomington: Indiana University Press, 2009), 149 tm.

33. This is the text of the final version of "On the Essence of Truth," composed in 1940. For similar thoughts in the earlier drafts of the essay, all written in 1930, see GA 80.1: 341, 365, 393.

34. Polt, *Emergency of Being*, 106–7, 215–17, 223.

35. See, e.g., GA 5: 64–65/48–49; GA 39: 3–4; GA 51: 108; GA 69: 156; GA 74: 12; Polt, *Emergency of Being*, 115–23.

36. Ó Murchadha describes the emergence of time as the obscure *kairos* in which truth, freedom, and action are born. "Just as birth is not experienced as such, so it is also with the event of emergence. Once the kairos is recognized, it is already past": *The Time of Revolution*, 112 (cf. 95, 196).

37. Heidegger, "Vom Ursprung des Kunstwerks: Erste Ausarbeitung," 14 = "On the Origin of the Work of Art: First Version," 140 tm.

38. Ibid., 15/142.

39. Polt, *Emergency of Being*, 76–77, 180–92.

40. See Richard Polt, "Ereignis," in *A Companion to Heidegger*, ed. Hubert L. Dreyfus and Mark Wrathall (Oxford: Blackwell, 2005). In 1970, Heidegger writes that *Ereignis* is "without destiny" and is not "in time": *The End of Philosophy*, tr. Joan Stambaugh (New York: Harper & Row, 1973), xii. Nevertheless, it "temporalizes" (xi).

41. Letter to Fritz Heidegger, March 2, 1932, in Homolka and Heidegger, *Heidegger und der Antisemitismus*, 26.

42. Letter to Elisabeth Blochmann, April 10, 1932, in Martin Heidegger and Elisabeth Blochmann, *Briefwechsel 1918–1969,* ed. Joachim W. Storck (Marbach am Neckar: Deutsche Schillergesellschaft, 1989), 48.

CHAPTER TWO: PASSING THROUGH THE POLITICAL

1. Heidegger's politics have generated great controversy in several cycles of discussion since the end of the war. Many important primary sources are accessible in GA 16 and in Alfred Denker and Holger Zaborowski (eds.), *Heidegger und der Nationalsozialismus I: Dokumente*, Heidegger-Jahrbuch 4 (Freiburg: Karl Alber, 2009). Zaborowski's *"Eine Frage von Irre und Schuld?": Heidegger und der Nationalsozialismus* (Frankfurt am Main: Fischer, 2010) also collects a great deal of pertinent evidence. There is a vast secondary literature, but no study published before 2014 was able to consider the *Black Notebooks*. The most controversial such study in recent years is Emmanuel Faye's *Heidegger: The Introduction of Nazism into Philosophy*, tr. Michael B. Smith (New Haven: Yale University Press, 2009). For discussion of Faye's work see Gregory Fried, ed., *Confronting Heidegger: A Critical Dialogue on Politics and Philosophy* (London: Rowman & Littlefield International, 2019).

2. Heidegger, *Übungen für Anfänger: Schillers Briefe*, 95–104, 112–14; cf. GA 43: 230.

3. See Richard Polt, "Eidetic Eros and the Liquidation of the Real," in *The Task of Philosophy in the Anthropocene: Axial Echoes in Global Space*, ed. Richard Polt and Jon Wittrock (London: Rowman & Littlefield International, 2018).

4. Löwith, *My Life in Germany Before and After 1933*, 60; Heidegger and Löwith, *Briefwechsel*, 201. After the war, Heidegger wrote a very positive recommendation for Löwith—with the significant qualification that "perhaps historical thinking in general" was "alien to him" (GA 16: 395).

5. Faye, *Heidegger*, 29–33; Johannes Fritsche, *Historical Destiny and National Socialism in Heidegger's "Being and Time"* (Berkeley: University of California Press, 1999); William H. F. Altman, *Martin Heidegger and the First World War: "Being and Time" as Funeral Oration* (Lanham, MD: Lexington Books, 2012).

6. Letter to Elisabeth Blochmann, March 30, 1933 (GA 16: 71).

7. Heidegger deleted this passage from the postwar publication of his Schelling lectures, so it does not appear in the English translation (cf. p. 23). For examples of similar deletions from the Nietzsche lectures see Gregory Fried, *Heidegger's Polemos: From Being to Politics* (New Haven: Yale University Press, 2000), Appendix.

8. Similar claims are found in the 1930 essay "On the Essence of Ground" (GA 9: 173/133). Heidegger was to explore the question of freedom further in his lectures on Schelling: GA 42 (1936) and GA 49 (1941).

9. Heidegger's encounters with Hegel include a 1927 seminar on Aristotle and Hegel (in GA 86); a brief treatment in a 1929 lecture course that focuses largely on Fichte (GA 28); his 1930–1931 lectures on the *Phenomenology of Spirit* (GA 32); a 1933–1934 course that aspires to a confrontation with Hegel but only has time for some telling remarks (in GA 36/37); a 1934–1935 seminar (in GA 86); a series of notes on negativity from 1938–1939 and 1941 (in GA 68); a 1942 discussion of the introduction to the *Phenomenology* (in GA 68); a two-semester seminar on the *Phenomenology* from 1942–1943 (in GA 86); and two late seminars from 1955–1956 and 1956–1957 on logic and thinking in Hegel (in GA 86).

10. In December 1931, Heidegger writes to his brother that Hitler "has an uncommon and sure political instinct, and already had it when we were all still befogged": Walter Homolka and Arnulf Heidegger, eds., *Heidegger und der Antisemitismus* (Freiburg: Herder, 2016), 22.

11. See Richard Capobianco, *Engaging Heidegger* (Toronto: University of Toronto Press, 2010), Chapter 3. Capobianco shows that Heidegger's late thought emphasizes home over homelessness.

12. Carl Schmitt, "Völkerrechtliche Großraumordnung" (1941), in *Staat, Großraum, Nomos: Arbeiten aus den Jahren 1916–1969*, ed. G. Maschke (Berlin: Duncker & Humblot, 1995), 317–18. For another translation see Carl Schmitt, *Writings on War*, trans. and ed. Timothy Nunan (Cambridge: Polity, 2011), 122. On Heidegger and Schmitt on spatiality and nihilism see Jon Wittrock, "The Social Logic of Late Nihilism: Martin Heidegger and Carl Schmitt on Global Space and the Sites of Gods," *European Review* 22:2 (May 2014): 244–57.

13. On affinities between Heidegger's ideas and those of some Jewish and Zionist writers, see Michael Fagenblat, "'Heidegger' and the Jews," in *Reading Heidegger's "Black Notebooks" 1931–1941*, ed. Ingo Farin and Jeff Malpas (Cambridge: MIT Press, 2016), 152–62; Elad Lapidot and Micha Brumlik, eds., *Heidegger and Jewish Thought: Difficult Others* (London: Rowman & Littlefield International, 2017), Part III.

14. Heraclitus is not mentioned in Carl Schmitt, *The Concept of the Political*, expanded ed., tr. George Schwab, foreword by Tracy B. Strong, notes by Leo Strauss (Chicago: University of Chicago Press, 2007). Schmitt discusses domestic enemies on 32 and 46–47, but in general the enemy is presumed to be external to the political community. In a 1936 essay, Schmitt takes Heraclitus as emblematic of a "warlike" attitude, for which war is an end in itself; for "political" thinkers (such as Hitler, claims Schmitt), war is only a means to an end: "Politik," in Schmitt, *Staat, Großraum, Nomos*, 137.

15. E. G. Kolbenheyer, *Lebenswert und Lebenswirkung der Dichtkunst in einem Volke* (Munich: Albert Langen/Georg Müller, 1935), publisher's unpaginated advertisements. Parenthesized citations in my next paragraph refer to this text.

16. GA 38 is based on student transcripts. Heidegger's original notes have reportedly been found, but have not yet been published: Silvio Vietta, "Wandel unseres Daseins: Eine unbekannte Vorlesung Martin Heideggers von 1934," *Frankfurter Allgemeine Zeitung* (October 18, 2006).

17. On Heidegger's ongoing concern with logic, see Daniel O. Dahlstrom, *Heidegger's Concept of Truth* (Cambridge: Cambridge University Press, 2001); Alfred Denker and Holger Zaborowski, eds., *Heidegger und die Logik* (Amsterdam: Rodopi, 2006).

18. According to *Being and Time*, in everydayness people "are what they do" (SZ 126, 239). Hence some interpreters, following Hubert Dreyfus, have emphasized the role of nondeliberate practices. But such "coping" is not supposed to exhaust the "who," since Heidegger's account of the everyday environment is not intended as the foundation of his ontology of Dasein; it is simply a first clue that can point us to the richer phenomenon of care.

19. Julia Ireland, "Naming Φύσις and the 'Inner Truth of National Socialism': A New Archival Discovery," *Research in Phenomenology* 44: 3 (2014): 315–46. The manuscript (reproduced in Ireland's article) is a tangle of deletions and insertions in Heidegger's minuscule and challenging handwriting, and the expression in question is abbreviated. Still, Ireland makes a good case for her reading, as well as for her interpretation of the philosophical context.

20. I will cite both Heidegger's notes (GA 86: 59–184) and the student transcripts and protocols (GA 86: 549–655). The texts by students are more coherent than the notes and are probably reliable reflections of what Heidegger said in the seminar, but they are not from Heidegger's own hand.

21. Faye, *Heidegger*, 204. Chapter 8 of Faye's book is devoted to this seminar. Some of Faye's positions are criticized by Peter Trawny in "Heidegger, Hegel, and the Political," in Heidegger, *On Hegel's "Philosophy of Right": The 1934–5 Seminar and Interpretative Essays*, ed. Peter Trawny, Marcia Sá Cavalcante Schuback, and Michael Marder, tr. Andrew Mitchell (London: Bloomsbury, 2014). This volume also includes several other studies of the seminar and its political and philosophical contexts.

22. *Hegel's Philosophy of Right*, trans. T. M. Knox (London: Oxford University Press, 1952), ¶149, p. 107.

23. Faye, *Heidegger*, 240.

24. *Hegel's Philosophy of Right*, ¶279, Remark, p. 182.

25. Giorgio Agamben even proposes that *Ereignis* could be translated as "adventure": *The Adventure*, tr. Lorenzo Chiesa (Cambridge: MIT Press, 2018), 78–82.

26. *Hegel's Philosophy of Right*, Preface, 4.

27. For discussions of various aspects of the text, including its politics, see *A Companion to Heidegger's "Introduction to Metaphysics,"* ed. Richard Polt and Gregory Fried (New Haven: Yale University Press, 2000).

28. Heidegger's reading of *Antigone* in *Introduction to Metaphysics* should be contrasted with his reading in GA 53 (1942), where the celebration of violence has been replaced by a Hölderlinian exploration of poetic thinking. See Clare Pearson Geiman, "Heidegger's *Antigones*," in Polt and Fried, *A Companion.*

29. On violence and *walten* in *Introduction to Metaphysics*, see Jacques Derrida, *The Beast and the Sovereign*, vol. II, trans. Geoffrey Bennington (Chicago: University of Chicago Press, 2011), 280–90; Eric Sean Nelson, "Traumatic Life: Violence, Pain, and Responsiveness in Heidegger," in *The Trauma Controversy: Philosophical and Interdisciplinary Dialogues*, ed. Kristen Brown Golden and Bettina G. Bergo (Albany: State University of New York Press, 2009).

30. Peter Trawny, *Adyton: Heideggers esoterische Philosophie* (Berlin: Matthes & Seitz, 2010), 38–39; Polt, *Emergency of Being*, 12–18, 20–21.

31. Quoted in Dieter Sinn, *Ereignis und Nirwana: Heidegger—Buddhismus—Mythos—Mystik; Zur Archäotypik des Denkens* (Bonn: Bouvier, 1991), 172.

32. Trawny, *Adyton*, 41.

33. Heidegger also touches on the sociality of language in his 1924 lectures on Aristotle, whose *Rhetoric* is a *"hermeneutic of being-there itself"* (GA 18: 110/75).

34. *Aristotle's Politics*, tr. and intro. Carnes Lord, 2nd ed. (Chicago: University of Chicago Press, 2013), 4 (1.2, 1253a8–18).

35. As Stuart Elden has pointed out, Heidegger's neglect of justice is apparent even when he directly and extensively interprets this passage from the *Politics* (GA 18: 45–64): *Speaking Against Number: Heidegger, Language and the Politics of Calculation* (Edinburgh: Edinburgh University Press, 2006), 33.

36. Cf. Lawrence J. Hatab, *Proto-Phenomenology and the Nature of Language: Dwelling in Speech I* (London: Rowman & Littlefield International, 2017), 1.

37. According to the *Black Notebooks*, "the concealed Germans" must learn to dwell with unsupported and defenseless beings and the concealment of being (GA 96: 31/25). The phrase "secret Germany," in contrast to "false present-dayness [*Gegenwärtigkeit*]," appears in Heidegger's notes for a Kant seminar in the Summer Semester of 1934 (GA 84.1: 337). On Heidegger's affinity for this idea of the secret Germany, which was promoted by Norbert von Hellingrath in his reading of Hölderlin and adopted by the Stefan George circle, see Charles Bambach, *Heidegger's Roots: Nietzsche, National Socialism, and the Greeks* (Ithaca: Cornell University Press, 2003), 241–46; Theodore Kisiel, "The Siting of Hölderlin's 'Geheimes Deutschland' in Heidegger's Poetizing of the Political," in *Heidegger und der Nationalsozialismus II: Interpretationen*, ed. Alfred Denker and Holger Zaborowski, Heidegger-Jahrbuch 5 (Freiburg/Munich: Karl Alber, 2009), 145–54.

38. Zaborowski and Denker, *Heidegger und der Nationalsozialismus I*, 13, 17. Heidegger's own questionnaire is reproduced on 240–43.

39. Cf. Ó Murchada, *The Time of Revolution*; Arun Iyer, "Thought, Action and History: Rethinking Revolution After Heidegger," in *After Heidegger?* ed. Gregory Fried and Richard Polt (London: Rowman & Littlefield International, 2018).

40. Arendt's view is essentially correct: at first Heidegger "explicates Nietzsche by going along with him," but his later lectures are "written in a subdued but unmistakable polemical tone"; the key to Heidegger's anti-Nietzscheanism is his conclusion (an exaggerated one, for Arendt) that "the will to rule and to dominate is a kind of original sin": Hannah Arendt, *The Life of the Mind*, One-Volume Edition (San Diego: Harcourt, 1978), vol. 2, 173. For a justifiably skeptical reading of the Nietzsche lectures and Heidegger's presentation of them after the war see Bambach, *Heidegger's Roots*, Chapter 5; but Bambach and I agree that the later lectures "see Nietzsche as merely a forerunner of the fallen and inessential versions of National Socialism" and see "official National Socialism as a pure form of Nietzschean will to power—and as a typical expression of modern nihilism" (266).

41. Letter to Kurt Bauch, August 9, 1935, in Heidegger and Bauch, *Briefwechsel 1932–1975*, Martin Heidegger Briefausgabe vol. II.1, ed. Almuth Heidegger (Freiburg: Karl Alber, 2010), 22.

42. *Inständigkeit* amounts to the same as *Existenz*: "standing in the ecstatic unity of transport [*Entrückungseinheit*]" (GA 49: 54). One can stand more or less properly, and so far, no human beings have attained true steadfastness (GA 49: 61).

43. "The *talk* about the disempowerment of *physis* can be misunderstood; the expression properly means that *physis* is displaced from its essence as *archē* (inception and mastery), because this essence remains an inception only in the inceptive beginning that grounds itself back into itself more originally, and *thus* develops the essence—in particular, grounds *alētheia* as belonging to *physis*. The expression 'disempowerment'

supports the illusion that *physis* belongs to the essence of 'power,' but in the sense of the 'will to power,' which actually comes to power precisely through the 'disempowerment' of *physis*": *Beiträge zur Philosophie (Vom Ereignis)*, photocopy of typescript and handwritten marginalia, Loyola University of Chicago Archives, Martin Heidegger-Barbara Fiand Manuscript Collection, accession number 99-13, box 2, folders 1–2. This marginal note refers to §96 of the GA edition (GA 65: 190). Cf. GA 66: 188, 193–94.

44. Fried, *Heidegger's Polemos*, Chapter 1.

45. References to Heraclitean *polemos* were not uncommon among thinkers aligned with Nazism. Alfred Baeumler, for instance, interprets Nietzsche in "Heraclitean" terms: *Nietzsche, der Philosoph und Politiker* (Leipzig: Reclam, 1937), 59–79.

46. In his 1945 text on "The Rectorate 1933/34," Heidegger claims that he always distinguished *polemos* from ordinary war (GA 16: 379–80/FT 21).

47. The 1955 open letter to Jünger, "On the Question of Being," refers to fragment 53 in connection with Nietzsche and the *Aus-einander-setzung* of being as the fourfold (GA 9: 424/321). The very last word in a collection of notes that range from around 1930 to 1970 reminds us that being is *das Strittige*, "the contentious" (GA 73.2: 1483).

48. In *The Emergency of Being* I provide a much fuller interpretation of this text. Other secondary literature in English includes *A Companion to Heidegger's "Contributions to Philosophy,"* ed. Charles Scott et al. (Bloomington: Indiana University Press, 2001); Daniela Vallega-Neu, *Heidegger's "Contributions to Philosophy": An Introduction* (Bloomington: Indiana University Press, 2003); Jason Powell, *Heidegger's "Contributions to Philosophy": Life and the Last God* (London: Continuum, 2007); and Parvis Emad, *On the Way to Heidegger's "Contributions to Philosophy"* (Madison: University of Wisconsin Press, 2007). My review of the 2012 translation of the *Contributions* by Richard Rojcewicz and Daniela Vallega-Neu can be found at http://ndpr.nd.edu/news/32043.

49. On selfhood in the *Contributions* see François Raffoul, "Rethinking Selfhood: From Enowning," *Research in Phenomenology* 37:1 (2007): 75–94; Polt, *Emergency of Being*, 156–80.

50. See especially GA 69: 62–71 and Fred Dallmayr, "Heidegger on *Macht* and *Machenschaft*," *Continental Philosophy Review* 34 (2001): 247–67.

51. Sidonie Kellerer, "Rewording the Past: The Postwar Publication of a 1938 Lecture by Martin Heidegger," *Modern Intellectual History* 11:3 (November 2014), 592. I make a more extensive case against Faye and Kellerer's reading of Heidegger on subjectivity in "*Un-wesen*: Tarrying with the Negative in Heidegger's *Black Notebooks*," in Fried, *Confronting Heidegger*.

52. Emmanuel Faye, "Subjectivity and Race in Heidegger's Writings," tr. Michael B. Smith, *Philosophy Today* 55:3 (Fall 2011), 269.

53. Ibid., 271.

54. Letter to Fritz Heidegger, October 22, 1943, in Homolka and Heidegger, *Heidegger und der Antisemitismus*, 92.

55. Letter to Fritz Heidegger and family, August 18, 1941, in ibid., 76. See Gregory Fried, "'Whitewashed with Moralism': On Heidegger's Anti-Americanism and Anti-Semitism," in Lapidot and Brumlik, *Heidegger and Jewish Thought*.

56. Diogenes Laertius IX, 3, quoted in GA 69: 88–89. But see GA 55: 11–12 on the possibility of a higher concern with the *polis* here.

57. The growing literature on the topic, and on the politics of the *Black Notebooks* in general, includes Peter Trawny, *Heidegger and the Myth of a Jewish World Conspiracy*, tr. Andrew J. Mitchell (Chicago: University of Chicago Press, 2016); Farin and Malpas, *Reading Heidegger's "Black Notebooks"*; Andrew J. Mitchell and Peter Trawny, eds., *Heidegger's "Black Notebooks": Responses to Anti-Semitism* (New York: Columbia University Press, 2017); and Homolka and Heidegger, *Heidegger und der Antisemitismus*. For a particularly thoughtful and wide-ranging investigation see Elliot R. Wolfson, *The Duplicity of Philosophy's Shadow: Heidegger, Nazism, and the Jewish Other* (New York: Columbia University Press, 2018).

58. In fact, Heidegger is not quite done with the phrase "history of being" (e.g., GA 98: 40, 46, 87), even though he has doubts about it as "a concealing expression" (GA 98: 168).

59. *Überlegungen* (excerpts), typescript, Loyola University of Chicago Archives, Martin Heidegger-Barbara Fiand Manuscript Collection, accession number 99-13, box 3, folders 2–3.

60. On Heidegger's errancy see Peter Trawny, *Freedom to Fail: Heidegger's Anarchy*, tr. Ian Alexander Moore and Christopher Turner (Cambridge: Polity, 2015). Trawny does not discuss the passage from GA 97, which was published after his book.

61. Heidegger, "Das Wesen der Wahrheit: Zu 'Beiträge zur Philosophie,'" *Heidegger Studies* 18 (2002), 10.

62. Compare the anecdote cited at GA 41: 74 and GA 73.1: 432: accused of always saying the same thing, Socrates agrees, and observes that his critic *never* says the same thing (Xenophon, *Memorabilia* IV.4.6; cf. Plato, *Gorgias* 490e).

63. However, a postwar entry countenances a turn to the "life and preaching of Jesus," which are "pre-Christian" (GA 98: 103).

64. For influences and affinities see Jeff Love, ed., *Heidegger in Russia and Eastern Europe* (London: Rowman & Littlefield International, 2017).

65. I retract the subtitle of my article "Beyond Struggle and Power: Heidegger's Secret Resistance," *Interpretation* 35:1 (Fall 2007): 11–40.

66. Letter to Fritz Heidegger, March 3, 1939, in Homolka and Heidegger, *Heidegger und der Antisemitismus*, 49.

67. All the following quotations are found in GA 97: "the National Socialist terror" (82); "the reign of terror of the bygone system" (84); "the reign of horror of 'Nazism'" (156); "The blunt brutality of the 'Third Reich'" (82); "the massive brutality of ahistorical 'National Socialism'" (87); "the criminal madness of Hitler" (444); "the irresponsible misdeeds with which Hitler raged around Europe" (250); "the wild willing of *nationalism*" (99); "the wildness of *National Socialism*" (100); "'National Socialism' very quickly and inexorably became *one* of the aberrations into criminality" (200–201); "the atrocities [*Greuel*] evident on posters [of concentration camps]" (84–85); "the atrocious business [*Greuelhaften*] of the 'gas chambers'" (99; cf. GA 73.2: 1179); "the atrocities of National Socialism" (98); "In 'National Socialism,' i.e. in the wretched aberration of its essence, 'the spirit' was simply despised" (209). For

Heidegger's denials that Nazism can be justified, see 129, 135 (with reference to Nazi "criminality"), 136 (Nazi "historical cluelessness"), and 150 ("Hitler").

68. Fried, *Heidegger's Polemos.*

69. Richard Polt, "The Question of Nothing," in Polt and Fried, *A Companion to Heidegger's "Introduction to Metaphysics."*

70. See Nancy A. Weston, "Thinking the Oblivion of Thinking: The Unfolding of *Machenschaft* and *Rechnung* in the Time of the *Black Notebooks*," in Farin and Malpas, *Reading Heidegger's Black Notebooks.*

71. Letter to Fritz Heidegger, September 24, 1938, in Homolka and Heidegger, *Heidegger und der Antisemitismus*, 46.

72. Letter to Rudolf Bultmann, October 2, 1939, in Rudolf Bultmann/Martin Heidegger, *Briefwechsel 1925–1975*, ed. Andreas Großmann and Christof Landmesser (Frankfurt am Main: Vittorio Klostermann and Tübingen: Mohr Siebeck, 2009), 201.

73. Letter to Fritz Heidegger, February 6, 1940, in Homolka and Heidegger, *Heidegger und der Antisemitismus*, 59.

74. Martin Heidegger, *Letters to His Wife: 1915–1970*, ed. Gertrud Heidegger, trans. R. D. V. Glasgow (Cambridge: Polity, 2008), 167 tm (written May 18, 1940, during the German invasion of France).

75. Letter to Kurt Bauch, August 10, 1941, in Heidegger and Bauch, *Briefwechsel*, 69–70.

76. *Letters to His Wife*, 186 (February 17, 1945).

77. Quoted in Trawny, *Heidegger and the Myth of a Jewish World Conspiracy*, 33. Trawny notes: "This sentence is lacking in the book [GA 69: 78]. It stands in the manuscript, but is not included in the transcript of Fritz Heidegger, who indeed had thus 'struck it out.' In keeping with the plan for an edition of the 'last hand,' the editor and the estate executor decided at that time not to publish the sentence. In light of the Black Notebooks, the statement spears differently. Chronologically, anyway, it belongs entirely in the context of the other anti-Semitic passages discussed here" (120n39). I have encountered the suggestion that Heidegger means that the Jews are destined to be *victims* of criminality. This interpretation does not strike me as plausible.

78. Heidegger's focus on *Untergang* might suggest that he is "channeling Spengler," as Richard Wolin has put it: "National Socialism, World Jewry, and the History of Being: Heidegger's Black Notebooks," *Jewish Review of Books* (Summer 2014), 41. Heidegger was interested in Spengler early on, and presented a talk on Spengler in 1920 that has not been located (GA 80.1: 558). In the *Black Notebooks* he supports Spengler's idea that Europe is "the actualization of the downfall of the West" (GA 96: 274/217 tm) and says that this insight cannot be refuted by external signs of progress (GA 96: 269–70). He gives Spengler credit for expressing "*a genuine power of his era*" (GA 95: 140/108) and resisting historicism (GA 97: 159). However, he also develops an extensive critique of various Spenglerian notions (GA 95: 137–40; GA 97: 171–73, 410). Heidegger's own conception of *Untergang* owes more to Nietzsche (e.g., GA 44: 62) than to Spengler, who depends on Nietzsche (GA 87: 283). On Spengler, see also GA 66: 27–28; GA 71: 96.

79. Letter to Kurt Bauch, November 24, 1939, in Heidegger and Bauch, *Briefwechsel*, 58.

80. E.g., Wolin, "National Socialism, World Jewry, and the History of Being."

81. Letter to Elisabeth Blochmann, May 10, 1930, in Heidegger and Blochmann, *Briefwechsel 1918–1969*, 35.

82. The infamous book burnings began at German universities in May 1933. In his *Spiegel* interview, Heidegger claims that he forbade the burning of books at Freiburg (GA 16: 658/HR 318). However, a 1933 letter from him to *Der Alemanne* (June 19, 1933, p. 5) objects to the inclusion of an anticommunist economist's writings among "the works to be burned"—not to the principle of book burning. The letter is reproduced in Sidonie Kellerer, "Antisémitisme et racisme dans le pensée de Heidegger: état de la recherche," *Revue d'Histoire de la Shoah* 207 (2017/2), 43.

83. A few years later, he will write that "I made many and great mistakes during my rectorate," but mostly he misjudged the vices of the professors, the students, and the ministry (GA 76: 216).

84. See especially Robert Bernasconi, "Heidegger's Alleged Challenge to the Nazi Concepts of Race," in *Appropriating Heidegger*, ed. James E. Faulconer and Mark A. Wrathall (Cambridge: Cambridge University Press, 2000).

85. As Eduardo Mendieta puts it, in this passage the Jew becomes the "personification of number": "Metaphysical Anti-Semitism and Worldlessness: On World Poorness, World Forming, and World Destroying," in Trawny and Mitchell, *Heidegger's Black Notebooks*, 44.

86. For Heidegger's sardonic comments on the supposed absolute correctness of official German military reports, see his letters to Fritz Heidegger of August 9, 1941 (Homolka and Heidegger, *Heidegger und der Antisemitismus*, 75), and to Kurt Bauch the following day (Heidegger and Bauch, *Briefwechsel*, 68).

87. Heidegger, *Introduction to Metaphysics*, tr. Gregory Fried and Richard Polt, 2nd ed. (New Haven: Yale University Press, 2014), Translators' Introduction, xxi. Original: Christian E. Lewalter, "Wie liest man 1953 Sätze von 1935? Zu einem politischen Streit um Heideggers Metaphysik," *Die Zeit*, August 13, 1953.

88. I find only one explicit reference to Jews in GA 98 (1948–1951): a dig at Jaspers as a "Judeo-Christian Church Father" who promotes "philosophical faith" (191). But it is not implausible to detect an implicit anti-Jewish animus in Heidegger's grumbling about the "profiteers" and "slave traders" who control "the global public sphere" (GA 98: 19).

89. Richard Wolin writes, "To place Heidegger's lifelong, philosophically grounded antipathy to Jews on the same footing as his rather unsystematic and piecemeal criticisms of the Third Reich is a macabre equivalence": *The Politics of Being: The Political Thought of Martin Heidegger*, 2nd ed. (New York: Columbia University Press, 2016), xxx. The fact is that Heidegger's explicit statements on Jews are "unsystematic and piecemeal," whereas his explicit critique of Nazism is far more extensive and developed. It is difficult to point out this fact without appearing to defend Heidegger, but well-grounded criticisms of his political thought must begin with a careful and accurate assessment of all his words.

90. Jean-Luc Nancy, *The Banality of Heidegger*, tr. Jeff Fort (New York: Fordham University Press, 2017), 43. See also Adam Knowles, "Heidegger's Mask: Silence, Politics, and the Banality of Evil in the *Black Notebooks*," *Gatherings: The Heidegger Circle Annual* 5 (2015): 93–117.

91. Cf. Robert Bernasconi, "Another Eisenmenger? On the Alleged Originality of Heidegger's Antisemitism," in Trawny and Mitchell, *Heidegger's Black Notebooks*, 177–78.

92. Trawny, *Heidegger and the Myth of a Jewish World Conspiracy*, 18.

93. Donatella Di Cesare, "Being and the Jew: Between Heidegger and Levinas," tr. Richard Polt, in Lapidot and Brumlik, *Heidegger and Jewish Thought*, 76.

94. Cf. Peter E. Gordon, "Prolegomena to Any Future Destruction of Metaphysics: Heidegger and the *Schwarze Hefte*," in Trawny and Mitchell, *Heidegger's Black Notebooks*, 140.

95. According to one anecdote, however, in 1944 Heidegger was angered by reports of killings of Jews in the East, and fulminated against the foolishness of the "party bosses": Paul Jurevics, "Meine Begegnung mit Heidegger und seiner Philosophie," tr. Agris Timuška, in Denker and Zaborowski, *Heidegger und der Nazionalsozialismus I*, 265.

CHAPTER THREE: RECOVERING POLITICS

1. Bernasconi, "Another Eisenmenger?" in Trawny and Mitchell, *Heidegger's Black Notebooks*, 181. Friedrich-Wilhelm von Herrmann argues that Heidegger's characterizations of Jews are "not anti-Semitic as such" because they apply to late modernity in general: "The Role of Martin Heidegger's *Notebooks* within the Context of His Oeuvre," in Farin and Malpas, *Reading Heidegger's "Black Notebooks" 1931–1941*, 91. But then there is a twofold problem: Heidegger's view of modernity may be pervaded by antisemitic tropes, and he may be applying this view to Jews with a particular vehemence and malice.

2. Heidegger, *Übungen für Anfänger: Schillers Briefe*, 130–31, 188n97.

3. Heidegger's "access to political space can come about only through the state of exception. In this sense, his politics is a poetics of emergency": Donatella Di Cesare, "Heidegger, entre apocalíptica y revolución," *Argumenta Philosophica* 2 (2017): 15.

4. Steven Crowell, *Normativity and Phenomenology in Husserl and Heidegger* (Cambridge: Cambridge University Press, 2013); Irene McMullin, Matthew Burch, and Jack Marsh, eds., *Transcending Reason: Heidegger's Transformation of Phenomenology* (London: Rowman & Littlefield, 2019).

5. Heidegger's most extensive discussion of Kierkegaard can be found in GA 49. While not denying Kierkegaard's insights, Heidegger sees him as overly indebted to metaphysics and limited by his Christian commitment.

6. Letter to Elisabeth Blochmann, August 8, 1928, in Heidegger and Blochmann, *Briefwechsel 1918–1969*, 25.

7. On Heidegger's often contorted thoughts on universality see Peter Trawny, "The Universal and Annihilation: Heidegger's Being-Historical Anti-Semitism," in

Trawny and Mitchell, *Heidegger's Black Notebooks*. Peter E. Gordon argues that we must transcend the finite, "holistic Umwelt . . . as the originary domain of analysis," without pretending to a view from nowhere: "Prolegomena to Any Future Destruction of Metaphysics," in Trawny and Mitchell, *Heidegger's Black Notebooks*, 147.

8. For a case that the United States is constituted by certain traditional conflicts, see Howard Fineman, *The Thirteen American Arguments: Enduring Debates That Define and Inspire Our Country* (New York: Random House, 2009).

9. For my defense of liberalism see *Emergency of Being*, 227–36.

10. The encounter with the Greek "first inception" is among Heidegger's lifelong concerns. On Germany and France, with some broader reflections on intercultural relations and on the need to counter the "uprooting" of Europe, see "Wege zur Aussprache" (GA 13: 15–21). For an introduction to the question of Heidegger and the East, see Bret Davis, "East-West Dialogue after Heidegger," in Fried and Polt, *After Heidegger?*

11. *Letters to His Wife*, 164.

12. Letter to Fritz Heidegger, March 3, 1939, in Homolka and Heidegger, *Heidegger und der Antisemitismus*, 49.

13. Letter to Fritz Heidegger, June 7, 1942, in ibid., 83.

14. Gregory Fried, "Back to the Cave: A Platonic Rejoinder to Heidegger," in *Heidegger and the Greeks*, ed. Drew Hyland and John P. Manoussakis (Bloomington: Indiana University Press, 2006); Mark A. Ralkowski, *Heidegger's Platonism* (London: Continuum, 2009); Francisco J. Gonzalez, *Plato and Heidegger: A Question of Dialogue* (University Park, PA: Pennsylvania State University Press, 2011).

15. For some attempts to think about the environmental crisis, often with Heidegger's help, see Polt and Wittrock, *The Task of Philosophy in the Anthropocene*.

16. For a similar judgment on the *Black Notebooks* see Krell, *Ecstasy, Catastrophe*, Part Two.

17. For a critique of the "history of being" see John McCumber, "Heidegger: Beyond Anti-Semitism and *Seinsgeschichte*," in Fried and Polt, *After Heidegger?* As I have noted, Heidegger himself rejects the concept in exasperation at GA 97: 382.

18. Miguel de Beistegui rightly observes that "everything Heidegger says about politics . . . is articulated from a position or a space that is itself *not* political, a space that, furthermore, defines and decides the *essence* of politics": "'Questioning Politics, or Beyond Power,'" in *The Movement of Nihilism: Heidegger's Thinking after Nietzsche*, ed. Laurence Paul Hemming, Bogdan Costea, and Kostas Amiridis (London: Bloomsbury, 2011), 54. Beistegui suggests that Heidegger thus challenges the "total politicization of our being" (55)—but the problem is his total ontologization of our politics.

19. For a few insightful studies of the two thinkers see Dana Villa, *Arendt and Heidegger: The Fate of the Political* (Princeton: Princeton University Press, 1996); Dana Villa, "Arendt and Heidegger, Again," in *Heidegger's Jewish Followers: Essays on Hannah Arendt, Leo Strauss, Hans Jonas, and Emmanuel Levinas*, ed. Samuel Fleischacker (Pittsburgh: Duquesne University Press, 2008); Peg Birmingham, "Heidegger and Arendt: The Birth of Political Action and Speech," in Raffoul and Pettigrew, *Heidegger and Practical Philosophy*.

20. For a concise explanation see HC 7–9. Labor, work, and action are explored in greater depth in Chapters III–V.

21. For a defense of this idea see Sophie Loidolt, *Phenomenology of Plurality: Hannah Arendt on Political Intersubjectivity* (London: Routledge, 2018).

22. Richard Polt, "Potentiality, Energy and Sway: From Aristotelian to Modern to Postmodern Physics?" *Existentia* 11 (2001): 27–41.

23. Hannah Arendt, *On Revolution*, intro. Jonathan Schell (New York: Penguin, 2006), 1.

24. *Republic* 501a. As it turns out, cleaning the canvas would mean exiling everyone over the age of ten (540e–541a)—a proposal that may very well be meant to sound ridiculous. If so, Plato is the first, all-too-subtle critic of the reduction of politics to fabrication.

25. Wallace Stevens, "Sketch of the Ultimate Politician," in *Collected Poems* (London: Faber and Faber, 2006), 294.

26. This famous concept from Arendt's *Eichmann in Jerusalem* was a misjudgment of Adolf Eichmann, who, as we now know from his diaries, was a malicious and deliberate mass murderer. But this does not invalidate her point that there is a way of participating in atrocities in a "banal" manner.

27. Further reflection on the question of acting and thinking would have to consider Heidegger's postwar statement that "the essence of action is accomplishment," i.e., "to unfold something into the fullness of its essence," and that by accomplishing the relation of being to human beings, philosophy acts (GA 9: 313/239). This thought requires us to reconsider both what we mean by philosophy and what we mean by action.

CHAPTER FOUR: TOWARD TRAUMATIC ONTOLOGY

1. For a spirited attack on such reductionism see Raymond Tallis, *Aping Mankind: Neuromania, Darwinitis and the Misrepresentation of Humanity* (London: Routledge, 2014).

2. Daniel L. Everett, *Don't Sleep, There Are Snakes: Life and Language in the Amazonian Jungle* (New York: Vintage, 2009), 131–34, 236.

3. Ibid., 129.

4. Ibid., Chapter 17.

5. An example is the commitment of love: "That once we told ourselves this tale / says what we ourselves long failed / to hear—but finally hear it asking, / calling us to bear it, tasking . . .": "*Amo: volo ut sis*" (GA 81: 109).

6. For at least a period in 1936, Heidegger rejects phenomenology because it is focused on describing what is given, what is present. Mere description excludes the element of risk and the leap into the possible (GA 82: 37–38, 41, 43).

7. In the thirties, at least, Heidegger clearly intends to liberate *Wesung* (essencing, essential happening) from its restriction to *Anwesung* (presencing) (GA 5: 155/116; GA 65: 31, 32, 75, 189; GA 73.1: 159). In his late texts he often appears to embrace a broader sense of *Anwesen* without limiting it either to the temporal present or to the

Western tradition, but one might ask whether such limitations are merely kept silent in these texts.

8. For a psychoanalyst's insights into trauma in the narrower sense—extreme, painful disruption and its aftermath—incorporating Heidegger's thought as well as personal experience, see Robert D. Stolorow, *World, Affectivity, Trauma: Heidegger and Post-Cartesian Psychoanalysis* (New York: Routledge, 2011).

9. "Trauma shatters the absolutisms of everyday life, which, like the illusions of the 'they,' evade and cover up the finitude, contingency, and embeddedness of our existence and the indefiniteness of its certain extinction": Stolorow, *World, Affectivity, Trauma*, 44. In my extended sense of "trauma," traumas need not shatter these absolutisms; they may also rattle them, jar them, or quietly glimmer through them. Jacob Needleman defines Binswanger's concept of trauma in suitably broad terms: "a traumatic experience is one in which the meaning to the individual of an event contradicts, or 'goes beyond' the transcendental experiential horizon; that is, the overarching meaning-context . . . makes possible an experience that leads to its own negation": "A Critical Introduction to Ludwig Binswanger's Existential Psychoanalysis," in Ludwig Binswanger, *Being-in-the-World: Selected Papers of Ludwig Binswanger*, tr. and intro. Jacob Needleman (New York: Basic Books, 1963), 90.

10. As noted in chapter 1, *Sinn* is translated as "meaning" in the English versions of *Being and Time*.

11. Thinking along these lines, Thomas Sheehan argues that Heidegger's *Sein* is best interpreted as the "meaningful presence" of things, and that the "question of being" asks about the basis of meaningful presence: Sheehan, *Making Sense of Heidegger*, xii, xiv, xviii.

12. Compare Sartre's concept of the "transphenomenality" of being: Jean-Paul Sartre, *Being and Nothingness: A Phenomenological Essay on Ontology*, tr. Hazel E. Barnes (New York: Washington Square Press, 1992), 9–10.

13. For a provocative account of the importance of this second half to an integral interpretation of Parmenides see Vishwa Adluri, *Parmenides, Plato and Mortal Philosophy: Return from Transcendence* (London: Continuum, 2011), esp. Chapter 5.

14. According to Frege, who did not use a separate symbol for the existential quantifier but laid the groundwork for modern symbolic logic, an existential claim asserts that a concept is "realized" or "not empty": "On Concept and Object," in *Translations from the Philosophical Writings of Gottlob Frege*, ed. Peter Geach and Max Black (Oxford: Basil Blackwell, 1952), 49.

15. "Existence is what existential quantification expresses . . . explication in turn of the existential quantifier itself, 'there is,' 'there are,' explication of general existence, is a forlorn cause": W. V. Quine, "Existence and Quantification," in *Ontological Relativity and Other Essays* (New York: Columbia University Press, 1969), 97.

16. On the fragility and finitude of Heideggerian *Sinn*, see Robert B. Pippin, "Necessary Conditions for the Possibility of What Isn't: Heidegger on Failed Meaning," in Crowell and Malpas, *Transcendental Heidegger*, 199–214.

17. Peter Trawny, *Adyton: Heideggers esoterische Philosophie* (Berlin: Matthes & Seitz, 2010), 80 (cf. 9, 70, 96, 106).

18. Jean-Luc Marion, *Being Given: Toward a Phenomenology of Givenness* (Stanford: Stanford University Press, 2002); *In Excess: Studies of Saturated Phenomena* (New York: Fordham University Press, 2004).

19. Alain Badiou, *Being and Event*, tr. Oliver Feltham (London: Continuum, 2006).

20. Hatab, *Proto-Phenomenology and the Nature of Language*, 25–28.

21. Jean Améry, "Torture," in *Art from the Ashes: A Holocaust Anthology*, ed. Lawrence L. Langer (New York: Oxford University Press, 1995), 124–26. For thoughtful explorations of Améry see Magdalena Zolkos, ed., *On Jean Améry: Philosophy of Catastrophe* (Lanham, MD: Lexington Books, 2011).

22. Ibid., 130–31.

23. Cf. Heidegger's discussion of "is" at GA 40: 95–98/97–100 and his discussion of Trakl's *es ist* and Rimbaud's *il y a* at GA 14: 48–49/39–40.

24. Blaise Pascal, *Pensées*, trans. Roger Ariew (Indianapolis: Hackett, 2005), 69 (Sellier fragment 262).

25. It is fair to say that Heidegger tries to "distance himself from . . . the transcendental paradigm . . . while still tacitly relying upon it and at times . . . reverting to its language and argumentative strategies": Eric S. Nelson, "Heidegger's Failure to Overcome Transcendental Philosophy," in *Transcendental Inquiry: Its History, Methods and Critiques*, ed. Halla Kim and Steven Hoeltzel (Cham, Switzerland: Palgrave Macmillan, 2016), 160.

26. See, e.g., Jeffrey C. Alexander, Ron Eyerman, Bernhard Giesen, Neil J. Smelser, and Piotr Sztompka, *Cultural Trauma and Collective Identity* (Berkeley: University of California Press, 2004).

27. Brian Sonia-Wallace, "What Happened When a Poet Was Sent to the Biggest US Mall to Write for Shoppers," *The Guardian*, October 10, 2017.

28. This problem is at the heart of Eugene Gendlin's project in *Experiencing and the Creation of Meaning: A Philosophical and Psychological Approach to the Subjective* (New York: Free Press of Glencoe, 1962) and his later works.

29. Cathy Caruth, *Unclaimed Experience: Trauma, Narrative, and History*, 20th anniversary ed. (Baltimore: Johns Hopkins University Press, 2016).

30. See, e.g., Charles Scott, "Trauma's Presentation," in Golden and Bergo, *The Trauma Controversy*.

31. See, e.g., Judith L. Herman, "Crime and Memory," in Golden and Bergo, *The Trauma Controversy*. Robert Stolorow recounts how, half a year after his wife's death, he began to come to terms with the event by embarking on "a project of attempting to grasp and conceptualize the nature of emotional trauma. This project has occupied me now for more than 20 years": *World, Affectivity, Trauma*, 49.

32. See, e.g., Idit Dobbs-Weinstein, "Trauma and the Impossibility of Experience," in Golden and Bergo, *The Trauma Controversy*.

33. John D. Caputo has denounced this tendency in Heidegger's late work to good effect: *Demythologizing Heidegger* (Bloomington: Indiana University Press, 1993).

34. For a comparable account that fuses Heidegger's concept of being-in-the-world with Kuhn's theory of scientific revolutions, see Haugeland, *Dasein Disclosed*, 177, 183, 215, 271.

35. See, e.g., Kierkegaard's *Philosophical Fragments* for the contrast between the Socratic (and Hegelian) notion of knowledge as recollection and the Christian (and Kierkegaardian) notion of a new revelation.

36. A number of interpreters indebted to Hubert Dreyfus have interpreted "death" in *Being and Time* in similar terms. "Death" is then the possibility that a way of life or set of practices may no longer be viable (e.g., Haugeland, *Dasein Disclosed*, 218). I disagree with this reading of Heidegger's text, but the concept is significant. For an application to Native American history, see Jonathan Lear, *Radical Hope: Ethics in the Face of Cultural Devastation* (Cambridge: Harvard University Press, 2008).

37. Michel Foucault, *The Order of Things: An Archeology of the Human Sciences* (London: Routledge Classics, 2002), 351. Foucault claims that the doublet "man" was invented in the late eighteenth century and is now on its deathbed. For an example of the empirico-transcendental problem, see Husserl's convoluted note on "the problem *man*" in *Cartesian Meditations: An Introduction to Phenomenology*, trans. Dorion Cairns (Dordrecht: Nijhoff, 1960), 52.

38. For examples of other philosophical uses of the concepts of natality and mortality, see Reiner Schürmann, *Broken Hegemonies*, tr. Reginald Lilly (Bloomington: Indiana University Press, 2003); Anne O'Byrne, *Natality and Finitude* (Bloomington: Indiana University Press, 2010).

39. Charles S. Peirce, "Some Consequences of Four Incapacities," in *The Essential Peirce*, vol. 1, ed. Nathan Houser and Christian Kloesel (Bloomington and Indianapolis: Indiana University Press, 1992), 29.

40. Wallace Stevens, "Long and Sluggish Lines," in *Collected Poems*, 456.

41. The theme has certainly not been underestimated by several thinkers inspired by Heidegger: see, e.g., Paul Ricoeur, *Time and Narrative*, tr. Kathleen McLaughlin and David Pellauer, 3 vols. (Chicago: University of Chicago Press, 1984, 1986, 1988); David Carr, *Time, Narrative, and History* (Bloomington: Indiana University Press, 1986).

42. Clarice Lispector, *The Passion According to G. H.*, tr. Idra Novey, intro. Caetano Veloso, ed. Benjamin Moser (New York: New Directions, 2012). For another account of this novel see Michael Marder, "Existential Phenomenology According to Clarice Lispector," *Philosophy and Literature* 37:2 (October 2013): 374–88.

43. Lispector, *The Passion According to G. H.*, 3.

44. Ibid., 85.

45. Ibid., 121.

46. Ibid., 189.

47. Ibid., 73.

48. Ibid., 189.

49. Ibid., 75.

50. Ibid., 111.

51. Steve Erickson, *Shadowbahn* (New York: Blue Rider Press, 2017), 244.

52. Ibid., 4.

53. Ibid., 153.

54. Ibid., 238.

55. Ibid., 248–49.
56. Tommy Orange, *There There: A Novel* (New York: Alfred A. Knopf, 2018), 122.
57. Ibid., 10.
58. Ibid., 62.
59. Ibid., 104.
60. Binswanger, "Introduction to *Schizophrenie*," in *Being-in-the-World*, 253.
61. Binswanger, "Dream and Existence," ibid., 247.
62. Orange, *There There*, 233.

Bibliography

Adluri, Vishwa. *Parmenides, Plato and Mortal Philosophy: Return from Transcendence*. London: Continuum, 2011.

Agamben, Giorgio. *The Adventure*. Tr. Lorenzo Chiesa. Cambridge: MIT Press, 2018.

Alexander, Jeffrey C., Ron Eyerman, Bernhard Giesen, Neil J. Smelser, and Piotr Sztompka. *Cultural Trauma and Collective Identity*. Berkeley: University of California Press, 2004.

Altman, William H. F. *Martin Heidegger and the First World War: "Being and Time" as Funeral Oration*. Lanham, MD: Lexington Books, 2012.

Améry, Jean. "Torture." In *Art from the Ashes: A Holocaust Anthology*, ed. Lawrence L. Langer. New York: Oxford University Press, 1995.

Ankündigung der Vorlesungen der Badischen Albert-Ludwigs-Universität Freiburg im Breisgau für das Winterhalbjahr 1929/30. Freiburg im Breisgau: C. A. Wagner Buchdruckerei, 1929.

Arendt, Hannah. *The Life of the Mind*. One-volume ed. San Diego: Harcourt, 1978.

———. *On Revolution*. Intro. Jonathan Schell. New York: Penguin, 2006.

Aristotle's Politics. Tr. and intro. Carnes Lord. 2nd ed. Chicago: University of Chicago Press, 2013.

Backman, Jussi. *Complicated Presence: Heidegger and the Postmetaphysical Unity of Being*. Albany: State University of New York Press, 2015.

Badiou, Alain. *Being and Event*. Tr. Oliver Feltham. London: Continuum, 2006.

Baeumler, Alfred. *Nietzsche, der Philosoph und Politiker*. Leipzig: Reclam, 1937.

Bambach, Charles. *Heidegger's Roots: Nietzsche, National Socialism, and the Greeks*. Ithaca: Cornell University Press, 2003.

Beiner, Ronald. *Dangerous Minds: Nietzsche, Heidegger, and the Return of the Far Right*. Philadelphia: University of Pennsylvania Press, 2018.

Bernasconi, Robert. "Being Is Evil: Boehme's Strife and Schelling's Rage in Heidegger's 'Letter on "Humanism."'" *Gatherings: The Heidegger Circle Annual* 7 (2017): 164–81.

————. "Heidegger's Alleged Challenge to the Nazi Concepts of Race." In *Appropriating Heidegger*, ed. James E. Faulconer and Mark A. Wrathall. Cambridge: Cambridge University Press, 2000.

Binswanger, Ludwig. *Being-in-the-World: Selected Papers of Ludwig Binswanger.* Tr. and intro. Jacob Needleman. New York: Basic Books, 1963.

Blattner, William. *Heidegger's Temporal Idealism.* Cambridge: Cambridge University Press, 1999.

Braver, Lee, ed. *Division III of Heidegger's "Being and Time": The Unanswered Question of Being.* Cambridge: MIT Press, 2015.

Buber, Martin. *Der Jude und sein Judentum: Gesammelte Aufsätze und Reden.* Intro. Robert Weltsch. Cologne: Joseph Melzer Verlag, 1963.

Capobianco, Richard. *Engaging Heidegger.* Toronto: University of Toronto Press, 2010.

Caputo, John D. *Demythologizing Heidegger.* Bloomington: Indiana University Press, 1993.

Carr, David. *Time, Narrative, and History.* Bloomington: Indiana University Press, 1986.

Caruth, Cathy. *Unclaimed Experience: Trauma, Narrative, and History.* 20th anniversary ed. Baltimore: Johns Hopkins University Press, 2016.

Crowell, Steven. *Husserl, Heidegger, and the Space of Meaning: Paths toward Transcendental Phenomenology.* Evanston: Northwestern University Press, 2001.

————. *Normativity and Phenomenology in Husserl and Heidegger.* Cambridge: Cambridge University Press, 2013.

———— and Jeff Malpas, eds. *Transcendental Heidegger.* Stanford: Stanford University Press, 2007.

Dahlstrom, Daniel O. *Heidegger's Concept of Truth.* Cambridge: Cambridge University Press, 2001.

Dallmayr, Fred. "Heidegger on *Macht* and *Machenschaft.*" *Continental Philosophy Review* 34 (2001): 247–67.

Davis, Bret W. *Heidegger and the Will: On the Way to Gelassenheit.* Evanston: Northwestern University Press, 2007.

de Beistegui, Miguel. "'Questioning Politics, or Beyond Power.'" In *The Movement of Nihilism: Heidegger's Thinking After Nietzsche*, ed. Laurence Paul Hemming, Bogdan Costea, and Kostas Amiridis. London: Bloomsbury, 2011.

Denker, Alfred and Holger Zaborowski, eds. *Heidegger und der Nationalsozialismus I: Dokumente.* Heidegger-Jahrbuch 4. Freiburg: Karl Alber, 2009.

———— and Holger Zaborowski, eds. *Heidegger und die Logik.* Amsterdam: Rodopi, 2006.

Derrida, Jacques. *The Beast and the Sovereign.* Vol. II. Tr. Geoffrey Bennington. Chicago: University of Chicago Press, 2011.

Di Cesare, Donatella. "Heidegger, entre apocalíptica y revolución." Tr. Facundo Bey. *Argumenta Philosophica* 2 (2017): 7–17.

Elden, Stuart. *Speaking Against Number: Heidegger, Language and the Politics of Calculation.* Edinburgh: Edinburgh University Press, 2006.

Emad, Parvis. *On the Way to Heidegger's "Contributions to Philosophy."* Madison: University of Wisconsin Press, 2007.

Engelland, Chad. *Heidegger's Shadow: Kant, Husserl, and the Transcendental Turn.* New York: Routledge, 2017.

Erickson, Steve. *Shadowbahn.* New York: Blue Rider Press, 2017.

Everett, Daniel L. *Don't Sleep, There Are Snakes: Life and Language in the Amazonian Jungle.* New York: Vintage, 2009.

Farin, Ingo and Jeff Malpas, eds. *Reading Heidegger's "Black Notebooks" 1931–1941.* Cambridge: MIT Press, 2016.

Faye, Emmanuel. *Heidegger: The Introduction of Nazism into Philosophy.* Tr. Michael B. Smith. New Haven: Yale University Press, 2009.

———. "Subjectivity and Race in Heidegger's Writings." Tr. Michael B. Smith. *Philosophy Today* 55:3 (Fall 2011): 268–81.

Fineman, Howard. *The Thirteen American Arguments: Enduring Debates That Define and Inspire Our Country.* New York: Random House, 2009.

Foucault, Michel. *The Order of Things: An Archeology of the Human Sciences.* London: Routledge Classics, 2002.

Frege, Gottlob. *Translations from the Philosophical Writings of Gottlob Frege.* Ed. Peter Geach and Max Black. Oxford: Basil Blackwell, 1952.

Fried, Gregory. "Back to the Cave: A Platonic Rejoinder to Heidegger." In *Heidegger and the Greeks*, ed. Drew Hyland and John P. Manoussakis. Bloomington: Indiana University Press, 2006.

———, ed. *Confronting Heidegger: A Critical Dialogue on Politics and Philosophy.* London: Rowman & Littlefield International, 2019.

———. *Heidegger's Polemos: From Being to Politics.* New Haven: Yale University Press, 2000.

——— and Richard Polt, eds. *After Heidegger?* London: Rowman & Littlefield International, 2018.

Fritsche, Johannes. *Historical Destiny and National Socialism in Heidegger's "Being and Time."* Berkeley: University of California Press, 1999.

Gendlin, Eugene. *Experiencing and the Creation of Meaning: A Philosophical and Psychological Approach to the Subjective.* New York: Free Press of Glencoe, 1962.

Golden, Kristen Brown and Bettina G. Bergo, eds. *The Trauma Controversy: Philosophical and Interdisciplinary Dialogues.* Albany: State University of New York Press, 2009.

Gonzalez, Franciso J. *Plato and Heidegger: A Question of Dialogue.* University Park, PA: Pennsylvania State University Press, 2011.

Grondin, Jean. "Why Reawaken the Question of Being?" In *Heidegger's "Being and Time": Critical Essays*, ed. Richard Polt. Lanham, MD: Rowman & Littlefield, 2005.

Hatab, Lawrence J. *Proto-Phenomenology and the Nature of Language: Dwelling in Speech I.* London: Rowman & Littlefield International, 2017.

Haugeland, John. *Dasein Disclosed: John Haugeland's Heidegger.* Ed. Joseph Rouse. Cambridge: Harvard University Press, 2013.

Hegel, G. W. F. *Hegel's Philosophy of Right*. Tr. T. M. Knox. London: Oxford University Press, 1952.

Heidegger, Martin. "Aufzeichnungen zur Temporalität (Aus den Jahren 1925 bis 1927)." *Heidegger Studies* 14 (1998): 11–23.

———. *Beiträge zur Philosophie (Vom Ereignis)*. Photocopy of typescript and handwritten marginalia. Loyola University of Chicago Archives, Martin Heidegger-Barbara Fiand Manuscript Collection, accession number 99-13, box 2, folders 1–2.

———. *Letters to His Wife: 1915–1970*. Tr. Rupert Glasgow. Polity, 2008.

———. *Überlegungen* (excerpts). Typescript, Loyola University of Chicago Archives, Martin Heidegger-Barbara Fiand Manuscript Collection, accession number 99-13, box 3, folders 2–3.

———. *Übungen für Anfänger. Schillers Briefe über die ästhetische Erziehung des Menschen. Wintersemester 1936/37*. Ed. Ulrich von Bülow, with an essay by Odo Marquard. Marbach: Deutsche Schillergesellschaft, 2005.

———. "Unbenutzte Vorarbeiten zur Vorlesung vom Wintersemester 1929/1930: *Die Grundbegriffe der Metaphysik: Welt, Endlichkeit, Einsamkeit.*" *Heidegger Studies* 7 (1991): 5–12.

———. "Vom Ursprung des Kunstwerks: Erste Ausarbeitung." *Heidegger Studies* 5 (1989): 5–22.

———. "Das Wesen der Wahrheit: Zu 'Beiträge zur Philosophie.'" *Heidegger Studies* 18 (2002): 9–19.

——— and Kurt Bauch. *Briefwechsel 1932–1975*. Martin Heidegger Briefausgabe, vol. II.1. Ed. Almuth Heidegger. Freiburg: Karl Alber, 2010.

——— and Elisabeth Blochmann. *Briefwechsel 1918–1969*. Ed. Joachim W. Storck. Marbach am Neckar: Deutsche Schillergesellschaft, 1989.

——— and Rudolf Bultmann. *Briefwechsel 1925 bis 1975*. Ed. Andreas Großmann and Christof Landmesser. Tübingen: Mohr Siebeck, 2009.

——— and Karl Löwith. *Briefwechsel 1919–1973*. Martin Heidegger Briefausgabe, vol. II.2. Ed. Alfred Denker. Freiburg: Karl Alber, 2016.

Homolka, Walter and Arnulf Heidegger, eds. *Heidegger und der Antisemitismus: Positionen im Widerstreit*. Freiburg: Herder, 2016.

Husserl, Edmund. *Cartesian Meditations: An Introduction to Phenomenology*. Trans. Dorion Cairns. Dordrecht: Nijhoff, 1960.

———. *The Phenomenology of Internal Time Consciousness*. Ed. Martin Heidegger, tr. James S. Churchill. Bloomington: Indiana University Press, 1964.

———. *Psychological and Transcendental Phenomenology and the Confrontation with Heidegger (1927–1931)*. Ed. and tr. Thomas Sheehan and Richard E. Palmer. Dordrecht: Kluwer, 1997.

Ireland, Julia. "Naming Φύσις and the 'Inner Truth of National Socialism': A New Archival Discovery." *Research in Phenomenology* 44: 3 (2014): 315–46.

Kellerer, Sidonie. "Antisémitisme et racisme dans le pensée de Heidegger: état de la recherche." *Revue d'Histoire de la Shoah* 207 (2017/2): 25–43.

———. "Rewording the Past: The Postwar Publication of a 1938 Lecture by Martin Heidegger." *Modern Intellectual History* 11:3 (November 2014): 575–602.

Kisiel, Theodore. "The Siting of Hölderlin's 'Geheimes Deutschland' in Heidegger's Poetizing of the Political." In *Heidegger und der Nationalsozialismus II: Interpretationen*, ed. Alfred Denker and Holger Zaborowski. Heidegger-Jahrbuch 5. Freiburg/Munich: Karl Alber, 2009.

Knowles, Adam. "Heidegger's Mask: Silence, Politics, and the Banality of Evil in the *Black Notebooks*." *Gatherings: The Heidegger Circle Annual* 5 (2015): 93–117.

Kolbenheyer, E. G. *Lebenswert und Lebenswirkung der Dichtkunst in einem Volke*. Munich: Albert Langen/Georg Müller, 1935.

Krell, David Farrell. *Ecstasy, Catastrophe: Heidegger from "Being and Time" to the "Black Notebooks."* Albany: State University of New York Press, 2015.

Lapidot, Elad and Micha Brumlik, eds. *Heidegger and Jewish Thought: Difficult Others*. London: Rowman & Littlefield International, 2017.

Lear, Jonathan. *Radical Hope: Ethics in the Face of Cultural Devastation*. Cambridge: Harvard University Press, 2008.

Lewalter, Christian E. "Wie liest man 1953 Sätze von 1935? Zu einem politischen Streit um Heideggers Metaphysik." *Die Zeit*, August 13, 1953.

Lispector, Clarice. *The Passion According to G. H.* Tr. Idra Novey, intro. Caetano Veloso, ed. Benjamin Moser. New York: New Directions, 2012.

Loidolt, Sophie. *Phenomenology of Plurality: Hannah Arendt on Political Intersubjectivity*. London: Routledge, 2018.

Love, Jeff, ed. *Heidegger in Russia and Eastern Europe*. London: Rowman & Littlefield International, 2017.

Löwith, Karl. *My Life in Germany Before and After 1933: A Report*. Tr. Elizabeth King. Urbana: University of Illinois Press, 1994.

Luchte, James. *Heidegger's Early Philosophy: The Phenomenology of Ecstatic Temporality*. London: Continuum, 2008.

Marder, Michael. "Existential Phenomenology According to Clarice Lispector." *Philosophy and Literature* 37:2 (October 2013): 374–88.

Marion, Jean-Luc. *Being Given: Toward a Phenomenology of Givenness*. Stanford: Stanford University Press, 2002.

———. *In Excess: Studies of Saturated Phenomena*. New York: Fordham University Press, 2004.

McMullin, Irene, Matthew Burch, and Jack Marsh, eds. *Transcending Reason: Heidegger's Transformation of Phenomenology*. London: Rowman & Littlefield International, 2019.

McNeill, William. *The Glance of the Eye: Heidegger, Aristotle, and the Ends of Theory*. Albany: State University of New York Press, 1999.

Meillasoux, Quentin. *After Finitude: An Essay on the Necessity of Contingency*. Tr. Ray Brassier. London: Bloomsbury, 2010.

Mitchell, Andrew J. *The Fourfold: Reading the Late Heidegger*. Evanston: Northwestern University Press, 2015.

——— and Peter Trawny, eds. *Heidegger's "Black Notebooks": Responses to Anti-Semitism*. New York: Columbia University Press, 2017.

Nancy, Jean-Luc. *The Banality of Heidegger*. Tr. Jeff Fort. New York: Fordham University Press, 2017.

Nelson, Eric S. "Heidegger's Failure to Overcome Transcendental Philosophy." In *Transcendental Inquiry: Its History, Methods and Critiques*, ed. Halla Kim and Steven Hoeltzel. Cham, Switzerland: Palgrave Macmillan, 2016.

Neske, Günther and Emil Kettering, eds. *Martin Heidegger and National Socialism: Questions and Answers*. New York: Paragon, 1990.

O'Byrne, Anne. *Natality and Finitude*. Bloomington: Indiana University Press, 2010.

Ó Murchadha, Felix. *The Time of Revolution: Kairos and Chronos in Heidegger*. London: Bloomsbury, 2013.

Orange, Tommy. *There There: A Novel*. New York: Alfred A. Knopf, 2018.

Pascal, Blaise. *Pensées*. Trans. Roger Ariew. Indianapolis: Hackett, 2005.

Peirce, Charles S. *The Essential Peirce*. Vol. 1. Ed. Nathan Houser and Christian Kloesel. Bloomington and Indianapolis: Indiana University Press, 1992.

Polt, Richard. "Beyond Struggle and Power: Heidegger's Secret Resistance." *Interpretation* 35:1 (Fall 2007): 11–40.

———. "Eidetic Eros and the Liquidation of the Real." In *The Task of Philosophy in the Anthropocene: Axial Echoes in Global Space*, ed. Richard Polt and Jon Wittrock. London: Rowman & Littlefield International, 2018.

———. *The Emergency of Being: On Heidegger's "Contributions to Philosophy."* Ithaca: Cornell University Press, 2006.

———. "*Ereignis*." In *A Companion to Heidegger*, ed. Hubert L. Dreyfus and Mark Wrathall. Oxford: Blackwell, 2005.

———. "Potentiality, Energy and Sway: From Aristotelian to Modern to Postmodern Physics?" *Existentia* 11 (2001): 27–41.

———. Review of Martin Heidegger, *Contributions to Philosophy (Of the Event)*, tr. Richard Rojcewicz and Daniela Vallega–Neu. Notre Dame Philosophical Reviews, July 24, 2012, http://ndpr.nd.edu/news/32043.

——— and Gregory Fried, eds. *A Companion to Heidegger's "Introduction to Metaphysics."* New Haven: Yale University Press, 2000.

Powell, Jason. *Heidegger's "Contributions to Philosophy": Life and the Last God.* London: Continuum, 2007.

Quine, W. V. *Ontological Relativity and Other Essays*. New York: Columbia University Press, 1969.

Raffoul, François. *Heidegger and the Subject*. Tr. David Pettigrew and Gregory Recco. Atlantic Highlands, NJ: Humanity Books, 1998.

———. "Rethinking Selfhood: From Enowning." *Research in Phenomenology* 37:1 (2007): 75–94.

——— and David Pettigrew, eds. *Heidegger and Practical Philosophy* (Albany: State University of New York Press, 2002.

Ralkowski, Mark A. *Heidegger's Platonism*. London: Continuum, 2009.

Ricoeur, Paul. *Time and Narrative*. Tr. Kathleen McLaughlin and David Pellauer. 3 vols. Chicago: University of Chicago Press, 1984, 1986, 1988.

Sartre, Jean-Paul. *Being and Nothingness: A Phenomenological Essay on Ontology*. Tr. Hazel E. Barnes. New York: Washington Square Press, 1992.

Schmitt, Carl. *The Concept of the Political*. Expanded ed., tr. George Schwab, foreword by Tracy B. Strong, notes by Leo Strauss. Chicago: University of Chicago Press, 2007.

———. *Staat, Großraum, Nomos: Arbeiten aus den Jahren 1916–1969*. Ed. G. Maschke. Berlin: Duncker & Humblot, 1995.

———. *Writings on War*. Trans. and ed. Timothy Nunan. Cambridge: Polity, 2011.

Schürmann, Reiner. *Broken Hegemonies*. Tr. Reginald Lilly. Bloomington: Indiana University Press, 2003.

Scott, Charles, Susan M. Schoenbohm, Daniela Vallega-Neu, and Alejandro Vallega, eds. *A Companion to Heidegger's "Contributions to Philosophy."* Bloomington: Indiana University Press, 2001.

Sheehan, Thomas. *Making Sense of Heidegger: A Paradigm Shift*. London: Rowman & Littlefield International, 2014.

Sinn, Dieter. *Ereignis und Nirwana: Heidegger—Buddhismus—Mythos—Mystik; Zur Archäotypik des Denkens*. Bonn: Bouvier, 1991.

Sonia-Wallace, Brian. "What Happened When a Poet Was Sent to the Biggest US Mall to Write for Shoppers." *The Guardian*, October 10, 2017.

Stevens, Wallace. *Collected Poems*. London: Faber and Faber, 2006.

Stolorow, Robert D. *World, Affectivity, Trauma: Heidegger and Post-Cartesian Psychoanalysis*. New York: Routledge, 2011.

Tallis, Raymond. *Aping Mankind: Neuromania, Darwinitis and the Misrepresentation of Humanity*. London: Routledge, 2014.

Tonner, Philip. *Heidegger, Metaphysics and the Univocity of Being*. London: Continuum, 2010.

Trawny, Peter. *Adyton: Heideggers esoterische Philosophie*. Berlin: Matthes & Seitz, 2010.

———. *Freedom to Fail: Heidegger's Anarchy*. Tr. Ian Alexander Moore and Christopher Turner. Cambridge: Polity, 2015.

———. *Heidegger and the Myth of a Jewish World Conspiracy*. Tr. Andrew J. Mitchell. Chicago: University of Chicago Press, 2016.

———. "Heidegger, Hegel, and the Political." In Martin Heidegger, *On Hegel's "Philosophy of Right": The 1934–5 Seminar and Interpretative Essays*. Ed. Peter Trawny, Marcia Sá Cavalcante Schuback, and Michael Marder, tr. Andrew Mitchell. London: Bloomsbury, 2014.

Vallega-Neu, Daniela. *Heidegger's "Contributions to Philosophy": An Introduction*. Bloomington: Indiana University Press, 2003.

Vietta, Silvio. "Wandel unseres Daseins: Eine unbekannte Vorlesung Martin Heideggers von 1934." *Frankfurter Allgemeine Zeitung*, October 18, 2006.

Villa, Dana. *Arendt and Heidegger: The Fate of the Political*. Princeton: Princeton University Press, 1996.

———. "Arendt and Heidegger, Again." In *Heidegger's Jewish Followers: Essays on Hannah Arendt, Leo Strauss, Hans Jonas, and Emmanuel Levinas*, ed. Samuel Fleischacker. Pittsburgh: Duquesne University Press, 2008.

von Falkenhayn, Katharina. *Augenblick und Kairos: Zeitlichkeit im Frühwerk Martin Heideggers*. Berlin: Duncker & Humblot, 2003.

Wittrock, Jon. "The Social Logic of Late Nihilism: Martin Heidegger and Carl Schmitt on Global Space and the Sites of Gods." *European Review* 22:2 (May 2014): 244–57.

Wolfson, Elliot R. *The Duplicity of Philosophy's Shadow: Heidegger, Nazism, and the Jewish Other.* New York: Columbia University Press, 2018.

Wolin, Richard. "National Socialism, World Jewry, and the History of Being: Heidegger's Black Notebooks." *Jewish Review of Books* (Summer 2014), https:// jewishreviewofbooks.com/articles/993/national-socialism-world-jewry-and-the -history-of-being-heideggers-black-notebooks/.

———. *The Politics of Being: The Political Thought of Martin Heidegger.* 2nd ed. New York: Columbia University Press, 2016.

Zaborowski, Holger. *"Eine Frage von Irre und Schuld?": Heidegger und der Nationalsozialismus.* Frankfurt am Main: Fischer, 2010.

Zolkos, Magdalena, ed. *On Jean Améry: Philosophy of Catastrophe.* Lanham, MD: Lexington Books, 2011.

Index

About the Author

Richard Polt is professor of philosophy at Xavier University in Cincinnati. His books include *Heidegger: An Introduction*; *The Emergency of Being: On Heidegger's "Contributions to Philosophy"*; and *The Typewriter Revolution: A Typist's Companion for the 21st Century*. With Jon Wittrock, he has edited *The Task of Philosophy in the Anthropocene* (Future Perfect series, Rowman & Littlefield International). With Gregory Fried, he has translated Heidegger's *Introduction to Metaphysics*; *Being and Truth*; and *Nature, History, State* and edited *A Companion to Heidegger's "Introduction to Metaphysics"* and *After Heidegger?* (New Heidegger Research series, Rowman & Littlefield International). Polt and Fried are the editors of the New Heidegger Research series.

9 781786 610508